Isaac's "Privateering" Tour Blog

Isaac Shabtay

© 2013 by Isaac Shabtay

Photographs by Jeroen Gerrits, Isaac Shabtay, Rivka Stein
Cover artwork by Isaac Shabtay
Back cover photograph by Ash Christopher

ISBN: 978-0-9868452-9-1

To everyone who made this trip possible.

Thank you.

Table of Contents

Preface	IX
What, Again?	11
Tel Aviv, Israel to Larnaca, Cyprus to Frankfurt, Germany to Bucharest, Romania (April 21–24, 2013)	11
Bucharest, Romania (April 24–25, 2013): Part 1	13
Bucharest, Romania (April 24–25, 2013): Part 2	13
Bucharest, Romania to Istanbul, Turkey (April 26–27, 2013)	16
Istanbul, Turkey to Sofia, Bulgaria (April 28–29, 2013)	21
Sofia, Bulgaria to Belgrade, Serbia (April 30, 2013)	26
Belgrade, Serbia to Milano, Italy (May 1, 2013)	29
Milano to Torino, Italy (May 2, 2013)	31
Torino to Milano, Italy (May 3, 2013)	34
Milano, Italy to Ljubljana, Slovenia (May 4, 2013)	37
Ljubljana, Slovenia to Zagreb, Croatia (May 5, 2013)	42
Zagreb, Croatia to Prague, Czech Republic to Łódź, Poland (May 6–8, 2013)	46
Łódź, Poland to Berlin and Bremen, Germany (May 9–11, 2013)	54
Bremen, Germany to Antwerp, Belgium to Delft, The Netherlands (May 12, 2013)	59
Delft to Amsterdam, The Netherlands (May 13–14, 2013)	61
Delft, The Netherlands to Luxembourg City, Luxembourg (May 15, 2013)	65
Luxembourg City, Luxembourg to Glasgow, UK (May 16–17, 2013)	68
Glasgow to Newcastle upon Tyne, UK (May 18, 2013)	75
Newcastle upon Tyne to Liverpool, UK (May 19, 2013)	80
Liverpool to Bournemouth to Cardiff to Birmingham, UK (May 20–24, 2013)	84
Birmingham to Brighton, UK (May 25–26, 2013)	90
Brighton to London, UK (May 27, 2013)	94
A Quick Note from London, UK	97
A Week in London, UK (May 27–June 2, 2013)	98
Delft to Zwolle, The Netherlands (June 7, 2013)	103
Amsterdam, The Netherlands to Helsinki, Finland (June 8–9, 2013)	107
Trouble in Norway	113
Helsinki, Finland to Hamar, Norway (June 10–11, 2013)	113
Hamar to Bergen to Stavanger, Norway (June 12–13, 2013)	121
Stavanger, Norway to Gothenburg, Sweden (June 14, 2013)	127
Gothenburg to Malmö, Sweden to Copenhagen, Denmark (June 15–16, 2013)	133
Copenhagen, Denmark to Hamburg and Frankfurt, Germany (June 17–18, 2013)	139
Frankfurt to Regensburg, Germany (June 19, 2013)	147
Regensburg, Germany to Vienna, Austria (June 20–21, 2013)	150
Vienna, Austria to Budapest, Hungary (June 22, 2013)	158
Budapest, Hungary to Bratislava, Slovakia to Salzburg, Austria (June 23–24, 2013)	163
Salzburg, Austria to Stuttgart, Germany (June 25, 2013)	171
Stuttgart, Germany to Paris, France (June 26, 2013)	176
Paris to Caen, France (June 27, 2013)	181
Caen to Rennes to Clermont-Ferrand to Dijon, France (June 28–30, 2013)	185
Heartbeat Check	191
Dijon, France to Köln, Germany (July 1–2, 2013)	192
Köln to Halle (Westfalen), Germany (July 3, 2013)	199
The 197th and 198th: Halle (Westfalen) to Dresden to Bad Mergentheim, Germany (July 4–5, 2013)	203
The 199th: Bad Mergentheim to Stuttgart, Germany (July 6, 2013)	212
The 200th: Stuttgart, Germany to Nîmes, France (July 7–9, 2013)	215
Nîmes, France to Locarno, Switzerland (July 10–11, 2013)	225
A Sign of Life from Italy	233
Locarno, Switzerland to Padova and Rome, Italy (July 12–13, 2013)	233
Rome to Napoli, Italy (July 14, 2013)	242
Napoli to Taormina, Italy (July 15–16, 2013)	247
Taormina, Italy to Valletta, Malta (July 17, 2013)	260
Valletta, Malta to Pisa and Lucca, Italy (July 18–19, 2013)	265
Lucca, Italy to Zürich, Switzerland to Lörrach, Germany to Saint-Julien-en-Genevois, France (July 20–22, 2013)	274
Better Late than Never: Facebook Comments Enabled	285
Saint-Julien-en-Genevois to Carcassonne, France to Barcelona, Spain (July 23–25, 2013)	286
Barcelona to Madrid to Málaga, Spain (July 26–27, 2013)	295
Málaga to Gijón to San Sebastián, Spain (July 28–30, 2013)	301
The Last One & Conclusion: San Sebastián to Calella de Palafrugell, Spain (July 31, 2013)	309

Isaac's "Privateering" Tour Blog

(July 24, 2013 @ Théâtre Jean Deschamps, Carcassonne, France)

Preface

Morning of August 2, 2013: I'm in Barcelona's international airport. Approaching Air Canada's check-in counter, I felt as if life started getting back to normal. The tiredness, weariness and exhaustion—unavoidable consequences of being more than three months on the road—made way to a refreshing feeling of rejuvenation: I was happy to, finally, be heading home.

A few days later, as I was getting reacquainted with my apartment, I finally sat down and started working on paper and e-book editions of the "Privateering" blog. Three years ago, I converted the "Get Lucky" tour blog into a book using a computer program that I wrote specifically for that purpose; fortunately, I was able to re-use much of it this time around, so the process was not as tedious as before.

Still, it was fun. Going through each and every post, I couldn't quite believe that I managed to follow an entire tour and get home in one piece. So many places, so much travel, so many challenges…

… And the further I got into the creation of this book, the more memories seemed to be fading away. As I am writing this preface, in September 2013, the "Privateering" tour feels as if it took place in the distant past. Sitting at my desk, looking over the beautiful city of Vancouver from above, it almost feels as if that entire tour was but merely a dream.

(A good one, that is.)

Thank you all for your readership. Those of you who have been following my blog throughout the tour—I hope that sifting through these pages will bring back some good, sweet memories; and those of you who have just been introduced to this little trip I had in Europe earlier this year—sit tight and fasten your seatbelts, as this is going to be a wild, bumpy ride.

One technical note: the original blog contained many hyperlinks—more than 700 of them. These hyperlinks are represented as text with a dotted underline. In the paper edition, tapping on such underlined text will lead you nowhere (although it would be funny to watch); in the e-book edition, these links should work, depending on your e-book reader's feature-set.

So let's get started, shall we?

Hello. My name is Isaac, 35 years old from Vancouver, Canada. I have set this blog up to document my journey following Mark Knopfler's 2013 "Privateering" tour, from April 25 (Bucharest, Romania) to July 31 (Calella de Palafrugell, Spain).

~~Due to~~ Despite the tour's obnoxious schedule (thanks, Mark), ~~I cannot be entirely sure that~~ I will attend all concerts. ~~That being said, I will try~~. You are more than welcome to sit back, relax, read, and comment.

Have fun,

Isaac

Wednesday, April 24, 2013

What, Again?

(If you are to read any post in this blog, then this should be the one, as it contains a very important disclaimer.)

So here we go again.

Three years after the epic Get Lucky tour, which I followed in its entirety, here I am about to do exactly the same thing for Mark Knopfler's Privateering tour.

I had many doubts before deciding to follow the Privateering tour in its entirety. Life circumstances being one thing; the other being my recollection of how difficult such an endeavour really is. I know, I know: once such an epic journey concludes, the sweet memories (France, Italy) usually dominate the bitter ones (Poland, Spain). Yet, I am a pragmatic realist and therefore cannot lie down in a bed of roses for long without feeling the thorns. When all is said and done, following the entire Get Lucky tour was **hard**; I would not recommend such a journey to most people I know.

Yet, as time progressed, it became increasingly apparent to me that, for me, following a Knopfler solo tour is a feat that appeals more than other circumstantial factors. It is simply an experience that I like going through, period. Whenever I tried to rationalize it by challenging it with plain down-to-earth pragmatic factors, I some got stuck with a "but still…" of some sort. It is that gut feeling that defeated all other factors before the Get Lucky tour, and it did it again now; who am I to argue, then?

Another thing that made this tour easier to digest was the fact that I am not going to follow it by myself. My dear friend Jeroen Gerrits has decided to suspend his *wakeup → slices of bread with some spread → work → some more bread with spreads → home → yet more bread with spreads → sleep* cycle, pack a bag and haul himself throughout Europe via any method of transportation known to man except for space shuttles and catapults. That made planning easier (although still *very* hard) and is certainly going to render the journey more enjoyable and manageable.

(No, he is not writing a blog.)

How Can You Help?

You didn't see that one coming, did you.

Well, constructive comments can definitely help. While you are free to comment in any which way you want, please try to keep it constructive and—to the extent possible—positive. Leave the negativity to me.

If you happen to own a residence that can host two strangers in a city along the way, and willing to offer some space for one night—that would definitely help.

You can also buy me some coffee. Had it been possible, I'd set up a PayPal-like "coffee fund" (hey, did I just come up with an idea for a start up?); that is impossible though, so find your own way.

Disclaimer

There are going to be some changes here, comparing to the last tour.

First and foremost, I am going to write less about the actual performances. Writing about a performance is very easy when you attend one performance, or three. When it's about 70 performances you attend, differentiating between them becomes very hard. Also, the performances themselves become a secondary factor in the overall experience: the actual travel captures top spot instead. I am going to write more about thoughts, experiences (though less about the actual food I eat. That's what *Instagram* is for), joys and grievances.

Second, about pictures. Expect (much) less performance-time pictures: I am hardly going to take any. Having attended so many performances already, I can conclude that the less cameras see the "light of day" (so to speak) during a performance—the better, not just for the viewer but more so for the band. Having said that, if you had taken pictures during concerts and would like them posted (and credited), feel free to share them with me (using Google Drive or Dropbox is preferred over email). Just please, avoid close-ups and attempt to capture situations rather than people; atmosphere rather than skin.

Third, please understand that occasional grumpiness is inevitable. I might, at times, become negative—especially around days when travel is very hard, and this tour definitely doesn't suffer from shortage in difficult transit. Grumpiness is a part of me, and so is this blog—and therefore you, the reader, are responsible to implement your own filters to what I write.

That's about it for now. Flying to Bucharest tomorrow (Wednesday), while the tour kicks off the next day.

Cheers,

Isaac

Wednesday, April 24, 2013

Tel Aviv, Israel to Larnaca, Cyprus to Frankfurt, Germany to Bucharest, Romania (April 21-24, 2013)

I vividly recall the last couple of weeks of the Get Lucky tour being rather obnoxious with respect to travel. I was tired, hungry most of the time, very nervous. It's not that the rest of the tour was much easier; but something happened in Spain that tipped the scale, making the last couple of weeks very problematic.

This tour, I can definitely say that the few days preceding the tour were so obnoxious, that I can hardly imagine anything more stressful later on down the road. It truly is a story of misfortune and agony.

Originally, I was supposed to fly from Tel Aviv (where I had spent a couple of weeks visiting my family) to Frankfurt on Tuesday, meet Jeroen there and head to Bucharest the next morning. Everything was planned out down to the atomic level; and when I say "everything", I mean *everything*. Train travel; hotels; flights; ferries; buses; even maps.

And that's when the immense clusterfuck took place.

All Israeli airlines decided to go on strike on Sunday, two days before the flight. Due to how workers' unions in Israel are organized (one superior union governing a bunch of lower level unions, with the superior union being managed in a manner not very different from the Sicilian mafia), it was clear that a strike within Israeli airlines is very likely to spread out to include other sectors, including the aviation sector in its entirety.

As soon as I had learned that a one day strike is coming, I started working on changing my schedule. I thought it may be worth the while to leave Tel Aviv earlier, as who the hell knows what's going to happen once the strike begins.

Then it turned out that not only Israeli airlines are going on strike, but also Lufthansa—which happened to be the very same airline I was supposed to fly to Frankfurt with. Lufthansa declared a strike for Monday, April 22.

On Sunday, April 21, the superior workers' union in Israel decided that they're striking and shutting down *the entire Israeli airport* (Israel only has one international airport) on… that's right: Tuesday, April 23, which is when I was supposed to take my flight.

Put yourself in my shoes on Sunday morning. You know you must be in Frankfurt by Tuesday (otherwise an entire travel schedule is at risk), there are *no flights* arriving to Germany on Sunday (I checked at the airport), there are no Lufthansa flights on Monday (due to Lufthansa's strike), and there are no flights leaving Tel Aviv at all starting Tuesday *indefinitely* (the strike wasn't bound in time).

What a fantastic kick-off for a tour, huh? dealing with two strikes in two countries.

To minimize the risk to the entire travel schedule, I had to fly out of Tel Aviv on Sunday. Luckily, I found the last ticket available, flying to Frankfurt through Larnaca, Cyprus. Packed quickly, bid my family goodbye and headed to the airport.

The same night, I landed in Larnaca. 2:00am, not a single soul on the street. A taxi cab driving around 120 km/h on roads that I would drive 80 km/h. Entering the city of Larnaca, the taxi cab took wild corners through narrow streets—I could swear that it's not Larnaca I'm in, but in *Jaffa* instead. For a moment, I was scared. Here I am in a place I have never been to before, by myself, 2:00am, trapped in a taxi cab that drives insanely through extremely narrow streets.

That 10 minutes taxi ride felt more like an hour. Eventually I made it to the hotel—a rather fine hotel though: Hotel Achilleos. Five hours of sleep, woke up, took my time and, in the meantime, checked my Frankfurt flight's status online.

It did not show up.

The morning routine is not quite the same when you realize that your intended flight's does not appear in the airline's website, I'll give you that.

Cyprus Airways' flight status website is rather unusual. Instead of entering your flight number or your route details (like with pretty much all other airlines I had flown with), you have to select an airport first, and then select whether you want to see departures from that airport or arrivals to that airport. Selecting "Larnaca Departures" showed me all Cyprus Airways' flights leaving Larnaca airport—mine wasn't there.

It often strikes me odd to find that people overestimate information technologists, as it is considered a respectable profession. Well, here's news for you: we have idiots in this industry as well. The way their website was structured, it was evident that it wasn't developed by the most capable minds in the industry. Therefore, instead of checking for all flights departing from Larnaca, I decided to check all flights arriving to Frankfurt.

Lo and behold, there it was. Scheduled to leave on time.

I muttered a few unpleasant verbal gestures, checked out from the hotel (I will *definitely* visit that hotel again next time I'm in Larnaca), hailed a cab and went on my way.

The airport was so empty, that upon entrance, it was evident that there were more staff people there than actual travellers. Within three minutes of arriving at the airport, I was already past security. Off I went to Cyprus Airways' VIP lounge (*not recommended*. If you can, try the *Star Alliance* lounge instead—however, you can only enter if you're taking a Star Alliance flight) to pass the time before the flight. Dull food and terrible coffee, but hey, free Wi-Fi and comfortable seats.

Flight left on time. A few hours later, I finally arrived at Frankfurt.

One of the best things in the city of Frankfurt is that it is extremely easy to get around in. Public transport in Frankfurt will take you from anywhere to anywhere—and, based on my past experience, this is not uncommon in Germany. Renting a car on a city trip to a major city in Germany is a pure exercise in wasting money, time and resources.

S-Bahn #8 to *Frankfurt Hauptbahnhof*, and then a few steps to my hotel for the night, Hotel Excelsior, conveniently located across the road from the station.

I had stayed in that hotel before and swore to never stay in it again. Unfortunately, with the rush of finding an impromptu hotel for the unplanned night in Frankfurt, I forgot everything even remotely concerned with vows and booked it.

The next couple of days were rather uneventful. A few pleasant things worth mentioning are a walk along *River Main*—it is pretty— as well as Urban Kitchen serving delicious food without having to take on a mortgage. *Coffee Fellows* on *Kaiserstrasse* is your place to go for coffee, tea, snacks—great location to chill out and let time pass by harmlessly.

On Tuesday evening, I went to the Ibis Airport hotel, which we had booked for the night before the flight.

Here's a tip for you if you're ever going to visit Frankfurt: *avoid staying in "airport hotels"*. North Americans are very likely to fall into this trap, especially those who live in the less populated areas, as an "airport hotel" is typically associated with "easy access to the airport from the hotel". While this may be of some advantage in many North American cities, it is completely useless in Frankfurt. It is easier and quicker to get from Frankfurt's airport to the city center, than it is to get from the airport to *any* of these "airport hotels". Simply board the *S-Bahn* #8 or #9 from the airport: the city center is within four stops—and there are quite a few hotels there, most of which are significantly better than the one I ended up staying in.

Was good to see Jeroen again, partly due to him being a great companion, but mostly due to the mere fact that he has, in his possession, more than half of our train tickets and concert tickets.

Did some more work, and off to bed.

Signing off this post while on board *Tarom*'s flight 302 to Bucharest. Today is a day off, which I'm going to be using primarily for work. The tour officially kicks off tomorrow, and my message to the band is simple: *getting to Europe was hell, and this tour better be worth it.*

(All in good spirit, of course.)

Later,

Isaac

Friday, April 26, 2013

Bucharest, Romania (April 24-25, 2013): Part 1

Part 1 of the Bucharest entry will be short, and only serves to let you know that will be a part 2 later on today. Things have been very busy. Currently waiting for the hotel room in Istanbul to be ready, and then off to see some of this exciting city. Will try to post later on today.

Isaac

Friday, April 26, 2013

Bucharest, Romania (April 24-25, 2013): Part 2

Here is an abridged list of things I knew about Bucharest and/or Romania before Tarom flight #302 touched ground here on April 24, 2013:

- It is a part of the European Union, but not a part of the European Monetary Union (practical knowledge: yet again dealing with esoteric currencies).

- They went through quite the unpleasant (to say the least) revolution back in the 1990's, after the country was led by a vicious dictator, Nicolae Ceaușescu. At the end of this revolution, Ceaușescu and his wife (who happened to be a big fan of shoes; either that, or she had many feet that nobody knew about) were executed by a firing squad. I watched it on the TV; I was eleven years old.

- Dracula.

Not much, is it?

That is to say, I didn't really know what to expect. The first structure I encountered upon landing—the main terminal of the Henri Coandă International Airport—was definitely a positive sign: clean, advanced terminal building, the result of an extensive airport improvement plan which cost the Romanian taxpayers about €150 million.

It is always nice to arrive at a spacious, nice airport. Gives you the feeling that everything's going to be OK—especially if "spacious & nice" is what you got so accustomed to. Over the last couple of years I have become a rather spoiled individual when it comes to defining my comfort bubble: much of it has directly to do with my moving from Canada's east coast to the wonderful city of Vancouver—a city that appears to go out of its way to strip its residents from most challenges in life (that is, the residents who could still afford living in this stupidly expensive city).

> To the uninformed visitor to Bucharest's international airport—that is, at least as uninformed as I was—here are a couple of tips:
>
> Currency exchange. As you make your way from the gate to the arrivals hall, you will encounter a few currency exchange stands with their exchange rates published on a sign. The closer you get to the arrivals hall, the worse exchange rate you're going to get. Best you can do is simply ignore them: as soon as you are at the arrivals hall, there are a couple of bank machines where you can get local currency for a better rate.
>
> Transportation to the City Center. The city center is about 20km away from the airport. You could do this by public transit for the price of about €1; however, if you were to use a taxi, this is a different story. You have two options:
>
> 1. Use the services of Fast Taxi, which is a taxi cab operator licensed to pick passengers up right upon exiting the terminal building.
>
> 2. Call a local taxi cab company. Local taxi cab companies (other than Fast Taxi) are not allowed to wait for passengers in the airport: instead, you need to call them, then wait for them outside and they come pick you up.
>
> The difference in cost is quite substantial: the Fast Taxi service costs almost three times more than most local taxi companies. Expect to pay the equivalent of about €20 with the Fast Taxi service to the city center area, much less with the local taxi companies.

Of course, we knew none of the aforementioned when we arrived. We chose the more convenient route, took the in-airport cab and off we went to the city center.

The conversation with the taxi cab driver was very entertaining. Not much because of the contents of the conversation, but more due to the fact that it wasn't really a conversation. The poor driver really did his best to communicate in English, but all that came out was a mixture of nouns, adjectives and adverbs, not entirely related to one another, and almost consistently failing to make any sense.

To the driver's credit, he was really trying.

Barely two minutes into the drive, the driver decided to inform us that Bucharest has "excellent women". That aligned with other things I had heard about this city, being some sort of a preferred destination for sexual extravaganzas.

I never really subscribed to the concept of sex tourism to begin with, but my position changed from ambivalence towards this subject to utter disgust last year, when I was involved with a lady who happened to be feminist. There is much that I am aware of now that I wasn't entirely aware of before. Using women's sexuality as means of "selling" a city—actually, using women's sexuality as means of selling *anything*—is gross, backward and wrong. Why we, as a society, allow this to happen—is entirely beyond me.

Anyway. The hotel for the two nights in Bucharest was the Z Executive Boutique Hotel, conveniently located right at Bucharest's old city area. Great hotel, highly recommended—although not cheap by any means. Quick setup and we were off for a walk in the city.

Three minutes later, I was on the ground.

What a nice way to start exploring European cities by foot—tripping over some inconsistent sidewalk, falling down and bruising a hip and an arm. What a violent fall it was, too: *BAM*, face touching the ground. A couple of days later, I'm still bruised and it's a bit painful to walk, but I'm pretty sure I'll survive this.

As equally annoying it was to fall, was to realize that no one around (and we're talking about a very busy street in rush hour) even bothered to lend a hand.

Guess I'm not in Canada anymore.

The city of Bucharest is the capital of Romania, as well as its financial and industrial center. It is a home for about 1.6 million people, and it is old—it dates all the way back to the 15th century. Parts of the older city have been destroyed over the years by the powers of mother nature, as well as the idiocy of one person who used to answer to the name *Nicolae Ceaușescu* before a firing squad put an end to his worthless life and his vicious dictatorship in December 1989. Ceaușescu decided, after visiting North Korea in 1971, to start a process called Systematization, involving mass (forced) relocation of people from the city to rural areas. As the Systematization process started in the more rural areas of Bucharest, it arrived to the capital city in the mid 1980's.

Other than just obliterating many buildings of historical value, Ceaușescu decided that he really needs a palace. The fact that people were living in the area where he wanted his palace set up, wasn't much of a hindrance: Ceaușescu simply issued an order for 40,000 people to evacuate their homes and relocate.

It was only unfortunate that those 40,000 people had exactly 24 hours to relocate.

The resulting palace was called Palace of the Parliament, and is considered to be the second largest building *in the world* after the Pentagon.

How big is it? Take a look (by the way, many pictures in this blog are courtesy of Jeroen Gerrits):

The city of Bucharest is busy. Very busy. Unfortunately, it is not the cleanest city in the world, to say the least. Dirt and garbage are rather commonplace. To the typical Canadian visitor, for instance, many sights of this city will appear aesthetically appalling. I am not entirely sure about how this affects the health of people living here, but I'm guessing that the answer is along the lines of "not very positively".

Infrastructure seems to be in poor condition as well. It is not uncommon to walk around and suddenly encounter an electricity cable hung from above, just because it fell off somewhere. Sidewalks are extremely dated, roads are rather uneven… and, by the way, nowadays the situation is better than it used to be not too long ago, as Bucharest is booming financially. By the looks of it, though, there still is a way to go.

One thing that was a good surprise was the people. I was forewarned, by some, that Romanians are "not very nice". I did not encounter this. I mean, OK, when I fell down and almost broke every bone in my body, nobody wondered whether I'm still breathing—but leave that aside for a minute; nothing too "rude" about people here.

(The preceding paragraph applies only to pedestrians. On the road, things are different. People drive like crazy fucking maniacs.)

A (planned) quick meal in Gargantua ended up taking much longer than expected:

Oh yes, if you are to visit Bucharest and are planning to eat in the more touristy areas, you better not be on a rush. Restaurants here are severely understaffed.

Not too far is the Romanian Athenaeum, a beautiful piece of land largely occupied by a concert hall.

Walking back to the hotel, the old city is literally around the corner so a walking tour was warranted. Dozens of bars, pubs and clubs catering to pretty much everyone on this planet with the exception of myself.

Spent the rest of the evening, and most of the next day, working. A couple of hours before the show, it was time for dinner at Cafe Van Gogh:

Then headed to the venue.

Sala Palatului ("The Palace Hall") is a conference center, as well as a concert hall, in Bucharest's city center. With the capacity of 4,000, the interior of the venue reminded me more of a theatre than a concert hall—not unlike the types of venues Knopfler plays in while in North America. Philipp and his friend Werner, who made their way from Switzerland for this, were already there. First time meeting Philipp after a few years of online communication—it's always (well, usually; OK, rarely; but true in Philipp's case) nice to meet the face behind the Facebook account.

Upon entering the venue, it felt as if I'm in the wrong place. Looking to my left, right and front, all I could see were stands of cosmetic products. Turned out that there's a cosmetics exhibition at the Sala Palatului over the next few days.

The next 30 minutes passed quickly and rather uneventfully; on 20:10, ten minutes past the posted time, Junior Parker's *Feelin' Good* started playing and the Privateering tour officially kicked off.

I am not an expert in these things, but it appears that this is the first time that Knopfler is setting foot in Bucharest as part of a solo tour. Perhaps related is the fact that the concert was sold out weeks ago. Hence, one could conclude that Bucharest is going to be very happy to welcome the band, which is precisely the impression that I received. Waves of applause even before the show began—highly unusual; I cannot recall when I last encountered this—and great audience support throughout the concert.

Structure-wise, the show seemed to be a continuation of the last two joint Dylan-Knopfler tour: similar structure (plus a few Dire Straits tunes; I guess you can't do without those), now featuring a rather neat fade from *Father and Son* ("Cal" soundtrack. Beautifully played live) into *Hill Farmers' Blues*. Some songs featured slightly different arrangements comparing to the Knopfler-Dylan tours' versions.

The concert lasted two hours, with the only break taking place before the encore (no band introduction). A sixteen piece set, concluding with a full rocking performance of Going Home—the audience couldn't have asked for more. Altogether a very good show, despite a few glitches here and there (it takes a few shows into the tour for the band to get running on full speed).

Easy walk back to the old city area after the show, quick dinner and off to bed, myself being extremely excited knowing where I was going to go next. More on that in the next post.

Isaac

Sunday, April 28, 2013

Bucharest, Romania to Istanbul, Turkey (April 26-27, 2013)

Disclaimer: This post is likely to end up being a long one.

Of all the cities going to be visited by this tour, Istanbul is the one—and only one—city, that I considered skipping.

The reason had nothing to do with not *wanting* to go, though.

To understand why, some background is needed.

I happen to have been born in a country named Israel. Israel, as most of you probably know, isn't exactly a problem-free country. I am definitely *not* going to delve into politics here—heck, that would take forever—but let's agree that, at the outset, Israel's problems (as reflected in worldwide media) revolve around international politics and security.

Turkey's population consists mostly of Muslims. That being said, it is—and has been, for a long time—generally secular. That allowed Turkey and Israel to maintain rather special relationship (Turkey was the first Muslim majority country to recognize the State of Israel after its establishment in May 1948). In a world when the words "Israel" and "Islam" can barely be expressed in the same sentence without igniting fire, the Israel-Turkey relationships were truly one of a kind, involving extensive trade and military cooperation.

Since the late 1980's until the end of the first decade of the 21st century, Turkey was an extremely popular destination for Israeli tourists. Around 500,000 Israelis toured Turkey *every year*, flocking its wonderful beaches, its all-inclusive resorts and its renowned markets. Many of my family members visited Turkey way more than once or twice; I never have.

Everything was just fine between the two countries until December 2008, when the Israeli military launched Operation Cast Lead against Palestinian militants. Turkey's stance during the conflict wasn't favourable to Israel; as a result, Israel's tourism minister at that time has decided to demonstrate his immense stupidity by advising Israelis to boycott Turkey as a tourism destination. That resulted in a significant drop in the number of Israeli tourists in Turkey—from 560,000 in 2008 to 110,000 in 2010.

Just when it seemed like things couldn't get any worse, there was the 2010 Gaza Flotilla Raid incident. In May 2010, a flotilla carrying aid to the Gaza Strip refused to listen to Israeli navy orders, ordering the flotilla to be inspected in Israel prior to the goods being shipped to the Gaza Strip (the Gaza Strip was under a blockade at that time; it still is).

The raid started with Israeli commando fighters being landed on the flotilla. Video footage shown that the commando fighters did not initially use power—to the contrary: they were brutally attacked by dozens of people carrying sticks, knives and whatnot—and ended with nine Turkish activists dead, and many others wounded, including Israeli soldiers.

What happened in between? that highly depends on who you ask. Turkey, Israel as well as the United Nations have all conducted their own investigations. The last investigation, also called The Palmer Report, was headed by New Zealand's Prime Minister and decided that, when all is said and done, neither side displayed perfect reasoning to its actions.

Israel refused to apologize to Turkey for the incident. As a result, The Israel-Turkey relationship deteriorated even further, to the point that it became unsafe for Israeli citizens to even visit Turkey due to the Turkish public's anger over the flotilla raid.

When the Istanbul show was announced, the Israel-Turkey relationship were still sour. That prompted me to heavily consider whether I should travel there at all, with the scale tipped towards "yes" primarily due to the fact that I also am a Canadian citizen. Needless to say, I was still pretty tight about the issue.

It wasn't until a few weeks ago—close to three years after the flotilla raid—that Israel's Prime Minister finally agreed to apologize to Turkey, much due to efforts by President Barack Obama. Since then, the Israel-Turkey relationship has been warming up again; still, there is a way to go.

Why can't we all just get along, it's what I say.

Early morning ride from Bucharest's old city to the airport, as the flight to Istanbul was scheduled to depart shortly before 9:00am. The worst thing about it was that I had to skip the hotel's breakfast, which was one of the best breakfasts I have ever had in any hotel, anywhere. Instead, we had to settle for a mediocre meal near the departure gate, with the seemingly usual Romanian approach towards service—one waiter per 8,000 diners. Close to an hour was spent there, out of which about 15 minutes were spent eating breakfast.

Back at the gate, I somehow was able to let go of the worries regarding visiting Turkey. I would expect to be very nervous, but oddly enough, I didn't really care anymore. I come in peace, and that's what really matters.

Short haul flight—less than one hour—and we arrived at Istanbul Atatürk Airport. Bags quickly collected, hotel's taxi driver quickly located, and off we left the terminal building en route to the city.

Welcome to Istanbul.

Istanbul is the largest city in Turkey and is its economic, trade and financial center. Population is a little short of 14 million. It is split between two continents, Europe and Asia, divided by the Bosphorus—which also happens to be one of the busiest waterways in the world.

I am trying to gather my thoughts about this city and, frankly, I don't know where to start. This city is so different from anything I had ever experienced before: westerners who are accustomed to western lifestyle are extremely likely to experience a massive culture shock (not necessarily a negative one!) once being faced with this beautiful city, its rich heritage dating back to around 660 BC, its genuine people and —of course—the food (we will get to that later).

This is a city with some rich history. Istanbul has been, at times, the capital city of not one but *four* different empires: the Roman, the Byzantine, the Latin and the Ottoman. Talk about heritage!

In 2010, Istanbul was the tenth most popular tourist destination in the world with 7 million tourists. Seven million. One city! Can't get my head around this.

Before coming here, I was told the following about Istanbul, from people who had visited here numerous times:

- Don't even think about driving a car in Istanbul. Never assume anything about traffic control: red lights and "no entry" signs don't do much more than serve as a guideline.
- Turkish drivers are the craziest drivers in the world.
- The Turkish cuisine is one of the best cuisines on the planet.
- The best way to explore this city is by foot.

The first two points took exactly 5 minutes to verify as we were making our way to the hotel. I have been to many countries before; I was certain that, of the countries that I had been to, Israelis are the worst drivers. I didn't really know what to expect.

So let me tell you: at least in Istanbul, there is not much difference between the road and a jungle. "Survival of the fittest"? Istanbul's road scene is a great case in point. The concept of "Right of way" doesn't exist here. Road courtesy? YEAH RIGHT. Speed limit? our driver drove 130km/h on a 70km/h road, just to catch up with the traffic in front of him.

Once the highway ride was over, there was no longer a reason to be afraid of the vast speed. The fear of crashing into a post in 130km/h has been substituted with the fear of crashing into other cars and—more than anything—pedestrians. As the taxi made its way towards the district of Taksim, the streets became narrower and narrower, literally flooded with people. Cars driving with the flow of traffic and against it; pedestrians *everywhere*. There are close to 14 million people in this city, which is, coincidentally, the same number of almost-accidents I was witnessing.

Finally, after about 40 minutes, arrived at the hotel: Plussuite Hotel, located a few minutes walk from the popular Taksim Square. About an hour later, got ready for some walking and left the hotel towards the old city area.

(The owners and operators of this hotel are of the nicest, most helpful hotel staff I have ever came across. It is strongly recommended.)

Long, long walking day. Walked all the way from the hotel down to the old city area, passing through the tourist-famous Istiklal Avenue. The latter is the very center of all tourist traps known to mankind, and aggressively caters itself to westerners. Worldwide corporate chains such as Gap, McDonald's, and other fashion and food chains (Starbucks included, of course) are common.

Crossed Galata Bridge to the old city…

Which things started to get really interesting. Istanbul's Old City area has so much to see and do that it would take a week or so to cover just the highlights.

In case you wondered as for the origin of the famous magic lamp, it's right here in Istanbul:

The Turkish cuisine is considered by many to be one of the best cuisines in the world. It is said that the best Shawarma (called "Doner" in Turkey) is made right here, and the desserts—well, that's an entire world right there. Walking through the streets of Istanbul, you'd encounter dozens over dozens of places selling "Turkish Delights", which is an expression covering a large variety of desserts.

Here you will find any type of Baklava one can think of.

The streets of the Old City are narrow, winding, *very* old and swamped with tourists. Definitely a pleasant walk in such perfect weather of 24–25°C.

Sat down for lunch. Can't remember the name of the place but here is how the meal started:

And then, off to the Grand Bazaar.

The Grand Bazaar in Istanbul is enormous. It is covered, and spans more than 60 streets spotted with about 3,000 shops. What's for sale in here? better ask what isn't. Everywhere you look, all you can see is a sea of people walking through yet another street within the market. This is certainly not the place for those with personal space issue: it *is* crowded. If you happen to travel in groups, better keep a good eye on the whereabouts of each other or you *will* get lost. I, myself, have never experienced anything quite like walking in Istanbul's Grand Bazaar. An experience to remember.

A long walk back to Taksim district—almost entirely uphill, mind you—and a brilliant, fabulous meal consisting solely of sweets.

What a great city.

The next day started late, as there was quite some sleep to catch after the very long preceding day. This time, a walk along the Bosphorus seemed to be the right approach.

A nice cafe by the water:

This is how tea is served in Turkey:

I got myself some Turkish coffee instead. Turkish coffee is different from North American coffee primarily in the way that it is prepared: cooked on the stove top, rather than being filtered. It is also served in insanely small cups:

Walked back to the hotel, chilled out for a while, and off to some dinner. Initially, I was very tempted to consume some Kokoretsi—a brief taste a day before proved to be extremely delicious—however, after reading about it, I decided not to. Turns out that, among one of the issues that Turkey will have to face if and when it joins the European Union, is that Kokoretsi will have to be banned for sale, as its cooking method is deemed unsafe by the European Union's standard. There's still a long way to go with this tour, and I am not in the mood for risking any food poisoning, so I decided to settle for Doner Kebob—that is, Doner cooked by coal (rather than regular, gas-based flame). A few deserts afterwards, of course. Paradise.

Back to the hotel and off to the venue.

Istanbul is split between two continents. The European side is generally where all the "action" is: the vast majority of tourist attractions are located there. That's the Istanbul you'd see in the movies. The Asian side, on the other hand, is more relaxed, laid back and thus boring (at least, that's what I was able to gather). Naturally, then, I preferred to stay in a hotel in the European part.

The venue, Ülker Sports Arena, is located in the Asian side. The distance between the hotel to the venue was about 18km, and involved crossing a bridge over the Bosphorus.

A traffic jam turned a 30 minutes ride into one hour. Surprise surprise: they drive insane even when there's a traffic jam. Again, the survival of the fittest: if you're not strong enough to push your own way through, you'll be left behind to rot, die and—in extreme cases—miss a concert.

The front of the stage was designated for general admission, which was happily passed on in favour of a seat in the tribunes. When purchasing the tickets, we knew that we would be very tired by the time the show starts, as we'd be spending a lot of time walking in Istanbul; therefore, the seated section seemed like a better approach.

The show started twenty minutes past the scheduled time, the venue not being too far from being completely sold out.

In the last post, I mentioned that it usually takes a few concerts into the tour for the band to start firing with all cylinders. Turned out that "a few concerts" in this tour's case equals the number "1", because the show in Istanbul was nothing short of brilliant. A truly great performance, led by a suspiciously upbeat Knopfler—he must have taken his Turkish coffee extra strong prior to the show.

Istanbul features a few popular soccer teams, such as Beşiktaş (named after a municipality within Istanbul, by the same name), Fenerbahçe (named after a neighbourhood) and Galatasaray (named after an Istanbul district). I don't know much about soccer; however, where I grew up, European soccer has always been very popular and the main thing I remember about Turkish sports teams is that their fans are borderline insane when it comes to their affection to their teams. Therefore, I wasn't extremely surprised to find the audience yesterday cheering in levels of intensity that make your ears bleed, giving the performance the feel of one real big party.

The band, as previously mentioned, cooperated fully. It was evident that they were having quite a bit of fun. The *Sultans of Swing* solo sounded like something I can hardly recall listening to, not to mention *Telegraph Road*.

The pinnacle of the evening, for me, was the introduction of a new song to the set—a song that I have never witnessed played live before. *Postcards from Paraguay*—one of my all-time favourites—beautifully played, with the show completely owned by John and Mike playing flute. Flute work in *Postcards from Paraguay*? I couldn't have seen it happening, but hey, it just fits. Brilliant arrangement.

A set of sixteen songs, very loud cheers from the audience and show was over.

As the taxi made its way back to Taksim district, it was evident that Istanbul is a very active city. It was around midnight when we arrived back to Taksim Square, only to find that *Istiklal Avenue* is as full of people as it was in 3:00pm. Amazing. So many people, so many stores and restaurants open—does this city ever sleep?

Unfortunately, no time could be spared exploring Istanbul at night. Only had four hours and a half to sleep before heading to the airport at 5:00am, to catch a flight to Sofia, Bulgaria.

I *will* visit Istanbul again.

Signing off this post at 6:00pm in my hotel in Sofia. Day off today, show in Sofia tomorrow, and then Belgrade.

Isaac

Tuesday, April 30, 2013

Istanbul, Turkey to Sofia, Bulgaria (April 28-29, 2013)

The following box shows an extensive list of everything I knew about Sofia before arriving here Sunday morning:

In other words: not much to work with. Not only have I never been here before, but I also can't recall any time in my life in which I said "I could really use a visit to Sofia right now".

Which is another positive thing in following a Knopfler tour: you end up visiting places you otherwise wouldn't think of visiting.

Arriving at Sofia presented the first mental challenge in the tour: waking up at 4:30am, in order to catch the 7:30am Turkish Airlines flight from Istanbul to Sofia.

It was harder than it already sounds.

As we left with the hotel's shuttle to the airport, looking outside the shuttle's window I was under the impression that I might be missing something. Sunday, 5:00am, and the streets are filled with people as if it's lunch time. What on earth is going on here? GO TO SLEEP, PEOPLE. It was as hard navigating the cab between pedestrians (and other vehicles) as it was hard doing so in sane, normal working hours.

Then we got to the airport—Istanbul's primary airport, named after modern Turkey's founder, Mustafa Kemal Atatürk (by the way, here is an interesting piece of trivia: in Turkey, it is illegal to criticize Atatürk and/or his legacy), which presents the fortunate traveller with quite the obnoxious airport experience.

> Here's a tip for you North Americans who are considering visiting Turkey and flying out of Atatürk airport: I know that some, if not most of you, ignore the fine print when flying within North America, advising you to arrive 2–3 hours prior departure.
>
> Once you're in Turkey, forget about it. Always be on the safe side. There are just too many things happening here.

First, you need to go through security *just in order to get into the terminal building*. I am not sure why—I've never seen it happening anywhere else—but I'm guessing it has something to do with safety precaution against possible terrorist attacks.

The problem (for the passengers) in this security line-up is that airport & airline staff have precedence. Hence, even a small line-up can end up taking long minutes to dissolve if a large group of an airline's staff enters the building.

Check-in seems to be a huge mess, so try checking in online.

Next up is passport control—*the first of two*. This takes a long time as each and every passport is thoroughly checked for your entry stamp, and you will be asked questions if your entry stamp isn't clear enough. Can take about one minute per passenger, so in a line-up of 50 people with 2 agents working in the passport control booths, you're looking at a potential 25 minutes wait.

Right after passport control, there's another, more thorough, security screening. Then, at the gate, there's yet *another* passport control process. That I have never seen done before, anywhere.

Much fun and hassle at 5:30am, after having slept about four hours the night before. Boarded the flight on time and passed out in my seat—a rare phenomenon, as it is extremely difficult for me to sleep during flights—being completely oblivious that the flight was delayed by about half an hour. An hour or so later, the plane touched ground in Letishte Sofia-Vrazhdebna, which, for all practical purposes, will henceforth be referred to as "Sofia's airport".

While Bulgaria belongs in the European Union, it is not a part of the European Monetary Union, thus it maintains its own currency (which is good for current EMU member countries; as if the Euro currency is not already in a huge pile of horse manure), called "Lev" and abbreviated "BGN". One BGN is worth approximately €0.50 and $0.68 CDN.

Hopped on a taxi cab to the city center. It was Sunday morning, hardly a living soul on the streets.

The hotel, Hotel Sofia Place, is conveniently located in the city centre, and save for having no air conditioning in the month of April, is quite good.

The last paragraph requires elaboration.

Weather forecast called for about 28°C. Having lived in Canada for the last ten years, with Vancouver's summer fluctuating around the 24°C mark, it was quite expected that the first thing I was going to do was to charge at the air conditioner and attempt to operate it—a rather simple operation that had triggered a very interesting learning experience.

Quite expectedly, nothing worked. Minutes after reporting it, we got a call from the front desk saying that the air conditioning will not work today, and possibly not tomorrow. "No problem then", I said; "let's move to another hotel", which is more or less when things started to get really strange.

As I was searching for a hotel, Jeroen went downstairs to talk to the front desk guy and inform him that we're leaving. Here's how the conversation went:

Jeroen: We are not happy with the fact that the air conditioning isn't going to be working, as the weather calls for 28°C and we are thinking about moving to a different hotel.

Attendant: What can I do for you?

Jeroen: Well, we would like to check out and go to a different hotel.

Attendant: Have you tried opening the windows?

<Silence>

Jeroen: No.

<Silence>

Jeroen: But we were specifically looking for a hotel room with air conditioning, so we're interested in moving to a different hotel.

Attendant: All other hotels in the city will probably have the same problem.

Now, I don't know about you, but I found the attendant's last statement to be somewhat puzzling. Yet, I checked. Called up the nearby Best Western—a respectable 4 star hotel—and inquired about the workability of their air conditioning system.

What do you know… Same issue. "We don't have air conditioning today, but we will most likely have it working tomorrow. But we can't promise anything."

(On a side note, opening the windows *did* help.)

More than I was frightened of the prospect of spending two days in a boiling hotel room, I was intrigued to know what the HELL is the problem this city has with air conditioning. After a few attempts to find out, it turned out that the reason has to do with how piping works in most hotels in the city center area. The same pipes are being used for both heating and cooling, and there's a system that is tuned to switch into "cooling mode" on exactly May 1.

Is it possible to set it to "cooling mode" earlier? probably. Can you get to anyone who would take such decision? no.

Also, the western visitor to Bulgaria is likely to discover that everything here is cheap. There's a sad reality behind this. Bulgaria's economy was never really strong, and is nowadays going through a difficult financial crisis: unemployment is high and electricity—while costing less than anywhere else in the European Union—is still very expensive considering the fact that the average wages are about €400 per month (that's $530 CDN) and the median wages are much lower, at the €250–300 range.

Recently, riots ensued in Bulgaria, demanding that the government is to be sent either to home or to hell, whichever is closer. I was told that people reached a situation when they can't pay their bills anymore. As finances is one of my hobbies, I had to inquire further; and as annoying people with in-depth examples is another one of my hobbies, here are some numbers.

€0.0846 per kWh (price of electricity in Bulgaria) means that a person consuming 100 kWh ends up spending €8.46, which, considering Bulgaria's average salary, is 2.115% of their wages.

Compare with Vancouver, Canada. But here, let's give Bulgaria a head start. Instead of comparing to Vancouver's average wage, we'll compare it to the *minimum wage*. The minimum wage is $10.25 CDN per hour. Assume 180 working hours per month, you get $1,845 CDN.

Electricity costs $0.068 CDN per kWh (according to my most recent bill); 100 kWh costs $6.80 CDN.

Hence, 100 kWh costs the Vancouverite earning *minimum wage* about 0.36% of their salary.

In total: the financial burden on a Bulgarian earning *average wages* when paying their electricity bill is almost 6 times (!!!) heavier than it is for the Vancouverite earning *minimum wage*.

To that, add the fact that Vancouver is the *most expensive city in Canada* when it comes to overall cost of living.

That, like many other things recently, set me off to do some thinking. Obviously, the initial reaction to finding out that air conditioning is kaput for the next two days is disappointment and frustration. But really, wouldn't it be considered selfish to feel bad about something like this? Perhaps these negative emotions are the direct result of myself taking things for granted.

Now, you might think that "electricity" is such a basic commodity that it's natural to take for granted; I know I did. But then you come to realize that, what you consider in life to be so basic and elementary, is more than likely a big bonus in the grand scheme of things. In other words: instead of bitching about not having enough electricity to cool you off in the hot summer days in Sofia, perhaps it'd be prudent if you shut the hell up and be thankful for having the privilege to have such elements so readily available to you in your own home.

After catching up with some much needed sleep, we set off to the central bus terminal to complete one of the two missing links in our travel plans: bus tickets from Sofia to Belgrade on April 30, as these could not be purchased online (the other missing link is the bus ticket from Trieste, Italy to Ljubljana, Slovenia next week).

Long walk to the central bus station:

Very handsome central bus station building. Too bad it's the domestic one; the international bus station is across the street, looking much less pleasant.

After spending about 45 minutes waiting in line, we were sent back in shame as it turns out that you need to present a passport when purchasing a ticket (makes absolutely no sense to me, but nevertheless).

Back to the hotel to do some work, and then decided to try the bus station once again and get the tickets' purchase over with. A subway ride seemed more appropriate. Sofia's underground system—at least, the part that runs south to north—is relatively new, less than a year old.

There, we met with Slavina, whom I met a few years ago in London and kept in touch with since. Slavina is local to Sofia, and was very helpful in ensuring that the tickets purchased were really what we were looking for.

(You would think that the *international* bus terminal in Sofia will be manned with English speaking personnel. Think again.)

After that, a stroll in Sofia's main entertainment avenue along with Slavina, taking a few shots along the way:

A few drinks on a curb-side patio, until Slavina's friend, Maya, joined and demonstrated to me that it is physically and mentally possible to drink coke and espresso at the same time and actually enjoying it. Bloody absurd, I'd say. In proper countries, doing something like this would cost you a night in jail.

Hours passed quickly until we all bid each other adieu at around 11:00pm. Back to the hotel to catch up with some work.

First day in Sofia turned from absolute boredom to quite the enjoyment thanks to Slavina and her friend Maya who joined us later. Hats off to them.

Dreading the upcoming nine days, which are going to be the hardest travelling days in the entire tour, a joint decision was made to keep effort levels to a minimum on Monday, the day of the show. Caught up with work, great lunch in Cactus conveniently located about a block away and I was all set to keep to myself in the hotel room until I realized that the next 9–10 days are going to be hell, and it's time to do the laundry.

I don't understand what's going on inside the head of a hotel owner when coming up with a price list for laundry. €1 for washing (drying not included!) a pair of underwear? You can't be serious. This is Sofia; you should be able to buy an underwear factory for €1. €4 for washing *one shirt*?

Naturally, we set out to look for a laundry place. Found it. "Do you speak English?", I asked. "No", she said. Goodbye.

Alright, Sofia, you wanna play tough? I'll hand-wash my underwear, I said. And I did. Now how do you dry them?

This is very simple to do when you happen to carry a 3 meters long LAN cable that you're unlikely to use. Luckily, the hotel room had a balcony.

Took the opportunity to take a few pictures of the view from the hotel's balcony:

Isaac's "Privateering" Tour Blog

Short stroll down the street for some coffee:

The night before, Slavina offered to join her and her friend, Maya, for a short trip to the nearby mountains.

I have a long-running romance with mountains. Mountains were the reason why I fell in love with the city of Vancouver in the first place, and is also why I decided to finally move there two years ago—the *Get Lucky* tour providing another great deal of motivation. There are at least four things I can hardly say "no" to, and being in the vicinity of mountains is one of them.

Sofia is surrounded by mountains, which look quite pleasant when viewed from the city centre and look even better up close. The destination: a desserts shop called "Romance" (although there's nothing romantic about it, at least not in day time), offering a very nice view of Sofia from the top.

Wonderful desserts, plus I got proof for the coke & espresso nonsense:

Headed back to the hotel, and then off to the venue for tonight's concert.

The National Palace of Culture consists of various halls and theaters, and as far as I am concerned, it wins the title of "the most poorly signed venue in the history of venues".

I have watched this band perform approximately 150 times before, in many venues in many countries. Never was the experience of actually obtaining the physical paper ticket so annoying and stressful. After about 20+ minutes circling this giant complex, I still had no idea where the tickets are to be collected. Luckily, Slavina was on site and showed us the way—a small hidden doorway, leading to a set of stairs, behind which there is one small counter (practically invisible).

Now back in the venue:

The stage contained this:

Which implied that a new song was going to be played. The show kicked off about ten minutes past 8 o'clock, to the sound of massive cheers.

When it was the time for the third song, Richard Bennett took a seat next to the pedal steel. During the joint Dylan-Knopfler tour, *Redbud Tree* was played with a lap steel guitar, so I thought we were going to hear that song again, until the opening C chord was played.

Redbud Tree doesn't start with a C, but *Seattle* does. Talk about a surprise—definitely a favourite from Knopfler's latest album. Beautiful live arrangement that just works, and by the looks of it, the band definitely enjoyed playing it.

Seattle is a nice city, but I'm much more in favour of that other city that is located approximately two hours and a half north of it, across the border. Homesickness kicked in and failed to depart until the next morning.

What else we had? an ecstatic audience, a cute young boy sitting on his father's lap at the front row, seeming to enjoy every minute of this wonderful show. We also had a *Sultans of Swing* solo that was rather different than the usual line, and an aggressive *Hill Farmer's Blues* solo worth listening to.

The second surprise came at the encore. As *Brothers in Arms* was skipped, *So Far Away* was played and I was under the impression that the show is over. Fortunately, the band had other plans. *Piper to the End*, the concluding song from *Get Lucky* that was played in 86 out of the 87 *Get Lucky* concerts in 2010, concluded the show. It was a real treat listening to this wonderful tune again, played live. Whoever went to a few shows in 2010 and listened to *Piper to the End* being played live, must know what I'm talking about.

After the show, we remembered that we need to buy some sandwiches for the next morning as we'll be taking an early bus drive to Belgrade. Stopped over at a local cafeteria for a sandwich and a couple to go, and off to the hotel to pack.

Concluding this post from the hotel room in Belgrade. What a hectic day, I tell you…

Isaac

Wednesday, May 1, 2013

Sofia, Bulgaria to Belgrade, Serbia (April 30, 2013)

Woke up at 6:00am, quick morning routine and headed straight to the bus terminal, this time taking a taxi cab. Nobody was quite in the position of walking 30 minutes carrying travel bags in 6:30am. Short ride and we were there.

There aren't quite enough words in the English language to describe the negative emotions I get when I even hear the word "bus". Yet, luck has it and this tour involves three bus rides:

- Sofia, Bulgaria to Belgrade, Serbia;
- Trieste, Italy to Ljubljana, Slovenia; and
- Prague, Czech Republic to Lodz, Poland. This one is going to be the hardest travel day of the tour and, for now, I prefer to not even think about it.

The only other way to get from Sofia to Belgrade by public transport is to take a night train, 9 hours or so. Infrastructure in eastern Europe doesn't allow for massive train schedules as western European countries do. In addition, there is a specific problem concerned with Bulgaria in that respect, as Bulgaria's poor economy results in a shortage of diesel supply. Diesel is somewhat required for the proper functioning of trains.

As I dislike night trains just as much as I dislike buses, we preferred the shorter ride. Two buses daily from Sofia to Nis (a city in Serbia; from there, connect to Belgrade using the Serbian public transport system), and we had to take the earlier one in order to make it to the show.

Bus left on 7:30am sharp. An hour or so later, we were stopped for passport control in the Bulgaria-Serbia border. Quite the impressive ride, actually: not far west from Sofia, the scenery takes a sharp turn into the green. Hills and small red-roofed houses. Pretty.

I tired to catch up with some missing sleep during the bus ride, with limited success. Well, after a couple of years of visiting my home country 3–4 times a year, flying 18 hours each direction, I'm quite used to sit down stationary for a long period of time. My luck.

Three hours and a half after departure, we arrived at Niš, which is of the only sizable towns en route to Sofia. There, we had to unload our luggage and wait in line to exchange our Bulgarian bus ticket to a Serbian bus ticket.

Of course, we had no idea that we were supposed to exchange the ticket. Luck has it and, in front of us, a nice Serbian lady who answers to the name Nada happened to speak English and explained to us how things work. Ten minutes later, we were already in the Serbian bus heading to Belgrade.

Nice ride again, lots of green hills spotted with red-roofed houses. The country side of Serbia appears to be as if it froze in time for a couple of generations. Through the bus windows, looking at the simple life in rural Serbia made me yearn for some peace and quiet myself. How would it be, I wondered, to live in such conditions? How would it be to leave the big city and live in a rural area for a while, take life slowly?

Then I remembered the eight years I spent living in Ontario's Waterloo region. The yearning stopped almost instantly.

Had a nice chat with Nada—it's fun to meet interesting people along the way—and the ride went by OK; not as terrible as I had expected.

Finally arrived at Belgrade's central bus station at 1:30pm local time.

It was warm.

Belgrade? Wait. What? Why? Where again? Belgrade?

That was, in general, my line of thought when I noticed that Belgrade was added to the tour's schedule.

My knowledge of Serbia was (and still is) rather limited, and revolves mostly around the various Yugoslav Wars that took place in former Yugoslavia during most of the 1990's. I also have two friends—ex-colleagues—who were born in Serbia and told me a few things about it.

Belgrade is the capital city of Serbia. During the 20th century, Belgrade's name was largely associated with wars. World War I started by Austria-Hungary declaring war on Serbia (after a Yugoslav nationalist assassinated the heir to Austria-Hungary's throne). The city was bombed in the summer of 1914, and in 1915 it was mostly destroyed before being taken back again by Serb troops.

During World War II, Yugoslavia signed an agreement with the Axis powers with the intention of keeping itself out of the War. That triggered protests in Belgrade, leading in the city being brutally attacked by the German air force on April 1941, resulting in 24,000 dead. Shortly after, Yugoslavia was invaded by the Axis powers.

The German military governor of Serbia, Franz Böhme, decided on a rule whereby for every German killed, 100 Serbs or Jews would be shot. He kept his word: Guerrilla attacks on the Axis powers in 1941 resulted in thousands of citizens being killed according to this vicious "rule", a true work of inhumane bullshit such that only Nazi Germany could come up with. The city was liberated from German occupation in 1944, and The Federal People's Republic of Yugoslavia was established in Belgrade shortly after.

From there on until the 1990's, Belgrade functioned as the capital city of Yugoslavia.

But it wasn't over. The Yugoslav Wars that took place during the 1990's, with an arch-killer by the name of Slobodan Milošević as the ruler of Serbia, resulted in mass killings of citizens through ethnic cleansing. Milošević was later indicted in the Hague and was accused in a long list of war crimes. He died in his prison cell during the trial.

Sometimes it seems that the worst thing that ever happened to mankind is mankind itself.

Avoiding the myriad of crooks pretending to be "taxi drivers", we found a taxi nearby and off we went to the hotel. While the vast majority of attractions in Belgrade are in the old city, we opted at a hotel in the new city as the venue would be close by. Enough time will be left to explore the old city on May 1, before the flight to Milano in the evening.

The hotel, Hotel Adresa, is a new hotel located in the new city. It is located inside a complex that involves a few stores, restaurants and cafe. Very poor signing resulted in us looking for the hotel's entrance for about 30 minutes: the immense heat did nothing to help, and by the time I located the hotel's entrance, I was just about to completely dehydrate.

Very helpful staff, and an *amazing* room. Quite far (about 3km) from the old city, but if you're looking for a place in Belgrade to stay the night, consider this place, if only for this *huge* walk-in shower.

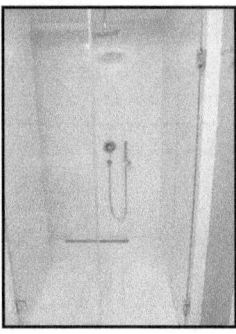

Having eaten just a small sandwich since morning, the first order of business was a meal in a nearby restaurant, then off to the room to chill out and regain some strength for the show.

The Kombank Arena is a general-purpose indoor arena in New Belgrade, and is one of the biggest indoor arenas in the world with the capacity of up to 25,000—depending on the event being held. It does look massive from afar.

The first item of notice in this arena was the entry procedure, which was much unlike security screening in airports—except that, here, you wouldn't need to present any boarding pass. Security is quite tight, I'd say.

(The three pictures above were taken after the concert. Not that it really matters.)

Arrived at the venue about half an hour before the show's scheduled start at 8:00pm. Five minutes before the scheduled start time, the venue looked like this:

More than half empty. I don't know whether this is typical to Belgrade, but it turns out that a concert's "scheduled start time" doesn't really mean much here. The concert started forty minutes (!) past schedule, and was well worth the wait.

The habit of being surprised with new set additions over the last few shows is a real treat and, fortunately, didn't stop in Belgrade. After a familiar opening of three songs, an unrecognized stage layout took place. Still, the first two bars of the song left no doubt: *5:15am*, from the album *Shangri La* of 2005, was played live for the first time this tour—and if my memory serves me right, *ever*.

A real treat. Of my few favourite songs in *Shangri La*, *5:15am* is a beautiful ballad telling the story of someone returning home after a night shift and noticing a dead body in a Mark Ten Jaguar—a mob hit, with the casualty being someone who stole money from the mafia. It features a warm Stratocaster rhythm, and as good as it is in the studio album, it is even better played live.

(It should be noted that some solo parts in this song, at least performed live, were performed by Richard Bennett, with Mark playing the rhythm. At least, that was my impression.)

Also new in Belgrade's show: for the first time in the last couple of thousands of years, *Romeo and Juliet* was not followed by *Sultans of Swing*. I am guessing that this omission was decided upon because there was this guy playing a ridiculously terrible rendition of *Sultans of Swing* outside the venue, featuring a mistuned acoustic guitar and a rather selective memory when it comes to the actual song.

Another addition to this tour's set shortly after: *Miss You Blues*, played in Seattle last October in the joint Knopfler-Dylan tour. That was played after an intro that is most often heard prior to *Donegan's Gone*, however Richard holding a Telecaster kind of gave me the impression that a different song was going to be played.

During *Marbletown*, Mike McGoldrick was suddenly seen fleeing the stage, returning with a flute shortly after. It is unclear why, though; the flute he came back with wasn't (to my knowledge) the flute being used for Marbletown. Still it was amusing to see him running back to the stage making it just in time for his pivotal part in the *Marbletown* jam—maybe three or four seconds prior.

Security before and during the show was quite strict. I didn't see any sign of over-aggressiveness, but security personnel did make a great effort to ensure that the stage area remains clear at all times—even before the show started. During the entire show, once could easily get the sense that they are being watched. As a result of this sort of intimidation, nobody from the front few rows stood up for a standing ovation at the end of the show: people were simply reluctant to express themselves. A standing ovation did take place eventually, after a minute or so of cheering.

After the show, back to the hotel and looking for a place to eat. The hotel is inside a shopping complex in a rather boring area of town: nothing to do here past 11:00pm, so that meant going to bed hungry.

Signing off this post at 9:30am, May 1. Today is a day off, flying to Milano in the evening for the night, then Torino the next morning for Thursday's show. Will catch up with some work and try to make some time to visit Belgrade's old city area.

Isaac

Thursday, May 2, 2013

Belgrade, Serbia to Milano, Italy (May 1, 2013)

The day-off in Belgrade came at the very right time. The day before, a long, boring bus ride from Sofia, arriving at the boiling hot city of Belgrade, and then a (great) concert at the Kombank Arena—quite the tiring day.

Woke up and checked the weather forecast, which called for 30°C—which is about 6°C more than I'm willing to handle in a good day. Still, I was interested in seeing some of Belgrade, having been told a thing or two in its favour.

The staff at *Hotel Adresa* wins the prize of the loveliest hospitality staff so far in the tour. Hats off to them for wonderful service and maintaining a hotel with stunning rooms.

We had a few hours to kill before leaving towards Belgrade's airport. A short walk, and then hopped on a bus to the city centre. Time constraints, as well as an apparent wish to conserve energy, prompted us to opt at a quiet walk around the city center: no elaborate sightseeing —I'll leave that to my next time here, which, judging by my life's circumstances at the moment, is likely to be never.

Walking in the city center area, you wouldn't be able to tell that this city was, more than once, the subject of merciless beating by various armies. It does look old and dusty, but nothing that would indicate savage military beating. Perhaps I didn't look hard enough.

It was May 1, Labour Holiday in Serbia. Labour Day in Serbia is a holiday; however, unlike most western countries (that I know of), Labour Day here is (also) celebrated by demonstrations commemorating Serbia's touch with communism and solidarity.

Rather vocal demonstration around the area of *Hotel Moskva*; I could not make any sense of whatever was announced through the speakers (carried by an old beaten car in front of the demonstrators), but from the voice's tone, I could tell that someone is pretty upset.

Altogether a rather negative tone of things, so we decided to abandon the premises.

The insane heat and the unbelievable humidity shortly got into me and I was pretty much content confining myself to some coffee place and let time pass, playing online chess with one of my closest childhood friends who wishes to remain anonymous, and thus will henceforth be referred to as Mr. L.

Oh, yes. I forgot about that. Chess.

I used to spend quite a bit of time playing chess when I was growing up. When I was 20 years old, Gary Kasparov arrived to Israel for promoting the business of a new mobile carrier in the Israeli market—the famous *Orange* brand. A part of the promotion included a simultaneous chess match against a few dozen players.

I was very close to score a draw. The game got to a point when Mr. Kasparov had to think for about a minute or two on his next moves. The game was very tight; at some point, I decided on a new strategy, and made a questionable move. Kasparov quickly replied with a killer move that left me no chance but resigning two or three moves later. I was devastated for a few days.

(Kasparov ended up winning all games that day.)

Recently, I started playing chess again—this time, almost exclusively online (as I have no Canadian friends who know how, or are willing, to play). I have a profile on chess.com, called "*isaac_s*". If you play chess and would like to keep me company during the tour, then by all means, let's play.

Until then, I'll keep on losing to Mr. L exclusively.

Back to the hotel via bus, took our luggage and off we went to Belgrade's airport, for another obnoxious airport experience which seems to be the general theme in east European airports.

Check in—quickly done, thank you. Then off to security (which was very quick, thankfully—probably because it was a holiday).

Then came passport control.

I happen to carry two passports, as I am a dual citizen of two wonderful countries. For convenience's sake, I hold them both in one leather-based passport case. The passport control officer, upon noticing my second passport, looked at me as if he was threatened by something.

"So you have two passports?" he asked, in a tone that implied some sort of trouble.

"Yes. I have dual citizenship", I replied.

I seem to recall reading somewhere that less than 1% of the global population holds more than one passport. Some research I conducted a while back indeed revealed the fact that the concept of dual citizenship isn't well recognized by certain countries, mainly in Africa. Why? beats the living hell out of me. I happen to have been born in one country, and later immigrated to another. Under no circumstances am I willing to give up any of my citizenships, as my life is (at the moment) quite balanced between the two and I fully accept the responsibilities derived from both.

(The single most important rule of holding more than one passport is that when you travel, *always exit a country with the same passport you used for entering it*. Makes a lot of sense, as countries keep record of incoming and outgoing passengers.)

But why is holding more than one passport still frowned upon in certain countries? I couldn't find an answer for this. If any of you knows, I urge you to share your knowledge as a comment to this post.

Once the officer got over the dual passport issue, he couldn't find the Serbian entry stamp—the reason being that such a stamp never really existed. When we crossed the Bulgaria-Serbia border by bus, passport control consisted of a Serbian officer boarding the bus, taking all passports, leaving and returning with all passports several minutes later. No stamp in my passport, none in Jeroen's as well.

That prompted the passport control officer to inquire Jeroen and I about the method by which we entered Serbia. Obviously we had nothing to hide. They seemed a bit non-believing at first, but after a while they let us through.

The malpractice of neglecting to stamp passports is not exclusive to Serbia, by the way. I have heard of cases of this happening before in eastern Europe, as well as a few countries in the far east.

Once that was done, off we went to the gate. A slight 30 minutes delay, but the obnoxious airport experience started getting to me (I suppose I became quite spoiled, getting used to how relatively flawless airport experience is in Canadian airports), and once that happened, all I really wanted was to just leave the place. The sight of various security personnel armed with pistols and clubs didn't make me feel any more welcome, neither did the second security check at the gate (with X-rays, body scanning and everything).

Richard Bennett wrote in his blog about the band's airport experience, and concluded with an inconvenient, yet perfectly valid, statement: we, westerners, are, after all, guests here; and we shall abide by our host's customs.

Still, I can't help but thinking how much better this sad blue planet would be, if people and governments, in general, would behave nicer to one another.

Meanwhile, reading the news I came to learn that May 1st didn't go quite well in Turkey. The Turkish government decided to shut down all public transport leading to Istanbul's city center, in order to avoid "unwanted" demonstrations in *Taksim Square*—coincidentally, two blocks away from where I was staying just a few days ago.

Demonstrations, however, did take place, which prompted Istanbul's police to use brutal means to control (read: oppress) said demonstrations. Various demonstration control measures were taken (helicopters included), resulting in many injuries and a total mess.

Makes me question, then, to what extent is Turkey's society really "free"? Criticizing Mustafa Kemal Atatürk is illegal. You know what? as odd as it sounds, I'm willing to accept it. Must be some sort of a cultural thing—you want to be able to positively commemorate the founder of modern Turkey—fine. I mean, borderline fine. Not perfect, but let's move on.

But shutting down public transport in order to avoid demonstrations? I don't know, something smells rather suspicious here. I'd understand if there was some sort of a terrorism concern or something of the like. But hey, pals, we're talking about a demonstration. To avoid demonstrations, you shut down public transport? And once demonstrations actually took place, what the hell is the deal with using brutal force to "control" them?

Pretty disappointing. I wish well to all people who were injured during the demonstrations.

On the positive note, I suppose it could have ended much worse, as it did in 1977.

Signing off this post while on board Jat Airways flight 416 to Milano; touching ground in about an hour or so, and then quickly to a hotel in the city center, leaving by train to Torino tomorrow.

Very excited to be in Italy again.

Isaac

Friday, May 3, 2013

Milano to Torino, Italy (May 2, 2013)

It felt great to finally arrive to Italy on Wednesday evening. How great? as great as it was to leave Serbia; and then some.

I have very fond memories of Italy from the last time I was here, in the summer of 2010 during the *Get Lucky* tour. While my senses of smell and taste were gone for a few days due to illness (must have been something I caught in Budapest, the night before arriving at Italy), rendering me unable to appreciate any sort of food, still—Italy made such an impression on me that I vowed to visit it again in the future.

The move from Serbia to Northern Italy within the span of a few hours did well to establish how different the two are. While, to the westerner visitor, Serbia may appear somewhat oppressed and gray—life certainly appears more vivid less than 800km away.

As soon as I left the aircraft in Milano's Malpensa airport, things started to seem significantly more upbeat, more open, more inviting; more intriguing. There's something about the air in Italy that makes me feel like home there.

That may not be as far fetched as it sounds. Many claim that Israelis and Italians are very much alike in terms of social interactions, body language and even looks (I was mistakenly thought to be an Italian quite a few times in the past, which is quite the insult for Italians); and while I did spend the last ten years in Canada, Israel is where I was born and raised.

From Milano's airport, it's a 45 minutes train ride to Milano Centrale. I should say that, after about a week of getting around using airplanes, it felt absolutely great starting to use trains again. Unfortunately, eastern Europe leaves much to be desired in terms of railway transport, which made the eastern European part of the tour excruciating to plan and execute (with the hell of all rides—the bus from Prague to Łódź—still lurking; that's next week). Here in western Europe, though, trains *are* the way to go.

From Milano Centrale, it is a ten minutes walk to Marconi Hotel—a hotel that looks very good on paper, very good from the outside, but was a complete failure. Like in Sofia, it turns out that air conditioning in hotel rooms in Milano start their "cooling period" in June—a fact that nobody bothered to mention when the hotel was booked; but even worse, there's an ongoing Wi-Fi connectivity issue in the hotel rooms, which, for certain people following concert tours, is more than a mild annoyance. Avoid it.

But hey, this is Italy, and when in Italy, first thing's first: pizza. Got a recommendation for a nearby pizza place. Ristorante Pane e Tulipani, just up the street from the hotel, offers a very interesting menu and a pizza that is of the best that I have ever had.

Sitting in the restaurant and gazing at people—diners, waiters, managers—I felt something. Just looking at how these people talk, interact, even their body language—you get the sense that these people know how to live. They seem free and joyful. No, it wasn't a fancy restaurant by any means; just a simple Italian restaurant, definitely not the place for the rich and famous to hang out in. Considering the fact that Italy's economy isn't exactly in its finest hour, you instantly know that happiness on people's faces here, in Milano, doesn't stem from finances and economy but from the knowledge of how to live well.

Pizza was devoured in a rather insane pace, then back to the hotel. No Wi-Fi in the room, so I opted at the next best thing—a good night sleep.

Regionale Veloce 2010 from Milano to Torino left at 11:18am, very well timed—past breakfast in the hotel (lots of desserts, of which I enjoyed none) as well as catching up with some work from the hotel's lobby, where Wi-Fi actually did work. Two hours in first class, and on 1:10pm, the train arrived at Torino Porta Nuova, which is Torino's main railway station.

I have never been to Torino before. I knew of its existence—the world famous Juventus soccer team calls Torino home—but never got around to see it, mostly because none of the recent Knopfler tours stopped here.

Dropped bags in the hotel—Hotel Roma e Rocca Cavour—and immediately set out looking for a place to eat. A quick search in TripAdvisor revealed a restaurant called Augusto Ristorante Pizzeria; unfortunately, due to a bug in TripAdvisor's Android app, the map took us about 1.5km away to *Piazza Cesare Augusto*, instead of to the restaurant which happened to be about 100m from the hotel. Still, it was a nice walk.

Piazza San Carlo is a beautiful square in Torino's city center, and a major attraction spotted with appealing cafes and restaurants.

Torino features beautiful narrow streets that are very typical, in appearance and appeal, to Italy: intimate, friendly, inviting—hell, I could definitely live here for a while.

Finally arrived to Piazza Cesare Augusto:

Isaac's "Privateering" Tour Blog

And then, upon realizing the navigation mistake, went back through an alternate route, revealing more of Torino's beauty.

It's these little beautiful cafes that I'd like to have my morning coffee. There's something appealing in sipping hot beverage in small, intimate patios like these: actually, the city planners of Vancouver took note of this, and tried to bring a similar concept to the (now-revitalized, previously a paradise for drug dealers) district of *Gastown* (ever heard of that famous steam clock of Vancouver? That's where it is. Never heard of it? then I suppose it's not famous enough). The result is pleasing, but still, no cigar.

By the time we arrived at the actual restaurant we had initially planned to go to, lunch time was over and most restaurants were closed until dinner time. Starving, we came across a self-serve type establishment that served good (though not great) food; that did the trick.

Back to the hotel to catch up with work, plus a short nap. 6:00pm arrived — time to head to the venue, this time located quite far from the hotel, about 4km away.

The plan was to eat a short dinner before heading to the concert: take a bus, stop by at a local famous pizza place along the way, then proceed to the venue by foot. Everything was planned down to the smallest detail.

There was only one problem with that plan: it was devised while I was asleep and I knew nothing about it before the Dutchman woke me up and told me "we have 12 minutes to catch a bus". Talk about rude awakening. Bus was missed, but with the help of the hotel's staff we found some alternate plan using another bus.

Now, here's a tip: in Torino, you can't buy bus tickets on the bus itself. You need to buy those in stores, such as convenience stores.

Neither of us was aware of this. Boarding the bus and asking how much it costs, we were told, in fluent Italian (that neither of us could make any sense of), that what we were trying to accomplish negates pretty much everything that Torino's bus system stands for. We knew what the driver meant by assuming that "No borda" means "not on board", but mainly thanks to the help of an English-speaking lovely Italian lady who stood by and informed us that we're clueless.

As I am not in the habit of taking free rides in buses, I was inclined to leave the bus but the lady urged us to stay on board, and explain the situation to the ticket maestro if and when they come on board. They didn't. Still, I may be purchasing bus tickets tomorrow and do nothing with them; I hate the idea of owing things to people, let alone owing money to entire cities.

Dropped off the bus, right in front of the pizza place, Pizzeria Vecchio Forno Garibaldi: rated #47 out of 1,449 restaurants in Torino, this place serves deep-dish pizzas, a far departure from Italy's normal thin crust ones. Delicious, but I think I'll stick to the thin crust pizzas from now on.

A short walk from there to the venue to pick up the tickets…

… then backtracked a bit for some coffee and tea in an extremely cute cafe near the venue — I can't find a direct link to the establishment's website (possibly because they don't have any) but you can see it here. A small tea, coffee & desserts place — local, not too fancy but extremely inviting. Baking everything on site. Tea, cappuccino and a few cookies for €3.30. I want to live here.

Back to the venue…

… and spent the next half an hour saying hello to many Knopfler fans I had met during previous tours. People from France and Switzerland made their way to Torino to catch the first show in the tour's Italian leg, was good to see them all.

Other than the food, the other reason I liked Italy so much during the last tour was the audience. The Italian audience is very passionate—more so in the south, but northern Italians aren't exactly the most reserved audience themselves. Much excitement in the venue: Knopfler's fan base in Italy is of the stronger ones. He is known to love performing in Italy, and I suppose it wouldn't be too risky to assume that the immense support he receives from Italian audiences is one of the main reasons for that.

The Torino show consisted mostly on fast, rhythmic, rocking songs. After being absent from the Belgrade show, *Sultans of Swing* made a comeback (I guess you can't do without this tune for too long), but for me, the definite highlight of the evening was the introduction of a new song to the tour's set: *Kingdom of Gold*, previously played a few times during the Knopfler-Dylan tour (if I'm not mistaken, only in its North American leg).

Kingdom of Gold is one of my favourite Knopfler tunes, both for its haunting melody and for its interesting lyrics, which **I am guessing** are a sarcastic stab at capitalism. There are many references to typical capitalistic economy elements in that song (ribbons, numbers, the Gods of the bought and the sold—these must refer to a stock market), and it appears to be telling the story of a money-driven society defeating perpetrators by using immense force, whereas such force is not necessarily needed. This is my own interpretation, and it might have popped into my head following all sorts of thoughts I've been having in the last couple of years about how modern society is affected by money—for good and bad, mostly the bad. I'll leave these thoughts for another post, but for now, here's an interesting article in which bankers explain why they couldn't possibly live on a $1 million salary.

Back to the show. Another new addition to the set—*Gator Blood*, not of my favourites but still sounds better played live. A rocking song, joining *I Used to Could* in setting the rocking theme for the entire concert.

The Running of the Bulls made its first appearance in the tour, when the audience attached itself to the stage barrier right after *Speedway at Nazareth*. Not much violence, though; I suppose we'll see some more violence in the vicinity of the stage once we reach the south.

Very good rocking concert, and here are some pictures, courtesy of the Dutchman:

After the show, a quick taxi ride back to the hotel and off for a good night sleep, before heading back to Milano.

Isaac

Saturday, May 4, 2013

Torino to Milano, Italy (May 3, 2013)

Only one day after leaving Milano to the beautiful city Torino, I had to bid Torino adieu and head back to Milano for Friday's concert. Same train ride as the day before, only in the opposite direction—quite the uneventful ride, with very little to offer in terms of scenery—two hours well spent resting.

The hotel booked for the second night in Milano was the Carlyle Brera Hotel, located in the trendy, pretty district of Brera in Milano's city center. This hotel turned out to be significantly better than the disappointing Hotel Marconi in which I had stayed just two nights before, which is not a huge surprise—it was me who booked it rather than the Flying Dutchman.

Upon arriving at Milano Centrale, hunger struck so the plan was to get to the hotel as soon as physically possible and head to lunch. The Dutchman took it upon himself to plan the route from Milano Centrale to the hotel, located some 2.5km away.

"Taking the subway isn't going to help us much", he concluded, thus sentencing us to walk 2.5km through Milano's busy streets, carrying luggage and "enjoying" the sun and humidity. I would not wish such a walk on you, whether I like you or not: you know the paddle of sweat you get on your back, when you're walking for 45 minutes in sunny, humid weather, carrying a backpack? oh, you know it? good. Just checking.

It was very nice to discover, once we arrived at the hotel, that there is a subway station *less than 30 meters away from it*. 3 stops from Milano Centrale, 5 minutes ride.

I looked at the Dutchman, the Dutchman looked back at me, with an apologetic facial expression that did very little to soften the frustration and very much to aggravate it.

"You have just lost your navigation privileges for this tour", I said.

Well, look at the bright side: I did lose a lot of calories during that walk.

First order of business upon arriving at the hotel was to look for a place for lunch. That had to be done quickly before restaurants close (most restaurants here are only open for certain hours around common dining times—lunch and dinner; if you'd like to eat something outside normal dining hours, you'd have to settle for a cafe, or a snack bar, serving sandwiches and other light foods).

A quick search in TripAdvisor's immensely slow mobile app revealed a proper restaurant by the name of La Rosa Nera—of course, an Italian restaurant (yes, smartass. I know. All restaurants in Italy are "Italian restaurants" as they are located in Italy. Work with me here), because who would even bother considering consuming non-Italian food in the very heart of Milano? The restaurant, located a few minutes walk from the hotel, in the heart of Brera district, offers superb Italian food, all made on the spot (including the pasta).

Italians appear to be very specific regarding how and where they want their Wi-Fi access. I didn't quite understand this sign:

Kept on walking around Brera…

Time for some after-meal meal. Still in Brera, there's a place called Panarello. The ordering process was quite frustrating (interestingly, almost nobody there speaks English even though this district is a major tourist area), but the food, desserts & drinks are good; €7.50 for snacks and drinks for two people, you can't go wrong.

Then back to the hotel, to catch up with some work.

Daria and Valeria, sisters, living in northern Italy, made their way to Milano for the concert. Two super nice ladies whom I had met a few years ago in past Knopfler tours. During the Get Lucky tour, I arrived at Italy being rather ill after catching some bug in Budapest; the two sisters were kind enough to host me for a few days and help me out with arranging a doctor visit, making my stay in northern Italy in 2010 quite the memorable experience. For that, I am grateful to them for eternity.

As the venue for Milano's concert was rather far from the city center, we agreed to meet in Navigli for a pre-show dinner. I knew nothing of Navigli district before, which goes to show how helpful it is to hang out with people who are familiar with the area you're in. This area in Milano is very pretty, boasting colourful buildings on both sides of a canal going through the district—and of course, millions of spots to enjoy good food, drinks and desserts.

The Navigli was a system of artificial canals constructed in the middle ages in order to make Milano accessible from the sea. Leonardo da Vinci, upon arriving to Milano in 1482, was commissioned with the task of designing a system that would make it possible to navigate, by sea, from Lake Como to Milano. The Navigli continued to be developed over the following generations, until it was deserted in the 19th century.

There's a specific type of risotto dish that Milano is famous for—*risotto allo zafferano* (risotto with saffron)—and the two sisters insisted that we all give it a shot. Not much convincing was needed—I am very easy to be convinced to consume Italian food of any sort, let alone local specialties. It was still rather early for dinner time (around 6:30pm) so most restaurants weren't ready for serving dinner yet, but eventually, we found one that was—Alzaia 26, which also happens to be the restaurant's address. Soft, delicious risotto, pleasantly consumed on the restaurant's patio looking at the canal and having conversation.

Of course, it didn't end there. Before heading back to the metro and to the venue, a quick stop for desserts was in place. Stopped by in a nearby gelateria called Amorino for amazing Italian-style ice cream. Salted pistachio. Can you imagine it? I couldn't. Yet, I tried it, and it was delicious.

A few more metro stations and we all arrived at the venue.

The venue, Mediolanum Forum, is located in Assago which is a small suburb of Milano. It is a sports arena with the capacity of 11,500.

We arrived early, so I used the time to do some thinking.

The concert started at 9:00pm sharp, featuring a similar set to the one in Torino: more on the rocking side, with *Gator Blood* making a second appearance in a row. Unfortunately for me, I suffer from some sensitivity in my left ear, and as I was seated at the left hand side of the stage by the speakers, I had to cover my left ear for much of the show in order to avoid sharp ear pain resulting from high frequencies. That undermined my own enjoyment of the concert, but still, it was a very good one.

(By the way, can someone provide sufficient proof to Jim Cox having no more than ten fingers?)

Knopfler appears to be in the habit of introducing a new song to the set in every show so far (knock on wood; that's one thing we don't want to jinx). Yesterday it was a superb live arrangement of *Back to Tupelo*, from *Shangri La* (2004), telling the story of a truck driver by the name of Elvis Presley who also aspired to be a movie star, other than being one of the iconic, most popular singers of the 20th century. The warm, fat guitar tone used on the studio version was replaced with a more conventional Gibson tone configuration (I prefer the former, particularly for this song) and it was evident that the guitar solo work for this song can be elaborated in many ways and wear many different shapes and forms.

Again, we're in Italy, and wherever there are Italians, there is the *Running of the Bulls*, which ensued in full force at the concert, well before the encore. While in Torino people at least made an effort to appear courteous, in Milano things looked totally different. Not wanting to take a part of this mess, I chose to remain behind and let those, who are not fortunate enough to be attending 70 shows this tour, get as close as they can to the stage.

Telegraph Road, the last song before the encore, was played with the entire audience on its feet, massive cheers from all over. *Piper to the End* concluded the concert, as it did 86 times during 2010.

Altogether a very good concert, that was somewhat ruined for me due to an event that took place shortly after the Bulls started roaming free.

Next to me, a nice quiet family consisting of a mature woman, young lady and a guy who I believe was the young lady's husband, were trying to catch a glimpse at the stage while the Bulls were standing up against it. The problem was that the mature woman was short, which meant that she couldn't see anything due to a relatively tall guy standing right in front of her. She asked him a few times to either move aside or do *something* to allow her to also enjoy the show—to no avail. Instead, the jackass was quite rude, dismissing her with sarcastic, cruel remarks.

That triggered a young man in the bunch to prepare for a fist fight, which was just about to break before the jackass' friend meddled and convinced his friend to move 10cm to the right.

You see, that I don't get. Not meaning to sound righteous or anything—as I am not—but for me, if a person with smaller physique than mine is having their concert enjoyment tampered with due to my presence in front of them, I do everything I can to help them out, by either moving away altogether, ducking, or have them switch places with me.

Seems elementary to me. Guys, yes, it's a great concert; but it is <u>JUST A FUCKING CONCERT</u>. You, yes—you, jackass; in front of you, there's a stage with eight musicians playing music. Behind you, there is a human, a person, who is asking for your help so they can enjoy the show as well—not to enjoy it more than you do, and not less; just to enjoy it. Will you not make the absolute minimum sacrifice to help them out?

Signing off this post from the hotel room in Ljubljana, Slovenia. Long travel day today, but not as long as the one coming up in a couple of days: 12 hours train ride from Zagreb to Prague. Aaaarrrrrrrgggggggghhhhhhhhh!

Isaac

Sunday, May 5, 2013

Milano, Italy to Ljubljana, Slovenia (May 4, 2013)

The journey from Milano to Ljubljana was the first smoke test for vicious travel: Waking up at 6:00am, in order to make it on time for the 7:35am train from Milano to Trieste (an Italian city right on the border with Slovenia) arriving 12:08pm, then wait for a couple of hours to take the bus from Trieste to Ljubljana, finally arriving at the latter on 4:15pm. That's 8 hours and 40 minutes total, out of which 75% are spent inside a vehicle of some sort.

What a way to spend a nice Saturday, but hey, it's not like there was another proper option to do this travel.

Woke up at 6:00am, and much unlike Richard Bennett, I didn't go to any gym, partly because I didn't feel like it but mostly because the hotel I stayed in had no gym.

Quick morning routine, and off to Milano Centrale. Breakfast? sure. Wait. What? Yes, need breakfast: there's a cafe-bar in Milano Centrale offering good sandwiches and good coffee. You can either take things to go, or sit down in the premises and have a waiter look after you.

What you can't (or, at least, shouldn't) do is seat yourself in the restaurant area and then decide to go grab two bottles of water from the fridge, pay for them at the cashier and return to your table. Do that and you get an angry look from a waiter whose tip prospects have just been decreased by 10% of €4. Ask Jeroen, he knows.

Two sandwiches (each) devoured within the span of approximately five minutes; very good cappuccino and off to *Frecciabianca 9707*, the train that would take us to Trieste, in the eastern tip of Italy.

For adults purchasing the EURail pass, buying a 1st class pass is the only option; 2nd class can only be purchased by youth and students. Granted, though, it does make a difference. If you are going to be spending hours after hours on trains, might as well spend those hours comfortably. The Frecciabianca offers a moderately good ride in 1st class—no complaints there. You can even buy Wi-Fi access for the staggering price of €0.01 (and later see that it doesn't work at all).

The first part of the journey was spent mostly trying to fall asleep. Shows in Italy start late and end late; combine that with early morning train rides, and you realize that not much time is left for this essential physical activity commonly referred to as "sleep"—and this "sleep" thing is important when you're going to be spending 3 months on the road.

Alas, falling asleep didn't work quite well. Completed the previous day's blog entry and enjoyed the view.

Free drinks are offered for 1st class passengers on this train; a staff member pushes a cart of drinks all throughout the train right after the train leaves each station. After being continuously ignored by the staff for about 3 or 4 stations, I finally got the guy's attention and asked for orange juice.

I got this:

Having been born and raised in a country when the word "orange" refers to a fruit that happens to also be of the color named "orange", I was surprised with the unidentifiable beverage that sneaked onto my tray.

I looked at the guy.

– "Orange juice", I said slowly, moving my lips in all direction in order to match the visual to the verbal, as if I was trying to explain Einstein's Private Theory of Relativity to my 78 years old grandmother.

– "Yes", he said, in fluent English.

– "This is not orange", I said, curious to know where my massive discovery is going to lead this conversation to.

– "It is a red orange", he said.

I wanted to ask him "If it is not orange, why are you calling it 'orange'?" but immediately decided to shut up.

So yes. It tastes (mostly) like an orange, but it is red. Looking into it later, I found out that I was drinking blood. Orange. Blood orange. Well, this.

The first time in my entire life that I heard about the city of Trieste in Italy was when I was trying to plan a route from Milano to Ljubljana to catch this show. As the train made its way closer and closer to Trieste, I realized that eastern Italy—at least the part that borders with

Slovenia—may as well be worthy of an in-depth visit. The area is made up of beautiful hills, rolling into the sea below, with red roofs spotting the valleys below.

A beautiful sight, when photographed properly.

Made it to Trieste's central station on time and decided to get the bus tickets' ordering over with. The bus ticket from Trieste to Ljubljana was the one and only travel leg in the entire tour that could not be pre-booked—Veolia (the bus company) still hasn't quite acknowledged yet that we're in the 21st century.

According to the map, Trieste's railway station and bus station are adjacent to each other. Still, you'd be surprised to learn how tricky it was to find out where bus tickets are actually being sold. The entire area was under construction and signing was as effective as it can only be in Italy, which means entirely ineffective altogether. Fifteen minutes were spent rolling luggage around until the bus station's office was located, a distance of about 50 meters away from the train station.

Decided to have a last Italian meal before bidding Italy adieu for the next two months. Located a restaurant online and started walking to it, a walk that revealed a pretty city.

The restaurant, Buffet e Trattoria Re di Coppe, is located close to the train station and provides a genuine, simple, Italian dining experience. It is owned by a nice couple, who, despite not being able to communicate well in English, did everything possible to explain the menu and provide recommendations.

Food was delicious as it was simple: seafood risotto, good espresso and panna cotta. More than enough to get going.

Unfortunately, slightly more than enough.

I made a crucial mistake to have two cappuccinos within five hours of waking up, plus consuming a large bottle of water. Now, caffeine is diuretic, and consuming caffeine *and* a lot of water right before boarding a bus is, well, how should I put it... insane, especially if the bus you're taking doesn't feature a toilet.

The pain started two minutes after we left the station. Miraculously, ten minutes later, the bus made a stop to collect some other passengers. Approached the driver (who left the bus to administer some luggage), and asked him if I could go into the bus station for a minute.

– "No".

– "OK. Can you tell me if there's going to be a break any time soon?"

He said nothing and just proceeded back to the bus. I figured that this guy is either completely stupid, completely ignorant or both, so I wouldn't want to take any chances. Boarded the bus and continued the ride with agonizing pain.

Half an hour later, the bus stopped again, to collect additional passengers. I noticed that the bus is stopped, people coming in, and the driver is busy with his phone, texting. Engine is on.

Minutes passed... nothing happens.

A few more minutes passed with even less happening.

Approached the driver again. "Hi. Can I go outside for a minute?", I asked.

– "No, I leave in one minute".

– "Please?"

– "You just had ten minutes. Why didn't you go?"

I told him that he is a fucking moron, because had he not been a fucking moron, he would simply announce that break, rather than sit on his ass texting the devil about how he's going to be spending his time in hell once he gets there, hopefully not too far ahead from now.

But not out loud.

– "One minute and I'm back."

Stormed out of the bus, did whatever needed to be done and, when I was back, the bus was already pulling out of the parking lot.

Once I was back at the bus, I was finally able to enjoy the view. I was told that Slovenia is beautiful, but didn't know that "beautiful" here also refers to natural scenery. Natural scenery wise, Slovenia reminded me a lot of British Columbia, and had you been to British Columbia before, you'd know how beautiful it is, nature wise.

As the bus made its way through narrow winding roads, I noticed that the driver was texting and driving. So, not only we're talking about a stupid and ignorant driver, but also a potential killer on the loose. Being a jackass towards a caffeine-drinking passenger is one thing: risking the lives of dozens of people because you *must* text and talk while driving a bus, is a completely different thing.

A complaint was filed with the bus company, Veolia Transport.

After a long travel day, finally arrived at Ljubljana's central bus station.

The nearby Apple Store caught our eyes.

Off to the hotel, City Hotel Ljubljana. Nice, clean, spacious—perfect for a city trip, with the only disadvantage of Wi-Fi not being available in the rooms (LAN access is available, though. Bring your own Wireless Access Point). On the way there, I realized that something is missing.

Something that every city has, and capital cities usually have more of.

People.

Saturday afternoon, beautiful weather; you'd expect Ljubljana's city center to have at least a decent number of people walking around. Alas, nothing. The streets appeared empty. Are we in the wrong place? is this the capital city of Slovenia? Puzzling.

I had heard before that Ljubljana is pretty, so decided to do some walking. It is, indeed, pretty.

Shoes, anyone?

I never quite understood this shoe tossing practice. It happens a lot in North America. I'm often intrigued, thinking what goes through the mind of an individual when they conclude "actually, I could use tying the shoelaces of two shoes together and have the product hanging off an electricity wire". Wikipedia doesn't offer much in terms of explaining where & when this practice had originated. If anyone has an explanation, please share.

Ljubljana's city center appeared, on this Saturday afternoon, as a very quiet, laid back, pastoral place. I should visit this place again for a more in-depth acquaintance.

Right at the city center, there's the famous Ljubljana Castle, which dates back to the 12th century. It was used by the Roman Empire's army in order to defend against Ottoman invasion. Later (and by "later" I mean 400–500 years later), it served as a military hospital and an arsenal, and later on—as a prison. In 1905, it was purchased by the Municipality of Ljubljana, with the plan of setting up a museum there. Once it was purchased, though, it was used as a temporary place to house poor families. That "temporary" arrangement lasted about 60 years. In the 1960's, finally, renovations started. Renovations took 35 years (!) to complete.

Nowadays, the Ljubljana Castle serves as a tourist attraction and a preferred location for conducting events such as weddings.

Took the funicular up to see what it's all about. As soon as the funicular arrived up the hill, it started raining so there wasn't much to do there except finding shelter. There's a restaurant up there in the castle, called Gostilna na Gradu. Fine, yet expensive, food.

Then took the funicular down, enjoying very pretty views of Ljubljana:

Time to head to the concert. The venue, Dvorana Stožice, is located about 4km away from the hotel. There's a bus that goes from the city center directly to the venue, and you can ride it for free if you show your concert ticket to the driver. As the tickets were in will-call, a nice young lad offered to give us his tickets, and he'll "get by" somehow. He ended up paying for his bus ride. For some reason, when we handed him back his tickets, he refused to accept any sort of compensation for the money he paid for the bus. I didn't quite understand why, but hey, that's a nice gesture towards visitors who are clueless about the public transport code of the city.

Minutes later, the entire population of Ljubljana made it into that bus, at least from a sonic perspective. The bus carried about 50 people, but these 50 people made the noise of 272,000. Still, look at the bright side: there are people in this city.

The venue was pretty to look at from the outside, designed like a shell. It is also huge, a fact learned the hard way through walking about half way around it to find the box office for ticket pickup.

The concert started fifteen minutes later than scheduled, featuring a similar set to the preceding show in Milano.

Sultans of Swing was in absentia again. I am not in the position to make any judgment regarding why this song is absent as this is none of my business and, frankly, I am not even interested in knowing; however, this particular blog is all mine and at the least, I can cast my feeling about it. The feeling is great. I know that I may be stepping on many sensitive toes when stating it: *Sultans of Swing* is a good, iconic song, but I personally prefer Knopfler's solo career over almost every Dire Straits material, *Sultans of Swing* included. You may throw rotten tomatoes at me now.

Another very welcome (in my eyes, at least) change was the substitution of *Speedway at Nazareth* with *Yon Two Crows*. The latter has way more options for "growth" than the former, and, to put it simply—I like it better, partly because it's easier on the ears.

Postcards from Paraguay seems to be serving as a platform for introducing band members, with each band member being introduced along with playing their part in the song's opening sequence. This song sounds better and better every time it is being played.

The *Running of the Bulls* took place in an odd timing: right before the encore, *after* the band returned to the stage. That's odd. At least, it wasn't violent this time. Still, I felt bad for the lovely handicap lady who was seated in the front row and had to miss the entire encore because people, standing in front of her, never really bothered to pay attention to the fact that there was a handicap person right behind them.

Left the venue as soon as humanly possible once the show concluded, as it was expected for roads to be jam packed with taxis, cars and buses after the show. Hailed a taxi and within ten minutes I was back at the hotel, preparing everything for the next morning's early ride to Zagreb, Croatia.

Isaac

Monday, May 6, 2013

Ljubljana, Slovenia to Zagreb, Croatia (May 5, 2013)

Woke up at 7:00am to the sound of nothing interesting. After a moderately annoying travel day in the day before—involving the most vile, ferocious, deprecated, unwanted and unwarranted type of vehicle referred to as "bus" in earth and as "who the hell rides this thing?" in other planets—it was good to once again be subject to train rides.

The train from Ljubljana to Zagreb left at 8:30am. The day before (Saturday), the city center of Ljubljana appeared as if taken from a futuristic movie where most humans are extinct and the handful that were left were seeking something to do with their lives. On Sunday morning, it was the same, except that not even a handful of people were on the streets.

Two hours train ride, could barely keep my eyes open, which was a shame because that train ride was quite a scenic one, especially while still in Slovenia. It rained, and the sight of rolling mountains, rivers and grey, wet skies took me back once again to some familiar scenes in British Columbia.

Finally arrived to Zagreb at around 10:30am, not knowing at all what to expect. As Croatia was a part of former Yugoslavia, I expected a similar experience to that of Serbia, which didn't really make me look forward for the day to unfold. It wasn't before long, though, when I realized how wrong I was.

Hotel rooms are rarely ready for check-in early in the morning, and the Best Western Premier Astoria hotel, located a few minutes away from the main railway station, was no exception in that regards. Had a couple of hours to kill before checking in, so we set off to explore some of the city center area.

Zagreb's city center is pretty, green, and has a small town feel. The city's square is the most popular starting point for touristic walks, as many of the old city's attractions are within short walking distance.

As it was a Sunday, we happened to just be arriving nearby a massive church, just as the bells were ringing, signifying that we were late for Sunday's prayer, which didn't matter much to either of us.

As I wasn't fully awake yet, coffee was in order and we set on a journey to find a Wi-Fi-enabled coffee place. That proved to be harder said than done, as it was a Sunday, in Zagreb's city center, many businesses are closed for a part of the day.

Eventually, found a nice cafe-bar called Kvazar, sat outside in the patio, gazing at the locals walking about.

The waiter comes up and starts talking in perfect English. Turns out that he was born and raised… in Toronto, Canada, which is not very far from where I currently live (about 4,300km away, in the same country). Nearby, a woman was seated with a couple of friends. She noticed the presence of tourists, and started talking to us, providing valuable and useful information about Croatia in general, Zagreb in particular, and many other topics… and, for a bet, was able to recognize, within two (!) attempts, the country where I was born and raised. She won free coffee.

On the way back to the hotel, stepping down a flight of stairs…

… A public market, with fresh fruit, vegetables and condiments for sale. Beautiful.

Off to the hotel, checked in and caught up with work. Looking online for a place to eat proved to be useless as virtually all restaurants worthy of a visit were closed on Sundays. The hotel's restaurant was open, though; delicious food and off for a nap, scheduled to wake up at 7:00pm, to make it in time for the concert beginning at 9:00pm.

Except that it didn't begin at 9:00pm.

6:45pm, as I lay down with one eye open, still more than a half awake, Jeroen informed me that he had read somewhere that the concert begins at 8:00pm, not 9:00pm. We double- and triple-checked all emails received from *markknopfler.com*; all stated a start time of 9:00pm.

Then I decided to be smart.

– "Check the ticket agency's link, there might be a start time there", I barked.

It showed 8:00pm.

Wonderful. It's almost 7:00pm, the venue is about 45 minutes away by tram, and I'm still more than half awake. Jumped out of bed like a monkey having been bit by a cobra; minutes later we were ready to go, yet acknowledging that taking a tram is not the best way to go about it.

OK, taxi, then.

Turns out that, in Zagreb, there are three big taxi companies, and a few small ones. Something went wrong with the hotel's line to the taxi companies, which resulted in about 15 minutes wait time until finally a taxi came by to pick us up to the venue. The cab driver arguably deserves the title "cab driver of the tour", as he was extremely helpful and agreed to meet us after the concert in an agreed-upon location, so we can quickly get back to the hotel not having to mess around with a huge taxi line-up after the concert.

The venue, Zagreb Arena, is a(nother) sports arena located in Novi Zagreb ("new Zagreb"), just south of the Sava river. For concerts, it can contain up to 24,000 people. It looks intriguing from the outside (unfortunately, due to being in a rush, no pictures were taken outside the venue), resembling a rib cage.

The concert didn't start at 8:00pm, as stated in the ticketing company's website, and it didn't start at 9:00pm, as stated in the ticket confirmation email.

It started at 8:30pm.

After a couple of concerts being seated in the worst seat in the venue, it was good to finally be seated in a place that offered a decent view of the stage. It was also good not having to block my left ear to avoid sharp pain resulting from high frequencies.

Concert started off as usual, and I was able to figure out Ian's daily puzzle.

The last statement requires an explanation.

Corned Beef City, performed live, begins with Ian drumming 8 bars before Guy breaks in with the dirty Gibson samples. That would be very easy for Guy to do if those 8 bars were played in a consistent pattern; however, Ian has been in the habit of drumming an inconsistent beat for the 8th bar, challenging Guy to break in with the Gibson sample in just the right moment. So far, Guy has been successful in all attempts. I have been successful in guessing it in all cases but one—I believe that the one I failed was in Belgrade, when Ian drummed something that threw me completely off balance.

This has "disaster" written all over it, but hey, it's fun!

A new song added to the set: *Prairie Wedding*, having been played dozens of time during the *Get Lucky* tour, was resurrected from the abyss and played for the first time this tour—with a slightly different arrangement, having Richard playing the pedal steel guitar instead of an acoustic. I am not sure if it was planned, but the pedal steel guitar was barely heard; however, when it was, it certainly added something positive to the performance.

Del McCoury, a famous bluegrass band from the United States, covered *Prairie Wedding* back in 2010. They chose to sing it one octave higher, which is most definitely the wrong approach.

Second night in a row that *Sultans of Swing* is in absentia. Good. Now, one can only hope that *Romeo & Juliet* is dropped in favour of a song out of Knopfler's solo repertoire and faith in humanity can be partly restored.

Kingdom of Gold was played again. While this is a beautiful song all throughout, its power to move lies mainly (at least in my opinion) at the outro. The outro this time around was more involved than before—a good sign. There is much left to explore and experiment with here.

No *Running of the Bulls* in Zagreb; however, that is not to say that people kept seated. Finally, a non-violent gathering by the stage, without running and smashing people and objects along the way. That's how it should be done, folks! Yet, something tells me that things are going to be slightly different in Italy.

So Far Away concluded the show, the usual rocking version. May I suggest a different approach, though? About a year ago, Rivka Stein, Leora Israel and myself gathered in a friend's apartment. Rivka videotaped, Leora sang, I played & "sang"—the only instrument being my much-beloved Taylor 414CE. One continuous audio take—no overdubs—mixed by my friend Oren Steinitz from Calgary, Alberta.

It was my first time playing in front of any sort of an audience involving more than one person, and I can't foresee a second time in the near future. It is also very unlikely that I will cover any Knopfler songs ever again; this one just begged for it.

(Due to a problem during the video/audio editing—wrong codec being used—there are a few "clicks" in the audio. If you're interested in the click-free version, please contact me.)

Quickly left the venue after the show, with the intention to make it to the hotel as soon as humanly possible due to the upcoming horrendous travel schedule. A quick bite in a pizzeria called Lira in the city center—delicious pizza, shared both ways for about €10 including drinks.

Signing off this post while on board the *EuroCity 158*. Long travel day—12 hours (!) train ride from Zagreb to Prague, with a brief 30 minutes stop in Vienna. That's the longest travel day in the tour, but not the hardest one: the hardest one is going to be the 9+ hours bus ride from Prague to Lodz, two days from now. If anyone has any better idea how to get from Prague to Lodz on Wednesday (flights are too expensive—already checked), please share.

Isaac

Thursday, May 9, 2013

Zagreb, Croatia to Prague, Czech Republic to Łódź, Poland (May 6-8, 2013)

Getting from Zagreb to Prague was the longest travel day in the entire tour schedule: Leaving Zagreb 7:25am towards Vienna, arriving 1:57pm; then depart Vienna 2:32pm, arrive Prague 7:21pm. Total time in transit: 12 hours minus four minutes.

While the option was there to split the train ride into two, spending the day off in Vienna, it was decided to get all travel done at once, during the day off, and enjoy two nights and one full day in the amazing city of Prague.

It was difficult getting out of bed at 6:00am. Hotel's breakfast starts at 6:30am, and what a breakfast it was—magnificent. So much selection that you're granted to find more than a thing or two to satisfy your hunger with. Very good, *Best Western Astoria*.

Unfortunately, breakfast had to be consumed in a rush in order to make it to the 7:25am train on time, which we did. Comfortable first class cabin on board the EuroCity 158 train, courtesy of *ÖBB*—the Austrian railway company. Was even able to catch a short nap.

Caught up with work and blogging, and enjoyed the view. Almost the entire train ride was an amazing treat for the eyes: I am inclined to say that this train ride, along with the one I took from Montreux to Locarno during the Get Lucky tour, are the two most scenic train rides I have ever been on.

As it is difficult to take proper photos from within a moving train, the following will have to do:

Hills, mountains, old houses, castles, rivers, lakes—what more could you ask for?

Oh, I know what else you could ask for: you could ask for a major railway clusterfuck to not take place 30km south of Vienna.

About 30km south of Wien Meidling—a major railway hub in Vienna—our train suddenly stopped, due to a "technical problem". The problem with such stoppages is that you can never really know what's going on, or any sort of estimate as to when (if at all) the train will move on. Such knowledge is necessary when you have a connecting train to hop on; in our case, the gap between the train arriving at Vienna and the one departing to Prague was about 35 minutes. In other words, we really wanted to know whether the delay is going to take less than 35 minutes (good) or more (bad).

Finally, close to an hour later, the train started moving again. That meant that we'd have to take the next train available to Prague, leaving 2 hours after our originally-scheduled train. Annoying, but not too much; we could have just spend the time at the train station having lunch.

But, no. ÖBB had other plans for us. An announcement (in German) was made that our train is going to stop its journey at the next stop, and that we should find alternative ways to get to our Vienna station.

Now, in an advanced country such as Austria, in a location so close to its capital city, you'd think that you would be able to get *some* help from on-site railway staff, as to which train you should be taking. Surprisingly, no such help was available. The result: hundreds of confused and frustrated passengers, completely oblivious as to what to do next. The departures board was confusing and completely useless, causing these hundreds of passengers (including us) to switch platforms many times before making sense out of this mess.

Now, when you read the phrase "switch platform", consider having to carry your luggage down a flight of about 20 stairs, then walk for about 20 meters and then carry your luggage up the stairs to get to the other platform. Now imagine doing this when it's warm outside. Once you are done imagining that, imagine that you're doing it with hundreds of people around you. *Four times.*

Fun? I'd say.

Eventually, we struck a conversation with two locals who were as frustrated as we were. A train came by, and we asked these locals whether this train takes us to Vienna, to which they said "yes".

We boarded, not knowing for sure whether the train goes at the right direction, and which stop to take. Fortunately, it sorted itself out: thirty minutes later, we were in *Wien Meidling*.

Next step: figure out which train to take next. Inquiring at the ticketing office, we were told that there's another train leaving just an hour from now. It has more than 300 vacant seats, so we should be able to find a place. Good.

As we're riding first class trains all throughout (except for the UK), we were allowed access to OBB's first class lounge, offering free drinks, snacks, Wi-Fi and comfortable sofas.

Our train, *EuroCity 74*, departed about 20+ minutes late. Turns out that something rather serious happened in the railway system just south of Vienna, screwing up many.

My ex told me, a while ago, that my life revolves around looking for problems and working on resolving them; that the very act of looking for a fault is what motivates me, and the act of fixing these faults is what builds my self image. I am still amazed how right-on she was.

I suppose that explains why I get frustrated when everyday breakages occur. In this instance, I was less frustrated with the resulting 2 hours delay, than I was frustrated over the fact that, in a developed country in the 21st century, a technical difficulty in one train or one track can still result in a chain of reaction adversely impacting the daily schedule of thousands of people. Moreover, it bothers me to acknowledge that many of such problems can be avoided by simply taking preventative measures against them, rather than reacting after the fact.

Finally, after a long, long traveling day, the train made it to Prague's central railway station. I was happy: Prague, in my eyes, is one of the most beautiful cities in the world, and definitely ranks very high among European cities worth visiting.

I have only been here twice before. The first time was about 13 years ago, on my first ever trip to any European destination, with my girlfriend at that time. In retrospect, the city left a much more lasting impression on me than did my ex-girlfriend: there's something in this city's beauty that makes you desire to explore it.

Here is myself playing the grand piano of the *Corinthia Hotel* 13 years ago. I used to wear a watch. I don't anymore.

The hotel, Falkensteiner Hotel Maria Prag, was the same hotel I stayed in during the *Get Lucky* tour. A bit pricey, but conveniently located right next to the central train station and a few minutes walk away from Prague's best known touristic areas. This time around, the stay wasn't as pleasant as it was 3 years ago, primarily due to the fact that air conditioning here is only available during the summer and the room in the top floor boasted two windows there were impossible to keep open for too long without them being slammed shut by the help of wind.

Having spent the day feeding exclusively on dry sandwiches, a proper dinner was in place. Very close to the hotel is Wenceslas Square, which, for tourists, is the main square to start exploring the city from. It is so touristic that it really isn't representative of Prague anymore: various over-priced restaurants offering poor-quality food for ridiculous prices; casinos; all sorts of establishments aimed at demeaning, objectifying and nullifying the value of 50% of the worldly population that only happen to be unfortunate enough to not carry the Y chromosome; and, of course, dozens and dozens of street peddlers, approaching you with all sorts of suggestions for drinks, drugs, parties and women. A remarkably beautiful square turned a touristic nightmare in the name of bullshit.

I suggest you avoid it.

The true beauty of Prague begins once you reach the northern point of Wenceslas Square and start exploring the myriad of small, narrow streets. The city of Prague is exceptionally beautiful at night due to the clever lighting that the city maintains over the old city's colourful buildings, making the entire old city area appear as if taken from a magical fairy tale.

The next day, after a good night sleep, it was time for some tour maintenance. Laundry first, and while waiting for it to be done, we went to a camera service store to fix my camera. The damnest thing, happening for the second time now: some dust, or a hair, somehow made it to the comfortable position of right behind the lens. If anyone can tell me what could cause this, please let me know.

(The second picture shows Wenceslas Square; the building at its end is the Czech National Museum.)

That required a tram ride, plus some walking in Prague's less popular areas.

Waiting for the camera to be fixed, we came across Cafe Pavlac, which is a pleasant spot for sipping hot and cold drinks while waiting for something else, more interesting, to happen.

Back to the hotel around noon…

… and it was time to take a walk and see some beauty in Prague's historic center, which was inscribed as a World Heritage Site in 1992:

Not far from Wenceslas Square, there is the Old Town Square.

Before heading on, stopped for a lunch in Pizzeria Ristorante Giovanni for delicious, reasonably priced food even though it's located less than a minute walk from the most touristic place in the city.

Not far from there, lies The Charles Bridge. The Charles Bridge crosses the Vltava River, connecting the Prague Castle with the Old Town. It was constructed in the 14th century by King Charles IV.

According to Wikipedia, the bridge tower in the pictures above is considered to be "one of the most astonishing civil gothic-style buildings in the world". It is indeed remarkably impressive, and so are the 30+ baroque-style statues on both edges of the bridge, which is approximately 600 meters long. Many pictures were taken, most of which aren't doing quite the good job in capturing just how inspiring this place is.

Tourists? name any sort of human DNA sequence, and it was there holding a camera. The place was absolutely flocked with tourists of all ways, shapes and forms. Of course, wherever there is a large concentration of tourists, there are also all sorts of street-side attractions such as caricature painters, street artists and whatnot. And this isn't even summer time yet.

One particular statue that made me wonder was this:

This is obviously Jesus being crucified, but what's interesting is the inscription above and around, which is in Hebrew. The top word means "Sacred", and the full phrase is קדוש קדוש קדוש יהוה צבאות, which is a phrase very often used in Jewish prayers—so often used that even I am aware of it. It means, in general "God is sacred" (the word "Sacred" repeated twice). Now, whoever knows a thing or two about how Christianity began, and how (according to belief) Jesus found himself crucified to begin with, can't help but wonder about the implied message.

I was intrigued. Upon further research, it turned out that this statue is called "The Crucifix and Calvary". The Hebrew text was put there as means of humiliating Prague's Jewish population, as a result of the accusation of a Jewish community leader of blasphemy at the end of the 17th century. Really interesting, and you can read about it here (search for "The Crucifix and Calvary").

Once reached the other side of the bridge, a new world of exploration possibilities open—unfortunately, though, time was tight before the show so this will be left for my next visit here.

Turning back and walking the bridge the opposite way was no less a pleasure.

So much beauty in one city… and this is just in day time.

The concert in Prague took place in the O₂ Arena, which is where the Get Lucky tour stopped for a visit three years ago.

The concert started a few minutes past schedule and featured the longest set so far in the tour—17 songs—with *Kingdom of Gold* done just about right and *Miss You Blues* played for the second time around. A good set altogether, despite the resurrection of *Sultans of Swing*. *Gator Blood* was played again, this time with a short introduction by Mark mentioning that this is a song about a music manager. I could have never arrived to that conclusion by reading the lyrics. Admittedly, not one of my favourite songs but sounds better played live than on the studio album.

To my right, a nice mature couple was seated. One of them—the male half—kept on turning to me before each and every song and letting me know which song he thinks was going to be played next. I nodded, especially when he announced that *So Far from the Clyde* is going to be played when Mark was holding the *Danelectro* guitar for *Miss You Blues*. I was not in the proper disposition to inform him that this certainly wasn't my first show this tour around, and that I would certainly enjoy the surprise element; so I shut up.

Behind me, a lady was screaming before and after, and sometimes during, most songs. Initially I was sure that she's in labour, or being bitten by an exceptionally aggressive alligator.

Again, a standing ovation before the encore, followed by a *Walking of the Bulls*, which is essentially the *Running of the Bulls* done peacefully without violence and without anyone getting hurt.

After the show, I felt the urge to see Prague at night once again.

Isaac's "Privateering" Tour Blog

Next to the Old Town Square, Zebra Asian Noodle Bar serves Asian food, including sushi. Triangular sushi.

A short walk around to sample a few sights…

And back to the hotel for an early night sleep, knowing that the next day was going to be a really tough one.

After only 30+ hours in Prague, it was time to leave this gorgeous city and embark on the hardest (though not longest) travel part of the tour: a 9.5 hours bus ride from Prague to Łódź.

The most annoying thing about travelling in Poland is, well, getting in and out of there. It is a bit puzzling at first: Poland isn't exactly located in a remote land, far off from civilization. It certainly is not "fly shit on the map", as someone said once in 2004. Still, during both the Get Lucky tour and in this current tour, the travel to and out of Poland has been rather difficult to plan, and more difficult to actually perform.

First, the railway system here is certainly not of the more developed ones in the world. In 2010, I had the misfortune of arriving to Poland by train, and I vividly recall it being an experience drastically different from the usual train experience in western Europe. It's not only about the actual trains that are old and out-dated; there simply aren't too many railways here. Unlike Germany, for instance, where you can travel from pretty much anywhere to pretty much anywhere else using trains, Poland decided to leave the railway system behind and use cars & buses as the main transportation method for the masses.

While you can fly out of Prague to a few destinations in Poland for a reasonable amount of money, Łódź's airport is still a small one and isn't well-served internationally. The other options were Wroclaw and Warsaw, but transportation from these airports to Łódź turned out to be either too expensive, too inconvenient, or both. The only option that made sense was to go on Polski Bus, which offers bus services involving Poland and neighbouring countries. It costs about $17 per person to get from Prague to Łódź—very cheap—and the bus includes a toilet and free Wi-Fi which, surprisingly, worked during most of the journey.

But for me, the most memorable experience between the time I departed Prague until I checked into the room in the Łódź hotel was my pursuit of a suitable place to urinate, so if you're not into reading about it, you better scroll down a few paragraph.

The bus journey was as pleasant and wonderful as Chinese torture must be. The seats' leg room was, indeed, leg room: you could place a leg there, and not much else. One refreshment stop only—2 hours after departure—so if you're like me and having trouble urinating in a moving bus, better rent a car. At some point I was so helpless that I posted the following on the company's Facebook page:

> Dear driver of the bus from Prague to Łódź: please stop the bus. We would all like to take a piss.
> Thank you.

Not that I intended the driver to read it—it was more of a statement—but still, a couple of Poles took it seriously and replied to my post telling me, essentially, to go fuck myself—which I would happily do had my bladder been empty, which it hadn't been. My post was later removed from Polski Bus' Facebook wall.

After close to ten excruciating hours of riding a bus, finally, Łódź's Kaliska coach station was in plain sight. Getting there took another 20 minutes because of a huge traffic jam right before the last traffic light.

As soon as the bus stopped and opened its doors, I stormed out of it like a maniac and right into the station, looking for a "WC" sign. None was found, but a small window was. A lady there referred me to a small building nearby, which looked like a cube, and told me to take 3 Zluti with me, which she happily changed for me.

Fine. Approaching the small cube-like building, I noticed someone trying to enter and failing. Repeatedly. Which wasn't surprising as he didn't put any coins in it.

As soon as he left, I felt superior. Here I am with my 3 Zluti in my hand, about to fulfil a 5 hours wish.

But hey, this is Poland. And whenever I'm in Poland, something just has to go wrong. Put my entire Zluti holdings into that thing. The door opened, but didn't close. There was a huge green button inside that just screamed "Push me". As the palm of my hand was on its way to push the button, the door started closing but it was too late for my brain to retract my hand. The big button was pushed, and the door broke open again.

Turned out that the big "Push me" button was the button that you should be pressing *once you're done*.

I didn't have additional 3 Zluti.

FUCK this world, I'm out of here. Back to the station, and we took a taxi cab to the hotel—1km away. Stormed into the hotel as if I was a privateer in search for some loot. "Bathroom is on the first floor, past the conference room". No further directions were given, and the first floor didn't really show you where that conference room was. Five painful minutes later I *finally* found it and faith in humanity was partly restored.

Arriving to the hotel at around 6:30pm, with about an hour left before the concert time, there was no time to even breathe: quickly changed and stormed out of the hotel, walking towards the venue.

The path from the hotel, Hotel Focus Łódź, to the venue, Arena Łódź, is about 2km. Thought about taking a taxi but decided to walk instead. Good decision, because the entire population of Poland made it to the (sold out) venue by car. Fifteen minutes later, arrived at the arena.

The arena is yet one of those multi-purpose arenas, used for sports, concerts and other events that involve including as many heads as possible under one roof.

Locating the ticket booth to collect the tickets was surprisingly difficult. I was told that the tickets should be picked up from a blue booth saying "KASA" on it. That's where I went. That box had 3 windows, all signed in Polish except for the middle one that had a sign saying "Clearing Point". What the hell is a "Clearing Point", you're asking? beats me, I have no idea. Waited in line for a few minutes, only to realize that the specific window I was waiting for isn't quite the window I should have been waiting for, and that I should move to the window that's located two meters to the right.

No, there was no way to predict that.

Tickets collected and within a couple of minutes I was finally standing inside the venue. Every step towards the concert felt like some sort of accomplishment: here I am again in Poland, just about to watch a concert, and there's no catastrophe yet.

As our entire food intake since 7:00am consisted of a small breakfast and one sandwich, we decided to eat in the venue. Total and utter garbage. Long line that took about 30 minutes to pass, as the people working there found a fantastically efficient way to work: two workers are working at the same time with the same customer, with the third one doing fuck all on the side. I measured: about two minutes per customer ordering a drink and a stinking bag of nachos, or a doughnut. There were about 5,000,000 people in line.

By the time I actually had an edible substance in my hand, it was 7:25pm—about five minutes before the concert's start time. Had to consume those like a hungry monkey who had just escaped the zoo, and rushed into the hall.

A few Knopfler fans from Poland, who happen to be reading this blog, approached and said hello. That did much to diffuse the immense frustration that has been building up during that awful travel day: it is always nice to meet friendly people, let alone at the end of a very frustrating day. A big thank you to Knopfler's Polish fans.

The concert started shortly before 8:00pm. There's something special in finishing up a terrible day with watching this band play: it serves to normalize everything, putting things in perspective and showing you that you're in the right place, at the right time, doing the right thing —listening to great music performed by eight musical masters.

5:15am was played again, beautiful, again with Richard playing solo parts with Mark in charge of the rhythm. Very similar set to the one before, with *Miss You Blues* replaced by one of my favourite Privateering tracks, *Haul Away*.

During *Postcards from Paraguay*, Mike decided that he can't possibly wait for his part to begin during the outro and started playing it a couple of bars before schedule, resulting in the entire band focusing on him as if to ask what was going on, then laughing it off. Funny moment. I'm not sure many of the audience noticed the fault.

I recall the Polish audience from the last tour being very vocal when it comes to cheering, so I wasn't surprised when I had to block my ears to avoid perpetual hearing damage when we all stood up against the barrier during the encore. Remarkably supportive audience in a sold out venue.

Good concert; glad I made it.

Back to the hotel, the city of Łódź seemed like a place where nothing happens. Absolutely no business open; the only option for dining was in the hotel. A mediocre fillet of salmon did the trick and off to bed before a 5:30am wake up. More on that tomorrow.

Isaac

Sunday, May 12, 2013

Łódź, Poland to Berlin and Bremen, Germany (May 9-11, 2013)

This post is published late due to an unexpected shortage in Wi-Fi connection in the Berlin hotel, plus being quite busy over the last few days. Sorry.

In the last post, I wrote about how inconvenient it was to travel into Poland by public ground transportation. Getting *out* of Poland by public ground transportation is not much easier: save for a few exceptions, trains aren't going to do it, which leaves buses as your only other option for ground transportation.

Thinking about it further, I'm not entirely sure that there is a justified reason to complain about the lack of trains. Canada has worse public ground transportation infrastructure than Poland. The USA isn't much better. Maybe, then, like mostly everything else, this is a question of cost vs. benefit.

Canada, for example, has a total area of (sit tight, a large number is coming) 9,984,670km^2, with a population of 33,476,688 (as of 2011). Just to get an idea of how big this country is, consider the entire continent of Europe with the landmass of 10,180,000km^2 (only slightly bigger) which are home to approximately 739,165,030 people (22 times more than Canada).

The population density in Canada is 3.41 people per square kilometer: take all of Canada's population, spread them evenly across Canada's area, and as a result, every square kilometer will have 3.41 people in it. The number for Europe is 72.5—that's more than 21 times over.

The reason, then, why Canada doesn't have a very advanced railway transportation infrastructure is because its cost would far outweigh its benefits. Setting advanced railway tracks to connect Canadian cities to one another will cost so much money and will be so underused (due to the low population density) that doing so makes as much sense as James Hetfield, of Metallica, had when he decided to do this.

Poland isn't much different. With a population of about 37 million, almost one third of them live in 8 metropolitan areas; the other two thirds of the population are so spread out, that installing and maintaining advanced railway infrastructure is simply way too expensive to make sense. I should note, that *within* the metropolitan areas themselves—and I can testify from my experience in two of them: Wroclaw and Łódź—public transport is not at all bad.

In the light of that, perhaps Poland deserves a little more credit.

At any rate, the original plan for leaving Poland was to take a train from Łódź to Warsaw on 6:30am, then connect from Warsaw city center to its airport, arriving at the airport around 8:40am and fly to Berlin on 10:40am. Not too difficult to execute. But after the horrendous travel day just 24 hours prior, neither of us was in the mood for any sort of mass ground public transportation so early in the morning. Once back to the hotel after the concert, a taxi was scheduled to arrive at 6:00am and take us directly to Warsaw's airport, some two hours and €70 away.

Woke up 5:30am and jumped out of bed like a tiger: quietly and on all fours. Tired like hell and unwilling to do much more than breathing. Morning routine, packed whatever was left to be packed and 30 minutes later boarded the taxi cab that was already waiting downstairs.

I noticed a sign on the taxi's window saying "Free Wi-Fi".

Went to the back and loaded my luggage.

Yawn. Twice.

Wait a second. What do you mean "Free Wi-Fi"? Who the hell did the driver steal this sticker from, and why?

But no, it wasn't a joke. Free Wi-Fi *in the taxi*, the entire ride. I have never come across anything like that before. And it worked, too; and just as it was working, it was also entirely useless for me as I had spent almost the entire two hours ride trying to fall asleep, consistently failing.

As soon as we entered Warsaw, traffic turned from being pleasant to being horrible. Traffic jams left, right, center and in both diagonals. Finally, we made it to the airport, paid the fare (which was suspiciously low. Meter showed about €140, we were charged €70), and went inside.

Warsaw's airport, called Warsaw Frederic Chopin (symbol: WAW) is named after the famous composer, Frédéric Chopin, who lived in Warsaw until he was 20 years old, during which he wrote much of his genius work. It is Poland's busiest airport: for most practical purposes, if you are going to fly into or out of Poland, you're likely to be present in this airport.

Starving after a 2 hours taxi ride with no breakfast prior, airport food was the only viable option. And some coffee, of course, just so I can keep my eyes open.

How do you pass the time until your flight? of course, by using the internet. The airport offers free Wi-Fi, but for that, you need to scan your boarding pass in order to receive a code, printed on paper (of course), that you then have to type into your browser. Where is the scanning machine? *AH*. Hidden somewhere. Took a while to locate it.

Clever. By the time one figures out how to use the Wi-Fi in this airport, they have no need in it anymore as their flight is already boarding.

Made me wonder: why would they require you to have a boarding pass in order to use their internet service? other than people who are just about to travel, who the hell is going to use it? is it such a common pastime in Warsaw for people to go to the airport for the sole purpose of firing up their laptops and read emails?

"Hey guys, how about we go out for a drink first, and then go to the airport, start our laptops and play"?—said nobody, ever, in Warsaw.

I guess I'll never know. One thing that comes to mind, though, is that it serves an excellent tool for Polish authorities to track your activities on the internet before taking off: By scanning your boarding pass and providing you with a unique code, which you later use to log in, it is very easy for system administrators to associate the boarding pass' owner with a list of internet activities performed whilst at the airport (of course that can be circumvented by using a few sophisticated tools).

Air Berlin flight 8039 from left Warsaw's airport having *X* people on board, but only *X-1* people were able to go about their business uninterrupted once the aircraft touched ground in Berlin.

It's a short flight, about an hour and a few minutes. On this particular flight, the crew consisted of three stewardesses that only happened, to their misfortune, to be drop-dead gorgeous. One of them in particular drew all sorts of vocal reactions from apes pretending to be men, to the point that I could definitely sense she wasn't very comfortable anymore. This happened about 20 minutes into the flight.

About 30 minutes to landing, I noticed quite a bit of tension in the area as the stewardesses were walking back and forth and having what sounded like a rough conversation (I couldn't make sense of any of it, as it was in either German or Polish) with one particular passenger who was seated two rows behind me. I seem to recall hearing a phrase resembling "my colleague" in some of these discussions, and the guy appeared to be rather shocked and ashamed.

The stewardesses then demanded an ID, or a passport, from that passenger, who initially refused to provide them with one. Then they proceeded to make a few calls from within the aircraft.

Once we touched ground, three German police officers immediately boarded the aircraft. Now, I don't know if you have ever been to Germany before and/or seen a German police officer: I have been to Germany a few times already, and if there's one thing I can say about German police officers is that they look like the last people on earth that you'd want to fuck around with. A minute later they were already outside, with that guy, questioning him.

These are the facts. What really happened there? I am much inclined to believe that it had something to do with sexual harassment of some sort, as that one particular stewardess looked pretty distraught the entire time.

Sometimes I don't want to live on this planet anymore.

Berlin Tegel Airport is Berlin's main international airport, and the most surprising thing about it (for me) was that there exists no train leading directly to it. Public transit from the airport to the city center involves taking a bus first—to connect you with the actual public transport system of Berlin. Dragged myself and my belongings through one bus and two metro lines until arriving to the hotel.

The hotel, TRYP Berlin Mitte Hotel, is located in Berlin's city center but not quite exactly in the middle of everything worth exploring. I would definitely recommend it if you're into staying in a relatively quiet place and want easy access to Berlin's interesting parts; but if you're a fan of staying right in the middle of things, then it's not for you.

Berlin is the capital city of Germany and is considered by many to be one of the most interesting cities in the world. When it comes to night life, many claim that Berlin is second to none. Other than night life, it has a very rich history, dating back to the 13th century. The list of things to see and do in this city appears to be endless in any guide book you'd pick.

But here comes the shocking part: due to being extremely tired after the hectic travel of the last couple of weeks, I have seen close to *nothing* of the city while being there. I spent most of my time in the hotel room, either catching up with work or resting. Dull, huh? well, I suppose that's some of the price you pay when you decide to follow a tour with a crazy schedule: sometimes you don't get to see much, and you realize how important and good it is to simply rest and chill out.

I am not concerned, though: I will have more than enough opportunities to explore more of this city in the near future. For now, I'll take all the rest that I can get.

As soon as I arrived at the hotel in Berlin, I grabbed my small backpack containing my laptop and went downstairs to the lobby to catch up with some work (no Wi-Fi in the rooms). Later, my friend Ingrid, from The Netherlands, came by: she drove that day from The Netherlands to Berlin to catch the show. Was good seeing her again. After some time catching up, I took my laptop back to the room and we all went out for dinner.

Write down the name of this place: Bonfini. Ended up dining there 3 (!) times, partly because it was *so good* and partly because I wasn't in the position to put more efforts into experimenting (again, the tiredness). Excellent Italian food, all made there on site. Delicious. We spent a couple of hours there catching up and chatting about all sorts of things.

It felt great, having a good time with friends and being completely oblivious to a tiny little fact that got me very close to be forced to take the next airplane back to Vancouver and forget about this tour altogether.

Once back at the hotel room, I decided to go downstairs to do some work (again). Grabbed my laptop, and was going to put it in the backpack, when I realized that I can't find the damn bag.

Small room. Where the hell could it be? a minute later, I realized: before going to dinner, I brought my laptop upstairs, but not the backpack—it remained in the lobby.

Now, that would be OK if the backpack didn't contain a few items of importance, such as my 3 months European railway pass (costs around $2,200, irreplaceable), as well as my two passports.

Whatever happened next, happened so fast that I didn't even have time to get stressed about it. Stormed to the lobby as if I was bitten by an exceptionally aggressive Cobra, I turned to the very first hotel receptionist I could find and asked, in the most begging voice that I could emit, whether anyone might have seen a small backpack that contains my entire life for the upcoming 3 months.

Luckily, it was located earlier by staff and put in the lost & found. As soon as I got my hands on this precious pack, I realized what a disaster it would have been had I really lost it.

The next day was as uneventful as the preceding one. Other than going out for breakfast and lunch, I stayed at the hotel room the entire time until it was time to leave for the concert. A couple of trains to *Berlin Ostbahnhof*, and from there I walked to the venue, the O$_2$ World, about 15 minutes away.

The street where the venue is located is the famous Mühlenstrasse, which also happens to be where the East Side Gallery is. The Gallery is a 1.3km long section of the Berlin Wall, and walking next to it was a somewhat moving experience. I was 12 years old when the Berlin Wall fell, and I still have the memories of watching TV and not quite understanding why people are so excited to be hammering a wall down.

A few weeks ago, I did some reading about that wall. That led me to read about the death of Peter Fechter—a disturbing, shocking story that goes to demonstrate how terrible, fucked up people can be. Peter Fechter was 18 years old, living in East Berlin, when he tried —along with a friend of his—to bypass the wall and escape to West Berlin. As soon as they both reached the wall and started to climb it, shots were fired at them by East German officers. Both were hurt: Fechter's friend managed to cross the wall, but Fechter couldn't and fell back to the east side.

There were hundreds of witnesses to the incident, including journalists: the ordeal was also filmed. He started screaming, but still, received no assistance whatsoever:

- The east's border guards didn't feel it was necessary to help out an individual bleeding to death.
- The west's border guards didn't feel it was necessary to risk confronting the east's border guards.
- The hundreds of onlookers from the west side feared that their lives would be at stake if they tried to help.
- A United States second-lieutenant on the field received specific orders to do absolutely nothing about it.

Falling victim to the stupidity of people from both sides of Berlin, Fechter remained on the ground, by the wall, bleeding for an hour until he died.

No words.

I have been to this venue before in 2010. It is a large indoor arena that can host up to 17,000 spectators. Beautiful from the outside and the inside, featuring a LED construction grid at the exterior equipped with more than 300,000 LED clusters.

Having arrived early, I decided to spend the time before the concert just sitting outside watching people go by, thinking about things. The modern, beautiful venue versus the grim reminder of a divided Berlin only a hundred or so meters behind me. Then entered the concert hall, spoke to a few kind people who happen to be reading this blog—thank you—and the show started shortly after: a 17 songs set, almost identical to the one played the night before only substituting one gem—*5:15am*—with another—*Back to Tupelo*.

Seated at the back, it was very amusing to witness the *Running of the Bulls* emerging and then happening at once. Dozens of people running towards the stage from all directions. It all happened so fast—maybe *Running of the Bullets* is more fitting. I waited until the Bulls settled in, then marched surely, slowly and safely forward, enjoying the encore. More than I enjoyed the actual songs played, I enjoyed the atmosphere—it's nice to look at so many people being tremendously excited and absorbing every note.

A short march after the concert to *Berlin Ostbahnhof* and back to the hotel. Tried to complete this post at the hotel's lobby, to no avail —Wi-Fi wasn't working.

Oh: and someone better explain this to me.

After two nights in Berlin, it was time to leave this beautiful city (of which I had hardly seen any) and travel a bit north. Felt good to wake up late with no intention to go to any airport: Bremen, in northern Germany, is only 3 hours train ride northwest of Berlin, and with Germany's train system being so efficient and helpful, nobody was in a rush. Decent breakfast in a restaurant across the street from the hotel, and then went to Berlin's central train station to catch the train to *Hannover*, then switching towards Bremen.

I have never been to Bremen before. I have been to other cities in northern Germany—Hamburg and Hannover—and both were beautiful; I was told the same about Bremen, however, unfortunately, didn't get to see much of it either due to time constraints.

Arrived to Bremen at around 2:00pm, then off for a 1.5km walk to Hotel Stadt Bremen, involving a one hour stop in a fantastic restaurant, Tendure, along the way. Beautiful, delicious Turkish food. We made a fatal error and ordered a full meal: the steep price (€23 per person) should have flashed a red light somewhere, and indeed, when the food arrived, the mistake was realized. That meal could feed an elephant. An insane amount of food, some of which wasn't even touched. The parts that were touched, however, were wonderful. Highly recommended, but do yourself a favour and buy individual items. A "full meal" there means way, *way* too much food.

On the way to the hotel, I noticed a strange sight: two buses filled with people, riding along, escorted with police cars on both sides. I didn't understand why. Later on, I was explained that these were fans of Frankfurt's soccer team, who came to Bremen to cheer for their team's game against the local *Werder Bremen*.

Weather was cool, windy, grey. Having lots to do, I resorted to once again stay at the hotel room while Jeroen went ahead to explore the city. He took a few good shots, which I am going to shamelessly use here:

Time flew by as I was busy catching up with the world, then headed to the venue at 7:00pm.

The venue, Bremen Arena, is a large indoor arena located just north of Bremen's central railway station.

To get there, we had to pass through the station, and I was baffled to find many groups of police officers, essentially dressed up and ready for battle: masks, clubs, shields, the works. Both outside the station and inside. The soccer game ended 1:1.

Sitting in a coffee place inside the station, I asked the barista whether this particular soccer game was of any importance. With such extensive police presence, I would expect this to be the World Cup or something, but no: just a regular game. It turns out that this practice, of flooding prominent public areas with police officers before, during and after soccer matches, is very common in Germany. This is done in order to provide fast response in case of people losing their temper (mainly with the aid of alcohol) and rioting. Whether this is proper use of taxpayers' money or not—I'll leave that to the Germans to decide, but here's my honest and brutal opinion: it isn't.

Long, *long* line-up outside the venue to get in, only to realize that the long line-up was a line-up to another line-up, inside. No problem. Went to my seat, left to buy a huge cup of water (€4 for 0.5 litre) and returned just in time for *What It Is*, the show's opener.

Again a good show, 17 songs set. After *Hill Farmer's Blues*, an unrecognized instrument handout took place. A *Bm* chord opening for a few bars left me struggling to figure out what the hell is being played here: I'm usually very good at this but I failed miserably this time. Turned out to be a stripped-down, a bit simplistic (but still pleasant) rendition of *I Dug Up a Diamond*, from Knopfler's 2006 album with Emmylou Harris. This rendition reminded me a lot of that of *Back to Tupelo*.

Quite frankly, while it was nice to listen to, something was certainly missing at the end. The missing thing, according to recent literature, is called "Gibson Les Paul in Richard Bennett's hands during the outro solo". Then again, thinking about it, this particular stripped-down rendition of the song wouldn't work well with a massive Gibson presence at the end, so I suppose that's why it didn't happen.

Still, nice surprise.

Concert ended at around 10:20pm. Jeroen, Maarten, Nelly, Ingrid and myself went on our way back to the hotel (turned out we were all staying at the same place), but decided to take a detour for some late night drink and snacks (I don't drink alcohol, but a cheer is a cheer. I cheered with my wonderful Nexus 4 phone).

Signing off this long post while still in Bremen. In a few minutes, we'll head to Antwerp with Ingrid in the driver's seat.
Isaac

Monday, May 13, 2013

Bremen, Germany to Antwerp, Belgium to Delft, The Netherlands (May 12, 2013)

The original plan for the day was to take the 7:44am train from Bremen to Köln; change in Köln, ride to Brussels; change in Brussels and eventually arrive to Antwerp at around 2:30pm. That's close to 7 hours in total. However, as Ingrid was going to drive from Bremen to Antwerp to catch the concert, and as I'd highly prefer Ingrid's company over train staff, we decided to hitch a ride with her.

Right after breakfast, I rushed upstairs to the hotel room to finish my previous blog post, which took another hour and by 10:00am we were on our way to Antwerp.

I was under the impression that I had a good night sleep the night before, looking forward for an extremely long day. Turned out I was a little off in my appreciation to last night's sleep: 30 minutes into the ride I was already passing out on the passenger's seat, consistently trying to fall asleep and even more consistently failing to do so.

Ingrid is a wonderful person, and knows her way around handling cars, especially fast ones. Also, Ingrid is not a huge fan of speed limits, which worked very well in Germany as some parts of the highways we took had no posted speed limit. At times, we were cruising at 170–180 km/h, which is about 60 km/h faster than the maximum speed I allow myself to drive back home in Canada. At such speeds, I often felt as if I was travelling through a time warp. Time stretched, space shrunk—and still, Ingrid somehow made it feel like a non-issue at all.

As it was the end of a long weekend in Belgium, Germany and The Netherlands, there roads were busy at times so we did spend some time in traffic; but altogether, we made it to Antwerp in about five hours and a half including two breaks.

Rumours had it that I actually fell asleep. I'm not entirely in agreement.

Arrived to Antwerp at around 3:30pm, five hours before show time. Left all of our belongings in Ingrid's car and went to see what's there to do nearby the venue.

I have been to Antwerp a few of times before. It is the capital of Flanders, a province in Belgium, and it is a very pretty city with a rich history that dates back to the 16th century. The last time was in 2010, during the Get Lucky tour, and I remember walking through the city's beautiful streets, featuring stunning buildings that make you feel as if you are walking into the past.

The venue—Sportpaleis—is located at a remote part of the city's north, in an area that looks shady at best and, quite frankly, ugly. Therefore, if you are to attend a concert in this venue and it's your first time ever in Antwerp, beware not to form an opinion about the city just by the sight of the ugly surroundings of this venue because you'll be doing a great disservice to yourself.

Nearby the venue, there is nothing interesting to see, do and/or eat. There are a few restaurants, none of which I would feel extremely happy dining in. The livelihood of these establishments highly depends on the events taking place in the *Sportpaleis* and its neighbour, the Lotto Arena: the restaurants aim at punishing those who weren't fortunate enough to eat somewhere else (say, at home), and the bars are there to sell beer that, apparently, it is impossible to do without these days. Take the two venues out of the picture and this entire neighbourhood dies.

Across the street from the venue, a place called Pizza Lounge sells a dough-based substance that some cultures would call "pizza". I don't belong in such culture. Still, I was informed that other dining options in the area aren't that much better.

Not far from there, there's a pub/bar/restaurant called Time Out; it is usually jam-packed before events and as I joined a few concertgoers there, I couldn't help but noticing a strong smell of sewage in the entire place—if Ninja Turtles are ever to be found in real life, they must be here somewhere. How could anyone drink, let alone eat, in a place that stinks of sewage? that's beyond me. I stuck to my guns and kept my stomach empty.

Moral of the story: if you are ever to visit the Sportpaleis or Lotto Arena for an event, then either eat somewhere else beforehand, or bring your own food.

An hour before the concert, it was time to leave the sewer and head to the venue, a march of a staggering 50 meters. The sewage smell still lingered and I'm pretty sure was the reason for me feeling a bit ill for the next few hours.

"Sportpaleis" in Dutch means "Sports Palace". It is an indoor arena mostly hosting sporting events but also fairs, festivals and other events. Now here's an interesting piece of Trivia: during 2007–2008, the Sportpaleis was the second most visited event hall *in the entire world* after the Madison Square Garden in New York. That came as a total shock to me: after all, the Madison Square Garden is located in Midtown Manhattan. Out of all places in the world, how come this deserted neighbourhood in Antwerp is home to the *second* most visited event hall? Puzzling.

The venue's facilities are in line with the facilities of other sport arenas I had visited before: nothing fancy, sticking to basics, with the alcohol selection far exceeding the selection of, say, food. Costs €0.40 to use the toilets here, which means that you have to add €0.40 to the price of every drink you buy in this venue. Clever!

The show started a few minutes after the posted start time of 8:30pm.

A 16 songs set, identical to the one played the night before with the exception of *Speedway to Nazareth* being skipped this time. I am guessing that it was skipped either because the band had to catch a flight to Amsterdam, or because someone up there finally listened to my ongoing prayers, or both.

Most likely, though, it was because of travel constraints. In 2010, the Antwerp concert was the only concert in the tour in which *Piper to the End* wasn't played at the encore, as the band had to fly to Amsterdam and thus was subject to the Antwerp airport's schedules. This time, however, the debt has been paid in full and *Piper to the End* was played.

Rather apparent during this show was the fact that Mark himself was in quite the good mood: either that, or he tends to emit cowboy-like vocal gestures for other purposes. The sight of the frontman often smiling, dancing and altogether having a lot of fun worked well with the audience.

The audience, as usually is the case in Knopfler's concerts in Antwerp, was very receptive. It should be noted that concerts in Antwerp typically involve audiences of mixed sources, as Antwerp is within a reasonable driving distance from The Netherlands, the west part of Germany and the northern part of France. A United Nations of concertgoers.

Concert ended at around 10:15pm, which was perfect: the plan was for Ingrid to drop us off in Breda (a city in the south of The Netherlands, from where we can catch the 11:39pm train directly to Delft, where Jeroen happens to own an apartment. The distance between Antwerp to Breda is about 52km, taking about 40 minutes for mortals to drive and about 4 minutes for Ingrid.

That didn't work.

As we were parked in the venue's parking lot, we were told that it's going to take about 15 minutes to leave the parking lot out into the open. That was taken into account; what wasn't taken into account, though, is that some people have a different interpretation to the concept of "minute". It took us close to an hour (!) to leave the parking lot. As we left the parking lot, the reason for the delay became apparent: there were two humans directing traffic instead of machines (that is, traffic lights), and they went about the worst way of doing so, allowing very little time in each cycle for parking lot traffic to clear out.

Once we were out of the parking lot, another challenge emerged. One of the major roads that was supposed to take us to the highway was blocked, so we ended up navigating for about 20 minutes through dark streets and alleys while Ingrid's GPS kept insisting on directing us back to the closed route.

Eventually we found our way out of that mess and were on the way to The Netherlands; however, we have already missed the last train to Delft, so Ingrid was kind enough to invite us over to her house in Goirle, near Tilburg, conveniently located right next to this:

Very kind of Ingrid to save the day. A short snack and off to bed.

I was so tired as I lay my head to sleep, that I don't even remember trying to fall asleep at all.

Signing off this post while seated at Jeroen's desk at his workplace. It's going to be a relaxing day in Delft today; concert in Amsterdam tomorrow, and two days from now—off to Luxembourg and then, *finally*, to the UK.

Isaac

Wednesday, May 15, 2013

Delft to Amsterdam, The Netherlands (May 13-14, 2013)

After allowing us to spend the night in her house in Goirle, gracious Ingrid gave us a ride on Monday morning to the train station in the nearby town of Tilburg. I was still half awake and three quarters asleep: it's a problem that I have, that one night's sleep is rarely enough to render me unwound and rested after a stressful day. Sometimes it takes a couple of days, or more, until I regain my physical and mental strength.

Some Dutch people told me that it's because I never take a shower in the morning (I only take showers at night). I may give it a shot.

At any rate, arrived at Jeroen's place just before noon. Quick shower and off to visit his workplace—essentially, a concentration of overly intelligent people doing all sorts of scientific programming, including making sure that the government of The Netherlands is notified as soon as it becomes a possibility that the country is flooded with water. Cool people. When it's lunch time, someone there hits a gong and everyone gathers at the dining room.

I wrote before about the Dutch people's obsession with breads, spreads and chocolate sprinkles. It was shockingly predictable that things hadn't changed much since I was here last. I was sitting at the table next to about twenty nice Dutchmen, took a couple of slices of bread, put some peanut butter on one slice and then asked a very simple question:

– "What should I put on this?"

I was shocked by the response. People started suggesting so many options, passing boxes and cans of strange materials for me to pick from. Ten seconds later, I was surrounded by containers:

Lovely people, great hospitality. Being there, you feel that this is a company worth working for—a rarity these days.

As Monday was a day off in a familiar city, I used it for touring maintenance. It helps to be able to revisit your packing strategy—leaving items behind, taking additional items with you—a couple of weeks into the tour: I already decided on a few items that I'm going to leave here and have them shipped to Vancouver as it became apparent that I won't be needing them.

Laundry—done. Also found a charger for my shaver, after forgetting mine at home.

Monday, a day off, in a familiar place. Batteries recharged.

Tuesday morning, woke up slowly to the sound of nothing and looking forward to take a walk in Delft's city center.

I have been to Delft a few times before already. I really, *really* don't know how why exactly, but there's something in this little city that makes me want to be in it. It's a combination of the cool, laid back Dutch mentality and the setting of a city where time slows down, nobody rushes anywhere and people are courteous and nice to each other.

It is also very easy to get run over by bicycles in here, but that's not entirely exclusive to Delft. In many cities in The Netherlands, your chances of being hit by a bicycle are not much lower than your chances of being hit by a car, and if you're not very well accustomed to the Dutch people's biking habits, then you really want to look to your left, right, forward, backward and in all diagonals before crossing any pathway here.

And Lord, the bicycles. By the thousands. Just to make matters a bit clearer, take a look at this picture:

What you see here is a picture of a one parking lot for bicycles, located next to Delft's railway station (there's another one like this nearby, plus another smaller one). People park their bicycles here before boarding the train, and picking them up once they're back. I will never understand *how the hell they manage to find their own bicycles when they return.*

By the way: Delft's population is about 100,000. I can't help but wonder what this would look like in, say, Amsterdam.

Came across this place, which makes a bold statement that it is in the cheese business:

Parked my bottom in Coffee Company—a cafe in the city center where I'm a regular whenever I'm in town—to catch up with work, writing and composing. Then, a short trip to a place called Pure Coffee: must be a new spot in town, as I have never seen it before—but will definitely revisit. They deal with raw, healthy foods—a dining option that is relatively easy to find in Western Canada but rather tricky to find around here (that, or I have been looking at all the wrong places).

After a superbly laid back day, it was time to get into concert routine again. Back to Jeroen's apartment to get ready, and left at 6:00pm to Delft's railway station. A few of Jeroen's colleagues decided to see for themselves what's so special about this band's performances that makes it worth the while to watch seventy times in three months. Delft to Schiphol airport, then connecting to Amsterdam Bijlmer ArenA (not a typo; that's how they spell it. A branding thing, I guess).

The Amsterdam Bijlmer ArenA railway station is a large one, and serves a few important entertainment establishments in Amsterdam —all of which are within short walking distance from each other. You'll find the Heineken Music Hall—a very popular concert venue— here, as well as the home stadium for the renowned Ajax football club. Nearby, there stands the *Ziggo Dome*.

The Ziggo Dome is a new indoor arena, opened less than one year ago. It seats 17,000 and, among all multi-use indoor arenas so far used in this tour, wins the top spot. For once, it is huge, which means that you are likely to find a way to walk around this venue without stepping on anyone's toes; second, the venue's facilities are clean, organized, well-signed and well-kept; and third, finally, there's a venue with proper food offering. While other indoor arenas focus on selling alcohol, leaving hungry people with the choice of eating garbage or stay hungry, this place offers—you may want to sit before reading this—proper, relatively healthy dining options such as sandwiches made on the spot, natural juices and the like. Beats the hell out of the *Beschuit Met Hagelslag* I had in Jeroen's apartment before we left—for the first time ever, I felt bad for not being hungry while at a concert venue.

As we all arrived late due to train delays, not much time passed before the lights went out and Paul Crockford took the microphone to welcome the opening act for the concert: Ruth Moody, who, coincidentally, contributed her stunning voice to a few tracks in Knopfler's latest album.

Winnipeg is the capital of the Canadian province of Manitoba. Manitoba borders with Ontario (Capital city: *Toronto*. Now there's a name you might have heard of) in the east and Saskatchewan (Capital city: *Regina*. Now there's a name you probably never heard of before) in the west. The provinces of Manitoba, Saskatchewan and most of Alberta (located to immediate west of Saskatchewan) are all referred to as the Canadian Prairies, and for a good reason: we're talking about vast areas that are for the most part flat and sparsely populated.

How vast? well, Manitoba's area alone is 650,000km², out of which approximately 102,000 km² (over 15%!) water. France is not too much larger with 674,000km². Quite the prairie, I'd say (Saskatchewan adds another 650,000km²).

As Ruth Moody mentioned while on stage, Winnipeg is cold at winters. How cold? unimaginably so. The lowest temperature ever recorded in Winnipeg was −47.8°C, recorded in December 1879. Days with insanely cold temperatures such as −25°C or −30°C were not too uncommon in recent winters.

If the winter there doesn't kill you, then the summer might. Winnipeg's summers are very hot. In addition, Winnipeg is dubbed the "Mosquito Capital of Canada", boasting mosquitos big enough to lift small children.

I have been to Winnipeg once before, in 2008, while following Knopfler's *Kill to Get Crimson* tour in North America. Back then, the itinerary included a few major Canadian cities, crossing Canada from west (Vancouver) to east (Montréal, which isn't exactly "east" in Canada. The true "east" is St. John's, Newfoundland, located a couple of hours flight east of Montréal). I followed that entire North American tour, mostly by car.

From Vancouver to Calgary, the scenery is brilliant, featuring mountains, lakes, rivers, valleys, snow peaks—the works. A couple of hours west of Calgary, you enter *Yoho National Park*, which marks the western edge of the indescribably amazing Canadian Rockies. Here's Peyto Lake, to demonstrate:

East of the Canadian Rockies, the scenery gradually changes from wild nature to rather dull nature, featuring very little except for prairies.

It's a common Canadian joke that, if you live in the prairies and the dog runs away from home, you can still spot it 3 days later because it is so flat. "Land of the Endless Sky", as depicted in the following picture taken in a rest stop somewhere in Saskatchewan:

One of the better things to come out of Winnipeg is Ruth Moody (well, not technically; born in Australia, raised in Winnipeg), a singer whom I was completely oblivious of before Knopfler released *Privateering* last year. Being home for Justin Bieber, it'd be fair to say that Canada has a lot to compensate for, and Ruth Moody is certainly a step at the right direction.

Moody was invited by Knopfler et al to be the opening act for the Amsterdam concert, as well as in a few concerts in the UK and France later on in the tour. Her opening act, presenting some of her own material along with an accompanying band, was pleasant to listen to although it did suffer from a few sound problems, including an almost complete outage during her beautiful rendition to Bruce Springsteen's *Dancing in the Dark*. Certainly deserves a closer listen; I shall give her albums a couple of spins and report back.

After a forty minutes' set, Moody left the stage. A few minutes later, the familiar band of eight took their spots and proceeded to perform the best concert so far in the tour.

The Netherlands has always been a warm spot for Knopfler, as his fan base here is quite strong. Knopfler's concerts in The Netherlands usually end up being either sold out or very nearly so, with the audience involving people in virtually all age groups. During the 2010 *Get Lucky* tour, Knopfler played the Heineken Music Hall three nights in a row—the only venue to be played in more than once during that tour with the exception of London's Royal Albert Hall.

Therefore, Knopfler's decision to drop *Sultans of Swing* from the set in Amsterdam can't be overlooked as if not indicative of anything. I'll let you draw your own conclusions and just state that I am happy with this.

After the usual five opening songs, something happened that I haven't seen in any of the previous ±160 concerts I had seen before: a guest artist being invited on stage to perform along with the band. After a few exceptionally warm introduction, Ruth made it back on stage, driving this concert to be the best one so far in the tour.

I Dug Up a Diamond was the first one in the sequence. Originally a duet with *Emmylou Harris*, I was curious to see how Ruth's voice fits here. Ruth's excitement was obvious, although she didn't did much to hide it—no need to. Beautiful performance, exactly what this song needed after being arranged to a somewhat stripped-down configuration.

Next up: *Seattle*, a beautiful track first played live in Sofia, made a comeback with Ruth playing backing vocals to it (she played backing vocals for this song in the studio album as well). What can I say? fantastic. Exactly what this song needs when played live.

Two duets in the same show were a great surprise I was very happy with, but then again, why suffice with two? *Kingdom of Gold*, previously performed in this tour (and the preceding one) with Guy Fletcher singing backing vocals, now with Ruth contributing her own soothing voice to the mix. The result? well, I strongly suggest that you get your hands on the official soundboard recording of the show and give it a listen.

Altogether, I think that whoever had the chance to be at the Ziggo Dome for this concert can (and should) call themselves lucky. It's not that previous concerts in the tour were bad: simply, this one—much thanks to Ruth's participation—was extraordinary. I can only hope that she joins the stage later on in the tour as well.

A short break after a powerful *Telegraph Road* performance; *So Far Away* and *Piper to the End* concluded this excellent concert and sent the Dutch audience home happy.

I was asked before what my opinion is about Jim Cox's performance comparing to Matt Rollings', as well as Ian Thomas' performance comparing to Danny Cummings'. Well, I am not a music critic and certainly don't aspire to be: what I write is based mostly on coarse-grained impressions that I get, and is often impacted by my overall experience rather than minutiae. While I do play guitar & piano, these guys are way out of my league and I consider myself lucky to be able to watch these guys play and somehow learn from them.

But if I were to compare Ian to Danny or Jim to Matt, I'd encounter a dead-end very shortly into the process as we're not comparing apples to apples here.

Comparing to Danny, Ian is certainly more aggressive and technical on the drums. Is it better? is it worse? neither. It's just a different approach that works well for certain songs and not as well for others. Certain songs sound better <u>to me</u> with the beat being softer and less aggressive (*What It Is* being a good case in point), while some seem to sound better with Ian playing them. My own personal taste generally favours softness over aggressiveness, yet I'm aware that my opinion is a minority one.

On the keyboard, there is a world of difference between what's being played by Jim Cox and what used to be played by Matt Rollings. Different style, different approach: Jim's style is generally softer, while Matt's is more technical. It seemed to me that Matt used to know exactly what he was going to be playing, while Jim is leaving more to improvisation.

It must be noted that piano involvement during this tour is considerably more visible than in previous tours: Jim is given much more space and freedom to demonstrate his style than Matt was, which makes it even harder to compare the performance styles of the two.

Plus, there is the difference in actual gear: I am not entirely sure what digital piano Matt used to play, but it certainly wasn't Roland's *V-Piano* that Jim plays. I had the opportunity to lay my fingers on a V-Piano before, and I can say that it is by far the best digital piano I have ever tried—it's fabulous, period. Unfortunately, its steep price (about $6,500 in Canada) rendered it irresponsible for me to purchase one, so I ended up buying a different Roland instead.

So, who is better? I don't know and I don't care. For sure, though, they are different. Very different. Listen for yourself and draw your own conclusions.

After the concert, different people in the group left the hall at different times (meaning: everyone else left together, I stayed behind), which wasted a few important minutes on the way back to the train station. Due to delays, a simple ride back to Delft revolved into taking a couple of extra trains in the middle, and a stop in Schiphol Airport for about half an hour. It was close to 1:00am when we made it back to Delft.

Long day, excellent show. Back to touring mode.

Signing off this post while at the hotel in Luxembourg. What a depressing place.

Isaac

Friday, May 17, 2013

Delft, The Netherlands to Luxembourg City, Luxembourg (May 15, 2013)

The morning after a stellar Moody/Knopfler experience, it was time to get back to touring mode: after getting rid of a few things I don't need, packing is now much easier. Batteries recharged, ready to go.

In the last post, I wrote that I am a big fan of the peaceful, lovely city of Delft. It was a pain to bid it farewell, and once again embark on train travel into the unknown—the good news being that I'll be back in Delft in about two weeks and a half, for a week long break after the London concerts.

Morning train from Delft to Rotterdam. I have awkward memories of Rotterdam's central station: whenever I happened to be there before, it happened to be under construction, making getting around the train station quite confusing and stressful. Turned out that it was a 5–6 years construction effort that is just about over: the station looks much better now, spacious and easy to get around in.

No place to sit down for a morning coffee. Knowing that the ride to Luxembourg is going to take about six hours, each of us bought a sandwich from La Place with the intention to keep it for lunch time—an intention that remained theoretical, as I am not the type of person who's going to let a warm sandwich get cold inside a backpack just because "it's too early". Superb sandwich, by the way. If you happen to come across a *La Place* shop in The Netherlands, use it.

The train ride from Rotterdam to Luxembourg passes through Brussels. For whatever reason, I had good memories of Brussels Midi/Zuid—I have been to this station a few times in the past.

Perhaps my memory is starting to betray me. Eagerly looking for my morning coffee, I found myself outside the station. Across the road, a sign with the promising name *SAS Cafe* appeared. Looks nice from the outside. Stepped in. About 20–30 tables, only one of which is occupied, by a lady sitting down reading the newspaper.

Caught the attendant's attention, which is where things started to go downhill. I asked an extremely involved, complex question.

– "Can I please have a cappuccino?"

– "Ah, yes. But we only make cappuccino with cream."

– "You mean, whipped cream?"

– "Ah… Pardon?"

– "You mean, *whipped* cream?"

– "It is not like an Italian cappuccino, with milk. We make it with cream."

I started suspecting that the difficulty revolves around the word "whipped".

– "Is it a sweet cream?"

– "Yes."

– "OK… can you make anything with steamed milk?"

– "Pardon?"

Obviously, the tricky word was now "steamed".

– "Can you make anything with hot milk?"

– "Yes. I can make a latte with hot milk."

Jackpot.

– "OK, thank you. I'll have one."

– "To sit down, or take out?"

– "To sit down, please."

– (Turning to Jeroen) "And for you?"

– (Jeroen) "Nothing, I'm OK, thank you."

– "Sorry, you can't sit inside then. If you want to sit inside, both of you have to order something."

– "What? Why?", I asked. Admittedly, my initial choice of words was different.

– "Because it's lunch time now, and we are very busy in lunch time."

We looked around. Nobody was there.

Not much in the mood to argue, I took the coffee in a paper cup and left. Now, I am not sure whether this is an acceptable business practice in Brussels, or in Belgium, or whatnot. Something like this happening in Vancouver would be very bad news for your business. I understand business owners' wish to make money, but to go as far as kicking a group of people out just because one member of the group doesn't want to order anything—excuse me, that's fucked up in many levels.

Took a sip. That resulted in my brain being overloaded with trying to find words to describe how disgusting the coffee was. €3 down the drain.

Back to the station, walked to the station's other end and found a familiar place, called Sam's Cafe. Another €3, another coffee that sucked.

Nothing worked for me there.

Went to the restrooms. Costs €0.50, I had three coins of €0.20. You can only put €0.50 coins there. How? AH. Good question. They have a machine there that you put coins in it and it changes them all to €0.50 coins plus whatever's left. Clever. Too bad that the machine had no written instructions on it other than a rather unclear diagram.

Finally, the train left Brussels. The travel plan said that the train was heading to Luxembourg, while the departures board showed that the train was heading to a town named Arlon, where there's another connection to Luxembourg. Fantastic, another challenge—as if the day wasn't challenging enough already. Of course, once arriving to Arlon, there were no instructions whatsoever as to which train exactly goes to Luxembourg. Connection time is 5 minutes. Go figure. Luckily, a nice lady who was going that direction herself saved the day.

It was around 15:40 when I was finally in Luxembourg's central railway station.

It was raining.

I have been to Luxembourg once before, during the 2010 tour. It was a short visit—getting into Luxembourg and getting out the next morning. That Luxembourg experience three years ago was far from leaving a positive mark in my memory, so I wasn't quite looking forward to visit it again. I seem to recall Luxembourg City being somewhat grey and depressing, with people wearing disturbed expressions on their faces.

As I arrived to Luxembourg this time around, it seemed like nothing changed. I don't know how to explain it: I just felt as if I am surrounded by people who aren't exactly happy. Therefore, I was determined to find out why: fired up Wikipedia and started reading.

I was shocked.

Luxembourg is a European country bordering with France, Belgium and Germany. It is small, in both area and population: about 2,600km^2 are home to about 530,000 people. According to the World Bank, Luxembourg has *the highest GDP per capita in the world*: income is high, inflation is low, and so is unemployment. According to The Economist's Quality of Life Index, Luxembourg ranks 4th in the world. 4th!

Due to its banking secrecy laws, Luxembourg has been (and still is) a tax haven for rich individuals and wealthy corporations worldwide. One famous case concerning Luxembourg being a tax haven was revealed in April 2012, when it turned out that the UK's arm of *Amazon* was able to avoid paying high taxes in the UK by channelling its revenues through Luxembourg. Also, Kim Jong Il—the dictator who, for decades, was in the habit of messing up the lives of millions of North Koreans—has been reported, in March 2010, to have about $4 billion in Luxembourg's banks.

On paper, yes, this is a rich country. Not only on paper: the hotel room for this one night in Luxembourg, in an average hotel with nothing special in it, cost about €140. Taxi to the airport from the city center—a distance of about 9km—costs around €40–50.

In other words, Luxembourg isn't quite the travel destination for those who aspire to travel on a shoestring.

I was intrigued. Clearly there's something to Luxembourg that I am not yet aware of. Perhaps it's just the area surrounding the central station being grey and depressing? The train ride itself shows a beautiful country, with beautiful houses spotted on green hills. Maybe the answer is there?

At any rate, as intrigued as I was, sadly, I could not afford the time to explore anything. This year, the tour's busy schedule restricted the stay in Luxembourg to one night only.

Upon checking in to the hotel, Hotel Carlton located a few minutes walk from the central railway station, we set out to get some food. A quick look in *TripAdvisor* showed a few worthy dining options around: sadly, none were open. Turns out that restaurants in Luxembourg (or, at least, at the city center area) follow similar habits to those in France and Spain: restaurants are only open for certain periods during the day. At other times, you'd have to suffice with bar- or pub-type establishments selling questionable food.

Eventually, we found one that was open: Alfa Brasserie, located right across the street from the railway station. This place caters to give you the best of a few dining options—Italian, French, Luxemburgish and so on. Prices were steep—starting at €16 for a main course and quickly climbing to the mid-€30's.

We both had a mushroom & parmesan risotto. I had it once, Jeroen had it twice. This will be explained below. Read on.

Then, off to the station to figure out exactly how to get to the venue. Back to the hotel to chill out and catch up with some things, and then took the 6:50pm train to the *Rockhal*.

The Rockhal is one of Luxembourg's main concert venues. It is surrounded by natural beauty, as depicted in the picture below:

Bah. Well. Essentially, the Rockhal is one big concrete-made shoebox, making it a perfect choice for events in which sound is not an issue, such as *Megadeth* concerts. Let's just put it this way: Beethoven isn't going to be played here any time soon.

Nearby the venue, there's a nice shopping mall. Looking for drinks, we stumped upon a nice restaurant that had a proper espresso machine.

Sat down.

Waitress came by, asking what we would like. We said we would like some drinks.

She pointed outside the restaurant, and then spoke in fluent French saying that this place is for eating: if it's not solid food that you'd like your body to consume, then you should go to the nearby drinks place.

That, ladies and gentlemen, was the second time in six hours that we were thrown out of a food-serving establishment because we were not seeking just the right thing. Rude, arrogant, screwed up… many words to describe this.

Having said that, well, I suppose that's what this trip is mostly about: getting out of your comfort bubble; experience new things; absorb them; learn from them. Fine. But the problem is that my comfort bubble, after having lived in Vancouver for the last two years, is just *so fucking comfortable* that getting adjusted to these quirks becomes a real hassle.

(During the last tour, I was a little more tolerant of such things. I used to live in the east coast back then.)

Mediocre coffee in the mall and back to the venue, very close to show time. The Rockhal is not the venue you're likely to desire to be in for more than absolutely needed.

Unfortunately I can't tell you much about what I saw in the concert because I didn't see much. For once, knowing in advance that we'd be after a long travel day when arriving at Luxembourg, we opted at the tribune in the back instead of standing up in the front. How back? a long way back.

Also, because the venue is not much more than a pile of bricks glued together, it's difficult to get good, balanced sound. I believe that the crew did their best with what they were given, and in the Rockhal, not much can be done. The concert didn't quite sound the same.

Nothing special happened during the show until *Haul Away* started playing, Jeroen turned to me and mumbled something.

– "What?"

– "Move, I need to go."

Jeroen and I attended many concerts together in the past—dozens of them. One thing he *never* did was to get up from his seat during the concert to go anywhere.

– "Where?", I asked, as if it mattered.

– "I'm not feeling well."

That's when the second tasting of that risotto came into play. He left the hall with a bad case of food poisoning, and didn't return until the encore. It was rather disconcerting. Not only a good friend of yours is going through hell, but you also happened to eat exactly the same things at exactly the same time over the last 12+ hours. That took away most of my enjoyment of the concert, as I had to leave the hall a few times to text the poor mate (no cellular reception inside the hall) to ensure he's still alive.

Quite expectedly, throwing up made a world of difference for the suffering Dutchman, and he returned, good as new, for the encore which we watched from the very back of the hall.

So Far Away concluded the show and we rushed back to the train station nearby to catch the train back to the city center.

Another stressful day, another stressful Luxembourg experience. Still, I'm hoping to get more time to explore this country in the future. I need to make amends.

Concluding this post from the hotel room in the wonderful city of Glasgow.

Isaac

Sunday, May 19, 2013

Luxembourg City, Luxembourg to Glasgow, UK (May 16-17, 2013)

Thursday morning. Flight from Luxembourg to Glasgow, through London Heathrow, is scheduled to depart at around 11:45am. I opened my eyes. Time: around 8:00am. No, please, let me rest some more.

Opened them again. Time: around 8:40am. Sprang out of bed as if my ass was on fire. "We need to go".

The Dutchman looks at me. "We have time".

Which we did. Luxembourg's airport is located around 10km from the city center. But I don't know why, I was rather stressed that morning. I don't know what I wanted more: to get out of Luxembourg, or to arrive to Glasgow—a city I am very fond with.

I think it was more about my deep desire to leave Luxembourg.

Quick morning routine, down to the hotel's dining room for a mediocre breakfast that failed to deliver, mostly because it didn't even try.

Stress. Rush. "Let's get out of here already". Unusual for me to be so stressed in the morning, and I didn't even have my coffee yet.

The hotel's receptionist, which I believe is also the owner who also lends a hand to preparing breakfast, explained to us that taking a bus to the airport is probably the best approach, considering the fact that for the price of a taxi ride to the airport we might be able to purchase Bulgaria's stock market in its entirety. Upstairs to grab the luggage, and within 10 minutes we were at the central station, wandering through the bus platforms to find bus number 16 heading to the airport.

It rained.

Do you know what it feels to be stressed out, outside, in the cold, 30 minutes after you wake up, and feel the drizzle on your face?

Good.

The bus took 20–30 minutes to ride 10km. During that ride, I got to see some pretty sights of the city center (around the City Hall area) as well as its surrounding areas, offering pleasant views of hills, trees and much greenery.

But I just wanted out; and once arrived at the airport, I felt as if some weight has been lifted off my shoulders.

Luxembourg's airport is small and is the only international airport in the country. It is also the only airport in the country having a paved runway.

Rushed into the terminal building and stood in the check-in line. A minute later I realized that we're surrounded by most of the band's crew: The two guitar technicians (Mark's and Richard's), plus various familiar faces—some of which I spoke with before but they all seemed very happy with the company of each other so I didn't quite feel like interfering. Turned out, though, that we were all booked on the same two-legged flight to Glasgow.

Check in—done. Security—done. Down to passport control, and there's a line-up. Three passport control booths, zero of which are active. Fifteen minutes passed until someone bothered to operate a booth, not before I realized that the flight was postponed by an hour.

These were not good news. Connection time in London's Heathrow airport was about 2 hours, which had to allow for switching terminals and going through passport control *and* security again (as you're switching between international & domestic travel).

"Well, that's fine. Let's just settle at the gate area, have a coffee or something", I said.

Well, what do you know. Once you're past passport control in Luxembourg's airport, there's nothing there except for a couple of vending machines, one selling candy and the other selling "coffee" and "coffee"-based products.

No Wi-Fi.

Yawn.

Ended up waiting for a couple of hours there, slightly cheered up by knowing that if I'm stuck in Luxembourg, then it means that the crew is stuck in Luxembourg as well and, without some of these guys, a concert simply can't happen. So let time pass; today is a day off, anyway.

Flight ended up being delayed by an hour and a half. As we arrived in Heathrow, we were told (by "we", I'm referring to Jeroen, myself, and most of the band's crew) that we missed our flight and we should go upstairs to customer service to see what the next steps are.

Whatever. I was really too tired to get pissed, and really, even if I was to get pissed, how could it help?

However, I must say that I was very impressed with how British Airways handled this. Customer service at the airport was fantastic. As the crew occupied the rest of the available seats on the 6:05pm flight, we had to suffice with the 6:50pm one. Got a £10 compensation voucher each, as well as free access to British Airways' Business Lounge.

Passport control… and now they take your picture here, too. It's a new system: they scan your boarding pass and take your picture. Upon boarding the aircraft, you have to look at a camera again so it can compare your face to whatever data it has about you in the system, in order to ensure that the person boarding the aircraft is indeed the person who went through passport control.

Security screening… again. Got all these procedures out of the way and then had to find a way to kill about four hours.

First order of business: lunch. Raised my head, looked around and what do I see? Wagamama. If you happen to be in the UK and come across a Wagamama, just go there. Been there many times before and was never disappointed: good, healthy, delicious and reasonably priced food.

Then off to British Airways' Business Lounge. Took a while to find that place—Heathrow Terminal 5 is *huge*, and all airlines' lounges are concentrated together in one part of the terminal. Turns out that British Airways has a few lounges in that terminal: one for first-class passengers, one for business passengers, one for other passengers… heck, they also have a travel spa there, on site. Oh, and a club, too. What do they do in that club? I should find out.

Entered the lounge… what can I say? no words. Fantastic. If you ever have an itinerary that includes a few hours' stop in Heathrow, buy access to that lounge. Free Wi-Fi, comfortable chairs, free (tasty!) food—including hot meals, cold meals, drinks, the works. I was impressed.

Used the time to catch up with things (as usual). Time passed quickly. Left to the gate about forty minutes before departure, which was good because Jeroen has misread "gates closing time" as "boarding time" (good one, mate. Good one). Boarded… taxi… take-off! on my way to Glasgow.

As soon as I left the aircraft in Glasgow airport, I already felt better. The familiar bus #500 to the city center…

As Jeroen was trying to chart the bus' route from the airport to the city center, we came across something weird. Now, we all know that one axiom in Euclidian geometry says that the shortest distance between two points (on a plane) is always a straight line, but *this* was a bit troubling:

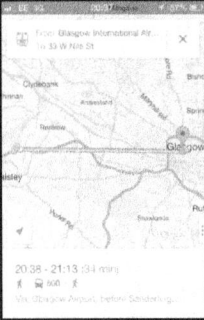

(the light blue line is supposedly the route that the super-bus, which apparently drives above vertical obstacles, is taking.)

Thirty minutes later we arrived at the hotel, Premier Inn, located on West Nile Street just steps away from Buchanan Street and George Square, both are major touristic spots in the city of Glasgow. Unloaded everything and, as it was still light outside, rushed back to the streets to get some fresh air.

Glasgow is the largest city of Scotland (though not the capital; Edinburgh is). It is located right on River Clyde, the third longest river in Scotland—the same river mentioned in one particular song that, to my dismay, isn't very likely to be performed live during this tour. It is home to about 600,000 people, while the metro Glasgow area is home to about 2.8 million—about half of Scotland's population.

It is rather intriguing to realize that some cities can cause you, somehow, to feel good about yourself while other cities can cause you feel anxious to leave. Of course, this is purely subjective: what makes my boat float might drown someone else's, and vice versa. Still, I'm wondering what is it, in a particular setting, that makes me feel comfortable in it?

Glasgow, in that regards, presents a sharp contrast to Luxembourg, as far as I'm concerned. This was my third time here, and the more I'm here, the more I want to stay.

For once, the city center area is beautiful, with massive old buildings looking brilliant at night time and fantastic in daytime.

It was Thursday night: most businesses were closed. Cloudy, cold, but still, walking in Glasgow's city center felt special.

As my EURail pass doesn't cover the UK, I had to pre-book all UK travel and collect the tickets in any UK train station. As I was walking past Glasgow's Central Station anyway, I figured I might as well just get it over with. The way UK train travel ticketing works is extremely inefficient (more on that in the next post, on which I'm working at the same time at the moment), and the ticket collection from the automated terminal also leaves some to be desired.

For once, I understand that our older generation may not be fully aware of the QWERTY keyboard layout which is found in each and every English keyboard on the planet (well, almost: some use a layout called *Dvorak*, which was patented in 1936 by Dr. August Dvorak while claiming that it reduces errors, improving typing speed and reduces fingers strain—all claims that were repeatedly proven wrong, leading to Dvorak's complete and utter market failure). But still, at least provide an option to change this ABCDE layout to QWERTY for those of us who are familiar (to some extent) with a keyboard.

For twice, if you have multiple itineraries to collect, you have to go through the entire process (credit card verification) for each itinerary separately. That turned a process, that could have taken one minute, into a ten minutes ordeal.

I would have designed it differently.

Ended up collecting 26 (!) stubs for 6 itineraries. An average of 4.33 stubs per itinerary. Here's a bright idea: how about *one*?

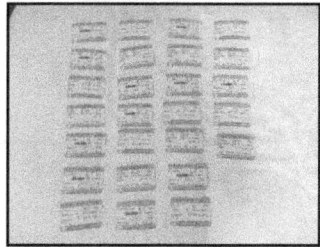

The Premier Inn hotel chain has it in its main slogan that it guarantees a good night sleep. I didn't get one, but not because of the hotel and its facilities, but mostly because of being overly stressed.

The next morning, the sun was shining. When the sun is shining, Glasgow is even prettier. A decision was made to obliterate morning hunger and then set out for a walk.

A look on the net brought up *Martha's* as the provider of a potentially good breakfast:

Martha's breakfast menu doesn't focus on selection, but instead focuses on simplicity and, well, taste. *Porridge* is a typical Scottish breakfast, and together with granola, flax seeds and all sorts of other healthy goodies, provides for a rather filling and healthy breakfast. Recommended. Go there.

Kept on walking, taking many pictures of this lovely city. The destination was River Clyde—for once, it'd be nice to see it in the sunshine.

Along the way, I made a disconcerting discovery: *KFC* is now in the business of serving espresso-based products.

(Skipped.)

Crossed the Glasgow Bridge as the grass looked greener there (well, there wasn't any grass on the city center's side), and then the *South Portland Street Suspension Bridge* back to the city center. The views were *amazing*.

Here's optimism at its best: "Thanks for Nothing Friday".

Back on Argyle Street…

Isaac's "Privateering" Tour Blog

Walking on Buchanan Street again, I noticed a familiar place: The Willow Tea Rooms. I have been there once before, during the joint Knopfler/Dylan tour in 2011. That place made a long lasting impression. We'll be back here soon for lunch.

I'll just dump most pictures here as I can't pick which ones to use.

Afternoon tea at The Willow:

And back to the hotel, as I had to catch up with a few things.

At around 5:00pm, James Morris, who had helped me planning some parts of the 2010 Get Lucky tour, made his way to the hotel for a get-together. A quick snack at Pret a Manger downstairs and we headed to the venue—an easy 25 minutes walk.

The venue—S.E.C.C (shorthand for *Scottish Exhibition and Conference Center*)—is located right next to the famous Clyde Auditorium (AKA "The Armadillo". Guess why):

It is the largest exhibition center in Scotland. A few halls inside are regularly used to host concerts, with the capacity of up to 12,500.

The S.E.C.C and the Clyde Auditorium and the nearby Crowne Plaza hotel are interconnected through a myriad of pathways. The Crowne Plaza there is ridiculously expensive to stay in, let alone in concert nights; however, its bar area is very popular among concertgoers for food & drinks before the show. Matt Duncan and his friend Chris were there, and we passed the time chatting for about an hour before it was time to head back to the venue. The concert started early—a few minutes past 7:30pm.

This tour around, the UK concerts are featuring Nigel Hitchcock, an English jazz saxophonist. He started collaborating with musicians when he was 18 years old, and had the chance to play with many glorious and famous.

After the regular opening, Nigel was invited to the stage. I wasn't quite sure what's going to be played next, as not many songs in Mark's recent repertoire seem to be accommodating of a saxophone. I was betting on *Your Latest Trick* from the Dire Straits days—actually, of the few Dire Straits tunes that I'm happy to listen to.

The band, however, had other plans. Nigel ended up performing *I Used to Could* in a rather minor capacity, and then, right after, *Romeo and Juliet*.

The first time I ever listened to a saxophone-featured version of *Romeo and Juliet* was when I bought *On The Night* some time in the beginning of the 2000's. I liked *On the Night*'s version of this song particularly because I thought that a saxophone fit the scene well. Therefore, it felt refreshing listening to Romeo and Juliet performed live yesterday featuring a saxophone.

Kingdom of Gold was certainly the evening's highlight—as it usually is (when it is played, that is). A lot of power at the outro, and it seems that Mark is getting less shy about squeezing every last breath out of that light blue Pensa.

A quick bathroom break at the beginning of Marbletown (that is, myself taking the break; the band stayed on stage), but when I returned, I realized that a few people are waiting to return to their seats as well, deciding to remain at the back in order to not interrupt other people with more efficient bladders. During the part when John & Glenn exchange notes between themselves, I noticed that the audience was laughing but couldn't figure out why. Later, I was informed that it was because John (who had just turned 40 the day before. Congratulations) decided to play *Scotland the Brave* for a brief few seconds during the exchange.

Nigel Hitchcock returned later on for the last encore, the (much expected, I should say; we are in Glasgow, after all) theme from *Local Hero*. Now here's a song where a saxophone adds a huge value. Very good—I certainly approve. Looking forward to more of these as the UK tour progresses.

After the concert, a walk back to the city center and a short late night meal in Wagamama, then back to the hotel for a good night sleep before traveling to Newcastle the next day.

Signing off this post from the hotel room in Newcastle. Heading for dinner and the concert tonight begins in about 3.5 hours.

Isaac

Sunday, May 19, 2013

Glasgow to Newcastle upon Tyne, UK (May 18, 2013)

After spending one day and two nights in the lovely city of Glasgow, it was time to bid this favourite city of mine farewell and get back into traveling mode. As the hotel was located close to Glasgow Queen Street station—where the train to Newcastle (through Edinburgh) was scheduled to depart from at 11:00am—it was a rather laid back morning. No rush. Almost felt like a vacation.

Quick walk downstairs to Pret-A-Manger for a sandwich and a yogurt (their berries' yogurt is great—I consume quite a few of those whenever I'm in the UK), then further down West Nile Street to Riverhill Coffee Bar which provided for excellent coffee the morning before and delivered fully this time as well. Back to the hotel, a few final arrangements and off to Queen Street station, an intense 6 minutes walk away.

Glasgow's Queen Street station has two parts: a lower level and an upper level. Both parts have trains that serve Edinburgh, only that the lower level trains are slower. It only happened that we entered the station through the lower level, which caused quite a confusion as we didn't see our train on the departures board, 15 minutes to departure. As Jeroen and I set off arguing which one of us is right (Jeroen, who has already lost his navigation privileges twice before has suggested that we take "any train" to Edinburgh because "any train" would just do, neglecting to consider the fact that the lower level trains may be *slower* and thus cause us to miss the connection to Newcastle), an attendant there decided to put an end to the nonsense and helped us realize that we're in the wrong part of the station. Up a few more stairs to the upper level, and got it all sorted out.

The EURail pass, offered only to non-European residents, doesn't cover UK travel. Therefore, whenever I happen to take trains in the UK, I get confused about their ticketing system. Eventually I get it, but I seem to forget all about it once I leave which leads to another frustrating learning curve the next time I'm around.

(Warning: mathematics follow.)

When you purchase a train ticket in the UK, depending on the type of ticket you purchase, you may get up to X number of printed stubs, where X is the number of connections in your overall journey plus *two*:

- The actual ticket displaying your overall journey & fare. You get this ticket once per itinerary.

- For each connection that requires a seat reservation (or for which you opted to reserve a seat), you get a seat reservation ticket (having paid for travel alone *does not guarantee a seat*).

- A receipt.

Therefore, if you have an itinerary with four connections, you may get up to six printed stubs: one displaying your overall journey; one receipt; and four stubs containing one seat reservation each.

Now, the fun part is that *all of these stubs look the same*: yellow stub with two horizontal margins painted orange. The font is the same, too. In other words, it is impossible to determine which stub is of what type (fare, reservation or receipt) just by glancing at it.

Obviously, the technologically-inclined individual may ask themselves whether there might be a better way to approach this. I mean, if the city of London got around to implement the *Oyster* card, then perhaps it'd be better to implement something similar for all train services in the UK (or, better off, the world; but let us take one step at a time).

Turns out that, indeed, transport providers in the UK have already reached the conclusion that printing millions of magnetic tickets might not be just the most efficient way to go about things, as it is both confusing *and* harming the environment; so, transport providers started working on rolling out smartcard-based ticketing systems.

"*Hurray,*" you'd say; "*it's just about time,*" you'd say; and I'd agree with you. But there's a problem: instead of coming up with *one* standard smartcard-based system, certain providers (or authorities) decided to come up with their own systems. Obviously, those systems are not integrated with each other. That means that if you live your entire life in London and using the Oyster card, then you're out of luck in Scotland: you'll have to use the Scottish smartcard instead.

As a large part of my professional career has to do with software systems' integration, it baffles me to repeatedly find out how clueless organizations can be when it comes to thinking about how one particular solution "fits" within a given domain. I mean, all of these decisions —about which computerized systems to come up with; their functionality; their capabilities—all of these decisions end up being taken by *people*. Hence, up there in the chain in the UK's transport authorities, there exist people who initially decided that coming up with different solutions to different parts of the country is a brilliant idea. The very thought that such short-sightedness exists in my professional field makes me lose faith in humanity a little bit more every time.

In other words: dear UK transport authorities—hire me. I will solve all your problems.

The train ride from Glasgow to Edinburgh was the first crowded train ride in this tour. I'll be riding trains mostly in 2nd class while in the UK—saved quite a bit of money—so I suppose that over the next week or so I'll have to let go of my privileged mentality and ride it rough. Train cramped with people. 50 minutes and we arrived at Edinburgh Waverley.

I have never been to Edinburgh before in my life, although I did hear that it's considered by many to be the prettiest city in Scotland and one of the prettiest cities in Europe. Unfortunately, there's no concert in Edinburgh this tour around, so my entire experience with Edinburgh took about 10 minutes, until the connecting train left Edinburgh Waverley station towards Newcastle.

Better ride this time. Train was, for the most part, empty. It rained—hard at times—and it was foggy, but the views were breathtaking. Northern England at its best. Here are what it looked like through the eyes of an exceptionally mediocre photographer:

An hour and a half after leaving Edinburgh, the train finally stopped in Newcastle.

Newcastle upon Tyne, often referred to as simply *Newcastle*, is a city in northeast England. It lies on the banks of the famous River Tyne.

Knopfler, while having been born in Glasgow, actually spent a good part of his life in Newcastle. His connection with north eastern England is evident considering the various references in his lyrics to places and elements related to that part of the country. The term Geordie—appearing more than once or twice in Knopfler's lyrics repertoire—refers to a person who lives in the Newcastle area, and is also the name of the English dialect spoken in the northeast. Tow Law, mentioned in *Hill Farmer's Blues*, is a town in the northeast. *River Tyne*, the river sorely missed by the English workers migrating to Germany described in *Why Aye Man*, is the same River Tyne that runs through Newcastle.

River Tyne is also mentioned in Jimmy Nail's 1995 song, Big River, describing (in wonderful lyrics) the story of the river's days in the sun and its later decline. Knopfler himself plays guitar there (if you never listened to this song before, then you should: other than the beautiful melody and lyrics, as well as Jimmy Nail's great voice, you're going to find one of the greatest Knopfler's work on a Gibson Les Paul).

The local soccer team, Newcastle United F.C, has Knopfler's *Going Home* played through loudspeakers during home games, when the players run to the pitch.

For Knopfler, then, Newcastle is, to some extent, home. He is known to be very comfortable performing here, which is why his concerts in Newcastle have traditionally been considered a treat. Therefore, I was looking forward to visit Newcastle again, both for its beauty and for taking part in a concert happening in Knopfler's home town.

The problem encountered while arranging travel to Newcastle was that hotels there, at the city center area, are ridiculously expensive. Last tour, Ingrid saved the day when she suggested that we share a twin room there; except for London, I can't recall hotel room prices being as high as in Newcastle. Even when planning *months* in advance, the best deal I could come up with was the Ramada Encore which is located on the other side of River Tyne (a place called *Gateshead*), about 15–20 minutes walk from the city center. Price? close to £100.

It was raining. Not knowing exactly which was the shortest route to the hotel, we ended up walking according to Google Maps' instructions, resulting in an additional half a mile or so of footwork, including the crossing of *Tyne Bridge*, offering nice views of River Tyne and its banks. Arrived at the hotel, just to find reception busy arguing with a group of youngsters who seemed to have had a problem with their reservations. Nobody was happy. I started considering paying for everyone's rooms just so I can get on with my day and check in. Fortunately, that wasn't needed. Checked in, and up to the hotel room.

From my previous visit here, I remember Newcastle being very pretty. Unfortunately, due to certain commitments (including completing the preceding day's blog post), I couldn't allow time for sightseeing so I remained at the hotel stuck in front of my laptop's screen for a few hours.

At around 4:30pm, we left the hotel room towards the city center. Plans were in place to meet Ingrid in a restaurant called *A Taste of Persia* close to the venue. Drizzling, foggy weather.

Newcastle's city center is located a few meters above the banks of River Tyne; found a stairway leading to The Castle. It felt strange walking those stairs: as if you're stepping into the past.

Finally arrived at the restaurant:

Adjacent to the restaurant there exists a pub, which was exactly where Jeroen decided to enter at first. It looked nothing like a Persian restaurant. The bartender looked at us, we looked at the bartender.

Awkwardness.

– "Is this a Persian restaurant?"

– "No. It's next door."

OK. Mental note: next time, before entering a door, ensure that it's the right one.

I have been a fan of Persian food for years. An ex of mine came was (well, still is. These things don't change) of Persian heritage and Friday nights with her family used to be true culinary delights. The secret is in the spices. This particular restaurant delivered well: good service, tasty food. Complaint list is empty.

After an hour and a half of feasting, it was time to head to the venue.

The Metro Radio Arena is a general sports and entertainment arena, located a few minutes walk from Newcastle's central railway station. It was first opened in 1995 and can seat around 11,000 for concerts.

Outside the arena, there is a line telling smokers exactly what not to do where:

Someone, though, decided to play it risky and live life on the edge:

Julio Bricio from Spain, who, during the last tour, provided me with invaluable help planning the Spanish leg of the tour, made his way from Valencia to Newcastle for the concert (he won't be attending any shows in Spain as he'll be very busy doing much, much more important things). Nice chap. Funny how people from all over Europe somehow run into each other in Knopfler concerts.

Tickets collected and, this venue being as dull as it is, no extra time was spent hanging around and I went to my seat.

A straight line view from my seat revealed a perfect view—

—of nothing. "Beyond Here Lies Nothin'", someone said back in 2009. Time was passed meeting and catching up with people who happen to have read the 2010 Get Lucky blog and graciously decided to come by and say hello, as well as catching up with Mikel Camps, who helped out during the last tour's concluding concert with a few logistics and flew in from Spain for this concert.

Concert started about 20 minutes past schedule to a roar of an exceptionally receptive audience: Knopfler is at home.

Indeed, being seated in one of the worst seats in the house does impede on one's enjoyment of the show, not because of the lacking visuals but mostly because of the mediocre acoustics in such edges of the stage. Still, I have been to venues with worse sounds.

The concert went very well. Relatively speaking, Mark communicated with the audience more than he has been so far this tour, giving a full explanation for his inspiration for *Gator Blood*. He did mention it before, but not at length. *Gator Blood* was inspired by the character of Colonel Tom Parker, who was Elvis Presley's music manager and fashioned quite the questionable character. *Back to Tupelo*, according to Mark, was also written about the same person.

The set was similar to the preceding night's, with the exception of *5:15am* and *Back to Tupelo* replacing *Kingdom of Gold* and *I Dug Up a Diamond*. Nigel Hitchcock showed up for the same songs he showed up for in the preceding concert, only this time he appeared to be more involved in the show.

In recent concerts, it became evident that the instructions provided by the band to security personnel aren't being consistently followed. First in Amsterdam—when security staff started pushing audience back to their seats (I was only informed about it later; I remained seated until later in the encore)—and then in Glasgow, when security staff prevented people from the back rows to approach the stage during the encore. In Newcastle, it seemed like instructions weren't entirely followed as well. A small group of people gathered in front of the stage during the last pre-encore performance, and security was sent over to try returning them to their seats. I didn't see any violence, though. Once *Telegraph Road* was done, though, the *Running of the Bulls* took place with people running from all over the venue towards the stage.

No casualties, though. As I have been trying to avoid these things myself, I walked slowly and surely towards the gathering. As the band returned to the stage, I realized that my immense six feet height blocked the view of a nice, shy looking lady behind me, so I urged her to switch places with me.

I'd like to say that I am not intending to preach, but that would be a lie. Please, people, be careful and courteous to one another.

Going Home, quite expectedly, concluded the show with a bombastic performance. The audience went nuts as the performance of this song was truly extraordinary. I don't think I'll be able to take the rocking version of this song anymore, unless Nigel Hitchcock is involved in it. Not many songs can gain beauty by adding a saxophone track to them, but *Going Home* can, and does.

Just a quick reminder: the vast majority of concert-time pictures here were taken by Jeroen Gerrits (read the disclaimer in my first post for an explanation why), including the following one which I think is fabulous, not because of the subject but because it manages to capture atmosphere brilliantly.

After the concert, I ran into my friend, Laurent Patry, from France, accompanied by his wife Carole. Laurent and I had plans to catch up in the venue before the show, but neither of us could locate the other. As they happened to be staying in a hotel in Gateshead, we decided to walk back to the hotels together.

Took the path along River Tyne. The weather was cold, foggy, misty. Still, the walk along River Tyne provided for some interesting views. This one is called *The Sage Gateshead* and located in… well… Gateshead:

The following is the Gateshead Millennium Bridge, gorgeous at night.

Sat down for drinks with Laurent and Carole. Two hours passed quickly. Wonderful couple, these two are.

Signing off this post while at my hotel room in Liverpool. Annoying travel day, and I'm very tired following last night's late night sleep.
Isaac

Monday, May 20, 2013

Newcastle upon Tyne to Liverpool, UK (May 19, 2013)

Having gone to bed very late on Saturday night, I woke up early feeling very tired. Schedule: take the 9:33am train from Newcastle to Liverpool, arriving 12:58pm. Direct train. What can go wrong?

7:30am wake up. Yawn, twice or thrice. Breakfast? what breakfast? no. Deferred that until we get to the central railway station area. Checked out of the hotel, and by 8:10am I found myself hungry, thirsty, 90% asleep waiting for the Q-Link bus to take me to the central station.

The plan was to find a place to sit down for breakfast in the central station itself. However, once entering the station, it turned out to be very cold: nothing to keep cold air from outside to enter the station, and nothing to heat it up. Highly preferring a covered, warm place for breakfast, I had no choice but to suffice with the Starbucks across the street. Nothing else seemed open so early in the morning; on the other hand, it's not like I dedicated much effort to even looking for an alternative.

You wouldn't catch me dead drinking Starbucks' disgusting coffee, but their sandwiches are acceptable. Sandwich, yogurt, tea… and I was ready for the 3.5 hours ride to Liverpool.

Well, not quite.

As I mentioned before, I'll be travelling mostly in 2nd class during the UK leg of the tour, in an attempt to cut costs. All travel has been booked already and is non-refundable. Little did I know that trains can be so crowded on Sunday mornings. The lucky Dutchman went off to enjoy his ride in 1st class (*Interrail* passes, applicable only to EU residents, are valid in the UK), while I was cramped into a corner seat in 2nd class.

That was hell. In front of me, two youngsters decided to feast on croissants and ham, making the immediate surrounding area stink. Tried to stretch my legs a few time, each attempt ending in someone in front of me being kicked.

As the train approached York, the two youngsters left the train and were replaced by a mature nice looking couple. The guy started coughing and didn't stop until the end of the ride. By the sound of it, he was in possession of some sort of a bug. I definitely hope I didn't catch anything. During the ride, he asked his companion to check on him whether he might have fever.

My take on it? if you're sick, either don't board a train full of people, or put on one of those filter masks. You'll look a little odd, but at least you won't make an entire coach sick.

I tried to catch some sleep, to no avail. 3.5 hours of torture, plus—of course—the inevitable delay at around Manchester; finally, arrived to Liverpool 20 minutes past schedule. Stretching my legs never felt better.

When I'm ignorant about something, I'm usually not shy about admitting it. Here is a summary of what I knew about Liverpool:

- It has two soccer teams that were successful back in the 1980's, when I was a child and actually cared about soccer at all. Maybe they're OK now as well, I don't know.
- The Beatles were born here.

Upon arriving at Liverpool Lime Street station—not the central station but definitely an important one in Liverpool—the immediate feeling I got about the city is that it is old, not very exciting, mainly catering to the middle working class.

The city seemed to be more bustling with action than Newcastle. Young people abound. The atmosphere reminded me of Toronto, not exactly sure why.

As we checked into the hotel—Printworks Hotel located right at the city center—and realized that the room's price is only £48, I started thinking. This either is a crappy hotel, or a crappy area in Liverpool, or the economy in Liverpool sucks the behinds of many goats. The hotel room turned out to be fine. Something's wrong in here. £48 for a hotel room in such location? what am I missing?

Once finding a proper place to sit down for lunch—Leaf on Bold Street—I fired up Wikipedia and started reading about the city. Much like in Luxembourg's case, it turned out that I may have missed something.

Liverpool is the home for just under 500,000 people, out of 2,000,000 people living in the Liverpool City Region. The city owes its development mainly to its port: by the early 19th century, 40% of the world's trade passed through its docks. It was unavoidable, then, for Liverpool to become a powerful, important city.

The Guinness World Records labelled Liverpool as the "World Capital City of Pop": if you were to group all number 1 hit singles by the artists' origin, Liverpool would come first. Not surprisingly, the fact that *The Beatles* were born and raised in Liverpool is a major contributor to that.

Music is not all, though: Art aficionados who happen to find themselves in Liverpool are unlikely to want to leave too quickly. Liverpool ranks second in the UK with respect to the number of important art galleries and museums (London being the the first). Nightlife? TripAdvisor's poll in 2011 yielded Liverpool as #1 in the UK for nightlife (London came as #3).

On paper, then, Liverpool has it all. For young people at least, Liverpool may as well be considered paradise.

But £48 for a decent hotel room?

Leaf on Bold Street offers a communal-style dining experience. You order at the bar, tell the cashier where you're sitting, and they bring everything to you. While 2- and 4-people seating areas exist, most seats are lined against long tables so you're likely to find yourself dining right next to people you don't know. Great way to meet new people, I'd say. Also a great way to be exposed to offensively disgusting body odours, though Food is reasonably priced and good. The coffee would be decent as well had they learned how to take that milk steaming wand out of the milk before it reaches earth's core temperature.

What Leaf do specialize in, however, is tea. All sorts of delicious(ly sounding) teas. Mint tea—my favourite refresher—and things started to feel better.

I then headed back to the hotel so I can keep up with blogging, as the Dutchman went ahead to explore some of the city.

The inconsistent diet of the preceding few days, as well as the stressful cramped train ride to Liverpool, started to get to me late afternoon. I also decided that all my future train travel in the UK (past this tour) will be 1st class, regardless of costs. A little weird how I can survive 18 hours flights in economy class but find it irritating to take a 3 hours train ride in the UK's 2nd class trains.

Close to 6:00pm, I left the hotel and started walking towards the venue. It was a bit cold, but sunny and beautiful outside.

Bold Street provides for a pleasant walk in Liverpool and is an excellent starting point for exploring the city center area. At its top there's the Church of St. Luke, dating back to the early 19th century until it was severely damaged in Liverpool Blitz during World War II. Down the street, cafes, restaurants and other entertainment establishments abound.

The venue, Echo Arena, is beautifully situated next to River Mersey, on what used to be the King's Dock.

It seats 12,000 and is considered environmentally sustainable, leveraging all sorts of features to conserve energy, including using rainwater for toilet flushing and the using turbines, operating on the nearby river, for power generation.

Ticket collection, however, presented a hassle. For a minute I thought I'm still in Poland. After standing in a never-ending line for 15 minutes, patiently awaiting my turn, I was informed by the attendant that ticket pickup is actually inside the venue, next door.

– "How about putting up a sign?", I advised.

I didn't get the response but I had a feeling that it wasn't pretty.

That "next door" was, indeed, a door; however it was completely unsigned. There was no way for anyone to know that beyond that door there's yet another line up for ticket collection. That took another five minutes that were lost forever.

Before entering the venue, I took some time to walk around the venue to see River Mersey. It was good to have some sun rays meet my skin, if only for a few minutes. Beautiful area to take a walk in, including at night (see below).

Time in the sun is up—concert starting in a few minutes.

Not much out of the ordinary happened during this concert, until some time in the middle of Telegraph Road. The usual set except for the beautiful *Seattle* coming back to life and… well… yes, *Sultans of Swing* is back after being in absentia for four concerts. Relatively reserved audience, comparing to what I would expect in such a young city that has seen a concert or two before.

This time I failed to solve Ian's daily riddle at the beginning of *Corned Beef City*. Guy didn't. But I was close. Here's a tip for Ian: I'm betting this will be much harder to guess once you introduce triplets to the beat… or try a *true sextuplet*. I really want to see this happening.

After a long *Marbletown* performance that saw John and Glenn pretty much making things up during their interchange and a very funny incident at the end as Mark made Mike run completely out of air, prompting Mike to bark at him with the flute and causing an uproar of laughter in the audience, there came the usual dose of noise with *Speedway at Nazareth*, and then Telegraph Road.

That must have been one of the best outros of Telegraph Road that I had ever encountered before. As it happened, I found myself moving my upper body in entirely random directions according to the beat. Was it just me? was it the performance? I don't know. Can't tell you. Remarkable.

Not much *Running of the Bulls* this time around as the seating structure didn't allow for people to run sideways (although I'm sure that in Italy or Spain it wouldn't matter at all). Still, it became crowded against the stage. *So Far Away*, and then another good performance of *Going Home* only that the saxophone wasn't very well heard.

Good concert, stabilizing an otherwise rather rattling day.

After the concert, I decided to head back to the hotel immediately to regain some strength. It was very cold. The view of the dock at night is fantastic—unfortunately, pictures came out a bit blurry but that's all I have for you.

Walked back to the city center…

And back to the hotel, very tired. I feel bad for not having the chance to see more of Liverpool—clearly, there's much more to it than can be covered in a few hours. I will be back.

Signing off this post from the hotel room in Bournemouth. It's been quite hectic recently; will use the rest of today & tomorrow to rest. Got many other things to catch up with, so the next post will be published after the Cardiff concert.

Isaac

Saturday, May 25, 2013

Liverpool to Bournemouth to Cardiff to Birmingham, UK (May 20-24, 2013)

Good to be back after a few days of silence. The last few days were very busy and I had to catch up with many important things—including sleep. Hopefully there won't be any blogging interruptions from now on. I know how vital this blog is for your well being.

I like Bournemouth.

The first time I heard anything about the city of Bournemouth was some time in 2009, when the 2010 Get Lucky tour was announced. Bournemouth? where is that? I remember I took a glance at the map and the only thing I could think of was "fortunately, there's a beach".

My idea of how the British coasts look like stemmed from my familiarity with Cape Breton Island's coastline, which is said to resemble much of England's: green-covered rugged cliffs over the beautiful sea. Standing upon them and looking at the water, you get the feeling that you have just reached the end of the world.

Ever since I first came here in 2010, I have been fond of Bournemouth. Hotels here are generally mediocre (except for the *Marriott* by the beach, which goes for around £160 a night. Never stayed there, but I know what the rooms are like), but other than that, it's a fine spot for relaxation by England's coastline.

Arrived to Bournemouth on Monday afternoon after a long train ride from Liverpool. A glance at *Google Maps* shown an easy one and so miles walk to the hotel, and the weather being cool, cloudy without rain, it seemed like an easy nice walk. However, what wasn't taken into account is Bournemouth's terrain: walking in this city is never boring, terrain-wise. Inclines and declines up the yin and yang, and by the time I reached the hotel, my shirts (two layers. As I said, it looked as if it was going to be cold) turned into a pile of sweat.

The hotel, *Best Western Connaught Hotel*, is located steps away from the beach and is surprisingly ranked #1 in Bournemouth by *TripAdvisor*—bypassing the Marriott. How? Beats me. The hotel consists of two buildings, one of which is where the reception is and I *think* was the fancy one. The other one—where I ended up staying in—is nearby and provides a typical English hotel experience: thick carpets in the hallway, hardwood (or laminate; not sure, didn't bother to check) flooring that makes sounds whenever more than one pound of weight is exerted on it. Aromatically, the room reminded me of my childhood as it smelled like old, cheap toothpaste.

Many hotels in Bournemouth are made up of very old buildings. You are unlikely to run into state-of-the-art modern architecture here. I am not sure whether this is due to some sort of a municipal bylaw or something else, but one thing is for sure—it helps (for the most part) maintain Bournemouth's authentic look. Unfortunately, some of them are both old and inconvenient to stay in. I mean, I'm OK with "roughing it up" but there's a limit. In comparison to my previous visit to Bournemouth (during the joint Knopfler-Dylan tour), though, this present hotel was certainly an upgrade.

Bournemouth's streets seemed to be rather vacant on Monday as we set out looking for food and drinks. It was a lovely walk in a sleepy beach town.

The city center is not far from the beach.

It was evening, and businesses around were surprisingly closed. Holiday? maybe. That, however, interfered with my goal of finding some coffee. Eventually I came across a *Costa Coffee* shop (they're everywhere) five minutes before closing time.

Costa Coffee and *Caffe Nero* are two major UK coffee chains. They both are everywhere, and often you'll run into situations when a *Costa* and a *Nero* are facing each other. Their coffee is OK. Not terrible like Starbucks, but not great. If you can't find any local, independent coffee shop, either a *Costa* or a *Nero* would do.

This particular one had a deal: balance a twenty pence coin on a lemon floating in water, and get a free drink.

I failed to deliver, and so did the coffee.

Back at the hotel, I decided to be enterprising and take advantage of the hotel's spa facilities. They have an 18 meters pool there, a Jacuzzi tub, a steam room and a sauna. A few short laps in the pool did much for cardio work alright, but at some point—I don't know why, perhaps it was the general look of the place which was quite depressing—I had a mysophobia attack and decided to imminently stop swimming in other people's urine. Hopped to the hot tub for a few minutes—realizing that the only difference between it and a swimming pool was that, in a hot tub, I'm sitting in other people's germs, whereas in a swimming pool I'm in motion—and then into the steam room.

I don't exactly remember when was the last time I was in a steam room. I think it was about 20 years ago when I visited a country club to which my family was subscribed. This particular one chose to add some eucalyptus extract to the steam, which was nice. Ten minutes later I was out.

It felt like Tel Aviv in June.

Next up: the sauna. The dry sauna's goal (as far as I understood) is to make you sweat, thereby cleaning your skins from all sorts of toxins.

It felt like Tel Aviv in August.

You know what? it worked, I did sweat. Unbearable heat, couldn't stand it for more than 5 minutes and I stormed out of there gasping for air—directly into the pool area which, quite frankly, stank.

The overall impression I got is that I possibly am not a big fan of swimming pools anymore—at least not ones that seem to be run down and not quite hygienic. The steam room & sauna, though, were an interesting experience. I shall make use of those more often.

The next morning was the morning of an easy day: the hotel, the city center and the venue were all located within a relatively short walk from each other.

The first order of business was to find some breakfast. One of the highest ranked places in Bournemouth for breakfast is *Frieda's Tearoom*, offering good breakfasts. Altogether a nice place for a quiet breakfast, really. However, it did get a bit annoying that we had to sit there for about 20 minutes before realizing that you will never get the bill to your table in this place—payment is at the cashier. During that time, I have seen the waitress there texting, talking on her mobile phone, hooking up her phone to a laptop to synchronize some tunes, reading the news... anything but divert her looks towards an impatient arse in a table nearby dying to pay the bill and go on with his life.

Kept walking through the city center area...

Came across this, and penned it down as the spot for a pre-show snack.

Came across *Camera Obscura*, which, at the time of checking, was the #301 restaurant in all of Bournemouth... out of 301.

Then, finally, arrived to this place:

Espresso Kitchen in Bournemouth is locally owned by an exceptionally cool lady by the name of Francesca. Provide me with an establishment like this one for every day during the tour, and I'm a happy camper. It takes guts to set up an independent, local coffee shop steps away from *Starbucks*, *Costa* and *Nero*, and it takes talent to bring this place to be #2 in *TripAdvisor* within two months. Delicious healthy cakes baked on site, and the coffee—hell, that's what I've been looking for.

Kept on wandering around…

Pre-concert snack in *Patisserie Valerie* and back to the beach area, where the venue is located.

The venue, *Bournemouth International Center* (usually referred to as simply "The BIC") is a general purpose arena—a boring one, but not more boring than most other general purpose arenas previously played in this tour—and is a major venue in southern England. It seats 6,500.

Good concert—nothing unusual except for *Our Shangri La* making its debut in the UK. As Nigel Hitchcock joins the band in the UK, he was involved in this song's performance, which added an entire layer of beauty to it. Well done.

Having gained some rest in Bournemouth, it was time to leave England's wonderful coast area for a few days (should be back here for the Brighton concert soon) and head north west to Cardiff, Wales. Easy wake up: nobody was in the mood for walking 30 minutes to the train station. Instead, (mediocre) breakfast was consumed at the hotel and a taxi was hailed to take us to the central railway station. Half an hour ride to *Southampton*, then change to a 2nd class only train heading to *Cardiff Central*. Not as cramped as my previous few experiences with 2nd class coaches, but still, I wouldn't classify the ride as being extraordinarily pleasant.

Now, here is something you need to know when you ride the trains in the UK, especially when you travel 2nd class: most train routes give you the option to reserve a seat. The fact that you hold a train ticket, doesn't necessarily mean that you will be seated (there are a few trains for which seat reservations are mandatory, in which case, everybody is seated). The pleasure of ensuring that your ass will be met with a seat (other than a toilet) while the train is moving usually costs an extra few pounds, on top of what you paid for the ride.

Seats are only possible to reserve up to a certain amount of time before departure (I think one hour). That's because the train's staff need to print seating stubs—a stub for each seat on the train, containing information about which sections of the train ride this seat is in a "reserved" status.

For example, if the train's origin is in point A, its destination is point F, and it stops in B, C, D and E along the way, it is definitely possible that seat number 23 will be reserved in the sections $B \Rightarrow C$ and $E \Rightarrow F$. It can also be reserved in the sections $C \Rightarrow D$ and $D \Rightarrow E$, by two different people.

All of these details are printed on the seat's stub and the stub is placed on the seat's headrest.

Now, the fun thing is that, more often than not, people boarding the train initially seat themselves wherever the hell they feel like, which is not necessarily the exact seat that they were reserving. For example, if you reserved seat 23, which happens to be adjacent to seat number 24; seat number 24 is occupied by an individual with an exceptionally offensive body odour and all sorts of swastika-shaped tattoos on their skin (this is not a random example); and there are fifty other vacant seats available in the coach—you are very likely to seat yourself somewhere else, preferably far away from the smelly Neo Nazi, say seat number 51. If the "true" owner of seat number 51 boards the train at some point and insists to take his seat, you would get up and find another vacant seat, or—if you have no other choice—return to your beloved and reserved seat number 23, next to the charming war monger.

This sort of arrangement is harmless in cases when the coach is sparsely occupied. However, the more people board the coach, the more probable it is for someone to insist on their reserved seat. The result: a few dozens of people shuffling around inside the coach (while the train is moving, mind you), along with their luggage.

The reason I'm telling you all of that is, that during the ride from Southampton to Cardiff, such mess ensued that took about 10 minutes to sort out. Naturally, luck had it and the coach was filled with old (yet charming. Well, mostly) English ladies carrying suitcases back and forth in the cabin (I helped some of them). Not one foot remained unharmed.

It was a fun morning exercise. I wish I could do it more often, but I don't want to.

Finally arrived to Cardiff. Sun! I don't think I ever got to see Cardiff in the sun.

Luggage placed in the hotel (can't check in yet; too early) and off to find some place to eat.

Cardiff is the capital city of Wales. In Welsh, "Cardiff" (spelled "*Caerdydd*") means "The Fort of Taff", where "Taff" refers to River Taff that runs through Wales. I have been here twice before—in 2010 and 2011—and there's something in this city that makes me... I don't know... makes me like it.

A glance in *TripAdvisor* showed up Cafe Citta as a promising Italian restaurant. Ranked #2 out of 572, expectations were high. The restaurant is owned and operated by Italian folks; the menu is simple and food is delicious. I have been to a few Italian restaurants in Cardiff before and this one ranks high. Go there.

But if you're going there and expecting to pay with cash, make sure you have enough change. For whatever reason, this place found it appropriate to take payment that was approximately 20% higher than the cost, never returning any change. At some point, while we were sitting there waiting for some change, the restaurant's owner looked at me and said "thank you". I didn't quite understand why; it only registered with me once I realized we're sitting there for 15 minutes waiting for something that is unlikely to happen.

One of the good things about money is that it helps you avoid dealing with awkward situations, especially when you have something more important to do with your life. A decision was made to leave the premises rather than getting into a deep discussion about ethical restaurateur-ship with the owners.

In the previous times when I was here, I skipped entering the Cardiff Castle and wanted to go for it this time around. Unfortunately it was closed. Still, it looks lovely from outside. It dates back to the 11th century and serves no purpose nowadays other than being a major tourist attraction.

Back for coffee in my favourite Cardiff coffee spot—Coffee #1, right by the central railway station—and back to the hotel.

The hotel, Royal Hotel Cardiff, was picked because I stayed there before and liked it. It is conveniently located right at the city center, and is spacious, comfortable and well-maintained.

Well, at least it *was*. The hotel was going through renovations over the last couple of years; the renovations have just ended two weeks ago so, if at all, I was expecting a better experience than last time's.

Hell, what a miserable experience, starting right from the beginning with a rather obnoxious receptionist. Room was at the 7th floor, and I'll leave you to guess which floor button didn't work in the (only) elevator. Windows were *locked shut*, expecting you to use the air conditioning system instead; guess what, it's turned on "heat" mode and you can't change it.

But you know what? fine. I have stayed in crappier places before. But what I really can't forgive any hotel for is poor Wi-Fi connectivity. We're in the 21st century already. Dear hotel owner: if you can't have proper Wi-Fi infrastructure in your hotel, then I don't want to stay there.

It was the first time ever that I had to manually set my network adapter's DNS settings to a custom DNS address, as the hotel's DHCP server provided me with a wrong one.

(If you don't understand anything in the preceding paragraph, that's OK.)

Internet connection was still slow despite all my attempts to remedy the situation. Couldn't even do proper lookups for the purpose of writing this blog entry, so we went for another walk outside. Weather became cooler, which might be explained by Iceman's decision to take a crap on Cardiff's sidewalk.

Back to the hotel, got ready and off to the venue, located a few minutes walk away.

The venue, Motorpoint Arena, used to be called "CIA"—Cardiff International Arena—until a car sales company by the name of "Motorpoint" purchased the arena's naming rights. Again, a general purpose arena used for exhibitions and conferences, with a full seating capacity of about 5,000.

A shorter, 16 songs set, was played featuring a beautiful performance of *Back to Tupelo* as well as another saxophone-accompanied rendition of *Our Shangri La*. An occurrence worth noting took place before the encore, when people started gathering close to the stage. Security staff started instructing people to go back to their seats. Mark noticed, referred to the security worker through the microphone saying "No, don't spoil it". The security worker didn't hear it at first, which prompted Mark to step towards the front of the stage, in order to gain his attention. Before that happened, the security worker finally understood what he was supposed to allow people to do and fled the scene.

Arrived to Birmingham on Friday, around noon time, *very tired* due to all sorts of events that took place in the preceding few days. Accidentally, we took the wrong train from London to Birmingham—the slow one that makes stops all throughout the UK before arriving to Birmingham New Street station.

I can hardly remember when was the last time I was *that* tired, but I surely recognize the symptoms: feeling as if your brain turns into some sort of a mush; inability to form a proper coherent sentence without it taking a hell of a lot of effort. I tried to pass out on the train, but couldn't.

Luckily, the Holiday Inn hotel in the city center is very close to the railway station. Not exactly sure how I made it safe and sound to the hotel, given the fact that I was only 10% awake. As I was just as hungry as I was tired, I had to resolve the more urgent problem first: Minmin is a Vietnamese restaurant nearby. Been a while since I had Vietnamese food. I ate it but was too tired to appreciate the taste.

Off to the hotel and I had one of the best two hour naps in mankind's history. The story of that nap will be taught in schools in years to come. Naps like that one, if left unattended, could cause you to wake up and not understand why everyone around you grew older by a couple of years.

Woke up and immediately headed to the train station, to get to the venue.

The LG Arena is a part of Birmingham's National Exhibition Center (NEC). The NEC is the largest exhibition center in the UK and the seventh largest in Europe, and inside the NEC, the LG Arena is where concerts take place. It is quite large, and can seat up to 16,000. I have been here before, too.

The NEC is located nearby Birmingham's airport. Access to it from the city center is best done using trains: most trains departing from, or arriving to, Birmingham city center, also make a stop in Birmingham International railway station, which serves both the NEC and the airport.

The concert started close to 8:00pm—almost half an hour past schedule. About 15 minutes prior, Paul Crockford took the microphone and explained that the reason for the delay is the terrible traffic outside the venue, which meant that lots of people are still on their way.

Good concert, ended shortly before 10:00pm. Train back to the hotel, not before having to walk outside for a bit (it takes a few minutes to walk from the LG Arena to the main NEC area). If it wasn't clear so far, I should tell you that England is going through one of its worst springs recently. Weather is actually winter-like: this isn't typical to the end of May. Hell, June is right around the corner!

While some might say that a long period of travelling is an excellent way to disconnect yourself from the everyday life, I hold a different theory: if you are looking forward to disconnect yourself from your everyday life, perhaps you should make some changes in it. The more I travel, the more I realize that I have my life right where I want it.

Sort of.

I miss home; well, both of them.

Isaac

Tuesday, May 28, 2013

Birmingham to Brighton, UK (May 25-26, 2013)

This post was posted late due to the Copthorne Tara Hotel's ridiculous Wi-Fi usage policy. More on that in the upcoming post that will be live later on today. Stay tuned.

After a cold, often rainy, day in Birmingham, woke up east around 8:00am feeling fantastic. Admit it: you were expecting me to whine about how tired I was, as I am in the habit of doing recently.

But no. I slept very well. That made me think that maybe my recent tiredness had to do with over-consumption of caffeine. Once you consume more caffeine regularly, your body becomes dependent on it. As a result, changes in your caffeine consumption (for example, not having your coffee "on time", when your body expects it) can lead to extreme tiredness, which opens a can of all sorts of worms—when you're constantly tired and unrested, your immune system weakens, and if there's one thing you want to avoid while following a concert tour, it is exactly that.

That led me to decide that, from now on until the end of the tour, all coffee that I consume is going to be caffeine-free. Tea-wise, I'll try to stick to low-caffeine variants. Time to get things back under control.

Breakfast at the hotel, and by 10:30am I was on the train to London Euston. This time it was the *Virgin* train. *Virgin* (the same company that owns the airline by the same name) boasts fantastic 1st class cabins, but it comes with a price: riding their trains isn't a cheap endeavour. For short haul rides, the price difference might not be worth it.

One hour ride to London Euston, then the Tube to London Victoria to catch the Southeastern train to Brighton.

Southeastern's trains' 1st class cabins, in contrary to Virgin's, are not really 1st class by any measure. The only difference between 1st class and 2nd class there is this piece of textile over the headrest:

Everything else is the same. If you happen to take a Southeastern train anywhere, don't bother paying extra for 1st class.

As I arrived in Brighton's central railway station and went outside, I realized that, at least weather-wise, this is going to be a pleasant experience. It was sunny and—listen to this—warm. Yes, it was warm. So warm, that shortly after starting the mile long walk towards the hotel, I had to stop, remove my jacket, remove my buttoned shirt and remain with a T-shirt—an activity that I had thought I'd never get to perform in England this year, as England is going through a terrible spring season.

The streets were flooded with people. Brighton's sidewalks aren't exactly huge, so that rendered navigating through a sea of people a rather tricky endeavour. At times, I was jumping sideways and sneaking between people (walking in both directions) in order to maintain my pace.

Felt like the character of George Costanza in that unforgettable *Frogger* episode, only I didn't crash into any truck at the end.

> In London, there's an unwritten rule whereby, if you take the escalator from a train station to the train's platform and choose to stand your entire way through, then you should align to the right hand side, so people with better things to do can easily bypass you and get to their destination sooner. How about we apply the same rule for sidewalks?

After a long walk…

Finally arrived at this place:

A sign said that this place is called "Brunswick Square". I remembered that the hotel was located in "Brunswick" *something*, so I was very happy. How pleasant, to stay in a hotel in such a beautiful complex.

Alas, my joy was short lived. Turned out that the hotel, Bow Street Runner, is located in "Brunswick Street", which is one short block away. It's actually a pub that owns a few rooms in the same building, upstairs. There are a couple of restaurants adjacent to it, and they all happen to be throwing their garbage through their back doors; those back doors face the narrow street that lead to the hotel. The result? as you approach the hotel, you feel like you're in garbage galore.

The staff is very nice, but the actual facilities… well, let's put it this way: it's not a hotel. More like a Bed & Breakfast. The rooms are tiny: good for one person, way too small for two. The "Breakfast" part of the "Bed & Breakfast" term consists of a dried croissant (placed on your desk *a day in advance*), two packs of cereal, a miniature fridge containing a jug of milk and a jug of orange juice, and a basket with semi-fresh fruit.

The idea here is to have your breakfast in bed. That is, since the room is so small, you can't possibly sit at the desk to have breakfast —you need to sit on your bed.

Altogether a rather questionable experience. The price? sit tight: £97 a night, and this is for a questionable place located about a mile away from Brighton's city center.

I have been to Brighton before, during the 2010 Get Lucky tour. My recollection of this city was generally positive, which made me look forward to visiting it again. That's why I chose to spend Sunday night—a day off—in Brighton instead of in London.

I don't know what I was thinking.

So here's the deal about Brighton: it is, when all is said and done, a seaside resort town.

It boasts a beach, which many consider to be the best in England (my foot. I'd take Bournemouth's beach over Brighton's any day of the week)—although it is made up of gravel rather than sand, which makes it look fake.

Along King's Road—which crosses Brighton from east to west, along the seashore—you will find gazillions of pubs, bars, dance clubs, restaurants (mostly substandard), cafes… you name it. As a resort town catering mainly to the young and the restless, most establishments you're going to be seeing will be leaning more towards serving alcohol and cheap food than serving anything else.

I am not entirely sure what's the deal behind picking two nouns—at least one of which is the name of an animal—and naming a pub after them. I think I have seen all possible combinations already: Fox & Fiddle; Duck & Goose; Sheep & Lawnmower; Fish & Spoon; Monkey & Banana; Fiddler's Elbow; Pianist's Pancreas; Violinist's mitre valve.

Another consequence of this city catering to the younger generation is that most hotels here are of quality that is just enough to be bearable. When you're a 25 years old human whose definition of a "good time" is to convert beer to urine, tip-top hotel experience isn't normally your highest priority. This is why so many hotels here can get away with offering junk rooms for an insane amount of money.

For me… I don't know, it just didn't click. It's not that I am *past* the stage in my life when I'm looking for parties, drinks and crap like that: I simply have never set foot in that stage to begin with. I'm not exactly sure how people find emotional outlets by partying and drinking in extremely noisy places; I tried it a few times in the last 35 years, and in all times I felt… well… stupid. Not something I wanna take a part in.

Saturday was a concert day, so I didn't do much. Rested for a bit and then took a walk to the city center. Last time I was here, I came across a wonderful coffee place called Marwood Coffee, located in Ship Street. This place is as strange as they come: as soon as you enter the place, you get the feeling that you're in some sort of a bizarre fantasy world. They have tables there made of old desktop PC's. Things hanging down from the ceiling. Really groovy. And their coffee is top notch. If you are ever in Brighton, pay them a visit.

Then, back to the hotel through Brunswick Square which looked lovely:

And then off to the venue.

The venue, Brighton Center, is the largest conference center in southern England, also used for concerts. It is located in King's Road, adjacent to a movie theater, a beautiful Victorian hotel by the name of The Grand and the fancy Hilton—hotels that cater to a slightly more adult (and rich) clientele.

I usually try to avoid spending too much time in the venue before the concert because I get somewhat anxious when surrounded by millions of people. Therefore, until 15 minutes before the concert, I was still outside the venue, sipping tea in the adjacent *Costa Coffee* with the Dutchman and with my friend James Morris who lives in Kent and made it to the concert.

Concert started about 10 minutes later than posted, and featured an identical set to the one played in Birmingham just the night before, except for *Our Shangri La* replacing *So Far Away* at the encore. I definitely prefer the former, especially when Nigel Hitchcock is involved as a saxophone adds a lot to that song.

Due to where I was seated—directly facing a loudspeaker—I had to watch *Speedway at Nazareth* from the door. Sound throughout the performance was very loud where I was seated, so I preferred to not take the risk.

Leaving the venue, I came to realize what Brighton is like on Saturday nights—essentially, representing everything I'm trying to get away from. I then opted to give up a gathering in a nearby pub and went back to the hotel for a good night sleep.

Well, I was going for a good night sleep, but I didn't get one. The cheap spring mattresses at the hotel didn't allow for a proper sleep, so I woke up Sunday morning a bit off. It was a day off that was planned to be spent in Brighton, so still, I tried to make the most out of it.

After a quick breakfast, took the bus east to see the Brighton Cliffs. Now this is something that should never be missed if you happen to be in the area.

These cliffs are designated as a "Site of Special Scientific Interest" for their geological characteristics—an interesting Wikipedia read; for us mortals, the cliffs provide a magnificent view of earth the way it could be had mankind opted to not fuck around with it.

Many pictures were taken and I'm not going to omit any of them:

There are a few things in life I can never get sick of, and one of them is ~~natural bodies of water~~ nature. The main reason I moved to Canada's west coast to begin with was that I fell in love with nature there. Walking ~~along natural bodies of water~~ in naturally-blessed settings is such an invigorating experience that it can do wonders to my well being, both physical and spiritual: fortunately, British Columbia certainly doesn't suffer from a shortage of lakes, rivers, creeks, mountains, cliffs—you name it, it's there.

Hence, when I travel, I can't miss on the chance to see nature at its best; the sea, specifically, attracts me. I must have been a starfish in one of my previous lives.

Or a freshwater eel.

Definitely not a Mantis Shrimp, though.

Long walk east along the cliffs until reached Peacehaven. Lunch consisted of a short visit to the nearby Sainsbury's supermarket, a few bread rolls and croissants for the staggering price of just under £4, consumed by the sea.

Half an our past due, the bus back to Brighton finally arrived and we made our way back to the city center. The closer the bus got to Brighton, the more people could be seen flooding the area and the less I wanted to be a part of this crowd. By the time the bus arrived at the city center, it became extremely crowded.

The Royal Pavilion is right at the city center. Its building started in 1787, for the Prince of Wales—just a nice seaside, you know, so he could sometimes just "get away from it all"; <sarcasm>it's tough life, being a prince</sarcasm>—until Queen Victoria decided that Brighton doesn't provide enough privacy anymore (once Brighton became accessible by train via London in 1841). A few years later, the land was sold to Brighton. A part of the pavilion was turned into a concert hall, nowadays referred to as the Brighton Dome.

Tourists, as well as locals, frequent the place. It's a nice environment for a walk, and the green there serves as excellent spot to just sit down, chill out with a good book (or, better off, an e-book of some sort. The end of the printed books can't come soon enough. I guess I'm a tree hugger now).

Back to the hotel, dinner in a Lebanese restaurant called Kambis, another walk along the shore and back to the hotel for a good night sleep.

Isaac

Tuesday, May 28, 2013

Brighton to London, UK (May 27, 2013)

Monday, May 27, was a day I was greatly looking forward to. After more than a month of intense travel—will I ever forget that 10 hours bus ride to Poland? probably not—finally, I get the chance to rest in *one* hotel for not one day, not two days, but for *six nights*.

And not only that there's an entire week free of travel, but also this week happens to be spent in one of my favourite cities on earth (I maintain a separate list for each planet)—the wonderful city of London.

Needless to say, then, I was quite eager to pack everything up and board the train from Brighton to London. After a short breakfast at Pret-A-Manger, inconveniently located more than a mile from the "hotel", ran some inventory check: it was just about time to do the laundry, and as there was a Laundromat across the street from the hotel, it was decided to get laundry work done with before heading to London.

That killed about an hour and a half. Well, didn't kill, really: just turned a hour and a half, which could have been used for fruitful purposes, into an hour and a half of watching this:

In the very first episode of Seinfeld, George joins Jerry to a Laundromat. During that scene, George is staring at the dryer spin and then saying: "Jerry? I have to tell you something. This is the dullest moment I've ever experienced". I relate. If you reach a point in your life when you are staring at a dryer spin for more than 20 seconds, and trying to guess the order in which your clothes are going to tumble over with every spin, then you are most likely not living life to the fullest.

Total cost of washing and drying—around £6, a price for which you can by a laundry machine in Bulgaria. Whatever. Let's just get it over with and get the hell out of here. Found the first bus to the central railway station, and took the 12:04pm train to London.

An hour later, left the train at *London Blackfriars*, then took the Tube to High Street Kensington, conveniently located a few steps away from the hotel, the *Copthorne Tara*, located in Scarsdale Place.

Exiting the High Street Kensington station, I looked above, looked to the sides... blue sky. Fantastic weather.

This is going to be a good week.

London.

Faith in humanity (partially) restored.

I had stayed in the Copthorne Tara hotel before, during the 2010 Get Lucky tour. It is a centrally located, well-maintained property. While planning the tour's schedule, the six nights stay in London was of the earlier planned legs which is why it didn't end up being too expensive (their "rack rate"—that is, the rate that you'd pay if you simply walk into the hotel without advance reservation and ask for a room—currently stands at £360 per night). Last minute bookings in such a hotel in such a location costs a fortune (less than the "rack rate", but still exceptionally ridiculous), which is why I decided to remain in Brighton during the day-off even after realizing that it sucks royal ass.

The Copthorne Tara hotel belongs to a chain called "Millennium Hotels", owning a few hotels in London and elsewhere. This chain has a very interesting pricing scheme for ~~logging into your Facebook account and get frustrated again witnessing people uploading pictures of dogs, cats, mice and Instagram photos of the food they're just about to eat~~ internet connection: it costs £10 per 24 hours—not per room, but per *device*. That means that for one person carrying a laptop and a smartphone would end up paying £20 (!) per day (!!) for Wi-Fi. Time it by six and you get £120.

Just to make sure you understand what £120 means, here's a list of things that cost (approximately) £120:

- €140; $181 US; $187 CDN; 672 ILS.
- Four times my recent *monthly* electricity bill.
- Almost five times my recent *monthly* high-speed internet bill (FiOS-based: 25Mbps download speed).
- 40% of one common stock of Apple (although, the way Apple is going, this percentage is likely to be raised soon).
- Not much less than the median monthly salary in Bulgaria.
- Approximately 60 cups of cappuccino from Starbucks.
- Three months worth of provincial health insurance in British Columbia, required to pay the doctors so they can heal you from the physical and mental wounds that you will surely suffer after drinking even one cup of cappuccino from Starbucks.

A few attempts to show how ridiculous this scheme was to the receptionist went unfruitful. Not because the poor lady didn't want to help, but mostly because she couldn't. It was decided, then, to postpone the fight for later on.

Quick setup in the room and we decided to go for lunch in a nearby Thai restaurant called Thai Terrace. I have been here before a couple of times and had good recollection of this place. As we were about to leave the hotel, Ingrid and Nelly were on their way in so we ended up going to the restaurant together. Shortly after, Philipp and his friend Werner from Switzerland joined us. Fun with interesting people.

Back at the hotel, armed with Ingrid, it was decided to once again attempt to demonstrate to this hotel that their Wi-Fi pricing scheme makes no sense for people who are staying there for six nights, and to use group power to try negotiating a deal that makes more sense. Once Ingrid explained the situation to the hotel's duty manager, in her own unique way, a much better deal was achieved and everyone was happy—the only caveat was that the arrangement was to start on Tuesday morning, not right away (which explains the delay in this post and the preceding one).

Knopfler usually plays more than one or two concerts in London during his solo tours. In 2008, for example, he played here six nights in a row. Same for 2010, and for the current tour. Therefore, the London stretch results in Knopfler fans pouring into London from various places on the planet, planning a vacation in England around the London tour dates.

While I am not active in any Knopfler fan forum (or any fan forum of any artist, actually), over the years I became acquainted with some. That might have something to do with the fact that I have attended more than a few concerts already. I was told that, in 2008, someone suggested the Stanhope Arms—a pub in Gloucester Road—as a pre-concert gathering place for concerts taking place in the Royal Albert Hall. Since then, it became a habit: whenever Knopfler touches ground in London for a concert, the Stanhope Arms is populated almost exclusively by concertgoers.

Due to a few peculiarities in my social upbringing (a skim Myers-Briggs I took once has shown that I'm an INTP. Some claim that so was Albert Einstein. Not that I'm trying to imply anything) as well as my drinking habits (that is, my non-existing drinking habits), I tend to feel uncomfortable in noisy, crowded environments and have very little to do in pubs as I hardly ever consume alcohol in any way, shape or form. I hope that this is not held against me folks, but that's the truth and that's what I am—I shy away from places I feel uncomfortable in.

Still, I remembered that there's a coffee place right next to that pub so I decided to pop in to say hello and then go sip some (decaf) coffee. The place was full of people, some more familiar than others. There were people from England; The Netherlands; Germany; Belgium; USA; Switzerland—an interesting setting. That must be what it feels like to attend a meeting of the Bilderberg Group, except that no wars and/or artificial economy crises are being planned out at this seemingly harmless English pub.

I had one half of one pint of beer. The last time I had beer before that was in the front yard of a friend of mine in Israel, who brought some beer that was home-brewed by a relative; that happened in December 2012. Before that, I can't recall when was the last time I had any sort of alcohol. That one half of one pint was enough to make me feel a bit off, so I joined my friend James for a snack in the nearby Paul cafe. Absolutely fantastic place for freshly baked goods—I will definitely revisit.

About half an hour later, it was time to head to the Royal Albert Hall, about 10 minutes walk away.

The Royal Albert Hall was opened in 1871 by Queen Victoria. It was originally named "The Central Hall of Arts and Sciences", but was later renamed by Queen Victoria to "Royal Albert Hall of Arts and Sciences", dedicating the place to her husband, Prince Albert.

In England, there's a concept of Listed Buildings; these are buildings that carry special architectural or historic interest. There are three "grades" of such buildings—1, 2* and 2—with Grade 1 defined as "buildings of exceptional interest". The Royal Albert Hall is a Grade 1 listed building for its architecture. It looks astonishing from the outside, but the real treat happens once you enter the hall and look around you.

This is, hands down, the most astonishing hall I have ever seen in my entire life. No photograph I took could ever do justice to how amazing this venue is from the inside, but here are a few attempts.

In the floor seating section, the front rows are exceptionally close to the stage. Moreover, the stage itself is very low. If you are seated somewhere in the front, you actually feel that the band is not playing for 5,500 people (the maximum capacity in the hall), but for one person: yourself. This is a remarkable experience that I would wish on pretty much anyone I am fond of.

Ruth Moody, who was last seen performing in Amsterdam making the Amsterdam concert the most memorable one in the tour so far, is also the opening act for Knopfler in all six concerts in London. Slightly less excited and trembling than she was in Amsterdam, she gave a remarkable performance, assisted by three band members, out of which two are from British Columbia. I should have a word.

About half an hour break, during which I went about to take a few breaths of fresh air. At around 8:45pm, the band took the stage…

… And gave the Royal Albert Hall the rocking of its lifetime.

In my post about the Amsterdam concert, I described that performance as being fantastic thanks to Ruth's involvement. Now, take that, and add the fact that London is Knopfler's back yard. To that, add Nigel Hitchcock and you end up with a product that I can hardly see how it can be beaten.

There was nothing in this show that I can say a negative word about. The Royal Albert Hall yesterday looked like one big happy party. Of course, the venue's special, intimate (at least at the floor section) layout contributed to the overall feeling that there's one hell of a party going on, but the music emitted by these ten performers was marvellous.

It's that type of energy that made the Toronto and Locarno concerts (2010) unforgettable. When the energy isn't there, or isn't there at its fullest, it is sometimes hard to notice; but when the energy is there, and all cannons are firing at full power, you see it. And you can see it despite having seen this band perform approximately 170 times before.

Quite expectedly, the highlight of this concert was Ruth's participation. *I Dug Up a Diamond* was played again with Ruth providing beautiful vocals as well as accompanying acoustic guitar work. It was evident that the excitement that was slightly holding her back during the Amsterdam performance was well under control now. Right next, *Seattle*, again with Ruth, minus Mark's guitar's tremolo effect, causing a bit of a stir at the side of the stage as Glen was trying to figure out what's wrong.

In Amsterdam, Ruth joined the band for the performance of three songs. Here in the UK, Nigel Hitchcock is also in the guests' line-up so some changes had to be introduced to the set.

Sultans of Swing was back, in a very good performance—good enough that even I enjoyed it.

Nobody wanted this show to be over. Off to *Telegraph Road*…

Followed by a crazed *Running of the Bulls* session when people from pretty much the entire floor area came sprinting by to catch a spot near the stage. When I thought it was safe to get up and march forward, two individuals who could hardly be described as "petite figured" came blazing through the wind, knocking me sideways.

I suppose I should look behind me next time, as well. Went back to my seat for the encore, when I noticed a lady struggling to watch the show as she was standing behind an exceptionally tall individual. I invited her to take my spot which had a better view of the stage, a suggestion which she couldn't quite comprehend at the beginning but eventually was very happy with. Turned out she came all the way from Brazil for this. Who am I to stand in the way?

The Royal Albert Hall's roof was close to being blown away with an energetic performance of *Going Home*. The entire audience—front, back, sideways—everybody were on their feet.

As good as this band is, performances as explosive as that one aren't very frequent to come by. You can have many good concerts, a few very good ones, fewer excellent ones… but not too many extraordinarily exceptional ones such as that one.

And then you ask me why I'm attending more than one show…

After the concert, a quick walk back to the hotel. Grabbed some Shawarma and started devouring it senselessly in the hotel's bar. By the time the waiter came by to tell us that hey, this is a restaurant and you shouldn't bring outside food here (fair enough. I honestly didn't know), I was already done. Minutes later, about 15–20 familiar faces—pretty much, whoever went earlier to the Stanhope Arms—came by for a drink and late night dinners. I went back to my room to grab my laptop, so I can catch up with blogging while others around me were busy talking in various languages I couldn't make sense of. It wasn't before 2:00am when it all ended and I went upstairs to catch a good night sleep.

It's days like these that make such a journey a memorable experience.

Signing off this post from my hotel room in London. Will go catch up with other things now, and then head to the Royal Albert Hall again for tonight's (**cough* Kingdom of Gold *cough**) concert.

Isaac

Friday, May 31, 2013

A Quick Note from London, UK

Oh hello.

Just a short one this time as a few kind readers emailed me asking what the hell is going on.

As there isn't any travel involved during the week in London, and I am using this week primarily to catch up with certain obligations (I actually hardly left my hotel room ever since getting here, except for dining. And buying underwear. I'll elaborate later), there isn't much to tell.

The concerts on Tuesday, Wednesday and Thursday (yesterday) were a treat. After an exceptionally tasty concert on Monday night—which I would definitely label as the best one yet in this tour*—the following experiences in the Royal Albert Hall were different, as the band seemed more relaxed and the audience (for the most part) exhibiting more of the typical London-ish reserved temperament.

> *One reader suggested that I recommend which USB stick(s) to purchase. Frankly, I am a little uncomfortable with that because enjoyment of these concerts is rather subjective and I wouldn't want people to take a blind bet expecting me to be the judge of things. So, let's get this out of the way: whatever I write reflects my own personal opinion. It's up to you to decide how to use your money—my opinions about the concerts are all described here and you're welcome to make your own judgement based on them.

Two exceedingly disconcerting violent incidents took place (so far), one on Tuesday and one on Thursday; I happened to be witnessing the first and being one of the victims of the second. I decided to do something about it and will keep you posted. People shouldn't have to attend concerts fearing for their lives, this just isn't right. All details (well, not all; whatever I will be in the liberty to publish) will be revealed in a blog post once the London week is over.

Bye for now,
Isaac

Monday, June 3, 2013

A Week in London, UK (May 27-June 2, 2013)

As I wrote in the last post, the week in London was originally planned to be absolute, completely filled with doing almost nothing. After more than a month of intense travel—from the aviation industry's clusterfuck in Israel and Germany, through the bus ride from hell to Poland and all other challenges along the way—finally, the time came for a most welcome break in one of my favourite cities.

Initially, I was planning on writing nothing during the week in London. That plan had to be altered following the exceptionally stellar concert on Monday, which was so good that I just had to share the experience somehow. Also, London's weather wasn't such that would build one's passion to walk around and experience anything, unless one was a fish: for the first three days or so, it was cloudy, cold and occasionally rainy—providing excellent opportunity to catch up with a few obligations and rest. So, there was very little to write home about anyway.

The week in London was less about the concerts (as good as they were) than about everything else: resting, working and socializing. Knopfler fans make it a habit to arrive to London whenever the tour parks there for a few days, as London is easily accessible from pretty much anywhere and the long stay (about a week) makes for an excellent excuse for a vacation. So many familiar faces and names from previous tours, making it to London from as east as Israel and as west as California. Many of them ended up staying at the same hotel I was—the Copthorne Tara Hotel, which will be forever remembered for setting the most ridiculous Wi-Fi payment and usage policy I have ever come across—so socializing during the week in London was more frequent than usual.

As the concert on Monday was absolutely stellar, I already knew that I should set my expectations accordingly. It is very difficult to produce such a fantastic concert once, let alone twice in a row. And indeed, Tuesday's concert was less extravagant, with everybody (band & audience alike) seeming more laid back than before.

Tuesday was also the only London concert that featured a performance of *Kingdom of Gold*. Just saying.

And then came that "man on a track", good performance of Telegraph Road and then something happened that made me post this. I was seated in the second row. I swear in the name of anything that might control this miserable planet that, within a blink of an eye, everyone just disappeared from the front row crashing into the stage. As if everyone was made of metal and the stage suddenly became a huge magnet.

I felt that something was a miss when I noticed that my friend Ingrid, who was seated in front of me on the front row, ended up being on the second row of people before the stage. Whoever has been to the Royal Albert Hall before (the distance between the front seats and the stage is about one meter), and/or knows Ingrid, should know that such an occurrence is not possible in normal working environments.

Seconds later, I figured it out—not by using much of my own brainpower, but by noticing that a few people (Ingrid included) were arguing with a tall, sociopath-looking individual who stood behind them. Turned out that the sociopath was pushing people around in quite the violent manner.

We will get to that sociopath later.

On Thursday, I decided to buy some new underwear.

I am not entirely sure why, but when I packed for this trip, I ended up packing less underwear than what would make sense. It hit me in Sofia (when I had to hand-wash my underwear and hang them on a LAN cable to dry out) but I never got around to buy new ones due to the lack of time and my complete cluelessness with anything revolving around buying clothes.

I don't know how to buy clothes. Any clothes. At the odd times that I am forced to buy some clothes for myself, I end up screwing it up and buying nonsense.

Luckily, my frequent visits home mean that I have access to the best ever clothing shopping engine in the world: my beloved sister. Whenever I'm at home, I drag her along, ask her to pick clothes for me and all I have to do is try things on and sign my name on the credit card receipt at the end. I rarely argue—both because I don't have enough fashion vocabulary to explain what I want, and also because it is virtually impossible to say "no" to my sister.

I am so clueless at buying clothes, that once I decided that I want (read: need) to buy underwear, I didn't even know how I should go about doing so—that is, where should I buy them?—even though I was located in central London.

So, I posted this. Suggestions came pouring in. As they were, I was sitting in a Paul's cafe in Old Compton street sipping coffee, when I suddenly heard someone calling "Isaac?". By chance, it was my friend Phil Bayliss who lives in British Columbia and often attends Knopfler concerts in the UK as well. Good to meet good people along the way: we had met a few times before during this tour but never outside any concert venue. Ended up chatting for about an hour and then I realized that, what the heck, I've been out all day and still no new underwear purchased.

As I exited the cafe, I looked through the suggestions on my Facebook post and, naturally, decided to visit the closest one first. The closest one was a place called Fifty & Dean, located less than ten steps away from the cafe I was sitting in. Now, I don't know if Michelle meant it as a joke when she suggested this place, but after spending less than one second inside I reached the conclusion that this is not the type of underwear I was looking for—partly because it was a sex shop but mostly because I happen to be (sit tight, this is going to hurt) heterosexual.

Thanks Michelle.

Ended up buying a few pairs in Primark—not before feeling the material of which each type of underwear was made of, a feat that I'm sure wasn't perceived as proper by others. Six good pairs for £14. Not much more expensive than doing the laundry here.

Back to the hotel and then off to the concert. I was seated at the left hand side of the front row this time, a bit stinging in the left ear whenever high treble sounds broke out of the speakers—so I had to watch *Speedway at Nazareth* from the stairs area in order to avoid terrible pain.

The concert was very good, with the highlight being the Marbletown outro session. I already thought that I had watched this song performed in any way, shape or form conceivable to mankind, but every once in a while I get surprised. John McCusker took this one to the next level, and the band quickly joined in playing in such harmony and accuracy that, really, goes to show exactly why I think that these guys are phenomenal and worth watching and listening to more than once or twice.

And then something happened, that hasn't happened yet in any concert I ever attended. Actually, such a thing hasn't happened since I remember myself: for a brief period of about 30 seconds, I lost my temper at a complete stranger.

As mentioned, I was seated at the left hand side of the front row. I knew what was going to happen as soon as Telegraph Road ends. I never run anywhere, never push or pull people—all I really wanted was to get up from my seat and make exactly one step forward, towards the stage.

Which is exactly what I did. I was happy to arrive safely, and looking around, I saw people approaching the other side of the stage, running. And then—*BAM*, someone crashed into me from behind, squeezing me quite violently into the stage.

I turned around to see who the hell that was so I can give them a piece of my mind, and I saw a rather familiar face of an otherwise innocent Dutchman right behind me. Something didn't look right: the chances of Jeroen intentionally pushing or pulling people around are lower than the chances of a live dinosaur being discovered in Manhattan. Turned out that he was pushed to distance of around 2–3 meters by someone, right onto me.

And by whom? that's right—the very same sociopath who caused havoc just two nights before.

Jeroen wasn't the only one pushed by that asshole. As the words *"what are you, a stupid fuck?"* came rolling out of my mouth—hell, I wasn't even aware that I can utter such a sentence towards a stranger; I was *that* shocked of being pushed that violently—I noticed other people arguing with that very same individual. He looked at me and just froze: didn't say a word to anyone around him, and only raised his hands as if to suggest "I have no idea what you want from me". He then proceeded to video-record the entire encore.

– "I don't think I'll ever get up from my seat again", said the Dutchman as the band started playing *So Far Away*.

– "Why, because of this fucking jackass?" I asked, diverting my look to the sociopath standing less than a a foot away.

The first time I ever watched this band perform live was on July 5, 2005, in the Molson Amphitheatre, Toronto. I was seated at the front row. In the Molson Amphitheatre, the stage is very high—about five feet and a half above ground. Back then, like nowadays, *Telegraph Road* was the last song performed before the encore. Everybody stood up afterwards, for a standing ovation. Now, that was Canada: Canadians are very polite, and you are very unlikely to come across people who would run recklessly to the stage, let alone inflict violence upon others. We all stood as my then-most favourite Knopfler song, *Brothers in Arms*, was played.

It was a mesmerizing experience. For weeks later, I couldn't stop replaying in my head the sensation of listening to *Brothers in Arms* performed live, standing amidst a sea of people with every note played through that Gibson Les Paul punching a hole through the air around. It was that night that I knew that it can't be the last time for me to watch these guys perform, and I ended up attending four more, including flying to Vancouver to catch the tour's concluding show.

Fast forward almost eight years later. I have seen this band perform more than a few times since. I can very easily relate to the excitement that this performance builds in people—after all, it's *Telegraph Road*'s outro solo that we're talking about, and it *is* a tension-building one (it would be silly to assume that Mark doesn't know exactly why he chooses to play this song before the encore). The experience of gathering nearby the stage is truly unique and touches an emotional nerve with many—this is undeniable; which is why, I think, the band's management instructs venues' security staff to allow the audience to remain standing up for the entire encore.

I have absolutely no problem with that.

However, just like with other areas in life, my problem begins when people treat others like garbage on their way to satisfy their own selfish emotional needs.

I am not religious, I don't practice anything and, if being religious is what makes you happy, then by all means, practice whatever you want. My problem begins once you let your own personal preferences interfere with the lives of others. A religious individual who inflicts violence on others as an ideology, interfering with their lives in the name of his/her "God", immediately loses—in my eyes, at least—any social privilege. I mock, despise, dislike, abhor, detest and loathe such people, irrespective of religious belief, race, gender or the colour of their underwear.

<u>Recklessly</u> running towards the stage, crushing everything along the way and completely disrespecting others' right to enjoy a concert without getting hurt, isn't much different than the practice of abusing others as part of a selfish ideology.

It saddens me to realize that, as a society, we are growing more and more tolerant to acts of violence. As mysterious it is to me what prompts someone to engage in violence (hey, parents nowadays allow 10 year old kids to play video games in which they kill prostitutes and shoot police officers. Maybe it's not that mysterious after all), it is far more of a mystery to me what prompts the *acceptance* of such violence without proper societal sanctions.

Having said that, I get the feeling that such incidents can be minimized (or avoided) by proper education (that is, teach kids in school less about useless stuff and more about how to avoid being cruel to one another), and proper sanctioning (charging such people with assault, plus having them barred from attending concerts for a period of time, say 95 years).

At the moment, I'm under the impression that none of these methods is actually practiced. You can be stopped by a police officer and given a hefty fine for jaywalking, but if you happen to be pushing people violently during a concert, most chances are that you're going to come out of it clean.

So what can we do? well, one thing we can *not* do is looking at the big elephant strolling around the china store and pretend that it's not there. If you see violence taking place in a concert, don't just ignore it. Report it. Act upon it. Insist that it's taken care of. The only way perpetrators are going to stop physically attacking other concertgoers is if they find out that it doesn't pay off, or is counterproductive. Accepting violence is bound to trigger more violence.

My friends from Arizona, Katrina & Lane, were spending a couple of weeks in Europe and made it to Knopfler's last two concerts at the Royal Albert Hall. Last time we met was during the 2012 Knopfler-Dylan tour in California; plans were made well ahead of time to get together and catch up, over afternoon tea at the Brown's Hotel—a staple in London's hospitality industry which dates back to 1837 and hosted many rich, famous and royalty.

As Lane made the reservation and forwarded the information to me a couple of weeks ago, I realized that this place has a dressing code called "smart casual". I know exactly what clothes I brought with me to this tour—none of it qualifies as "smart casual".

> Quite frankly, I think that the entire concept of "dress code" is stupid to begin with (as long as you're dressed, why the hell would I care if you're "smart casual" or "stupid formal"?) but that's a different story.

The point is that jeans and a buttoned shirt was the best I could come up with, so the Arizonians promised that it will all be OK.

Arrived at the Brown's Hotel on Friday afternoon, 4:00pm. Quite expectedly, meeting this wonderful couple was a pleasure. The four of us spent about two hours sitting at the wonderful tearoom snacking on delicious sandwiches, extraordinary desserts and great tea, all the while catching up on so many things that time was really flying by.

The two live in Flagstaff, Arizona. They travel a lot together and they work together. According to them, since they became a couple, they never ever spent even one night apart.

The latter statement wouldn't be so baffling had they not been together for 20 (yes, twenty) years now.

Now, I am no stranger to relationships—good or bad; neither am I an expert on the subject. But when I look at these two; see them interact with each other—verbally and physically; when I am in their very presence, I simply feel that if a perfect couple exists out there in the world, it must be them. They repeatedly claim that they are, in fact, one; and it doesn't take more than an hour with these two to realize exactly what it means.

The very act of observing all of this is fulfilling and inspiring. Maybe not all hope is lost. Inevitably, delving into this issue, I can't help but thinking about myself and my own status: where I am going to end up, and in the presence of whom, if at all. Only time will tell, I suppose; however, so far, time has been giving many clues but I consistently fail to connect the dots between them.

Before leaving the hotel, we went to see the room where Alexander Graham Bell made the first ever successful phone call in Great Britain: it happened right there at the Brown's Hotel, and the room where Bell demonstrated his invention we call "phone" now serves as a touristic attraction.

Instead of taking the Tube from the Brown's Hotel to the Royal Albert Hall, we decided to hop on a taxi. That was my first time ever in a London taxi, which explains why I was completely shocked when I noticed the peculiar spacious interior that allows passengers to sit *facing each other*. That seemingly small taxi could hold up to seven (!) passengers and I could have *never* guessed so just by looking at the taxi from the outside.

The show on Friday was a treat. Just before the concert started, I felt a tap on my shoulder and someone saying "Shalom".

When such a thing happens, I already know that I'm going to be happy once I turn around. Travelling intensely for so long makes the very sound of your mother tongue feels like a handle for holding on to reality. Turned out that it was an Israeli couple I had met three years ago in Chicago by complete accident as I was taking an elevator in a shopping mall and was recognized as "that guy". They flew to London from Israel to catch the show and it was certainly good to see them again.

Friday, then, was a good day, and all that was left for it to end well was for some random band of eight musicians, accompanied by two guests, to perform well—which they did. The bulls did run, but no extraordinary violent incidents witnessed.

Saturday arrived way too quickly. Waking up Saturday morning, I couldn't believe how quickly that week has been flying by.

My Israeli friend, whom I met during the concert the night before, spoke highly of a coffee place by the name of Monmouth Coffee, claiming that it is the best coffee in London. Reviews appeared be generally supportive of that statement, so I decided to pay a short visit.

What I didn't know was that the coffee place is located in Borough Market, which happens to be one of the most renowned food markets in the UK.

It was also sunny. And it was a Saturday.

Combine the aforementioned together and you should understand why the entire area was flooded with millions of people. As soon as I exited the London Bridge station and started walking towards the market, I realized that this was going to be an interesting experiment in drowning in a sea of people. Approaching Monmouth Coffee, I saw something a had never seen before in my entire life, anywhere: a *long* line-up. When I say "long", I mean this:

The line-up started outside, around the corner from the store. Looking at how it progressed, I figured that it might take another 30–45 minutes until I'll be able to order anything. As no coffee in the world is worth 45 minutes of my time waiting for it, I fled the scene and grabbed a good cup from a nearby coffee place (less than 20 steps away), much less crowded but still very good coffee.

Wandered around Borough Market…

… and on my way back to the train station, I couldn't help but laugh at this:

Someone please remind me what prompted the 2007 economic meltdown in the United States…

Back in Kensington, I decided that I couldn't take this anymore. I know I stated before that I wasn't going to cut my hair until the tour is over. I lied. I used to have long hair in high school (past the shoulder line) and for a brief period ten years ago, but not anymore. Paid a visit to a place called Cool Creative in Kensington.

I am not a big fan of getting my hair cut, especially in an establishment I had never been to before. The reason is that I'm having a hard time explaining what it is exactly that I want done: I can only explain after the fact. Hence, trial and error are a necessity here, and the more establishments I go to, the more such trials and errors are required.

Back in Vancouver, the only reason why I ended up cutting my hair where I do is that I know the owner through a mutual friend. Luck had it and she turned out to be fantastic at what she does. In my first time there, she asked me "what are we going to do today?", and I responded with "I don't know. Make me dateable". She did. But I didn't do anything with it.

This time, I simply said flat out that "from what I currently have on my head, the only way is up, so go nuts".

I normally shy away from small talk. I'm not good at it; never was. That probably (partly) explains my mediocre dating history as well as the fact that my circle of friends grows slower than the continental drift. Somehow, miraculously, the individual, who was in charge of cutting my hair back to the realm of sanity, sensed that. At first I thought he was rude; he wasn't. It was really all me and what my expression conveyed. He did a great job. If you're in Kensington and would like to lose some weight through cutting your hair, go there.

Back at the hotel, and then headed out to the last concert in the Royal Albert Hall for this tour.

Ruth Moody, once again, gave a very good performance. She and her band will be missed, until later on in June when they return to perform as an opening act for Knopfler in France.

The band, perhaps fuelled by knowing that a week long break is ahead, gave everything they had and the result was a truly remarkable performance, ranking together with the first concert that week in London as the top ones in the tour so far. Really, wow.

A couple of seats to my right, a man was seated along with his little daughter. As the people who are most likely to get hurt by violent bull running are the ones seated on the sides, I was a little concerned with how things might develop.

Surprisingly, the run to the stage started much earlier than usual, about 20 seconds before the end of Telegraph Road. People around hypothesized that this was a result of a significant presence of Spanish and Italian fans in the audience, which may be true—Knopfler enjoys a rather vocal and loud fan base in these countries. It all happened very fast, but by what I saw, there were no casualties.

That little girl was safe, by the way.

It felt sad to bid this wonderful venue goodbye. Not just the venue: heading back to the hotel after the concert, it occurred to me that once again I have to pack things up. Back to travelling mode—but only for a day, before a long week break.

Signing off this post from Jeroen's apartment in Delft, The Netherlands. Will do very little writing in the next following days. Next up: June 7th in Zwolle, The Netherlands—followed by a flight to Tallinn, Estonia and a ferry to Helsinki, Finland right after.

Can't wait to see Laura again.

Isaac

Monday, June 10, 2013

Delft to Zwolle, The Netherlands (June 7, 2013)

As expected, it was sad to leave London: not only because it's one of my favourite cities, but also because it meant packing yet again. Alas, every good thing must come to an end (interestingly enough, the same isn't true for bad things). After having breakfast with a friend

Sunday morning, we headed up to London's St. Pancras station (no, it's not spelled "St. Pancreas" as I had seen someone spelling it before). Arrived early and killed some time in the terminal, then boarded the Eurostar train to take us back to mainland Europe.

I have taken the Eurostar train a few times before. It is the only train that takes passengers from England to mainland Europe, spending much of the ride underwater, traversing the Channel Tunnel. Complete darkness around—it'd be nice had they designed the entire tunnel to be a see-thru aquarium, but hey, nobody listens to my suggestions anymore—and of course, the occasional sensation of pressure in the ears. Then, as if out of nowhere, the train emerges from the tunnel right into the vast greens of northern France. First stop is in *Lille*, and the next one is in *Brussels*.

Only two and some weeks prior, I had the displeasure of consuming two cups of coffee here—that is, tasting one; throwing it away; tasting the other one and just consuming it without listening to my taste buds—so, this time I didn't even try.

On my Facebook wall, a friend has suggested that Brussels is not a true representation of Belgium and therefore it'd be improper to draw conclusions about the country based on my impression of Brussels alone, let alone if I were to judge by Brussels' *Midi* train station (that discussion later led to a quarrel).

Lucky Belgium, then. I find it hard to describe the level of depression I get every single time I set foot in that train station: everything—everything!—looks bleak and hopeless. Everything from the floor, through the people and to the ceiling. This place must be a black hole sucking worldly good mood. World War III is likely to start here.

Half an hour wait to the connecting train seemed like taking forever. Eventually, we were on our way to The Netherlands. Shortly into the ride, an announcement was made that due to problems in the Dutch railway network, we'd have to leave this train in Roosendaal and proceed with a different train. Whatever, really; just take me to Delft already.

Arrived in Delft late evening. On one hand, I was very happy: finally, a familiar place in a city I like a lot, an apartment of a good friend of mine. On the other hand, hey, that meant sleeping on a mattress on the floor for a few nights. That's fine, I guess… I've had worse.

The next few days in Delft were almost entirely vacant of any challenges—just as I was hoping those days to be. That break came in a good time, almost half way into the tour: rest was definitely required as the second part of the tour is unpleasant when it comes to travel schedule. No amount of rest could therefore be deemed as "enough".

The weather in Delft was perfect. Sunny, cool wind—basically, every day was good for taking walks around this beautiful city and sipping coffee in various places, enjoying the weather and the lovely Dutch atmosphere.

Also took a short trip to The Hague for a couple of hours. The Hague is located about 10 minutes train ride north of Delft:

By far, the greatest challenge I put myself through during this break was making a perfect *Duo Penotti* sandwich, during lunch with Jeroen's colleagues:

In the morning of the last free day in Delft, I decided to go to the city's main square once again, sip some coffee in the sun. Little did I know that the city of Delft had other plans for that square—setting up an outdoor market:

I of course wasn't impressed much from the fact that my beloved quiet spot suddenly became flooded with humans. Found a nearby spot away from the crowd and peace was restored.

June 7th arrived; the Delft break is over, back to touring mode. Everything charged—toothbrush; phone; tablet; laptop; everything washed and dried up. Everything ready to charge at the tour's second leg with full power and vigour.

Originally, the itinerary was to fly on June 6th to Moscow, Russia through Tallinn, Estonia, as there were two concerts scheduled in Russia (Moscow & St. Petersburg). Some time in March, Mark decided to cancel his two concerts in Russia due to the Russian government's crackdown on Human Rights Watch and other human rights-related organizations.

The cancellation of the Russian dates raised a few problems in the itinerary: the flight from Moscow to St. Petersburg was only partly refunded; train tickets from St. Petersburg to Helsinki were non-refundable and therefore lost. Also, money paid to the Moscow hotel for the first night was lost, as it had to be prepaid for issuing the invitation required to get a Visa for Jeroen.

> Getting a Visa to Russia is a long, tedious process; in the light of Russia's attitude towards the west, I wouldn't be surprised if the process of getting a Visa is intentionally tedious as means of deterring visitors in the first place.
>
> First, you need to fill out an online application. Application? more like the bureaucratic equivalent of a full-on rectal examination. The amount of data they're looking for, about you and your family, is ridiculous. Among other things, they want to know the details of each and every country you have been in over the last *ten years*, including arrival and departure date from each. If you entered a country more than once—all arrivals and departures must be specified. This is particularly painful for Canadians who happen to cross the border to the USA frequently, sometimes even for just a few minutes in order to pick up a package.
>
> Filling that online form isn't enough. You also need to get an actual, formal invitation from the establishment that is going to host you. If you're there for a conference, an invitation must be provided by the conference center. If you're going to be staying in a hotel, the hotel itself must generate such invitation. Of course, these invitations cost money, and if you're staying in a hotel, then most hotels will require you to pre-pay for your first night's stay as a condition to getting that invitation (which, of course, you have to pay for separately). All of these payments are non-refundable. To add some more cruelness into the mix, most hotels are willing to provide you with an invitation that covers *only the dates in which you're staying in that hotel*. If you're staying in multiple places in Russia, you might end up having to get a separate invitation from each hotel.
>
> Think you're through? no. Once all of the above is completed, you need to appear for an interview in your nearest Russian embassy or consulate. *Then* you get the Visa.
>
> Citizens of a few countries are exempt from requiring a Visa; Israeli citizens fall into this category (Canadian citizens don't), so I didn't have to go through this bullshit.

As soon as the cancellation was made public, we changed our plans accordingly: we changed the Amsterdam-Tallinn-Moscow ticket so instead of departing June 6th, we'd be departing on June 8th with the same route—except that we'd simply check out in Tallinn instead of proceeding to Moscow. From Tallinn, it's less than two hours ferry ride to Helsinki.

As our flight to Tallinn the next morning was scheduled to depart in the morning, it made much more sense to stay the night in Schiphol than anywhere else. Late in the afternoon, we bid the beautiful city of Delft adieu and boarded the train to Schiphol airport. From Schiphol, it's a short 10 minutes shuttle ride to the Steigenberger Hotel; checked in and almost immediately left back to Schiphol, to meet Philipp and take the train to Zwolle, about an hour and a half train ride east.

Zwolle? what?

I have never heard of Zwolle before in my life. The city, with the population of about 120,000, is located in the province of Overijssel (pronounced: *O-ver-ai-sel*) in The Netherlands (just FYI, even though the term "Holland" is often used to refer to The Netherlands, it is misleading. "South Holland" and "North Holland" are two provinces in The Netherlands).

The city's name originates from the word "*Suolle*", which means "Hill". That "hill" refers to, well, a hill that is located between the four rivers that surround the city (the city actually sits on that hill). Those rivers used to get flooded every now and then, and that "hill" was the only part of the land (between the four rivers) to remain dry.

Here's an interesting bit of trivia: during World War II, Zwolle's liberation from Nazi Germany is mainly attributed to the actions of *one* soldier, corporal Leo Major from… Canada. The story of how he ("singlehandedly", according to Wikipedia) went about doing so is very interesting, I suggest you give it a read.

I didn't get much time to look around the city but it is a treat to the eyes:

Typical Dutch city landscape.

As time was pressing, there wasn't the luxury of picking a proper place to eat so the three of us went to a place called Kota Radja, suggested by TripAdvisor as a good place to fill up. It is an Asian fusion restaurant, in a prime location and very interesting menu.

Getting food in this restaurant is the culinary equivalent of applying for a Visa to Russia. The table gets a card, listing all available dishes. The card has five columns, each representing a "round" of ordering. A table can order up to five rounds of food in total, with each round containing up to three dishes per diner (are you following? good. There's a quiz at the end of this post). The restaurant's staff simply visits your table occasionally, checking whether the form is filled with orders for the next round (you're supposed to shove the card into a special metal holder to signify "we're ready"), picking it up and serving the dishes as soon as they're ready.

Lots of work, but it paid: the food was very good. I was starving and completely gave up after four rounds. I figure it'd be very hard to finish five full rounds in that restaurant and remain hungry. Cost is quite expensive (about €26 per person), however.

The Netherlands being a very strong fan base of this band, naturally we ran into more than a few familiar faces on the way to the venue, including Ingrid of course. Ten minutes away, we arrived at the venue.

Wikipedia has the following to say (as of this writing) about the venue, IJsselhallen:

> IJsselhallen is a building in Zwolle, Netherlands. It is a conference centre, and has hosted many concerts. It hosted Legoland 2010.

That isn't much, and indeed, there isn't much that can be said about this huge box of concrete appearing as if out of absolutely nowhere right in the middle of absolutely nowhere. It is huge, as it contains of multiple halls inside, some of which are separated by curtains rather than by any hard material, for flexibility.

Entering the venue and walking towards the concert hall, I already felt that something in this venue is strange. Passed through what seemed to be a place for wedding receptions, and just before entering the seated area of the hall, I saw this:

In case you are wondering what this is: it's a bulk food stand, selling bulk candy for about €1.50 per 100 grams. Have you ever seen such a thing in any concert venue? I haven't.

Entering the area in the venue where the concert was to take place, the feeling of strangeness intensified.

Immediately I couldn't quite point my finger at what didn't ring well. Then I found it: the layout of the seating area wasn't symmetrical (not even close) with respect to the margins. If you click on the image above and look at the left hand side, you'll see a curtain stretching from the left hand tip of the stage all the way to the back. On the right hand side of the picture, you won't find such a curtain. Conclusion: this venue's seating layout was intentionally rearranged to allow for less audience than usual. Either that or I'm missing something basic. It looked very odd.

One other thing that was obvious—this time, for everyone—is that whoever was running this venue wasn't a big fan of… well… fans. I mean this type of fan:

The heat in the venue was simply unbearable and air circulation wasn't working to any satisfactory capacity, which negatively affected my enjoyment of the concert (and I bet I'm not the only one). Two bottles of water consumed during the concert just to maintain sanity. Heck, I feel warm just writing about it.

The concert, however, was good. The band seemed fresh after a vacation of almost a week. As neither Ruth Moody nor Nigel Hitchcock were present (Ruth will make a comeback for the Paris concert; I'm not sure about Nigel, but I seem to recall that he was only scheduled to appear as a guest during the UK shows), the set got back to the pre-UK days.

Apparently, the audience wasn't alone in feeling the intense heat inside this pile of concrete: Mike McGoldrick was spotted with his back completely and utterly wet of sweat. The performance itself wasn't much affected by it all, though.

In this venue, the distance between the front row to the barrier positioned before the stage was huge, about 3–4 meters. You could easily add a few rows there but you'd have to either equip people sitting there with earplugs, or pay for their healthcare bill afterwards as some of them would have lost their hearing. The sound was very loud where I was seated. Either way, the long gap between the seated area and the stage's barrier allowed for the *Running of the Bulls* to go on without casualties. Warm, sweaty encore and the concert was over.

Trains at night run less frequently than during the day. As we were walking back to the train station, we realized that we could save a few minutes from the overall itinerary if we run to the train station, a distance usually made by 7–8 minutes of walking, within 3 minutes. I ran fast, very fast—but arrived last: still, we made it. The train's doors were closed shut as soon as I boarded. Back in Schiphol airport, the hotel shuttle was unavailable anymore, which left no choice but take a taxi to the hotel.

Long, long day.

Signing off this post from my hotel room in Helsinki, Finland. Got here yesterday, concert ended just a couple of hours ago, and the last two days were fantastic—during which, unfortunately, I didn't have the time to write. More on that in the next post, hopefully to be completed tomorrow.

Heading off to bed: flight to Oslo leaves at 7:15am (!!), scheduled to arrive to Hamar, Norway at around 10:00am.

Isaac

Monday, June 10, 2013

Amsterdam, The Netherlands to Helsinki, Finland (June 8-9, 2013)

Arriving exhausted to the Steigenberger Hotel after the concert in Zwolle, I took a shower and went to bed immediately. I was so tired that I'm not sure I even finished showering before embarking on my first trip to dreamland.

The flight to Tallinn was scheduled to depart at 9:15am, and Schiphol Airport being a major European transportation hub, nobody wanted to risk long security line-ups: therefore, it was decided to take the 7:00am shuttle to the airport, which meant waking up at around 6:15am. Not much time to sleep.

Everything went according to plan. Made sure that the necessary adjustments are made upon check-in, as we were originally booked for a flight to Moscow through Tallinn (to catch the shows in Russia, which were later cancelled), and were going to break the itinerary in Tallinn.

> If you happen to book a flight with multiple connections, and later decide that you would like to drop off somewhere along the way, you should mention it to someone when you check in, unless you want to be separated from your luggage as the latter proceeds to the original final destination.

The flight from Schiphol to Tallinn took less than three hours.

Tallinn's airport is small, having only one runway. Locals call it "Europe's cosiest airport". I don't know about cosy, but it is indeed very nice. Gate seating:

I have heard before that Estonia is beautiful. That's why, once the Russian concerts were cancelled, I was debating whether I should spend June 8th in Tallinn or in Helsinki. Eventually I decided in favour of Finland as my friend Laura agreed to have me over and show me around (we'll get to that).

From the airport, it's an easy 20 minutes bus ride to the ferry terminal. The bus goes through the city center, which, I must say, doesn't look too astonishing. Once arrived at the ferry terminal, about two hours prior to departure, it turned out that there is more than one ferry terminal in Tallinn and the one serving *Linda Lines* (*Linnahall*) happens to be a couple of kilometers away from where we ended up (*Terminal-D*). Too tired to walk, a taxi was hailed and ten minutes later I was in the correct terminal.

The *Linnahall* ferry terminal is small. Very small. Inside the terminal—I have seen bigger cafe's, actually—nothing to either see or do, except a rather desperate cafe serving "food" and "drinks" to whomever had the misfortune to arrive at that ferry terminal hungry (or thirsty). Well, I suppose there's a reason why ferry fares in *Linda Lines* cost about 50% less than those of the bigger companies.

When you're hungry and thirsty, however, you eat and drink whatever's available. An hour or so later, the check-in counter was opened and we all boarded the ferry.

I mentioned before (I'm pretty sure) how fond I am of water in general, and the sea in particular. Perhaps not coincidentally, I love ferries. My first ever ferry ride was in British Columbia, taking the ferry from Vancouver's lower mainland to Vancouver Island, in the summer of 2002 (before I moved to Canada; it was "just a trip" back then, which happened to be when I originally fell in love with that wonderful country) and I remember it vividly. Here's a negative scan (see the printed date):

Once seated upstairs, I somehow managed to work the on-board Wi-Fi but not for long.

A particularly suspicious individual who happened to be taking the same ferry struck a conversation with Jeroen and myself. I made it clear that I wasn't in the mood for any chit chat as I have much to do; unfortunately, Jeroen wasn't as lucky and was dragged into being endlessly pestered by an individual who clearly had absolutely no conversation skills whatsoever. I excused myself a few times to the ferry's deck, both to avoid that annoying passenger as well as enjoy the view of the water and the cold, revitalizing wind.

As you approach Helsinki, many tiny islands start appearing. I took quite a few shots, generally failing to capture the atmosphere.

Finally arrived in Helsinki. I was very happy to finally be in Helsinki, even though I was planning on spending the minimum amount of time possible in the city.

I met Laura in March 2007, when I was living in Waterloo, Ontario. Waterloo is a students' town; students from all over the world take their studies in one of the two universities there. Laura was one of them. Back then, I rented out a couple of rooms in my house to students, so that's how the connection was made.

I usually wasn't much into establishing friendships with people who cohabitated with me. I have my own life; my circle of friends is small and changes slower than the earth's landmass as it is. Laura, however, was an exception as she struck me as a rather unusual lady. Very quickly, we became very good friends—spent tons of time chatting about all sorts of things, reaching conversational depth that I could rarely reach with others at that time.

I was sad, then, when Laura finished her studies in Waterloo and decided to head back to her native Finland. She came back to Canada (Vancouver this time) while I was busy scorching Europe's railways following Knopfler's Get Lucky tour, and left back to Finland before I decided to move west. In total, then, we haven't seen each other since August 2007.

When the concert in Helsinki was announced, it was time for me to pay an old debt: visiting Finland and have Laura show me around her home town of Hämeenlinna, located about an hour north of Helsinki—which is precisely what I ended up doing.

Arrived at Helsinki's ferry terminal, where Laura and her friend Outi were already waiting. Was great to see them both—hugs, the works. Jeroen headed out to a hotel in the city, and the three of us—Outi, Laura and myself—headed to Laura's car, and drove to Hämeenlinna.

First, of course, we drove circles in the city. Turned out that the city of Helsinki decided to welcome me by calling an impromptu samba party in the city center, resulting in traffic chaos. Took about 20 minutes to find our way out of this mess, during which I got to see some of the city's landscape—clean, tidy, but really nothing way out of the ordinary.

Heading north, though, the scenery changed. Leaving the big city, the landscape took on a lot of green and the terrain became hillier. Even during the ride, I still couldn't believe that I was *actually* headed to Hämeenlinna after all these years.

> If you ever used a computer program named *Sibelius* for transcribing music, then you should know that the program is named after Jean Sibelius—a famous Finnish composer who was born and raised here in Hämeenlinna.

Arrived at Laura's apartment, unloaded everything and the three of us immediately went out again, not before Laura packed a few snacks. Laura, much like myself, is a big fan of nature, so we headed to a nearby place called (take a DEEP breath) Aulangon Luonnonsuojelualue.

A picture I posted on Facebook, showing the view in relatively low resolution (using my phone's camera), turned out to be rather popular. Here's what the view looks like when taken with a proper camera:

A few steps away, there's a tower that you can climb to get a better view of the surrounding area, but it was already too late—it closes at 7:00pm.

"7:00pm?" you might ask; "look at the sky. Isn't it noon?"

No. It's 7:00pm.

The closer you get to either of earth's poles, the more variance you get with respect to daylight vs. darkness hours. The more you're headed north, the longer daylight time is during the summer time of the northern hemisphere (heading towards the south pole, it's the other way around). Finland is, I think, the most "north" that I had ever been before. In Finland's south—that is, the Helsinki area—sunset time on June 8th, 2013 was—are you sitting?—10:40pm. That's just for *sunset*; when the sun sets, it's still not dark. When is it dark during June? well, that depends on what you consider "dark". As far as I'm concerned, it doesn't get completely dark in June (see below).

On the other hand, once winter hits, things turn around: it gets dark (that is, completely dark) very early—as early as 3:00pm (!). The sun hardly ever shines.

Freaky, isn't it? and that's just the *south* of Finland. In the north (for example, in *Lapland*), the situation is more extreme. Around the time of this writing, *it doesn't get dark at all in Lapland*.

HELL. I need to see this. Added to my bucket list: experience Lapland in both the summer *and* the winter.

Drove down the hill into a nearby lake for a very pleasant walk.

It wasn't before 8:30pm or so when we arrived to Laura's apartment again. Next up: dinner. Delicious pasta with a sauce involving avocado bits and other goodies (sounds strange? I know. Try it. It's extraordinarily good), followed by good white wine—excellent.

At around 11:00pm—still light outside, yes?—the three of us headed to a nearby pub. Alcohol consumption is a national sport in Finland: according to Laura, the Finnish are used to drown their misery, resulting from prolonged winters and the accompanied never-ending darkness, in alcohol. Small, cosy pub in the city center—I let the girls drink up while I stuck to my guns and avoided alcohol altogether (that glass of wine after the pasta was more than enough, thank you). We kept on chatting on just about everything for a couple of hours, until the pub became so noisy that we just had to leave.

(I drove.)

(A manual shift. Still got it, apparently.)

It's past midnight already. Looking at the sky—yes, it is obviously darker than before but still not a complete darkness. Dropped Outi at her place (thanks Outi—was great to see you again!) and went back to Laura's apartment, then out again for a walk in the bush conveniently located steps away from the building. Funny, it was about 1:00am when we were walking through that forest and we could still see our way. Here is what it looked like at 1:03am:

Headed back and off to a good night sleep after a perfect day.

June 9th, woke up to a beautiful sun (well, it was there all along anyway), quick breakfast and we went to climb that tower we had missed the day before. Here is what it looks like. Sit tight:

And… a panoramic one (this one you should click):

Mama Nature… I love you.

Afterwards, it was time to bid Laura goodbye. It wasn't pleasant: I dislike bidding people I like farewell.

Thank you, Laura and Outi, for everything, and see you soon in British Columbia!

Booking the Helsinki stay on June 9th—the day of the concert—was tricky: we were looking at a very early (7:15am) flight the next morning, so it made a lot of sense to stay in the airport area. Jeroen's hotel for the preceding night was at the city center, which is south of the airport. Therefore, we made plans to meet somewhere between—well, actually, closer to Helsinki than to Hämeenlinna—and get to the hotel from there. This is a bit scary when you don't have *any* way to communicate with the outside world (for example, if a train is delayed, or something else pops up. My SIM card didn't work *at all* in Finland—not for data, not for voice calls, nothing). Luckily, everything went according to plan and we met in Tikkurila—a short 20 minutes ride north for Jeroen and a 50 minutes ride south for me—and from there, took the bus directly to the hotel: Cumulus Hotel Helsinki Airport.

The main problem with hotels in Helsinki is that they are ridiculously expensive (the same holds for the rest of Scandinavia). A hotel room in the city center can easily cost €250–300 a night (that's $340–400 CDN), and we're talking about a *hotel room*. Outside the city center, prices become more manageable, around the €100 mark.

The Cumulus Hotel provided good value for money, although I didn't get to enjoy much of it. Shortly after checking in, we made our way to the hotel's restaurant for an early dinner (cheapest entree in the venue: a vegetarian dish for about €15. Steaks went for €50–60), and then headed out towards the venue. That required taking a bus, plus walking about a kilometer and a half.

Phew.

The Hartwall Areena (not a misspelling) is a gigantic multi-purpose arena located at the north of Helsinki. It was built to host the Ice Hockey World Championship in 1997 and can seat about 13,000 for a concert.

After picking up the tickets, killed some time in a nearby grassy point enjoying the sun and the perfect weather. Entered the venue about half an hour before the show, and we split up: Jeroen was in charge of buying two bottles of water, and I was in charge of looking for the nearest restrooms. When we finally met at our seats, I was informed that the water wasn't there.

Apparently, this venue allows you to buy water on-site (€3.50 a bottle, thank you very much) *but you are not allowed to bring any drinks to your seat*. Hell. So far, I have encountered venues who wouldn't allow you to carry bottles to your seat (emptying your bottle into a plastic cup instead); I also encountered venues where you may take a bottle with you to your seat, minus the cap (because, apparently, some people are in the habit of throwing full bottles of water onto the stage to express some sort of idiocy). Not allowing to bring *any* liquid in *any* sort of container? that's a first for me. Ridiculous.

Somehow, however, an arrangement was made whereby the cup of water was waiting for me with a venue staff member who agreed to watch it. Headed there, consumed the entire thing on the spot, thanked her for watching over my precious water and headed in for the concert, which started a minute later.

After the sauna-like conditions in the Zwolle concert, it was good to be in a properly air-conditioned, ventilated venue. Band members appeared to be more comfortable with the temperatures being lower than the earth core's, and proceeded to deliver a great concert, featuring a similar set to the preceding one with the exception of *Song for Sonny Liston* replacing *Gator Blood*.

As Mark currently uses *Postcards from Paraguay* to introduce the band, with each band member starting to play right after they are introduced, it is always a challenge for the last two being introduced—John and Mike—to synchronize with the rest of the band and start playing exactly when they're supposed to. This is mostly due to the chords' structure of the repeating intro, which gives John and Mike the opportunity to join on a ~~16~~ 8 bars' interval (in other words: the intro consists of ~~16~~ 8 bars, repeating; John and Mike can only join once an entire ~~16~~ 8 bars sequence is played).

Watching closely, you can see John and Mike using all sorts of facial gestures in order to be in sync and start playing exactly at the right moment. Yesterday, Mike was just about to start playing in entirely the wrong time (at the 8 4 bars' mark), signalling to John. John's response was priceless: a huge smile and an even bigger nod for "hell no, not now".

That was the point when I started laughing uncontrollably for about a minute. One of the funniest incidents I ever witnessed in a concert. At some point, Mike noticed me laughing and started laughing himself, two seconds before he had to play again—sorry Mike, didn't mean to throw you off balance.

It was interesting to witness the difference between the Finnish audience and the Dutch audience from just two nights prior. The audience appeared to love the show and threw much love, hugs and kisses at the band, but even then, you could see that these people are different: more reserved, less expressive.

Remember the *Running of the Bulls*? the concert in Helsinki provided for a new term to be coined: the *Walking of the Swans*. At the beginning of *Telegraph Road*, a few people from the back approached the stage. Slowly, more and more people joined in, almost each one of them looking hesitant. No violence, no running, no pushing, no shoving—all was done beautifully and in good spirit. Thumbs up to the Helsinki audience for being great that way.

Concert ended after slightly less than two hours. Walked back to the bus station—full daylight, again—and hopped on the bus back to the hotel for a very short night.

Signing off this post from the lobby of the HI (Hostelling International) hostel (yes, hostel!) in Hamar. Chose to spend the day-off here—it's always better to get travelling done on a day-off.

Isaac

Wednesday, June 12, 2013

Trouble in Norway...

Just a quick note. Unfortunately, as much as I was looking forward to visit Bergen, things got screwed up and today has been quite hectic so far. Jeroen had to pay a visit to a nearby hospital due to some ear-nose-throat condition (which turned out to be an ear infection; he'll survive and should be OK within a few days, with the aid of some penicillin), which triggered a chain reaction of all sort of things. All will be described in an upcoming blog post which will have to wait another day or so. Sorry I couldn't complete yesterday's post yet.

Isaac

Thursday, June 13, 2013

Helsinki, Finland to Hamar, Norway (June 10-11, 2013)

First thing's first: I recently received a few pictures taken by my friends Lane and Katrina during our time together in London. Good to reminisce... wonderful people:

Getting back to the hotel in Helsinki very late at night, no time was left for anything: the itinerary for the next morning included a flight from Helsinki to Oslo, leaving Helsinki's airport at 7:15am, arriving Oslo at around 8:00am (two hours flight; Finland's time zone is one hour ahead of Norway's). From Oslo's airport, there's a train leaving every hour towards Hamar.

Being constantly on the move hones your skills at packing, unpacking and repacking. It takes time to get adjusted to it, even though the "rules" are simple:

- Don't spread your belongings around the room; concentrate them all in one location.
- Don't unpack anything before you actually need it. Repack it as soon as you're done with it.
- The night before departure, pack as much as you can and also prepare your clothes for the next morning.

These are extremely important when you don't have much time to sleep. It's easier to get logistics done with before going to bed when you're still kind of alert, than getting them done as soon as you wake up when you're still yearning the sensation of your head resting upon a pillow.

This particular hotel had included breakfast starting (get this) 4:00am. By 5:00am, I was already in the dining room transporting edible substances from large containers into small plates. Ate quickly, back to the room, brushed teeth and got my stuff together.

As I was preparing to leave the room, Jeroen was busy checking us in online, through his mobile phone. Eventually, I received an email with a link, saying that this is my "travel document". I opened it and found instructions in Norwegian.

I should mention that I don't understand Norwegian. Also, nobody bothered to ask me whether I understand Norwegian (unless they tried asking me that in Norwegian and I didn't understand, because, again, I don't understand Norwegian).

Saw my name there, with a link. Clicked it and got a barcode, along with further instructions in Norwegian. No way to change the language.

> I think I had written before about how surprised I am to find that people regard software engineers as overly intelligent. However, this industry, of which I have been a part for the last 17 years (formally; informally, around 25 years), doesn't really lack its own population of idiots. It bothers me, to no foreseeable end, that someone in Norwegian Airlines—an airline that actually puts a lot of effort into becoming more and more efficient, yielding most check-in and pre-flight work to the passengers—

thought, at some point, that putting an "English" link is not really necessary. It further bothers me that whoever tested this company's mobile check-in process never actually considered this to be a problem.

Decided to sort this out at the airport. Stormed out to catch the 5:40am shuttle to the airport, which arrived late.

Helsinki's airport was very busy at 6:00am. After being completely confused regarding which line we should be standing in, things were sorted out. Apparently, with Norwegian Airlines, you can't fully check in online if you have any baggage to check. You have to use the special check-in machines located in the terminal.

Security check… as usual, I picked the line that ended up being the slowest. Coffee was skipped as I wasn't willing to pay €5 for coffee that was most likely going to turn out a failure; bite me, Finland. Off to the gate for boarding with no delays.

During check-in, there was an option for better seats so we took it—to adjacent aisle seats. Most passengers were already inside the aircraft when I suddenly heard a deep voice speaking to me in an accent that was so depressing, so condescending and so suspicious that it must have something to do with Russian.

– "YOU WANT TO SIT BY THE WINDOW?"

Interesting. Some people usually begin a conversation with a "hello".

– "No."

– "OOOH. I HATE TO SIT BY THE WINDOW."

– "Me too."

– "OOOH. YOU ARE FROM HERE?"

– "No."

– "OOOH. YOU ARE FROM UNITED STATES?"

I looked at him, squinting, trying to phrase my answer. Thought about it carefully until I came up with the absolute best response, which I conveyed using the most conversation-discouraging tone I could have ever emitted.

– "No."

A friend of the suspicious fellow, an older guy around 60–70 years old, took the window seat and the suspicious guy (who had quite the large figure) took the middle seat, next to me. For the first thirty minutes of the flight, this guy was irritatingly noisy; and by "noisy", I am not referring to him talking, but to all sorts of weird hums and other mutterings. You know that voice—that hum—that you emit when yawning really hard? imagine that, continuously, for thirty minutes, until he decided to cover himself with his jacket and take a nap.

> Note to self: email *Bose*, asking them to add a feature for blocking yawn-induced hums with their next generation of noise-cancelling headphones.

Flight arrived to Oslo almost 30 minutes *ahead* of schedule (how can a two hours flight be shortened by a quarter? beats me. No wind can be that strong. Maybe Philipp can answer?). Luggage quickly collected and made our way to the train station located just beneath the airport, ending up riding a train that left one hour prior to the one we were originally planning.

Norway is considered by many to boast some of the most beautiful natural scenery on the planet, which is another reason why I was happy to get here. The train ride to Hamar takes about an hour; there was a 30 minutes delay somewhere along the way, conveniently right next to this:

So it wasn't a total loss after all. Here and there, I managed to doze off for a few minutes. At around 9:30am, finally arrived to Hamar.

Hamar is a small town located about 130km north of Oslo. Its history dates back to the 11th century: it used to be an important trade center during the Middle Ages, until it was hurt badly by the Black Plague in 1349, along with the rest of Norway (60% of Norway's population was killed by the Black Plague). 200+ years later, most of Hamar's trade was moved to Oslo, and Hamar stopped existing as a town until it was re-founded in the 18th century.

Due to its geography, Hamar is susceptible to floods. A major flood took place here in 1789; few more have occurred since. Actually, only a couple of weeks ago there was a flood in the area, although not even close to the 1789 mayhem.

I did not know any of this before arriving here. As soon as I arrived in Hamar's train station, the following issues felt rather burning:

- I wasn't holding any local currency; must get some cash from an ATM somewhere. Where?
- I was dead tired.
- I was starving.

- My mobile phone had no data connectivity as my SIM card's roaming plan doesn't cover Norway.

    It doesn't cover Sweden or Denmark either. If anyone reading this post is from Sweden or Denmark, perhaps you could tell me which mobile carrier(s) I should go to in order to get a pre-paid SIM with data connection? only data connection matters: I don't make/receive phone calls or text messages.

Located a Seven Eleven nearby; ATM inside. Cash out—done. Next, walked to the hotel—well, actually a *hostel*, belonging to the world famous Hostelling International (HI) federation. It is located about 15 minutes walk from the train station and just across the street from the venue—actually, with the exception of the concert in Temecula, California during the Get Lucky tour, I don't think I ever stayed so close to a Knopfler concert venue.

Upon arriving at the hotel, I went ahead to resolve the other burning issues as Jeroen headed to catch some sleep (unfortunately, Jeroen hasn't been feeling well at all during the last few days. Getting better, though). Miraculously, an electronics store nearby sold SIM cards for a local mobile carrier (*Telenor*)—purchased and I'm a happy camper. Then I went off to a nearby supermarket that also had a cafe on site: ridiculously expensive sandwich (see below) and coffee and I was even a happier camper. As Jeroen decided to stay in the room for the entire day due to his illness, I did some shopping in the supermarket so the Dutchman doesn't starve to death.

Back at the hotel, dropped the groceries and went outside to explore the surroundings. Somehow, I wasn't tired anymore.

Norway is not a part of the European Union. Traditionally, Norwegians have been against joining the European Union for a variety of reasons. Polls are showing that, over time, the sentiments against joining the EU have been almost consistently growing (a poll from July 2012 shown close to 75% against joining).

Norway also maintains its own currency, called *Norwegian Krone* (abbreviated NOK) with the exchange rate currently standing at around 1 NOK per €0.13 / $0.18 CDN / $0.17 US.

> I have a confession to make.
>
> Economics is one of the few subjects that are of special interest for me. When I visit countries—even regions within countries—I always find myself becoming interested in issues such as cost of living, cost of real estate, cost of products / services, taxation, wages and such. Why? I don't know, it's just very interesting to me.
>
> I have only visited Norway once before, during the 2010 Get Lucky tour. Back then, there were only two concerts in Norway—one in Oslo and one in Bergen—plus an unforgettable day-off. From back then, I remembered Norway being ridiculously expensive for the traveller, and was wondering why.
>
> Never got around to do more than a superficial research, though. I attributed the high costs to the fact that taxes in Norway are very high (when taxes are high, business owners often raise prices; they need to make money *somehow*. Also, sales tax here is at 25% in general, with the exception of food which is taxed at 14% and certain travel-related services which are taxed at 8%).
>
> Another thing I kept in mind is everything I heard about Norway being very advanced with respect to the social services provided to residents here. In other words, taxes are indeed high, but residents here get much back from the government in certain ways.
>
> One error I did make, though, was to assume that Norwegians earn a lot of money. It made sense to me: heck, if you are to afford spending $35 on a pizza in a restaurant, you must be bringing quite a lot of cash home every month. Not to mention hotels: hotels in Norway are so ridiculously expensive that, at first, I thought my vision was impaired when I looked at hospitality prices.
>
> I have to thank my friend Philipp Zeller who sent me back to do some research before I assume all sort of things. Norwegians, it turns out, do earn more in relative terms, but not by that much—not enough to justify the whopping difference in the restaurant and hotel prices. Norwegians themselves acknowledge the fact that certain "things" are simply ridiculously expensive—that's how things are and they accept it. Food in restaurants is too expensive? fine—they simply don't dine out as often as people in other countries (notably in the United States and Canada). Hotels are too expensive? fine—they simply don't stay in hotels all too often anyway.
>
> Groceries, for example, aren't that expensive. I bought enough food for two people for one day for the price of just under €20.
>
> To summarize: Norway *is* an expensive country to travel in. Ridiculously expensive, even. But that doesn't have much to do with wages around here: that's simply the way things are, period.

The hostel (and the venue) are located about a kilometer and a half from the town's center. The path to the town's center is surrounded by greenery, and water is almost always in sight.

From the east, the town's center area begins with the central train station:

From there, exploring the area is very easy by foot, simply because it's small. It was around 6:00pm—perhaps a bit more—and almost everything was closed.

Hungry, I was looking for a place to eat. This is tricky if you're on any sort of a budget as restaurants in Norway are ridiculously expensive. A 12" pizza in a restaurant here can easily cost around $30–35, and I'm not talking about a full-on Italian restaurant. Eventually, that pizza was the only sane thing to go for.

It wasn't that good.

Nothing left to do in the city center area, I just walked back to the hostel, taking some more pictures to show off with:

The last picture shows a metal tower, located by the water nearby the venue. Here's what you see from up there:

... And, of course, a couple of panoramic ones:

Nothing very dramatic, but still a natural beauty that, I think, would be better off just left alone.

Next morning—concert day—sun was shining bright over clear blue sky. Fantastic weather, great for exploring some more. Accompanied by an unhealthy Dutchman, I went back to the city center area to see if I missed anything the day before.

Glad I did.

First, just to demonstrate the distance from the hostel to the venue:

Morning view of the hostel. What a quiet, wonderful place:

Took similar pictures to the ones taken the preceding day—only now, the sky were completely blue:

Isaac's "Privateering" Tour Blog 117

Stopped for a morning snack at a local bakery. That was one of the weirdest bakery experiences I could recall. Food was very good, coffee was very good, but something was missing… the bakery smell. It didn't smell at all like a bakery, even though fresh goodies were constantly brought in from the back. Very strange.

Kept on walking and then reached the waterfront. Fantastic walk.

At some point, came across this:

This monument shows the water levels during Hamar's more serious floods. See the top one: July 24, 1789. Can you imagine? water as high as this?

Steps away, came across this:

This is a result of the more recent flood that took place here, just a couple of weeks ago (to my knowledge). Either that, or some morons found a really stupid way to pass the time.

Came across further evidence to the flood that took place here recently:

See this island? see the benches on it? well, it's not really an island. This piece of land can usually be accessed by a narrow strip of land —you can notice how the "island" slowly fades into nothing at the right hand side of the picture (the shore is a few meters further to the right; unfortunately it wasn't captured in this photograph).

Terrible. Just terrible. Well, I suppose that's what happens when people screw around with Mother Nature: Mother Nature strikes back. Global warming still occurs, and governments still don't seem like giving a crap. What prompts mankind to shoot itself in the foot... that I'll never understand.

That's not the world I was hoping to live in.

Finding a place for lunch took some walking, as no place seemed quite "right". Eventually we settled for a good Italian restaurant in the city center. Tasty, good food—unfortunately, Jeroen couldn't enjoy much of it as he has lost some of his sense of taste due to his illness.

Back to the hotel to bide the time before the concert.

The concert venue for Hamar is the *Hamar Olympic Hall*, but is usually referred to by the name *Vikingskipet* ("The Viking Ship") for its design.

This venue was designed to serve as the speed skating rink for the 1994 Winter Olympics, not before raising some uproar due to the decision to build it in an area that was (and still is) included in an international treaty for the conservation of wetlands.

This venue is huge: it can seat up to 20,000 (!) for concerts. For this particular concert, the venue was arranged in a rather unusual way —the stage was set up along the longer edge of the venue, rather than the shorter one; huge, vast space to the left and to the right.

I tried taking a panoramic photo to capture how huge this venue is:

The concert started a few minutes past schedule. The lights went out but the venue was still pretty lit because it was full daylight outside, and rays of sun made their way inside through a few windows that remained unsealed. Similar set to the usual, except for the much-awaited return of *Kingdom of Gold* and the less awaited (well, I have my own taste) *Gator Blood*.

The beginning of *Privateering* is when Mark usually interacts with the audience. This time, he went ahead to inform the audience that they live in a beautiful country (indeed, they do), suggesting that the Norwegians are keeping it secret (may be true; otherwise, mankind would probably find a way to screw it up).

Another comic relief was provided at the beginning of *I Used to Could*, as Mark started strumming his guitar but something appeared to have been missing in the guitar's tone. Then he stopped playing. "Did you like it?" he asked, to the sound of cheers. He then hinted something towards the right hand side of the stage—I'm guessing he was referring to the crew—and within a few seconds everything went back to normal.

Another mishap took place at the beginning of *Marbletown*, when Richard's amp seemed to not be making any sound, triggering a swift response by the crew; issue was resolved before anyone noticed.

The audience here is typically reserved and polite (so I have been told, and so I have witnessed in the Norway concerts during the last tour). Still, many times, people just found a reason to move from one side of the stage to another, holding cameras, taking photographs… rarely, if ever, pissing anybody off. It was all done in good spirit, nobody seemed to mind. People were also gathering in the aisles during some songs, for good photo-ops.

> I was once thinking to myself—what makes people take so many photographs during a concert? forget the discussion about whether it is annoying or not; distracting or not; useful or not.
>
> Consider a hypothetical venue that provides an interesting service—top-of-the-line professional photographers taking pictures during the show using bleeding-edge equipment; at the end, all photographs are provided to the audience completely free of charge. Would that prompt concertgoers to stop taking photographs?
>
> My guess is a solid strong "no".
>
> The reason people take photographs during concerts has very little to do with the end result (the picture), and much to do with the actual process (taking the picture) and—more than anything else— the senses of belonging and ownership. They want a photograph that *they* took. When they look at that photograph years from now, they don't want to remember getting that photograph from someone else: instead, they want to reminisce the actual situation of holding up a camera and pressing the shutter.
>
> What motivates people to do what they do has always been a fascinating subject for me.

Something very peculiar happened during *Haul Away*. Mark was busy focusing on John playing, when a lady approached the stage holding a paper. She put the paper on the stage and went back to her seat. I am not entirely sure that Mark noticed where that paper came from, but once he noticed it, he approached it, being evidently rather annoyed. He then proceeded to slide the paper away from the stage using his foot. That took a few attempts (it's rather tricky to do, let alone when you're busy performing in front of thousands of people), but at the end, the paper found its rightful destiny—the floor.

Some *other* lady later approached the stage and took the paper away.

Strange. I suggest the next one will try their luck by placing not a paper, but something more interesting. Like a book.

Telegraph Road, as usual, concluded the first part of the show—not before a few people from the audience started approaching the stage right before the outro solo. Similar to how it was done in Helsinki, there was no violence involved whatsoever. Nobody (that I could see) was running, pushing or squeezing anyone. Everything seemed to have been done in good spirit.

I should say, though, that once the audience got up, the show started becoming a blast. Beautiful *Telegraph Road* outro followed by the usual encore of *So Far Away* and *Piper to the End*, played in front of an exceptionally receptive audience.

The concert concluded just about two hours after it started. The venue being so huge and spacious, it didn't take too long for people to leave; five minutes later, I was already at the hotel.

Tried to do some writing in the hotel's garden, when I was approached by a group of local Knopfler aficionados who somehow recognized me. Lost some writing time but gained some good socializing time with nice people. Thanks fellas for coming to say hello, and see you later in the tour.

Signing off this post the hostel room in Bergen, Norway. Today was supposed to be a good, easy day of exploring one of the most beautiful cities I have come across; instead, it turned into a nightmare. More on that in the next post.

Yawn. (A quiet one.)

Isaac

Saturday, June 15, 2013

Hamar to Bergen to Stavanger, Norway (June 12-13, 2013)

I have very fond memories of Bergen, as I had spent two days in that eye-candy of a city back in during the 2010 Get Lucky tour. For the three years after that marvellous day-off in Bergen, almost exactly three years ago, the name "Bergen" was engraved in my mind and soul right next to these:

No wonder, then, that I was *really* eager to get to Bergen. I could already see myself take the funicular up to that mountain again—a dear reader who answers to the name Lars has, in his kindness, provided me with the exact name of that viewpoint so I can look it up on the map (last time, I came across that funicular completely by accident and just took it)—it's called Ulriken 643.

The flight out of Oslo airport was scheduled to leave at 10:40am. The train from Hamar to Oslo leaves every round hour, and takes an hour to get there. Nobody wanted to take risk of any train delays so, instead of taking the planned 8:01am train, we ended up taking the 7:03am one, knowing that, if everything's going according to plan, we'd have almost three hours of wait in Oslo's airport.

That's fine. I just wanted to get to Bergen.

Of course, no train delays whatsoever and we ended up in Oslo's airport right on time. Busy airport. Armed with knowledge of how Norwegian Airlines expects people to check in themselves (after the nonsense that took place the day before), checking in went like a breeze and it was time to kill two hours in the airport.

I was tired. Very tired. To make the 7:03am train, I had to wake up at 5:30am, as there's about 20 minutes walk from that hostel in Hamar to Hamar's train station. I managed to doze off for a few minutes here and there while on the train—actually, I was half asleep when the train's announcer announced the Oslo airport stop (and I'm pretty sure Jeroen was passed out as well), which could have been rather problematic—but still, I missed the sensation of a long, good night sleep on a mattress.

Time passed slowly, flight left on time and arrived earlier than planned. Interestingly enough, a similar thing happened a couple of days earlier, again with Norwegian Airlines—arriving almost 30 minutes before schedule. I'm wondering if they're trying to impress anybody.

Welcome to Bergen.

So, after three years of bearing Bergen in my memory as the representation of everything that is beautiful about sunny weather and beautiful nature, it finally dawned upon me that Bergen is actually rainy. *Very rainy*. The average annual rainfall there is 2,250mm (89 inches). Hence, my three years old experience in Bergen—two sunny days in a row—was actually a complete miracle.

Upon arrival, taking the bus to the city center, it was still dry. Roads were busy, and it took about 30 minutes until arrived at the hotel for the night—Citybox Bergen.

The Citybox hotel is located a couple of blocks away from where things start getting interesting in the city center. Last tour, I stayed in a hostel high up on a mountain, which was very good as far as peace & tranquility were concerned, but rather mediocre with respect to facilities—which is why I was willing to get rid of a few more dollars to stay in the city center area. Another reason was that the venue for this tour was also located in the city center (the 2010 venue was very far away).

A bit of a rough-looking environment but still definitely manageable. Checked in, put the luggage down and prepared to leave towards the city center.

– "I can't hear anything through my left ear", I heard stereophonically.

I remember what it is to be sick while following a tour. For me, this happened during the 2010 Get Lucky tour, as I was leaving Budapest towards Italy. I remember waking up quite off that morning, and my situation worsened; by the time I got to Italy (long train ride that day), I was sick like a dog. As my illness progressed, I lost my senses of smell and taste. Luckily, this all happened during a five days break in the tour, and I happened to have my friends Daria and Valeria—the two beloved Italian sisters from northern Italy—to take good care of me.

Being sick is terrible.

Being sick away from home is worse.

Being sick while you're following a busy concert tour, then, is a bloody nightmare. If whatever they're saying about Satan is true, this must be how Satan punishes people he *really* dislikes. It's a huge physical and mental challenge.

This time, it wasn't me who was sick, though. Jeroen has been feeling ill ever since the day we departed Delft towards Zwolle, a week ago; what started as a cold because more and more severe. As we landed in Bergen's airport, the Dutchman realized his hearing turned mono, which meant that perhaps it was about time to do something about it.

The first guess was that we're talking about an earwax build-up. Out of the hotel to the city center for some lunch, some wax dissolver was purchased, and was attempted during lunch—to no avail. Rightfully concerned, the Dutchman decided to seek medical help; for tourists, it seemed at that point (not sure if it's fully correct) that a hospital's emergency room is the only option (in Canada, it is possible for anybody to step into any walk-in medical clinic). Decided to keep in touch as our ways were split and I headed to the city center.

Bergen's city center is very pretty, featuring beautiful coloured buildings with the background of magnificent green-rich mountains. Tourism is a major source of income to the city of Bergen, and to my taste, they took it a bit too far as the city center seems, at times, overdone. This reminds me of the town of Banff, Alberta in the Canadian Rockies: Stunning natural setting, stunning everything—but so touristic that I can't spend more than two days there without wanting to leave. That's why Jasper (also in Alberta, also in the Canadian Rockies) is my favourite spot—underdeveloped, beset by second-to-none, wild natural beauty.

When exploring Bergen's city center, you are bound to, eventually, hit the harbour. Bergen's harbour is one of the main point of interests in the city, for locals and tourists alike. It provides for postcard-like scenery of colourful houses, beautiful mountains and, of course, water partly hidden by marine vessels of all sorts.

At that day, there happened to be a food market thing going on in the harbour. All sorts of foods—mostly seafood—sold on plastic plates to passer byers.

Walking back, I was contemplating whether I should be going to the *Ulriken 643* funicular. Considering the cloudy weather (expected to rain), the time it'd take to get there and back, and the fact that I was very tired, I decided to pass; instead, I decided to head back to the hotel to catch some sleep.

Once at the hotel, my desire to sleep had a short battle with my desire to write, which meant that I kept awake a little longer—long enough to notice a message from Jeroen saying that he's still in line for medical treatment with no particular expectation of how long it was going to get. Plus, as he's been having problems with his ear, we decided that it would be worth the while to at least check whether it's feasible to make the next days' travel without flying.

On top of everything, the tickets for the Bergen's concert were under Jeroen's name, which meant that none of us could attend the concert unless the Dutchman was present on site.

That's a lot to deal with when you're tired, about six hours before the concert. I let go of any desire to do anything else and switched into focus mode.

Jarle and Kay, two nice fellows from Norway whom I had met just the day before after the concert in Hamar, were saying, that same morning (we met at the airport as well), that they would be taking a ferry from Bergen to Stavanger. I recall feeling utterly frustrated: as we were planning the tour's itinerary, we overlooked the option of taking a ferry and instead opted for an early 7:00am flight, which was both much less convenient *and* more expensive.

Fortunately, there were still seats available on that ferry (though not very cheap). Kept an eye on those, while looking for non-air travel option for the day after (Stavanger, Norway to Gothenburg, Sweden): no luck there. The only way to travel between these two cities and still make it to the concert is by air, at least from Stavanger to Stockholm (and then a train connection to Gothenburg is possible).

At the meantime, a few emails were sent asking to change the name under which the tickets were registered, so I could pick them up ahead of time.

That being done, I grabbed my stuff and headed back to the city center. My tasks: find out where exactly the next day's ferry was leaving from (in the rush of things, I couldn't quite get it from the ferry company's website); find out about their cancellation policies (if we decide to take a flight after all); and pick up the tickets.

Of course, once I arrived to where I *thought* the ferry terminal was, I noticed that it was vacant. One security officer on site, behind a glass window. When I asked him where the ferry to Stavanger is leaving from, he looked at me with a big smile reserved specifically for the cases when one looks upon another human being with extreme mercy. "It's on the other side of the harbour", he said, pointing at a location about 25 minutes walk away.

It rained.

Decided that I don't care much about cancellation policies anymore, and headed to the venue to pick up the tickets. Fortunately, the name change took place and within a few minutes I was on my way back to the hotel, not before verifying the show's start time (originally 7:30pm; then, an email sent out by *markknopfler.com* said 9:00pm; and the ticket office at the venue said 8:30pm).

> I'd like to thank Mark's management team dearly for helping out in resolving the ticket pickup issue in such
> a short notice. Hats off to you, folks. Love you all to pieces.

On my way back to the hotel, I got a message from the Dutchman saying that he's on his way back to the hotel. Figuring the poor fellow might be hungry, I stopped by a bakery to grab some food. Fifteen minutes walk and it was good to be in a dry place again.

The diagnosis ended up being an ear infection that started in one ear and was now spreading to the other. That's the thing about ear-nose-throat illnesses—things start in one location and then spread all over the place. With the aid of penicillin, we should have a healthy Dutchman within a few days.

The concert in Bergen was a general admission one; *markknopfler.com* organized ticket buyers with early entry starting 5:30pm or so. The day was already very tiring and therefore it was decided to skip the early entry altogether and enter the venue a few minutes before show time. At around 8:00pm, we made our way back to the city center.

The venue, Bergenhus Festning ("Bergenhus Fortress"), is located right by the harbour. It dates back to the 13th century—when Bergen used to be Norway's capital—and contained a royal residence, churches and a monastery. Nowadays, the fortress is under the command of Norway's Navy, which might explain why uniformed soldiers were seen hanging around the place during the concert. The area appears to be beautiful and very interesting—that is, when it is not infested with loads of food stands, alcohol stands, an impromptu seating area for consuming said food and alcohol, and—of course—millions of people. Wish I had the time to explore this fortress in normal conditions. Maybe next time.

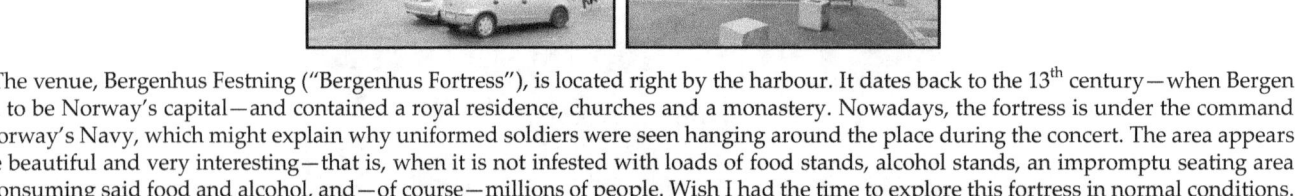

Arriving late, a decision was made to simply stand in the very back, leaning against the fences and enjoy the concert from a distance. The disadvantage of distance is offset by the advantage of better sound, and better freedom to walk around listening to the music. This venue being outdoors probably prompted the resurrection of *Cleaning My Gun* and the omission of *Haul Away*; in general, the set was more on the rocking side this time.

It rained occasionally—well, not really "rained"; more like "drizzled"—but people didn't seem to be very concerned about it. I learned my lesson from last tour's concerts in Helsingborg, Sweden and Middelfart, Denmark and came prepared with my rain jacket which turned an otherwise annoying experience to a pleasant one.

The audience—those who stood close to the stage as well as those who stood afar—loved the show; people were seen dancing (by themselves or with others) and having a good time regardless of the weather. When you live in a city where it rains most of the year, I suppose rain is seen as yet another "thing" you get used to so it doesn't really annoy you anymore.

Being standing in the far back was a good change. Not that I would like to spend too many concerts located so far from the action, but once in a while, I'm perfectly fine being far off the crowdedness. Of course, that also depends on the city I'm in: the more there is to explore around town, the less I am likely to opt spending hours over hours at the venue just to catch a good spot against the stage—many, *many* people deserve it more than I do as, for me, there's always a concert the next day.

In other, boring places, I might just show up early and enjoy the concert from the front.

We'll see.

Concert ended shortly before 11:00pm. Quick walk back to the hotel, hoping for a better day to come.

It didn't. Thursday morning, the Dutchman woke up reporting that he feels worse than the day before. Great. Well, at least we didn't have to wake up at 4:30am to catch the 7:00am flight to Stavanger; instead, woke up at 6:30am and by 7:30am we were at the harbour, waiting for the ferry.

The ferries from Bergen to Stavanger (as well as a few other routes) are operated by a company named Norled, offering—among others—trips around the famous Norwegian fjords. The particular ferry taken to Stavanger, though, doesn't go near any fjord. Four hours ride in a ferry where it's impossible to visit the deck—and even if you could, you'd rather not as it was raining most of the time.

Long, boring ferry ride was spent in repeated attempts to fall asleep and repeated failures in doing so, due to the particularly uncomfortable seats which wouldn't recline. An hour left to the journey, I somehow decided to see what it'd be like to sit in one of the seats in the middle, rather than by the window. Turns out that the seats located in the middle of the ferry are much more comfortable than the ones by the windows, and, hell, they even recline!

It'd be very helpful if there were signs on the ferry telling people "for ridiculous, uncomfortable seats, please turn towards the window. For a much more pleasant ride, seat your ass anywhere else on this ferry. Welcome aboard".

Arrived at Stavanger at around 12:30pm.

Stavanger is the third largest city in Norway. Like Bergen, it is located in the country's west. Located on a peninsula, Stavanger dates back to the early 12th century. Wooden, coloured houses are aplenty; these houses, located mainly in the city center, are protected and considered a part of Stavanger's heritage. For that reason, there is not much building opportunity left in the old city area—leading to the city's growing population settling outside that area, further increasing the landmass of what's considered "Greater Stavanger".

Norway itself can't be considered a "poor country" by any reasonable mean. Even within Norway, though, Stavanger is considered a wealthy city. This is not surprising as Stavanger is dubbed the "Oil Capital of Norway": the oil industry is what drives the city's economy, which makes me think what would happen once mankind finally ends torturing Mother Nature and becomes independent of this commodity.

Rich city… expensive city… and as such, hotel choices were limited. Originally, I booked the Myhregaarden Budget Apartments, which is owned and operated by the Myhregaarden Hotel. The hotel is located about a kilometer away from the apartments, and as checking in must be done there, we went to the hotel.

The hotel is located in an absolutely fantastic location, right in the old city area and less than five minutes walk from the ferry terminal. A stroke of luck came in the form of a particularly nice receptionist who actually offered to switch our booking so we stay in the hotel instead. Four thumbs up. The hotel also offers 24 hours coffee/tea, great comfortable rooms, free breakfast, free light supper and an exceptionally helpful staff. Oh, gas fireplaces as well. If you happen to be in Stavanger, stay in this hotel.

First order of business: lunch.

Wandering the beautiful narrow streets of the old city, a couple of potentially good restaurants turned out to be closed. By chance, came across a Thai restaurant by the simple, straightforward name "Thai Cuisine". This place, currently ranked #8 in Stavanger by *TripAdvisor*, provides excellent food for surprisingly reasonable prices. A large plate of Pad Thai and the world seemed to be smiling again.

Being very tired due to the rush of the past couple of days, I took a painful decision and decided to go to for an afternoon sleep instead of exploring this pretty city. It's a shame; this city *is* beautiful. I think I'll visit again at some point.

Afternoon sleep proved to do wonders. Woke up full of energy, tiredness went away as if it never existed. Dressed up and off to the concert, not before sipping some mediocre coffee in a nearby cafe.

Close to the old city area, there is a very pretty park called *Byparken* ("City Park"):

On the other side of this beautiful pond, Stavanger's central station is located, from where many buses take you to the *DNB Arena*. Boarded a bus and within 10–15 minutes we arrived at the venue, bypassing lots of cars that were struggling to find parking nearby.

The venue, DNB Arena, is a ice hockey rink located south west of the city center. It is less than one year old, owned by the Stavanger Oilers (a ice hockey team) with the naming rights owned by DNB, which is a Norwegian bank.

The venue can seat around 6,000 for concerts, as 4,500 are seated and about 1,500 more are standing. The standing, general admission area was on the rink itself. When planning the tour, we consistently preferred to sit in venues that offer seating, and the DNB Arena was no exception. Hence, we were seated somewhere on the side, first row above the rink. Sound was so-so, but again, these deviations from floor area seating give you yet another way to enjoy a concert.

Good concert, featuring a set that has been played before with no special surprises. As usual, I was watching Mike & John trying to synchronize their entry into *Postcards from Paraguay*; Mike decided to start early—about a second after Mark finished the introductions—

while John preferred to wait for those 8 bars to finish. Alas, when one plays, the other must join: that resulted in John jumping forward towards the microphone in order to make it in time. Funny moment. These two crack me up each time.

Mark seemed to have started *I Used to Could* before Richard was even ready, which prompted Mark to stop and restart, to the sound of roaring cheers.

Altogether a good show, ended within two hours; back to the bus station, long wait and off to the hotel.

Signing off this post from the hotel room in Gothenburg, Sweden. Re-reading the text above, I noticed the slight negative tone of it all. Well, it's been quite hectic here for the last few days. Fortunately, things appear to be picking up now. Should be an easy day today, and easier tomorrow and there are *NO MORE FLIGHTS PLANNED FOR ME FOR ABOUT A MONTH*, Praise the Lord.

Isaac

Saturday, June 15, 2013

Stavanger, Norway to Gothenburg, Sweden (June 14, 2013)

Stavanger to Gothenburg… finally.

I was looking forward to this.

Not because I was so eager to get out of Stavanger (I wasn't), and not because I was so eager to arrive at Gothenburg (I wasn't).

The reason I was looking for this day was that, after this day, there would be no more flights in the itinerary until some time in mid-July; and after so many flights so far this month, I was eager to get the last flight (well, two; short layover in Stockholm) over and done with and start making use of trains again.

Woke up at 6:00am. Quick morning arrangements. 6:30am—breakfast at the hotel. To ensure arrival at the airport on time, breakfast had to be done with by 6:54am, as the shuttle to the airport was scheduled to leave 6:55am.

Stavanger is a beautiful city. Its airport is located in Sola, about 10km away, and even the ride to the airport gives you the right dose of green. Something in Stavanger makes me want to revisit it in the future. I may.

The flight was scheduled to leave 8:50am. Plenty of time to spend over coffee. Found this coffee bar in the terminal's lower level, offering good yogurts and mediocre coffee for prices that only make sense in Norway.

An hour or so were efficiently killed until departure, which commenced on time. The aircraft was of the smaller ones: one column of one seat; an isle; and one column of two seats per row. Altogether three seats per row, and about 20–30 of them. It's a Saab 2000, operating on turboprop.

I dislike turboprop aircrafts with passion. Rides tend to be bumpy, and this time, it surely was. I was happy to be done with it.

An hour and a half later, arrived at Stockholm's airport.

The first thing you see when you leave the aircraft and enter Stockholm airport's Terminal 5 is a puppet display of *ABBA*, which is (still) considered one of Sweden's major contributions to the world of music.

Apparently, Stockholm's airport is a sponsor of the ABBA Museum, which opened in Stockholm just about a month ago.

The layover was for just an hour; however, as we were flying from a different country and our end destination was in Sweden, we were supposed to actually exit the secured area and go through security again. Actually, that's how it works in every country (that I had the chance visiting): if you're flying from airport X to airport Z through airport Y, and airports Y & Z are in the same country (which is different from the country in which airport X is located), then your luggage *may* make it all the way to airport Z but you, yourself, must go through security again in airport Y.

Unfortunately, as much as it made sense, we forgot all about it and were therefore rather annoyed to find ourselves outside the secured area, having to go through security again with only 25 minutes left to departure. In Stockholm's airport, check-in is done at the ground level, and there's a set of stairs leading to the second level, where security screening is being done. The line-up to security stretched all the way through the stairs and to about 20 meters beyond.

Needless to say, I was stressed. A backup plan was already prepared (it is possible to get from Stockholm to Gothenburg via train; 3 hours, direct), at least I had that. Still, missing that flight would cause a chain reaction about baggage handling (if you check into a flight but neglect to actually board, your luggage must be ejected from the aircraft. That's not done in order to make your life easier; it's done as a security precaution) and I really didn't want to mess around with that.

At the bottom of the staircase, a sign said "Waiting time from this point on: 5 minutes". Looking up, I concluded that there was no way in bloody hell that all of those people could go through security in 5 minutes. To my amazement, though, they did. The continuing flight to Gothenburg was already boarding when we arrived at the gate.

An hour later, we safely arrived at Gothenburg's airport. It certainly looked like a tiny airport—heck, the domestic terminal's baggage claim area has *one* (!) baggage belt—which is why I was surprised, reading about that airport later, that it's actually the *second busiest* airport in Sweden (after Stockholm's). More careful reading showed that it's the international terminal there which gets most of the traffic.

No train station at the airport; instead, a shuttle bus takes you to Gothenburg's city center for about 100 SEK.

> Sweden is a part of the European Union, but does not use the Euro currency. The local currency is called *Swedish Krona*, abbreviated as *SEK*. Current exchange rates: 1 SEK = €0.12 / $0.16 US / $0.16 CAD.

Bus, loaded with people; poor ventilation; nightmare. Traffic condition on the highway leading to Gothenburg's city center prompted the driver to take an alternate route, prolonging the ride and shortening my will to live. Was as happy as a man can be when I left that stupid bus, right in the city center.

Welcome to Gothenburg.

The city of Gothenburg (written as *Göteborg* in Swedish, and pronounced *yuo-te-bor*; although, the city actually has two formal names —"Gothenburg" being the foreign one and "Göteborg" being the domestic one. Both are in use) is the second largest city in Sweden, and located at the country's west. About half a million call Gothenburg home, with another half a million living in the immediate surrounding area.

The city is famous for its universities—primarily the University of Gothenburg—as well as for the various famous events hosted there on an annual basis such as the Gothenburg International Film Festival.

The main avenue in Gothenburg is called Kungsportsavenyen, stretching for about one kilometer right in the city center. That's where most of the nightlife action in Gothenburg takes place as that avenue (typically referred to simply as "The Avenue") is absolutely loaded with businesses catering to people who are hungry, people who are thirsty, people who feel like dancing and people who want to do pretty much anything except for being at home.

The hotel for the night was Hotel Poseidon, located at the city center, a short walk from The Avenue. Great location. Quick check-in and went to the room, unloaded everything and off to grab something to eat.

Walking by the University of Gothenburg en route to the #1 rated Gothenburg restaurant according to *TripAdvisor*, I realized that Gothenburg is, while not as eye-candy-ish as Bergen or Stavanger, still a pretty neat place. A few cafes encountered along the way but were skipped as my mind was set on trying some Italian food.

Alas, it was closed, as well as some other restaurants we tried around. Starving, we just went inside the first cafe unfortunate enough for me to pass by: Cafe Garbo, ranked #316 in Gothenburg and I have no idea why. All food there is made on site, tasty food, very cheap (possibly because it's located right across the street from the university), great service.

Massive lunch consisting of all sorts of healthy materials, and back to the hotel to try completing the previous post. It was then when I realized that the hotel's Wi-Fi sucks in levels rarely before seen. That was very frustrating. It was already time to head out for a pre-show coffee; figuring that waiting around for the Wi-Fi connection to just work out of nowhere would be a terrible way to use my time, I turned my computer off and headed out to the street.

My friend James Morris from the UK decided to make it to a few concerts in Scandinavia. He was mentioning that he "knows a good coffee shop in Gothenburg so let's meet there". I obliged. Only later it occurred to me that James doesn't even drink coffee, and that by "good coffee shop" he referred to "a coffee shop that is good", rather than to "a shop of good coffee". Fortunately (for him, more than for anyone else), the place ended up serving really good desserts and excellent coffee. It's called *Frank's Coffee & Co*, located just off Kungsportsavenyen. Go there.

Minutes to 7:00pm, it was time to wrap things up and head to the venue, located a few minutes walk south on Kungsportsavenyen.

No better driver to the invention of "copy & paste" exists in this world, than the word *Kungsportsavenyen*.

The venue was called Trädgårdsföreningen and I hope nobody ever puts a gun to my head demanding that I pronounce it correctly. This long word means "Garden Society of Gothenburg"; it is a park, dating back to 1842 and boasting a rose garden, a few restaurants and cafes.

markknopfler.com provided a street address of where the venue's ticketing office was. At least on Google Maps, that address made absolutely no sense at all. Ticket pick-up was actually done inside the venue—a few steps past the main entrance.

The tickets were under my name. A gorgeous Swedish lady looked at my ID with a big smile.

– "Oh, you came all the way from Canada for this?"

I was contemplating whether I should tell her exactly what it was that I had been doing lately, and then proceed to ask her what she was doing in life, her dreams, aspirations, objectives, willingness to immigrate to Canada and, of course, marital status—but instead opted at emitting an incredibly pathetic smile accompanied by an even more incredibly pathetic "Yes".

From the entrance, it's a short walk to the area where concerts take place; "short", that is, if you happen to be by yourself rather than surrounded by millions of people. On your way, the first notable scene one comes across is what I call the *PTA*—*P*ortable *T*oilet *A*rena—a large square consisting mostly of those blue portable toilet bins I grew to hate ever so passionately during the 2010 Get Lucky tour.

Amidst those, there stood a few of those infamous unobstructed urinals. I have only seen this stupendously horrid construct once before —in Nijmegen, The Netherlands, four years ago in a Coldplay concert—and the memories still haunt me. These are, effectively, plastic-made poles, where males can simply stand and urinate against. Each such pole serves three or four, depending on the number of dividers.

Obviously, I couldn't take a photograph of this. I mean, I could, but that might have been perceived offensive by certain people. Therefore, in order to better explain what I refer to, I drew this sophisticated diagram that shows how this construct looks like from above:

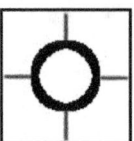

I am not entirely sure that a planet where such urinals exist is a planet in which I'd like to spend most of my time.

The concert was a standing, general admission one. *markknopfler.com* ticket buyers received access to a special area called *Golden Circle*. The *Golden Circle* was a fenced area at the front of the stage: general public could not get access to that area. In addition, *markknopfler.com* buyers received special "early entry" access to the Golden Circle, so they could catch a place right in front of the stage earlier than all other people who got Golden Circle access. Of course, that meant arriving even earlier to the venue (at around 5:30pm, before the general public is allowed entry)—a proposition that I wouldn't even consider in a beautiful city such as Gothenburg.

Still, arriving shortly after 7:00pm, we got pretty good spots within that Golden Circle—not before each of us was made to wear a fancy wristband.

The weather was good at the early evening: sunny, some clouds, slightly cold wind that was generally harmless as there were lots of people around. At 7:25pm—the scheduled start time—the stage wasn't even completely set up yet, which raised some concerns as there's a limit to how long I can be standing up without starting to question life, universe and everything.

(The stage's top, by the way, wasn't round; it was flat. What you see is a distortion resulting from how I took the panoramic picture. I just included it here because it looks so peculiar.)

Not much of a delay, though. Concert started about 15 minutes past schedule as the band took the stage, evidently a bit concerned of the wind (there was no curtain behind the stage to block the wind from circulating around).

Concerts performed standing audiences tend to be more rhythmic and exciting than concerts performed against seated ones. This concert wasn't an exception as we ended up receiving a dose of rhythm with a set identical to the one played just a few days before in Bergen— also a standing venue.

Good concert, during which it was evident that certain band members were experiencing some cold. Crew members were seen hanging around with jackets, as well as bringing other jackets to the stage area—possibly as an option for band members so they could pick some up if the cold becomes exceedingly annoying.

In the audience—at least in the Golden Circle—the cold wasn't felt much.

Another consequence of having an outdoor concert in a northern country during the summer is that light works really don't add much as they are barely noticeable at all. The only times when you would realize that light works actually take place were if you happened to look at the stage's ceiling or look at other surfaces, such as the guitars. See here:

I thought Mark would just give in to the cold after *Father and Son*—

—which he didn't. The concert, however, wasn't affected at all by the temperature: good guitar riffs—and whoever here plays guitar, should know how difficult it is to play in a cold environment; good tempo; great receptive audience... everything combined into one tasty experience. Lots of fun.

During *Speedway at Nazareth*, I was caught doing this:

Good *Telegraph Road* solo, a break…

And for the encore, apparently it was already too cold for some people.

Someone was asking for a pick.

Concert ended and it was time to head out. Took about 20 minutes to leave that park, partly due to the fact that the pathways are narrow but mostly because people simply took their time, walking slowly and holding everyone else hostage. Once out, we went back to Frank's Coffee & Co for a post-concert snack.

Back at the hotel for a mediocre night sleep.

Signing off this post from the hotel room in Malmö, Sweden. Starving. Going hunting for food.
Isaac

Monday, June 17, 2013

Gothenburg to Malmö, Sweden to Copenhagen, Denmark (June 15-16, 2013)

On Saturdays, there are direct trains from Gothenburg to Malmö every two hours in forty minutes past the hour (7:40am, 9:40am and so forth). Slightly more than a three hours ride, I wasn't exactly in the mood to catch the 7:40am one (I have been waking up early every morning for the past week, thank you), and the 11:40am one would mean not enough time to rest in Malmö before the show, so 9:40am it is.

All of these things—resting time; distance from train station to the hotel; distance from the hotel to the venue; dining time; dining location (hotel? train station? anywhere else—where?) and so many more—are the things that make planning such a journey so challenging. When you use public transport, you give up a lot of independence; unlike following a tour in North America, when you can simply take the next highway exit in order to feed yourself, here everything needs to be planned out carefully otherwise you get into obnoxious situations (hunger, thirst, tiredness).

It's hard to do, all of that planning.

Anyway, sunny beautiful morning in Gothenburg, and I wished I could have stayed. Alas, Knopfler et al had different plans, so shortly after 9:00am I was already walking towards Gothenburg's central railway station, accompanied by a slowly recovering Dutchman and our friend James who flew from the UK to catch a few concerts in Scandinavia.

Took the time to take a few photographs, now that the sun was dominating the sky:

Into the train station and boarded the 9:40am train which left right on time.

Tired, I did my best to fall asleep in the train—to no avail. I am one of those people who can't possibly sleep unless lying down: the occasional five minutes nap is possible, but not much more than that. Flying to my home country involves being airborne for about 18 hours each direction; I have done that route many times in the past and still can't bring myself to get a good sleep.

(No. Never tried sleeping pills, and never will.)

Arrived at Malmö a few minutes before 1:00pm.

I was a bit anxious.

The city of Malmö is the third largest city in Sweden, located at the country's south western tip. It dates back to the 13th century, as it was founded… in Denmark. The city was under Danish possession until the 17th century, when a treaty was signed to end the Second Northern War.

As its economy was based mostly on manufacturing and shipbuilding, the Swedish economy's recession in the mid-1970's—severely hitting such industries—started a chain reaction that eventually led many residents (about 14% of the population) to leave the city for its suburbs. Another country-wide financial crisis—now in the 1990s—hit Malmö very hard resulting in massive job losses in the city.

Towards the end of the 1990s, Malmö started regaining some of its past glory, much thanks to the construction of the Øresund Bridge, connecting Malmö with Copenhagen, Denmark.

> NOTE: This is my own personal blog, and does not aim to please anyone in particular. Whatever is written in the following paragraphs represents my own opinion which may well differ from yours. At any rate, I'll be happy to stand corrected and learn more, if you have some interesting information to share.

The first time I heard of Malmö, though, was some time in the year 2009. Even though I was (and still am) living in Canada, the vast majority of the people I love and care for—including my entire family—live in Israel which is why I am very aware of whatever is happening there.

Anti-Semitism is still alive and kicking in many countries, Sweden included—which is surprising, as Sweden has traditionally been considered a peaceful, tolerant country. Why and how did Sweden bring itself to the situation when Anti-Semitism flourishes there—that I'll leave to the Swedes themselves to answer and reflect upon (I suppose, though, that when Swedish Parliament members attend rallies where the Israeli flag is spat on, torn and set on fire, then acts of hatred aren't very unlikely to follow); the bottom line is that it exists, and the city of Malmö "shines" in that regards.

The Jewish community of Malmö (about 700 people. No, this is not a typo. 700 people, as of 2010; and shrinking) has long been subject to repeated harassments by certain groups (read the linked Wikipedia article above). All and all, the idea that Malmö is not a safe place for Jewish people to hang around in has travelled well: Israelis prefer to stay away from Malmö in particular (and Sweden in general) as they fear being targeted based solely on their country of origin and/or religion. That's 1939 again. Great.

> In the 2009 Davis Cup (tennis), a match between Israel and Sweden had to be played without any audience due to "security concerns", with certain Swedish Parliament members calling to cancel the match—an idea that was then turned down for the sole reason that such an act would result in Sweden's automatic drop from the tournament. I suppose that boycotting a tennis match to support

an agenda is acceptable—as long as your team still has a chance to win the tournament. Hypocrisy, anyone?

Arriving at Malmö, weather was great and I was looking forward to see the city. The hotel for the night, Elite Hotel Savoy, was conveniently located right across a small bridge from the central railway station. Beautiful hotel, inexpensive, convenient. I wish all hotels for this tour were like this one. By chance, James was booked for the same hotel. Checked in, unloaded everything and off we went to explore the city center.

Steps away south of the hotel is the first tourist trap of the day—the *Malmö Stortorget*: a nice looking square surrounded by all sorts of high-cost, low-quality dining establishments. My traveling history taught me that, while such places might be visually lucrative, dining options there usually range between terrible and mediocre.

Having said that, hunger struck and, with the advice of *TripAdvisor*, we were going to the following restaurant—

—which turned out to be closed.

Looking for a place to eat when you're hungry is never pleasant so I informed the group that, while they're more than welcome to continue scouring the place for a proper restaurant, I'm off to a coffee place to grab a short sandwich just to keep me going. In central Malmö, it seems like you can find an Espresso House shop every other block. Great bagels, good coffee (if you know what to order. What you'd call a "latte" in Canada is called "cortado" here).

From there, went on for a stroll in the city center area. Malmö is a pretty city—not drop-dead gorgeous but there are pleasant places to hang around in.

Malmö's city center includes a few parks as well, which make for pleasant walks, especially when the weather is cooperating:

The extended walking—as pleasant as it was—took its toll and I started becoming rather tired. Off to the hotel for an afternoon nap.

Only an hour or so later, waking up and looking outside the window, I noticed that the weather has turned to the worse. As pleasant as it was in the afternoon, things went haywire and, around 6:00pm, it was cloudy, windy and, of course, rainy.

Off to the central station and hopped on a train to the venue. The venue was located a couple of train stops away from the central railway station; trains going that way were absolutely jam packed with people. Alas, I had to put my personal space issues aside (in a nutshell: I need my personal space, and I need much of it. All the time) and feel like a sardine for about 8 minutes until the train's doors opened and millions of people flooded the platform on their way to the venue, located about 50 meters away from the train station's entrance.

The venue, Malmö Arena, is a general indoor arena. Opened in 2007, this arena is used for all sorts of sports, as well as concerts. Only a month ago, this arena hosted the Eurovision Song Contest (Denmark won). It can seat up to 15,000 in a concert.

Back to an indoor, seated arena after an outdoor, standing experience just the night before, I was very happy to not have to watch this concert outside. Couldn't appreciate two standing concerts in a row, thank you very much. I'm good with the seats.

Concert started a few minutes past schedule. Similar set to the one usually played in seated venues, with *Back to Tupelo* popping by for a most welcome visit and a *Hill Farmer's Blues* outro that seemed to be longer than usual by a few bars.

A group of 3–4 noisy blokes were seated right behind me. I never thought people would actually chew on popcorn during a concert (can you imagine listening to the *Marbletown* instrumental part while someone is digesting popcorn right behind you? oh, you can't? good. Lucky you), but apparently some do. One of these dudes was also in the habit of emitting incredibly loud whistles, making me feel sorry for not bringing some ear plugs with me.

Before the encore, no bulls were running to the stage. In the typical Scandinavian manner, people simply got up and walked towards the stage (or, to be more precise, towards the red ribbon that was placed about one meter away from the stage). Even the popcorn aficionados that were seated behind me were walking patiently, not pushing / pulling anyone.

Good.

Great performance, ended two hours after it started and it was time to head back to the train station, then the hotel. As expected, the train platform was jam packed with people: as the destination was the city central railway station, many people had to take the train there in order to connect to other parts of the city. So yes, it was crowded, but still civil.

Back in the city center, took a short walk around to look for a place for some evening tea, to no avail.

Isaac's "Privateering" Tour Blog

Back to the hotel for a good night sleep.

Finally, after almost a week of intense travel, there was *absolutely no rush* in the morning: no train to hurry to (Copenhagen, the next destination, is about 25–30 minutes by train), no airports, no buses… nothing. "All you can sleep".

Much needed.

Much done.

Sunday morning. Woke up I-don't-know-when, got up around 10:00am or so. Great day to do as little as possible. Off to breakfast in the hotel—wonderful breakfast!—and another piece of good news: the hotel allows Sunday check-outs at 6:00pm (!) during off-peak season (which ends next week). Could I ask for better than that? no.

The plan was, then, to do the minimum needed for mere survival until around 2:00pm, then head to Copenhagen as the concert was to start early—6:30pm (the earliest start time for a concert during this tour. The latest, by the way, is in Malaga, Spain: 10:30pm. Add a few exclamation marks here).

Weather was a bit cold but sunny as we left the hotel towards Espresso House again. Good coffee and chat in the patio, biding the time doing nothing special and nothing worth telling the world about.

And then it started pouring intensely.

Crazy weather. Back to the hotel to do some writing; by 2:00pm, we were all checked out and heading to the central railway station. James had a flight to catch back to the UK, and we decided to hop on the same train. Was good to have James along for a few days—stay strong mate and see you soon.

(Please, however, stop setting me up with women.)

Arrived at Copenhagen at around 3:15pm.

Copenhagen is Denmark's capital as well as its biggest city. I have to plead complete ignorance concerning Denmark: the only two cities I have ever heard of in Denmark are Copenhagen (trivial knowledge; give me some credit) and Middelfart—and the only reason I am even aware of the latter is because Knopfler performed there three years ago (and, of course, I was there).

I have never been to Copenhagen before in my life, although I do seem to recall passing through its train station (or changing trains in its train station) back in 2010. I did hear, however, that it is a pretty city, and as a fan of pretty cities, I was curious to see it.

Alas, arriving to Copenhagen's central railway station, it was cloudy, cold and raining. Quick walk to the hotel—Saga Hotel—and I became utterly depressed as the hotel rooms here are… how to say it… not very scenic. There's apparently a good reason why this hotel is (currently) ranked #63 out of 110 hotels in Copenhagen, by *TripAdvisor*.

(I will have a word with Jeroen about this, as he was the one booking it.)

Weather being so mean, I did nothing but writing until 4:30pm when it was time to go eat. A few locations were attempted and ended up being closed, either because it's a Sunday, or because they have weird dining hours here, or whatever. Ended up landing in a Chinese restaurant right by the hotel; too bad I can't find its name so I can warn you, lest you make a grave mistake and dine there. Slow service, poor quality food. I feel bad just writing about it, so how about I don't.

> Now, I don't know where Copenhagen's beauty is, but if it is indeed there, it certainly isn't at the central railway station area. If at all, the area looks run down, uninteresting, as if asking you to go away already.

After a terrible meal, it was about 1.5 kilometers walk to the venue.

The venue, Forum Copenhagen, is yet another big box of everything and nothing: indoor arena used for any sort of activity that involves… well… people gathering in one place together. It was built in 1926 and renovated in 1996–97, and, in my humble opinion, is due for another renovation.

What struck me about this place is that it is located so close to a residential area. During the walk from the central railway station area towards the venue, I started speculating whether Google Maps is leading us astray again: a concert venue? *here*? it's all houses and apartments around.

But it was there.

Tickets picked up, and as there was some time left, I decided to walk around the venue and search for some coffee. As I was walking, I realized a line forming for about 100 meters outside the venue. I wasn't entirely sure what people were waiting for: as we were picking up the tickets, three or four venue staff were standing there scanning tickets for people and there was no line-up whatsoever. I'm guessing, then, that people chose to line up simply because they saw a line-up and decided that joining that line-up is probably the best course of action.

> Here's a tip: before you choose to waste your life in a line-up, at least check *what you are lining up for*.

Didn't want to take any risks, though: went immediately back to the venue and to my seat.

The concert was scheduled to start at 6:30pm. At 6:29pm, the three immortal pre-concert songs started rolling—nice, for a change, to start a concert on time—and I noticed a couple of differences:

- Usually, there is a gap of a few seconds before The Louvin Brothers' *Broadminded* to Howlin' Wolf's *44*. That gap was skipped this time.
- Howlin' Wolf's *44* faded out after one verse.

You need to be attending many concerts to notice these differences.

Anyway, seems like someone was in a hurry.

Good concert—a bit "slower" than the previous evening's but, for me, a performance of *Kingdom of Gold* can cover for any fault. What a beautiful piece of music. Perform this song at every concert and I'm a happy camper, really. Though I'm not a huge fan of that otherwise beautiful blue Pensa guitar (sorry. I know I'm stepping on a few toes here but no, its sound isn't much to my liking. It is, however, externally gorgeous), this song builds up to an outro that is no less powerful than that of *Telegraph Road*.

If you were to purchase any of those official guitar-shaped USB sticks (forget about bootlegs. Go for the real thing), pick one that has *Kingdom of Gold* in it. Or pick all of those with *Kingdom of Gold* in them. Of all songs played so far in this tour, this one is the most mesmerizing one to listen to.

Concert ended at 8:30pm (I can't believe I'm writing this. 8:30pm. So early). On the way out of the venue, an individual who answers to the name Magnus, who happens to be following this blog, approached and introduced himself. It's good to meet nice people along the way. As Magnus is from Malmö, he had to go back to the central railway station, which happened to be on our way, so we walked there together having a good chat.

Now, I'm a curious person. I'm also upfront, and at times, even too upfront. As Magnus seemed to be a reasonable interesting fellow, I asked him what his opinion is about the Anti-Semitism situation in his city.

Not a lightweight topic to bring up when talking to a person you had never met before, but as I said, I am curious. Fortunately, though, Magnus took it well and provided an interesting point of view on the subject, which helped me form a more balanced and slightly less emotional opinion on the subject. I will not quote Magnus' opinion here as I am not in the habit of quoting (named) people about political and other similar subjects without their permission; Magnus is of course more than welcome to add a comment to this post.

Regardless: thank you, Magnus, for sharing your opinion. See you soon.

Originally intending to head to the hotel, Jeroen remembered that it is immoral for him to go to sleep prior to consuming some sugar. Attempts to locate a suitable place for desserts went unsuccessful. A 7/11 shop provided some yogurts and it's back to the hotel for an attempted good night sleep.

Haven't seen anything pretty in Copenhagen today. Hopefully tomorrow.

Signing off this post from my hotel room in Copenhagen.

Tomorrow: a free day in Copenhagen until 6:46pm when I'm going to face the worst.

My enemy. My nemesis. My kryptonite.

The worst form of punishment known to mankind.

The invention that made Satan himself say "are you serious? well… OK, I guess".

An experience so vile, so mean, so cruel, that the world would have been a much better place had it not been invented.

The first thing the world needs to get rid of, even before reducing greenhouse emissions.

A night train.

Isaac

Wednesday, June 19, 2013

Copenhagen, Denmark to Hamburg and Frankfurt, Germany (June 17-18, 2013)

The last post, uploaded in the wee wee hours between Sunday and Monday, concluded with a short demonstration of how resentful I was of sleeper trains. My hatred towards this means of transportation isn't just made up: it is based on experience. During the 2010 Get Lucky tour, I had the utter displeasure of riding sleeper trains a few times, and I remember not being able to sleep at all through one ride, and being awakened multiple times during the night through the other rides. The common for all my previous sleeper train rides was extreme tiredness that took days to remedy.

The hotel I stayed in while in Copenhagen, Hotel Saga, proved to be a total flop. Woke up many times thanks to doors being slammed, drunken idiots being too vocal… basically, the entire package of displeasure inherent from picking a budget hotel that also happens to be located near a central railway station. Stay away from it. Pay more and sleep better elsewhere.

They also had the following sign posted in the breakfast room:

And I say… a hotel that posts such a sign is, most likely, not in the habit of catering to the same sort of clientele that I wish to be a part of. Call me a snob, but if you are a hotel owner and you find it appropriate to presume that your clientele is stealing food for use as lunch, then perhaps you should class up your hotel a little. Posting a sign like this shows a great deal of disrespect.

When I opened my eyes in 6:30am—about four hours and a half after uploading the last post—I knew that there was no way in hell that I was going to be surviving the next twelve hours awake (the night train from Copenhagen to Frankfurt was scheduled to leave at 6:40pm); moreover, I just knew that was not going to be sleeping at all during that entire twelve hours ride. In summary, I was looking at spending the next 24 hours awake, after having slept for about 4 hours the night before (including being rudely awakened multiple times).

I didn't even bother getting out of bed: grabbed my phone and started looking for alternatives. Ten minutes later, I had an alternative itinerary: take the train from Copenhagen to Hamburg (just over four hours), spend the night there, and continue to Frankfurt the next morning.

Had I realized that it's possible to cut the Copenhagen → Frankfurt trip into two, right in the beautiful city of Hamburg, I would most likely not even bother booking the sleeper train in the first place. Unfortunately, when planning such a journey, there is only so much that your brain is capable of processing.

I also knew that Jeroen was very content with going on that sleeper train: the Dutchman is a heavy sleeper, nothing wakes him up. He's the type of person who would sleep through an entire World War and then wake up asking where the hell everybody went. The change in plans was going to incur additional costs, so I was assuming that I was going to be on my own with this new itinerary. Quickly packed everything, got dressed and was ready to hit the hotel's dining room for breakfast when the Dutchman woke up.

Fortunately, no convincing was needed whatsoever. Minutes later we were downstairs at the dining room discussing the details.

Another item of major concern was brought up. Apparently, the next week in Germany is going to be insanely hot as temperatures are expected to be in the 30°C area. Therefore, it made a lot of sense to ensure that the hotels we're staying in actually have air conditioning. This is something we were making sure of (or, at least, I thought we were making sure of) while booking all hotels for the tour, but it was worth double checking.

Good thing I checked. The hotel booked for Frankfurt—only 24 hours ahead—didn't have air conditioning. Great.

Right after breakfast, two travel ninjas were presented with a series of tasks:

- Research and book a hotel in Hamburg for the night.
- Research and book an alternative hotel in Frankfurt for the next night.
- Cancel existing hotel reservation in Frankfurt.
- Plan railway route from Copenhagen to Hamburg.
- Plan railway route from Hamburg to Frankfurt.
- Find out about the cancellation policy of the sleeper train.
- Make reservations for trains that carry a compulsory reservation policy.
- Look into cancelling the next sleeper train scheduled for next week, from Salzburg to Paris.
- Book a different hotel in Salzburg, as that one didn't show to have air conditioning either.

It's amazing, though, how easy these things become the more you do them. A few minutes later, the Frankfurt hotel switch was already done, and we headed out to the central railway station, where we reserved seats for the train from Copenhagen to Hamburg.

Having more than two hours to kill, we went to Andersen Bakery—a desserts shop we had seen the day before but couldn't check it out as it was closed. This bakery is ranked #19 out of more than 900 restaurants in Copenhagen and for a good reason—baked goods are delicious and even the coffee was great. Go there.

Only while writing this blog, I did some research and found out that Andersen Bakery has four locations in the entire world: Hiroshima, Tokyo, San Francisco and… Copenhagen. Interesting.

Using the Wi-Fi connection in the bakery, we completed the rest of the tasks: hotel in Hamburg—booked; train reservation for the Hamburg → Frankfurt journey—done. Looked into the Salzburg → Paris ride, and decided to break it in half by spending the night in either

Strasbourg or Stuttgart, about half way. (Cancellable) Hotel reservation in Strasbourg—booked; alternative hotel reservation in Salzburg—booked; cancellable hotel reservation in Stuttgart—deferred for later, when we finally decide where to break the Salzburg → Paris ride.

And there was ample time afterwards to sip coffee and catch up with the world.

Travel ninjas, indeed.

The Intercity Express (ICE) train ride from Copenhagen to Hamburg takes a different route than the sleeper train. I neither knew nor cared for it until I woke up from a short nap while in the train and informed Jeroen that I'll be going to the toilet for a second, to which he replied that it may not be such a great idea, as we're about to hop on a ferry.

A ferry?

Yes, a ferry.

The ICE train crosses the Fehmarn Belt—a stretch of water in the Baltic Sea—between Rødby, Denmark to Puttgarden, Germany. It does it by being loaded in its entirety onto a ferry! Shortly after boarding the ferry, all living things are required to leave the train and get to the ferry's deck: as a security precaution, nobody's allowed to remain in the train while it's on a ferry, and it remains locked until five minutes before the ferry arrives at its destination.

Up to the ferry's deck to hunt for some food. The ferry has a restaurant on board selling miniature dishes for exaggerated prices—skipped. It also has a self-serve shop where you can buy traditional junk food (sausages, hamburgers, fries etc.) as well as some cold sandwiches and yogurts. That was a good opportunity to both eat *and* get rid of the Danish currency I had left. Short meal and up to the ferry's upper deck to get some sun.

At the ferry's upper deck, a seagull was gliding by right above us, keeping perfect pace with the ferry's speed so it looked as if the seagull was completely stationary.

I then noticed the seagull gliding above the water, by the ferry. A group of people was throwing bits of food towards the seagull. I was completely and totally shocked to witness that seagull catch each and every bit of food thrown at it—a tremendous feat considering how many parameters are involved: the direction and speed of the ferry, the seagull and the wind; the wind's speed and direction; the mass of that food bit and its shape (the shape would affect its aerodynamic behaviour). In a few instances, food bits were actually on their way to sink into the sea, and that brilliant seagull dived more than a few meters and caught them!

Unbelievable. If you throw food bits at me, while I'm stationary and there's no wind at all, I'm more than likely to miss it. This seagull does it all while flying. It's an unfair world.

I should say that feeding seagulls by throwing food at them is not something that I would do. Animals living in the wild (and the sea should be considered as "the wild" in this context) should live off the wild and feeding them often produces more damage than benefits. There, I ruined another party.

Back to the train, which took about 10 minutes to depart the ferry. Goodbye Scandinavia, hello again Europe's mainland.

There was something soothing in touching ground in Europe's mainland again. For once, there is much less water "in the way", which means that it's possible to get pretty much anywhere with trains (comparing to Scandinavia, where the abundance of water makes it at times very difficult, if not impossible, to travel by train); for twice, my Israeli SIM card, which doesn't work in Scandinavia, works perfectly in Europe's mainland which meant that I'm back into 3G connectivity mode, thank you very much.

Train arrived in Hamburg and first thing's first: off to Deutsche Bahn's reservation center to check a few items off the list.

The sleeper train for the night—which we obviously were not going to take—cancelled. Should get a partial refund.

The next task was to attempt to book the only remaining train journey for the tour: the train from Madrid to Gijon (July 28). Tickets for this train only went on sale a few days earlier, but unfortunately, Deutsche Bahn couldn't help us as they couldn't even find that train in their systems.

I had heard before that Spain's train travel system isn't very well integrated with the rest of Europe. Therefore, I decided to email my friend Julio, asking for his help—which was kindly and promptly given. Hopefully everything will be booked by the week's end.

Out of the train station… welcome to Hamburg.

I have very fond memories of Hamburg. I was there three years ago during the 2010 Get Lucky tour: I remember the weather being sunny, warm and clear—as well as a few pleasant walks by the Außenalster. Arriving to Hamburg, then, was accompanied by a relief: I'm in familiar territory.

From Hamburg's central railway station to the hotel, Suite Novotel Hamburg City, it's less than a kilometer walk on Steindamm, a major street in Hamburg. Walking in Steindamm, I wasn't sure, at first, that I was indeed in Germany: so many Middle Eastern restaurants, and a few fruit and vegetable stores offering their goods right on the sidewalk—of those sights you'd encounter so frequently in Istanbul, Jaffa, Tel Aviv and Jerusalem. There's something charming and invigorating in walking down an avenue filled with the scent of fresh fruit and vegetables all along. I recommend it.

I was dead tired upon arriving at the hotel, but still, it's Hamburg so why not make the most out of it. Off to a walk by the Außenalster, crossing the Kennedy Bridge and on towards the old city area.

The old city area is tourist-centric, which means many restaurants with a ridiculous ration of price vs. quality. *TripAdvisor* suggested a restaurant by the name of Friesenkeller, and on the way there, I saw this:

I know of so many people who would wish to switch places with me just so they could jump into one of these tents and enjoy the traditional German habit of consuming insane amounts of beer along with cheap mediocre food. I just can't quite "connect" to it: can't think of myself having a lot of fun sitting along long tables surrounded by people I don't know, let alone while drinking beer which I generally dislike with passion. I'm not sure whether this is due to my resentment towards beer, or my built-in defects when it comes to socializing — either way, you're unlikely to find me dead in such places (although I have nothing much against those who are into it, of course).

Dinner was pleasant, good poached fish consumed on a terrace floating on the water.

Off for a short stroll in the old city area (which didn't reveal much; or perhaps I was looking in the wrong place)…

… another sit-down for tea and desserts when it was already getting late.

Knackered. *S-Bahn* back to the hotel…

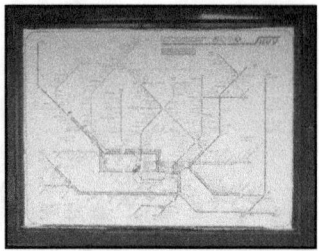

… and a *glorious* night sleep.

Screw you, sleeper trains. You and I need to see other people. It's not me, it's you.

Tuesday morning, the usual morning routines and off to Hamburg's central railway station. Breakfast wasn't included in the hotel's rate so the plan was to grab a short sandwich for the morning and buy some food for later on, as the train ride to Frankfurt takes about four hours. All went according to plan, save for a 10 minutes train delay. Hopped on the 1st class coach and spent almost the entire train ride writing, as well as deciding upon whether to break the Salzburg → Paris ride in Strasbourg or Stuttgart. As much as I'd prefer Strasbourg (we're going to be spending a couple of days in Stuttgart later during the tour anyway), getting there by train from Salzburg is rather tiring: through Stuttgart, it's a whole different story — much easier — so Stuttgart won. Congratulations Stuttgart; see you June 25.

Weather forecast called for temperatures around 32°C in Frankfurt. It has been quite a while since I had experienced such temperatures: inhumane, ridiculous and borderline illegal. Anything over 24°C is redundant as far as I'm concerned; 27°C is already something I'm not willing to cooperate with. 32°C? you must be kidding.

> Where I was born and raised, temperatures such as 32°C or even more (I faintly recall temperatures in the low 40°C's) weren't so unheard of. You just had to learn to live with it. In central Israel, you get about 330 days of sun every year, and weather starts being irritatingly hot some time in April and gets back to tolerable realm some time in October. In between, air conditioners are used pretty much everywhere so you only feel the heat (and humidity) when you're transitioning between air-conditioned locations.

Therefore, I do have the knowledge of what such heat feels like, as well as the knowledge that I do not welcome it at all.

What I do remember vividly is the feeling you get once you exit an air-conditioned place into a hot, humid environment: you feel as if the sun, the wind and all other elements have joined together into one big palm and just smacked you silly right in your face. Of course, the same happened in Frankfurt: leaving the train towards the platform, I felt as if I'm entering a huge sauna.

Passed by Le Crobag for a good sandwich:

(Le Crobag is a German fast-food chain specializing in sandwiches [some of which are actually healthy] and baked goods. They're everywhere in the German railway system.)

Quick walk to the hotel—Star Inn, located about 200m from the central station—and finally, a proper hotel (for its price) in the central railway station area.

> When you exit Frankfurt's central railway station through the main exit—facing east—you are presented with a crescent-shaped avenue containing many, many hotels. I used to stay in these hotels before until I realized that, for their price, they offer ridiculous quality. The reason these hotels are so expensive (comparing to what they offer) is simple: they are very easy to find. They are literally *in your face* when you exit the station.
>
> Luckily, now I know better.
>
> When looking for a hotel in Frankfurt, don't settle for those junk hotels facing the station. Total waste of money.

Great rooms, air-conditioned of course. No free Wi-Fi, but wired (LAN) internet is free—however you need to punch in a code. Phoned reception.

– "You'll need to come to reception to get the code."

– "What? Why?"

– "Because you need to sign something."

Sigh.

> When you access the internet through a hotel or many other sorts of public places, you usually get presented with a digital form asking you to read the term of service, check a box and click to "agree". That "I agree" box is probably the most prevalent lie in the history of lies: do you know of anybody who ever read those terms, to the fullest?
>
> Me neither.
>
> In a nutshell, people who go about surfing the net have the potential to cause a lot of damage, to themselves as well as to others. Often, one doesn't require to have malicious intent in order to cause damage (for example, consider all those cases of internet "worms" that keep popping up every once in a while).
>
> The reason you are required to "agree" on a bunch of legalese text is in order to release the hotel (or whatever public place you're in) from any sort of liability concerning your use of the internet. For example, if your computer gets infected with a virus while surfing the internet from the comfort of your hotel room, forget about suing the hotel.
>
> Also, such public places want you to commit to not commit illegal acts through the internet while connected through their facilities. Such acts might put the public place at legal risk, so the purpose of the "agreement" is to roll such liability onto you.
>
> Seems reasonable. However, while all public places I've been to so far were prompting me with that "agreement" form online, it was very strange to be required to actually sign a paper.

At around 4:00pm, it was decided to go about doing the laundry. Laundry is yet another element that has to be carefully considered while following a concert tour with a busy schedule. As Frankfurt is notorious (at least in my eyes) to be exceptionally boring, it would make sense to do the laundry here than, say, in Vienna.

No self-serve Laundromat in the area. Instead, we found a location nearby the hotel that agreed to give us a deal—€30 for everything. "Come back at 6:00pm". OK.

Back to the hotel, did some writing until wonderful Ingrid came along. Ingrid made her way to Frankfurt from The Netherlands despite having some back problems. Ingrid is such a strong individual—one of the strongest-willed individuals I know—that she'd probably have to be bound to a stretcher in order to be convinced to alter her plans. Was good seeing Ingrid again—as it always is.

5:00pm: time for lunch. *TripAdvisor* suggested Pizza 7 Bello as a great place for... well... pizza. Steaming hot everywhere, and a good pizza was consumed in the open air patio outside. This simple-looking restaurant offers good food for very reasonable prices. Go there.

Back to the Laundromat to pick up the clothes, where I lost a bit more of the very little faith I had in humanity to begin with. Of course laundry wasn't ready at 6:00pm. Fifteen minutes later, the lady came out asking whether we need the clothes right away, as they're "a little damp". We said "that's OK", and she started loading the clothes (surprisingly, they were *already folded*—which means that they were folded before she even asked whether it's OK for them to be damp. Weird) onto paper bags. The bags seemed to be heavy. Arriving at the hotel, it turned out that the clothes weren't "a little damp". They were "very damp", or—the way people usually call that level of humidity—"wet".

Brilliant. Clothes were now spread out all over the hotel room, with hopes that they will dry out by the morning.

Off to the venue.

The venue, Festhalle Frankfurt, is located in Frankfurt's city center, about 10 minutes walk west of the central railway station. I have been there before, during the 2010 Get Lucky tour.

The first thing I noticed when entering the venue had nothing to do about how beautiful the ceilings were: instead, the first thing I noticed was the heat. Ventilation was next to non-existent. Remember what I wrote about the concert in Zwolle? The Festhalle was even worse.

It was certain that a normal human being wouldn't survive this concert without water. €3.30 for half a litre of water, poured into a cup. Thank you very much.

> Have you ever wondered what allows concert venues to forbid you from bringing your own water—thereby forcing you to pay ridiculous prices for the transparent liquid—and get away with it?
>
> I'm not even talking about getting water for free; I'm talking about bringing my own decent bottle of cold water. Why can't we do this?
>
> As I see it, concert venues may provide two excuses:
>
> - The desire to prevent people from bringing in certain types of liquids. For example, someone might abuse this "privilege" and bring in a bottle filled with flammable material of some sort.
> - You want free water? go ahead and drink from the toilet sink.
>
> The first point, then, is basically a form of collective punishment. Why should most people be forced to pay ridiculous prices for water just because some idiots *might* break the law?
>
> Then again, in our day and age, innocent people often have to pay the price for the criminal / immoral acts of a few.
>
> Drunken screw-heads throwing bottles of water onto the stage? "let's disallow the entire population of concertgoers from entering the venue with bottles".
>
> Such collective punishments are commonplace, and the only reason they're commonplace is that we, as a society, are too weak (or too politically correct, at times) to fight back such nonsense back.

The second point is harder to dispute. It should be, then, within the venue's responsibility to ensure and to prove that water coming out of toilets' sinks are safe and drinkable. So far, I can't recall any sort of "these water are safe for drinking" notice in any venue I had been to.

P.S. Interestingly enough, there actually is a country out there who is in the process of passing a law whereby you could bring your own drinks and food into a concert venue (or a movie theatre and other similar establishments) under one condition: you could only bring in items that are up for sale in the venue. For example, you'll be able to bring in water bottles, but won't be able to bring in the chicken cordon bleu that you just prepared at home.

Israel, of course. Turns out that, sometimes, that country does make sense.

I wish I could tell you much about the concert, but I can't. Unfortunately, while the concert itself was as good as many others, the concert *experience* was, hands down, the worst so far in the tour and one of the worst ever for me. First, due to where I was seated, virtually all audio was played into my left ear which is sensitive to high treble audio, so I had to block my left ear for most of the time. Second, the immense heat eventually made me get up from my seat and watch the concert from the back of the venue. At times, I even went outside for a breather. It was *that* hot.

I watched a great deal of the concert from the side of the stage, standing up. There were less people there so temperature was at least manageable. I then saw a few stretchers leaving towards the seated areas—wouldn't be surprised if a few people simply gave in to the ridiculous heat and passed out.

What a terrible experience.

After the show, some post-concert snack (well, a salad) and drinks with Ingrid in an Italian restaurant by the venue, then back to the hotel for a glorious shower followed by an even more glorious sleep.

Signing off this post from the lobby of my hotel in Regensburg, Germany. Most of the afternoon was spent in a nearby hospital. Got to upload this and head out for dinner, then to the concert.

Isaac

Thursday, June 20, 2013

Frankfurt to Regensburg, Germany (June 19, 2013)

Wednesday morning, good morning after a good night sleep. Woke up earlier than really needed as I had an important phone call to make. That done, grabbed everything, checked out from the hotel and out into the hell that is Frankfurt.

By "hell", I mean weather-wise. It was so hot that the heat made me tired again. Went to Kamps, right across the street from the central station's north entrance, for a tasty sandwich and some fruit. Then off to the train station.

The itinerary: Frankfurt → Würzburg, 10 minutes connection time, then Würzburg → Regensburg.

On the departures board, a scrolling marquee showed that the train leaving Frankfurt is delayed by at least 15 minutes.

Doesn't take a math genius to figure out that this weren't good news. A quick check of the trains' schedule shown that, if we miss our connection in Würzburg, we're talking about a delay of about a couple of hours arriving to Regensburg.

With the help of Deutsche Bahn's staff, we made a few adjustments to the itinerary: leave Frankfurt about 30 minutes past original schedule, connect in Nürnberg instead of Würzburg, then proceed to Regensburg.

Train arrived on time, boarded it, sat down, and decided that it's time to visit the hospital.

About a week and a half ago, while in Delft, I stumbled upon uneven surface (yes, again. What the hell is going on with uneven surfaces in this continent? can you not build things so they're just straight?) and fell down, hands first. I remember feeling some pain in my right hand afterwards—which wasn't that unexpected—but it was one of those sensations that you'd assume were going to pass after a while.

Over the last few days, though, the pain seemed to have worsened. As I am rather paranoid when it comes to my health, I decided to not take any risks. Last thing I need in my life is trouble with my wrist. That decision was taken while on the train out of Frankfurt to Nürnberg; meanwhile, I was reading some information online about what could be the reason for my pain, which got me quite depressed so I took my frustration out by writing.

The 30 minutes connection time in Nürnberg were used to locate a public phone and attempt making a collect call to my travel insurance company. Alas, the T-Mobile phone stand on site still wanted money for an international call. The €2 I put inside the damn thing were barely enough to ask the person on the other end of the line to call me back: one second after providing the last digit of my phone number, the call was terminated.

Sorted it out: got clearance to go to a hospital and take care of things.

Train to Nürnberg left on time. Shortly before 3:00pm, arrived at Regensburg's central railway station.

Regensburg is a city in the wonderful, eye-candy state of Bavaria, Germany. I knew absolutely nothing about it before I saw Knopfler's tour schedule: I didn't even know its name. Regensburg? what's that?

I didn't even get the time to read anything about it. The night before, as Ingrid, Jeroen and myself were sitting for a late night snack after the hideous Frankfurt experience, Ingrid pulled out her phone, looked Regensburg up and mentioned that the city's medieval center is a UNESCO World Heritage Site.

That got me listening. While I'm no fan of that corrupt, screwed-up organization that goes by the name "United Nations", UNESCO World Heritage Sites are of interest to me.

So, I was looking forward to visit the city and explore some of its medieval area. That was, of course, before I decided to go to the hospital instead.

Arrived in Regensburg and it was bloody hot. Blimey, what the hell is going on in here? according to a few people I already asked, these temperatures aren't normal for Germany in June. There's some sort of a heat wave going on. Whatever it is, please make it stop. It's ridiculous.

From Regensburg's central railway station to the hotel for the night, you need to cross one road. Still, when I arrived at the (air-conditioned) hotel, the only way for me to know I wasn't on fire was the paddle of sweat all over my upper body.

Checked in, and informed the receptionist that we'll be right down again so she can hail a taxi for us to the hospital. Up to the room, turned the room's thermostat to the lowest temperature possible and then some, then immediately downstairs.

The clock was ticking—it's impossible to predict how long the hospital visit was going to take. The receptionist was busy pouring beer into exceptionally large glasses for some fellow. "Hey, you can take your time pouring beer for that gentleman while I'm in pain here and in need to go to the hospital", I said, but nobody listened to me—partly because nobody listens to me anyway, but mostly because I didn't say it out loud.

OH! Good. Beer guy got all the beer he wanted—which looked equivalent to the total amount of beer I had in my entire 35 years of living—prompting the receptionist to finally hail a taxi. 10 minutes later we were at the hospital.

> Jeroen was joining as he was supposed to go for a check-up anyway, one week after his hospital visit in Bergen. Two travel ninjas in a hospital. How pathetic.

The hospital, Caritas-Krankenhaus St. Josef, is located about a kilometer away from the central railway station. It was opened in 1950 and can lay down up to 300 patients.

Oh, wait, it's not a concert venue.

Told the receptionist (very cute! OK, let's move on with it) the history of my entire life, focusing specifically on what happened a week and a half ago. Waited about an hour for my turn in the X-ray room (more urgent cases, obviously, took priority). The entire ordeal took less than two hours. The result: no visible fractures on the X-ray—it is probably a trauma-related pain that should go away with time. I was advised to let that wrist rest, got my wrist and palm wrapped with bandage and some cooling gel and instructed to visit a hospital again if the pain doesn't go away within two weeks, as a CT scan might be required then.

Tour goes on, for now. Let's all hope that everything gets back to normal over the next couple of weeks.

> Jeroen, by the way, didn't get his check-up done as the hospital didn't have an ENT doctor on site; he'll have to have his check-up done in Vienna instead. Still, he stayed along with me. Hats off to a good friend.

Walked back to the hotel (not such a long walk after all). Along the way, I saw this:

38°C in the shade.

Finalized my previous post and spent some time trying to upload it using the hotel's crappy Wi-Fi connection, to no avail. Time was up: got some stuff together and off to the nearest bus station, to catch a ride to the venue—not before stopping for some quick dinner in the central railway station.

The venue, Donau Arena, is located north east of the city center. It is named after the river Donau, which is also known by the name *Danube*. The reason might have something to do with the fact that the Danube is right nearby.

This venue is primarily used for ice hockey and can contain up to 7,600 for concerts. There's really nothing special about it. Actually, the venue's surroundings are much more interesting than the venue itself—lots of green, carrying that special "green" scent that (I think) can best be smelled when the weather is hot and humid.

And it was hot, and it was humid.

Crossing the bridge towards the venue, noticed two lanes of traffic below, two lanes were moving slow:

Went to pick up the tickets. Tickets pick-up is right at the entrance: it was so hot inside that, for a minute, I was sure that this show is going to break the record in sucking set just the night before in Frankfurt. Grabbed the tickets and immediately exited the building to catch some cooler atmosphere outside in the shade.

As show time approached, I felt like I'm going to be executed. Here I am, Isaac Shabtay, 35 years old with some really interesting life history, and I was just about to enter hell on earth. Really, just kill me now and get it over with.

THE HEAT. TAKE AWAY THAT HEAT!!!

Miraculously, it turned out that, once inside the venue, ventilation *did* work. It wasn't cold or nice, but certainly a lot, *lot* more tolerable than the *Festhalle Frankfurt*.

Concert started shortly after 8:00pm. Good concert—enjoyed it more than the night before simply because I could actually manage staying in my seat for most of it (bathroom break towards the end; I *did* drink a lot of water).

At the concluding *E* chord of *What It Is*, something went wrong in Mark's guitar as the low E string apparently went haywire and lost a couple of tones, prompting Mark to correct it on the spot. I'm pretty sure that was the first time I ever witness Mark tuning any guitar. He did manage to bring it back to an almost perfect E.

On the terraces, to the right hand side of the stage, a young couple was standing and dancing *during the entire show*. Not stopping for a second. Lots of energy in the audience overall: the audience loved the show. No *running of the bulls* at the end—looked more like a social gathering. The entire encore was spent standing up by the stage, the way it needs to be spent.

The venue's staff did everything within their powers to prevent people from even touching the stage. Was strange. I mean, there were people videotaping the entire encore *all over the place*—in contrary to the venue's (and the band's) guidelines—but that was OK, as far as the staff was concerned; but touching the stage with your finger? that would immediately prompt angry venue staff to charge at you mercilessly, lest your unholy fingertips touch the sacred stage of gold.

As this tour progresses, I lose my faith in humanity a tad more at a time. Good thing I have these concerts to peg me into the realm of what really matters: it's not the idiots around. It's the process of creating, and executing, something beautiful.

We were planning on walking back from the venue to the hotel, a distance of some 3.5km. As we exited the venue, we noticed a bus parking by the venue, showing *"Hauptbahnhof"* (meaning "Central Station". It's one of the very few words I know in German. I also pronounce it really, *really* well) as its destination. Hopped on it, thank you very much. Twenty minutes later I was happy to be back at the hotel.

Finalizing this post at 1:00am from my hotel room in Regensburg. Tomorrow—Vienna for two days!

Isaac

Saturday, June 22, 2013

Regensburg, Germany to Vienna, Austria (June 20-21, 2013)

Stayed up late after the concert in Regensburg as I decided to catch up with my blog: uploaded the Frankfurt entry and completed writing the Regensburg entry, preparing to publish the latter just before leaving Regensburg the next morning.

From Regensburg, it's an easy 3.5 hours direct train ride to Vienna. The train being scheduled to depart 9:27am, together with the fact that Regensburg's central railway station is located right across the street from the hotel (I could see the railway station through my hotel room's window), allowed for a wake-up alarm set to 8:10am. Easy morning procedure, and we were at the station before 9:00am.

The Regensburg central railway station is connected to a shopping mall. There are a few interesting dining options in that mall (well, everything is relative. By "interesting", one should take into consideration just how "interesting" dining options in a mall can be): grabbed a sandwich from one of the many bakeries on site, together with some coffee from San Francisco Coffee Company (which, by the way, is a German company having nothing to do with the city of San Francisco, California)—both consumed with ease on site.

The train arrived a few minutes later. Intercity Express, 1st class, like a boss. Did a bit of writing on board and enjoyed the view: the train ride from Regensburg to Vienna shows postcard-perfect views of Bavaria, featuring hills, a tremendous amount of green and, of course, the Danube.

Bavaria is indeed gorgeous: even a mere train ride through the state is enough to demonstrate that nature freaks are very likely to fall in love with this place.

Germany, in fact, is of the few European countries that I actually feel comfortable in. I'm not saying that I miss Germany or anything like that (let's not get carried away); what I mean is, that in a multi-country trip across Europe, Germany is of the few countries I'd feel much less stressed out in (Poland, for example, would be on the other end of the scale). I can certainly see myself having a short, few days trip to Bavaria's natural scenery.

Bye for now, Germany; see you again July 1st.

Hello again Austria (last time here was a little more than a month ago, as I passed through Vienna en route from Zagreb to Prague).

Unless my memory is betraying me, the 2010 Get Lucky tour didn't include too much time in Austria. I remember getting to Vienna after what was possibly the most stressful day for me in that entire tour, involving riding a taxi for about 200km in order to catch up with a train.

Fortunately, getting to Vienna this time around wasn't anywhere near as stressful. Train arrived at *Wien Westbahnhof* ("Wien": "Vienna" in the local language; "Westbahnhof": western train station) right on time. From there, it was a long 2km walk in the searing heat to the hotel—a walk that could have been saved had any of us bothered to look at the map and realize that there's a tram that takes 10 minutes to get from the train station to the hotel.

The heat... blimey. The heat! the sun mercilessly pounding on the skin, and the humidity so high that my sweat was emitting its own sweat. By the time I made it to the hotel, it was already after cursing on living things on our solar system and all I wanted was to just bury myself under a glacier.

Such as this one.

> When you are going to stay more than one night in one location, it is very important to book a better quality hotel than you'd otherwise book: it's OK to be stuck in a stupid hotel for one night, but being stuck in a crappy hotel for more than one night can adversely screw things up.

Booking the hotel for Vienna was under Jeroen's list of tasks, and I have to admit that he scored it big time. The Austria Trend Hotel Park Royal Palace (such a catchy, easy-to-remember name; isn't it?), located far from the city's touristic center but very close to a nice park and within easy access to public transportation, offers great value for the money. Brilliant hotel room that was already cold when we got there. Surprisingly fast (and free) Wi-Fi. Spotless rooms. What else could I ask for?

Last week, while in Bergen, Jeroen was terribly sick and went to a hospital where he was diagnosed with an ear infection. As he was due to a follow-up within a week, and the hospital in Regensburg couldn't offer an ear-nose-throat doctor, he had to go for a follow-up in Vienna. Minutes after checking in, then, the Dutchman went on his way to the nearest hospital and I was left to my own.

The first task at hand—that is, after restoring my body's core temperature to normal levels—was to head out, eat, and buy a proper brace for my right wrist. Took a look at *TripAdvisor*, listing a few possible dining places; grabbed a few things and went outside.

To the hotel's immediate south, there lies a nice park—*Auer-Welsbach-Park*—offering a pleasant walk amidst some greenery, better than having to walk by Vienna's busy roads.

At the southern edge of the park, there lies the huge Schönbrunn Palace. This palace dates back to the 16th century, and is labelled a UNESCO World Heritage Site. The word *Schönbrunn* means "beautiful spring", named after a well of which waters were used to water the gardens.

The Schönbrunn is considered a major touristic attraction in Vienna; however, the busy schedule, as well as the fact that hunger was starting to be a major annoyance, caused me to care very little about the area's touristic value.

Inside the Schönbrunn was my destination for lunch—Cafe Residenz—which turned out to be focused mostly on desserts so I had to leave (although things looked wonderful). My search for food—consistently following *TripAdvisor*'s recommendations and even more consistently finding out that dining places, at that part of the city, were closed until later in the evening—took about an hour and a half (!).

At the least, I was able to find a drugstore and bought myself a fancy, shiny wrist brace. Let's hope I am in the position to get rid of it as soon as possible.

After wandering around for a while, sweating my arse off, I came across a complex called *U4* which had a few restaurants and cafes at the lower level, right on the street. Entered a cafe that turned out to be air conditioned.

A few people were seated in the smoking section of the cafe, behind shut glass doors. Nobody was seated in the non-smoking section.

One worker there, not even looking at me; instead, she was typing something on her phone.

And typed.

And when she was done, she typed again.

I was standing there for a long minute, not understanding whether I arrived at a cafe or at a public display of everything that is wrong with humanity. Finally she was done, and looked at me with a punishing look as if she wants to smack me for interrupting her texting extravaganza.

Schnitzel with rice for €7. I was setting my expectations low—what quality could you really expect from a schnitzel that costs €7?—but it was surprisingly delicious. Either that, or I'm not quite the schnitzel connoisseur. Entire contents of the plate were devoured in about 5 minutes.

Jeroen was periodically in touch, informing me that the hospital experience was ridiculously inefficient. Minutes after I was done eating, while making my way back to the hotel, good news beeped on my phone: Jeroen's illness was over and done with. Met in the hotel room after half an hour, and immediately left to head to the venue—some 2km away.

The venue, Wiener Stadthalle, is an indoor arena built in the 1950's. It has six halls, used for sporting events and concerts. I was here before in 2010, although it took me a few minutes to get oriented as this time I approached the venue from a different direction than I did the last time.

Not much time was left for the show to start: therefore, I had to pass on the opportunity for some coffee in the nice looking cafe conveniently located right next to the ticketing counter, and headed to the entrance instead.

In this venue, there are two entrances to the floor area: north and south. The indication as to which of the entrances was applicable in our case was, indeed, marked on the ticket. However, at the entrance, there was only one sign leading to the floor area so we followed it. Line up… warmth… humidity… the entire package. Great, here's the usher.

She checks the ticket, looks at me and mumbles something in fluent German. In German, mind you, ever single word sounds to me like some sort of a command, so I became anxious even before I understood what she wanted to say.

– "Sorry, I only understand English."

She then proceeded to instruct me, in broken English, that the entrance I should be taking is at the other side.

OK, fine. Well, but I'm past all this queue already. This is the floor area. Once you're in, you can get anywhere in the floor area. I understand that I'm a complete human failure—just let me in.

But no. Instead of just letting us in, she decided that it's a much better idea to force us to backtrack—of course, bumping into other people along the way, thus increasing the total amount of anxiety in the venue—just in order to teach us a lesson.

> Power clouds compassion, and it clouds it most when said power is given to an individual who would otherwise be rather powerless in their everyday lives. Dear attendant: if you're reading this, kindly go screw yourself.

Once past the obstacle of stupidity involved in entering the venue, I came across this:

Last time I saw a bulk food stand in a concert venue—which also happened to be my first time ever witnessing this—was in Zwolle, The Netherlands, just two weeks prior. I was sure that this is so peculiar that I'm unlikely to come across it again in the future, so I cherished that moment. Apparently, though, I may be the crazy one and selling bulk foods in concert venues isn't such an insane idea.

Concert started a few minutes past schedule—maybe because people kept trying to enter the floor area through the wrong entrance and were sent back to the other side of the venue; who knows—and offered a similar set to the usual except that *Seattle* was back after a long absence.

I was seated in the second row. Behind me, two or three small children (couldn't be more than 10–12) were seated along with their parents and kept on talking through most of the show. At times, they were trying to emit loud whistles, to no avail; but it didn't stop them from keeping on trying, not only between songs but also during actual performance. At some point, the guy seated next to me turned to them and barked something at them in German. It helped for a couple of minutes.

Having consumed quite a bit of water before the show, I left for a bathroom break after *Romeo and Juliet*, just around the time I started feeling a strong sensation of complete tiredness. As I was going back to the venue, I started feeling very weak so I remained in the hall for about ten minutes, sitting down on one of the now-empty vending tables. At some point—I believe it was between the middle of *Song for Sonny Liston* and the end of *Haul Away*—I *think* I passed out. Found myself coming back to my senses at once, as if struck by lightning. Headed back into the hall, but decided to watch the remainder of the concert from the side door, instead of heading to the seat, as it was cooler there and, frankly, I didn't feel like being surrounded by people.

First part of the concert concluded with a mild *Running of the Bulls* carrying no casualties. A happy lot near the stage celebrating a good encore—*Our Shangri La*, for the first time after the London shows. Beautiful performance, but honestly, once you listen to it live with Nigel Hitchcock on stage, you can't go back to the saxophone-less version without feeling that something's amiss. *So Far Away* and the show ended.

Long walk back to the hotel. It was still hot and humid outside, and I was simply *dying* for a shower. That long-awaited shower finally arrived: I was waiting for it for so long (since morning!) that I think I actually sang. Jeroen did report hearing a few unidentifiable vocals coming from the shower's direction.

Caught up with a few things and chatted online with a friend until the wee wee hours; the next day was a day off spent in Vienna—nowhere to hurry to.

Bliss.

When planning the tour's itinerary, we had to decide whether we spend the day off, June 21, in Vienna or in Budapest. The distance between the two is about three hours train ride. Eventually we decided on Vienna, and I'm happy we did. It was one of the best day offs in the tour so far, almost entirely because it contained so little.

Woke up late—around 10:00am (!)—and off to the city center. From the hotel, it's a short walk to the *Schönbrunn* U-Bahn station, and then another few stops until you get to Karlsplatz, which is an excellent place to start walking around this gorgeous city.

First call of the day—breakfast at The Breakfast Club, for good breakfast followed by a good cup of cappuccino (well, this is Vienna. Coffee here is known to be excellent)—done. Headed back north towards the more touristic area of the city.

Only recently I was told about the Sachertorte. The Sachertorte is a torte invented by Franz Sacher in 1832 to please some royalty, prince Wenzel von Metternich. The "Original Sacher Torte" is sold in a few locations in Austria, however the recipe of the version sold in Hotel Sacher itself is secret. According to Wikipedia, the difference is in the icing: in Hotel Sacher's version, the icing is made up of three different types of chocolate, produced by three different vendors for the sole usage of being a part of that icing.

Naturally, a visit to Hotel Sacher was definitely called for.

Seated on the patio in the shade, beautiful weather (the sun was only warming up for the day), and asked for two slices of that so-called sensation and a bottle of water.

I ate it.

Is it good? yes, certainly. Is it extraordinary? well… no. I'll put it this way: consuming this cake did not result in an explosion of colours in my brain. It was good but, really, I didn't understand what the fuss was all about. My one and only sister, Natali, bakes much better cakes—better in appearance, better in texture, better in taste and better in aftertaste—than this one (at least to my taste), with her eyes closed and possibly while talking on the phone the entire time. Every time I visit home I gain a few pounds mostly thanks to the cakes she keeps feeding me with. And she wasn't even formally trained for it (unless you consider "learning the basics from our mother [who had learned the basics from her mother]" to be "formal training)—just natural talent for these things.

If you want a really good cake, then, forget about Hotel Sacher and fly three or four hours east to Tel Aviv.

Hotel Sacher claims to be selling 360,000 slices of this cake *every year*. That's about 1,000 slices a day, selling for €4.90 each. Revenue of about €5,000 a day for selling a good (even very good), but not great, cake.

Nice.

Kept on walking at the touristic area of the city center.

Came across this guy:

I'll let you figure out how this one works. Next time I'm there, I'm going to show up with a huge magnet and a can of termites. Walking on, came across this:

This is the St. Stephen's Cathedral, dating back to the 14th century. According to Wikipedia, this is the most important religious building in Vienna. The Archbishop of Vienna is seated here. As impressive it is from the exterior, it is absolutely gorgeous inside.

Walked on to the river…

… and once scorched by the sun, decided to head straight back to the nearest U-Bahn and off to the hotel. A few hours spent at the convenience of the hotel's lobby, doing some work and writing. Back outside—now, for dinner.

The destination: Gasthaus Pöschl, located again in the city center. Took the U-Bahn, and from there it's a pleasant ten minutes walk, primarily through a park.

The restaurant is located in a small square, along with a few other cafes—each of which has its own seated area in the square. Other than the occasional peddlers passing by trying to sell you weird things because you look like an ignorant tourist, the experience is quite lovely. Food is a bit pricy but a great schnitzel nonetheless.

From there, continued exploring the city center area. Some desserts in Cafe Imperial, again on the patio overlooking this busy city:

Kept on walking, now back to the St. Stephens Cathedral area:

And, of course, before boarding the U-Bahn—some coffee and tea to call it a day.

So… yes. After a few days of feeding almost exclusively on sandwiches, the day off in Vienna was payback time. Vienna offers thousands of dining options and standards here are relatively high. Coffee? fantastic.

Liked this city a lot; this day off was revitalizing, invigorating, a huge energy boost. Bring on the rest of the tour, I'm ready.

Signing off this post from my hotel room in Budapest, Hungary. A bit of a travel hiccup earlier. Off for a snack, dinner and then to catch tonight's concert.

Isaac

Sunday, June 23, 2013

Vienna, Austria to Budapest, Hungary (June 22, 2013)

After two nights in the wonderful city of Vienna—which, unfortunately, I didn't get much opportunity to explore due to the immense heat wave going on in Central Europe nowadays—it was time to decamp.

Nowadays, with the ongoing pain I have in my right hand (I am right-handed), it takes me longer to prepare in the morning. Due to some negligence on my part, I stayed asleep past the wake-up time Jeroen and I had agreed upon, which meant that I had to prepare in a rush. Let me tell you this: it wasn't fun at all. I think I over-stressed my tired right-hand wrist during the process, which caused some pain.

Checked out and went to the tram station nearby.

Beautiful morning: sunny (of course), around 24°C—why can't it always be like this?—and the roads were relatively peaceful as it was, after all, Saturday morning.

Tram ride to *Wien Westbahnhof* takes less than ten minutes.

On to the station for the usual routine of buying enough food to keep us going until the travel for the day is over. Two sandwiches from Le Crobag usually do the trick.

The Railjet is Austria's main high-speed train network, featuring great 1st class experience (equivalent to the German's Intercity Express network). Boarded the train about 20 minutes prior to departure, simply because it's nicer to sit and wait in an air-conditioned 1st class cabin than inside the train station along with hundreds of people.

Train left a few minutes past schedule. Itinerary: three hours direct high-speed train to Budapest. Couldn't be easier than that, could it?

Almost naturally, though, something had to go wrong. Due to the serious floods that hit Europe a few weeks ago—floods that caused, among others, shutting down a few major high-speed railway links in Germany, causing havoc—a particular section of the track, between Győr and Tatabánya (both are in Hungary, and both are cities about which I had known nothing before), could not be traversed by train. Instead, passengers were instructed to leave the train in Győr, take a bus to Tatabánya, and take a train from there to Budapest.

The distance between Győr and Tatabánya is about 66km, which meant spending an hour inside a bus. Not a big deal in absolute terms—heck, I'm still carrying the scars from that tantalizingly horrendous bus ride to Poland, in the earlier part of the tour—but still, after a relaxing day off and with more than half of the tour behind me, travel challenges are less and less welcome.

But hey, what can you do.

Left the train in Győr, seriously expecting everything to go wrong. Something in Hungary's air—just like Poland's—told me that things were bound to somehow get screwed up.

I was wrong. I suppose that, as some time has already passed since the floods started affecting the Hungarian railway system, the travel authorities were already prepared to deal with the train → bus → train complication. Bus was found within an instant; five minutes later we were already all on our way to Tatabánya. Fortunately, as it was weekend, roads were pretty clear. Bus ride went just fine, save for two particularly annoying kids sitting somewhere behind and being way too noisy to be considered charming.

Arriving in Tatabánya, I was stressed again. Now what? looking up at a train schedules' app on my mobile, I realized that a direct train leaves Tatabánya towards Budapest once every two hours. Just like the entire population of the world (minus the population of Tatabánya itself), I did not want to stay in Tatabánya. What do I do? take a bus to Budapest? taxi? perhaps walk?

Wrong again. Turns out that a train was already waiting for us on the platform. To my complete surprise, that train was identical to the train I left Vienna with—same structure, same cabins, same seat numbering—maybe it was actually the *very same train*? I don't know. If it was the same train, why weren't we allowed to simply stay in it?

Puzzling. Still, I was very happy that the potentially annoying change in travel plans turned out to be much simpler and less intimidating than expected. Boarded the train in Tatabánya, and 20 minutes later it was on its way to Budapest, arriving Budapest's Keleti station about 40 minutes past original schedule.

Not bad.

Left the train onto the platform to the sensation of searing heat, and immediately sought a place to register myself as a Jew. Couldn't find any so I went on my way.

Oh, come on. Don't tell me you didn't know.

I have been to Budapest before, during the 2010 Get Lucky tour. That visit was brief: it ended badly (as I caught a virus there which made me feel sick for about four days) but, really, during the very little time that I was walking around that city, I noticed that it had great character and beauty.

That was 2010. Fast forward three years, and in the Hungarian Parliament there exists a neo-fascist, neo-Nazi party that, in the recent elections, received (sit tight; if you had never heard this before, you're going to be shocked) 16.67% of the votes in the first round. A second round was then needed, in which they won 12.26% of the votes and, consequently, 12% of the seats in Parliament.

This party (called *Jobbik*. Their motto: "*The Movement for a Better Hungary*") has some significant history in leading a racist (particularly anti-Semitic) and even homophobic agenda. You are more than welcome to read about their bent ideas and screwed up agenda in Wikipedia; I will just highlight a few.

- In 2012, a Jobbik parliamentarian decided it would be a great idea to commemorate the 1882 Tiszaeszlár blood libel... while in Parliament. That blood libel claimed that a 14 years old girl from a Hungarian village was killed by Jewish fanatics for her blood to be used for a Passover celebration, and then triggered a series of pogroms against Hungarian Jews, which lasted even after it was proven that the Jewish community had nothing to do with it.
- In April 2012, the party submitted to Parliament an amendment to ban "gay propaganda" (this isn't much different from what's going on in Russia nowadays).
- In November 2012, another Jobbik parliamentarian by the name of Marton Gyöngyösi stated that the Hungarian government should create a list to include "all dangerous Jews who are posing threat to Hungarian national security".
- They demand that the Székely Land in Romania is given *territorial autonomy* (the Székely Land is a territory in Romania which is primarily inhabited by Hungarians). Combine that with Jobbik's insane idea of the Hungarian National Guard—an idea they, of course, implemented in practice—and it doesn't take a paranoid to predict a war going on in the future.
- The party is against globalised capitalism. That by itself isn't such a despicable idea. However, Jobbik made it clear that it specifically opposes Israeli and Jewish investments in Hungary. In May 2013, when the World Jewish Congress announced its plan to have its 2013 congress in Budapest, the party's chairman (!) said the following: "The Israeli conquerors, these investors, should look for another country in the world for themselves because Hungary is not for sale". I fail to find the connection between deciding to hold a congress in Hungary and buying out the entire country, but I suppose that Nazi asses follow their own logic.
- A newsletter published by an organization headed by a Jobbik candidate to the European Parliament (!) once had the following written in it: "Given our current situation, anti-Semitism is not just our right, but it is the duty of every Hungarian homeland lover, and we must prepare for armed battle against the Jews". Gee, thanks.

Now, you may choose to challenge me by saying that I shouldn't generalize an entire country based on the votes of 12% of the population. Oh well: in the 2006 elections, this party got 0.007% of the votes in the final round. So, no: I don't generalize saying that "all Hungarians are Nazi": absolutely not. Instead, I'm saying that something in the Hungarian society must be sick to the bone if it allows a Nazi party to multiply its relative power by 1,713 in four years (between two consecutive elections).

Admittedly, I was initially considering making my own protest by skipping the concert in Hungary. Eventually, I decided that my admiration of this wonderful band still supersedes my feeling of disgust towards Hungary's politics, so I shall go ahead and attend the concert. Instead, I decided to protest through this pathetic blog and attempt to contribute as little as possible to Hungary's economy.

I will leave it to the Hungarians to figure out what went so broken in their society. It's the Hungarian people who are going to suffer the consequences of their bent politics: I just hope that minorities in Hungary—not necessarily Jewish, of course—are going to survive this with minimum casualties.

The hotel for the night, Royal Park Boutique Hotel, is conveniently located less than 100 meters from the central railway station. Due to construction going on around the central railway station (and, in fact, spanning much of the same street westbound all the way to the

Danube), the station's huge main entrance is closed until further notice, sending people scrambling around for solutions how to get the hell out of that station and, more importantly, how to cross a single road without being killed. Construction, really, all around: fences everywhere and totally unclear signage as to where you should be going. That, together with the immense heat and Budapest's ferocious air pollution problem, wasn't exactly chicken soup for the soul.

Those 100 meters to the hotel were enough for me to determine that something's wrong in this area of Budapest. Looking around, you get the feeling that you don't want to be in this place at all, and that the place doesn't want you in it either. Groups of dusty, transparent people roaming the streets with empty looks in their eyes; garbage everywhere; poor infrastructure and the smell of rotten *something*; in one word, "the works". Fortunately, however, Jeroen did his homework well and the hotel turned out to be very good. €58 a night—a bargain —for a well-equipped hotel, beautiful inside. This hotel certainly doesn't belong in this area of the city.

Checked in, did some writing for slightly more than an hour, uploaded the previous post and decided to hit the streets looking for some more interesting scenery.

Once outside, decided to head west towards the Danube. That's where the "inner city" is, and to my recollection, that would be where things start being interesting here. Unfortunately, a look in the map showed that the "inner city" is about 2km away.

Bothers me to no end why neither of us thought about taking a bus there, or the metro. Instead, we simply started walking. Perhaps we had hopes of discovering anything worth the while along the way? who knows. Regardless, no; we didn't. Instead, we spent precious time walking through stinking streets, the sun reducing my life expectancy one step at a time, with the terrible, TERRIBLE smog-filled, disgusting Budapest air making me feel like vomiting.

Along the way, ran into Elian and Arnaud, who flew in from France to catch the concert. Both informed us that there's absolutely nothing interesting to see around, and that most interesting things in the city are on the other side of the Danube.

Things start becoming slightly better as you approach the "inner city" which is, perhaps not surprisingly, where tourists to Budapest are usually headed to.

The city of Budapest actually consists of two parts: *Buda* and *Pest*. The two are separated by the Danube river: *Buda* is the prettier, more affluent part; *Pest* is where the central railway station is, and where we ended up staying. Most interesting things to see and do are in *Buda*; still, the plan was originally to only spend one night here, knowing that there'll be no time to explore much anyway. If you are heading to Budapest for a few days, try to stay west of the Danube.

The more you approach the various bridges connecting Buda and Pest, the prettier things become.

As plans were to have dinner before the concert in a restaurant near the hotel, time pretty much ran out already. Decided to walk on the bridge of a few shots before heading back.

Backtracking, we decided to take a bus back to the hotel. A quick look in Google Maps revealed that it takes less than ten minutes to ride that entire disgusting stretch that we suffered so much walking through just an hour earlier. Boarding the bus, I asked for two tickets.

The driver looked at me and mumbled something in a language which I have a very strong reason to believe was Hungarian.

Needless to say, I don't understand Hungarian.

The driver refused to accept money. I didn't really know what else I should be doing. An impromptu decision was made to simply remain on the bus and see what happened. Nothing happened. The bus went on its way, and ten minutes later we were at the hotel.

Of course I had to find out what the hell the deal was with buses here. Turns out that buses are not free here. You can't, however, purchase tickets on the bus itself: you can buy those in kiosks, or in the reception of certain hotels.

Fine. I'll remember that for the next time I'm in Budapest, which I estimate to be at some point between "in two thousand years" and "never".

Back at the hotel to get ready for the concert, and out again for dinner.

Maarten and Bruno—heading to the Budapest concert from Germany and Switzerland, respectively—suggested, the day before, that we get together for dinner before heading to the show. The Dutchman took it upon himself to do the research and ended up with a place called Huszár Étterem, located about 10 minutes walk from our hotel.

Walking towards the place (plan was to meet the folks there), I started mocking the Dutchman. This entire area of Budapest looks so unfriendly, so uninviting, so dusty—heck, you lose your appetite just walking the streets around here. I spent the time walking there thinking about the tone I'm going to use in my voice when I finally tell the Dutchman "good choice, pal".

Bruno was there—good to see him, such a nice fellow—so, starving, we entered the place and got a table for four. Maarten showed up a few minutes later, and we were scanning the menus while catching up.

In the corner, we noticed a couple of folks holding musical instruments. You know, of these duos / trios who force their horrible music upon you while you're dining, expecting you to tip them. As soon as I noticed that, I was determined to simply ignore this despicable sales tactic; unfortunately, it was much harder to ignore the terrible "music" that the duo so violently forced out of their poor instruments.

As this is Hungary, I decided to try the goulash. Hungary is the home country of the goulash: as many Israelis have roots in Hungary (I don't), the goulash is also a very popular dish in Israel. I never really quite "connected" to it, but heck, I'm in Hungary, so why not give it a chance here?

After a bowl of "fruit soup" (sounds strange, huh? I know. It tastes even stranger. Basically, it's water with a few unidentified fruit swimming inside, plus whipped cream. Not ugly, but not something I'd try again without a gun pointed to my head), there came the goulash.

And it was hands down the best goulash I had in my entire life, and one of the tastiest meals I had in the tour. How *on earth* did they get to make it so tasty is way beyond me. That particular goulash involved some good amount of *sauerkraut* and steamed onion, as well as sour cream and some fresh herbs on top. Hell, it's 1:47am as I'm writing these lines and I'm drooling just *thinking* about that meal.

In one word, WOW. I don't know if it's something that this particular restaurant does well (when all the mockery about the surroundings is said and done, still, this restaurant is currently ranked #59 out of about 1,200 restaurants in Budapest, according to *TripAdvisor*), or maybe I grew up experiencing all the wrong types of goulash.

If you're in Budapest, go to that place. Service is great, it's operated by the owners. Cute little restaurant and the food is delicious.

Prices?

> Hungary is a part of the European Union, but not a part of the European Monetary Union. Over the years, the Hungarian governments were debating whether they should be joining the Euro zone; at the moment, it's unclear when Hungary is going to join the Euro zone, if at all.
>
> The local currency is called "Hungarian Forint", abbreviated *HUF*. The exchange rates reveals much about the inflation that took place here during the 1980s: as of this writing, 1 HUF = €0.0033 / $0.0044 US / $0.0046 CAD / 0.016 ILS.

For the westerner tourist, things here are ridiculously cheap. In the most touristic area of *Pest*, a bottle of mineral water costs €1. Earlier at the ATM, I was given a series of 2,000 HUF bills as well as one bill of 20,000 HUF. I decided I need some change, so I handed the 20,000 HUF bill to the cashier, who, in turn, choked.

Food here is, too, very cheap. A full three course meal in that wonderful restaurant, including drinks, went for about €11 per person.

From the restaurant, it was a short taxi ride to the venue. The taxi driver's English was pretty good and he seemed like he knows a thing or two about the city. He also appeared to be very nice and welcoming. Good chap.

I just had to ask.

– "Tell me something… this area of the city… is it a good area? a bad area? what's going on in it?"

The taxi driver went ahead to explain that this particular part of the city is now run down, much due to (are you sitting? I'm not making this up) *blacks, gypsies and all sorts of other "people" who decided to settle in this place*.

And that was in a taxi cab carrying four passengers.

I looked at Jeroen, Jeroen looked at me.

– "Oh. I see", I mumbled.

The venue, Budapest Sports Arena, is really called "Papp László Budapest Sports Arena". Papp László was a Hungarian boxer back in the 1950s, which was a little problematic for him as Hungary used to be a Communist country back then, disallowing boxing. He was, then, forced to travel to Vienna in order to practice and fight.

I have been to this arena before, during the 2010 Get Lucky tour.

Picked up the tickets, entered the venue.

The venue's arrangement: general admission, standing, in front of the stage; seated everywhere else. As usual, we had picked the seated option, leaving the general admission area to those who were going to attend less than 70 shows in this tour.

Concert started a few minutes past schedule, with the set including *Cleaning My Gun* (as customary for shows that involve standing audience) and excluding *Haul Away*. Good show—nothing out of the ordinary, really.

   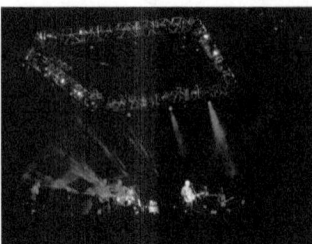

Those who have attended a few concerts before could tell you that, in the beginning of the show, one of the band's sound engineers travels along the venue holding a laptop in his hand. I'm guessing that this is done in order to measure the sound levels in different parts of the venue, so it can be fine tuned later. I have seen this guy almost 200 times before and don't know his name (maybe one of the readers can help out?). Anyway, he happened to have finished travelling through the floor area and decided to climb up the stairs to the seated area.

However, according to this venue's rules, this wasn't permitted for the audience. If you had a ticket to the floor area, it's the floor you're going to be in; if you had a ticket to the seated area, you can't access the floor. The venue placed staff in each and every passage between the floor and the seated area, to prevent people from moving between those two sections.

The staff member, mistaking the sound engineer to be a delinquent concertgoer, grabbed the sound engineer's arm preventing him from climbing the stairs (are these people even *allowed* to touch anyone?). As it was already during show time—*Corned Beef City* was playing, which kind of impedes the possibility of a quiet dialogue—it took him some time to explain to the staff member that she should leave him the hell alone as he's doing his job. He seemed to be pissed about it all.

Justifiably, I think. I wouldn't tolerate anyone grabbing my arms preventing me from going somewhere before fully explaining to me what it is that I'm doing wrong (unless, of course, they are just about to save my life).

Concert ended; a short metro ride—one station—back to the hotel, when I realized that I have quite a lot of local currency that I have nothing to do with.

Sat down at the hotel's bar for a drink and a chat with the nice lady in charge there. Started talking about things: Hungary… life here… the economy. Somehow, I got to ask about that neo-Nazi party I wrote about earlier in this post.

Turns out that Hungary's economy is in the toilet. Years of corruption in all levels of government have seriously eradicated the middle class: middle class—at least according to this nice lady—virtually doesn't exist anymore. For the most part, it's either you're working long hours just to make ends meet—or you're rich. Nothing in between.

A deteriorating economy has always been a fertile ground for extreme right wing political parties. When the public is in distress, it is very easy to gain popularity by throwing the blame at certain groups who are "not like us". That's exactly what the Nazi party did in Germany during the 1930s. Hungary's *Jobbik* party decided to do exactly the same, and… lo and behold, it worked.

I truly and genuinely feel sorry for the Hungarian people. Let's all hope for better times.

Signing off this post from my hotel room in Budapest. Yes, still. It's 2:30am here, and I decided to not go to bed before finishing up this post.

Tomorrow: Bratislava, Slovakia. Another place on earth that I had never been to before.

Isaac

Wednesday, June 26, 2013

Budapest, Hungary to Bratislava, Slovakia to Salzburg, Austria (June 23-24, 2013)

The Budapest hotel located where it was, it was decided to have breakfast at the hotel despite its ridiculous breakfast charge (€10 per person. More expensive than breakfasts I had in certain hotels in western Europe). The central railway station area in Budapest does not service well any of the five senses, which went to demotivate me from even considering looking for a breakfast place.

As our room was booked without the breakfast "privilege", we were told, upon check in, that we'd need to go through reception and notify them of our breakfast plans before heading to the dining room—which is what we did. However, arriving to the reception in the morning, the reception's staff was occupied handling all sorts of requests and bequests from other guests.

Looked at the clock (well, not really a clock. My Android phone's clock app). It was ticking.

"Hurry up", I didn't say.

They didn't hurry up, most likely because I didn't really say anything. So, I decided to try getting into the dining room and telling the attendant there to charge the damn breakfast to the room. That should be possible in any normal hotel.

But no, not here. The lady here needs a small ticket that you can get from reception. Without this ticket, you may as well starve to oblivion.

A ticket.

Felt somewhat like requiring a note from my parents the next day after missing class in third grade.

Well, she got the ticket alright. What did I get in return? a breakfast not worth the ticket allowing me into the Royal Breakfast Pavilion.

Ah, whatever. My second visit in Budapest: the first one ended with me being sick to my stomach for almost a week, so I suppose this visit was a step up in the ladder of joy. Settled the hotel's bill and off to the central railway station, happy to be heading off to a place that would (hopefully) make more sense.

Boarded the 1st class cabin of the EuroCity train. These EuroCity trains are regular-speed trains, usually old, and the 1st class cabins there (on routes that actually offer 1st class cabins) leave much to be desired if you're used to the 1st class cabins of the more modern high-speed trains. It's very common for cabins in these trains to consist of compartments, rather than the traditional row-based seating layout: each such compartment is basically its own little room, offering six seats. Some like it (Jeroen does), some don't (that would be me).

With us in the cabin, there were two mature men who didn't quite seem to be travelling together. The older one kept pestering the other with facts about places along the way, which didn't quite trigger any sort of appreciation by the receiving end.

The train ride from Budapest to Bratislava is scenic, showing old, modest houses on lush green hills. Old signs saying things in languages I can't make sense of, I didn't quite know when it was when the train left Hungary and entered Slovakia. What I did know, however, was that my SIM card doesn't provide discounted data roaming in Slovakia, so I was careful enough to turn data connectivity off while my phone was still connected to a Hungarian mobile carrier.

Finally, about three hours after leaving Budapest, arrived at Bratislava's central railway station. Welcome to yet another country and another city that I had never been to before.

The only context in which I heard about the city of Bratislava was when my father once went there on a trip with a few friends. That's all I knew about this city: it's name. Plus, of course, the fact that it was the capital of Slovakia since Czechoslovakia peacefully dissolved into two separate countries—Czech Republic and Slovakia—on January 1, 1993 (Prague was the capital of Czechoslovakia, and remained as the Czech Republic's capital after the dissolution).

Bratislava, then, is Slovakia's capital and largest city. It dates back to 200 BC (!) and changed hands many times since. Who has ruled this place since Europeans decided that they were in the habit of declaring wars on one another? better ask who hasn't. Reading about this city's history in Wikipedia, I lost my way around within minutes.

It was a Sunday, and as such, the path from the central railway station to the hotel—about 1km—seemed to be rather vacant of humans and vehicles. Frankly, the sights of that part of the city weren't that lucrative—maybe not as borderline appalling as Budapest's central railway station area, but still nothing that would make a typical tourist say *"this* is where I want to be". Weather was more forgiving than the day before in Budapest: still very warm, but not hot enough to make you feel like peeling your own skin off.

The hotel, Hotel Saffron, was located about a kilometer away from Bratislava's old city area. You could easily spot it from the distance as it is adjacent to a building that is painted in saffron yellow, which, I am guessing, wasn't a complete coincidence. A very good hotel for the price of around €70. Checked in and went for the elevators.

> One of the things I find interesting in this tour is encountering all sorts of oddities and peculiarities in how things work in different places. In particular, as I am staying in a different hotel almost every night, I find it astonishing that I need to get accustomed to small differences in the way hotels are designed. I know this may sound strange and trivial, but still. It fascinates me to see how differently different people can think and how they go about implementing solutions.
>
> So, in this hotel, there are two elevators. Usually, you'd just push the "up" or "down" button, and the system will decide which elevator to send over to you, based on all sorts of parameters (were you ever wondering what happens when you push the "up" or "down" button in an elevator? that is, how does the system decide which elevator to send over? I know I did. There are actually a few ways that elevator designers can go about implementing this, but the basic approach is the one that is implemented the most). Here, though, each elevator had its own "up" and "down" buttons. If you wanted to be sure you get to your destination the fastest, you had no choice but pressing both buttons and see what happens.
>
> If everyone is "greedy" (that is, pushing buttons for all elevators), the average waiting time (for all hotel guests) is expected to increase.
>
> Someone actually *designed this and thought it's a great idea.*
>
> Why are some people stupid?

Stuff unloaded in the room. It was early, which left ample time to explore Bratislava's old city area, about a kilometer away.

On my way, I saw this sign:

This club hones your English skills to deal with real life situations. That's quite the unique value proposition over all other language schools, which cater to prepare the student to deal with imaginary life situations.

A quick search in *TripAdvisor* suggested a place by the bombastic name of Bratislavský Meštiansky Pivovar. As of this writing, this place is ranked #6 in *TripAdvisor*, and for a very good reason. Interesting Slovakian dishes in the menu, tough to choose. Smoked meat dumplings with sauerkraut and sour cream—delicious. Full meal for two for under €20. I'm sold. Go there.

From the restaurant towards the old city area, the scenery gradually becomes more interesting.

Then, a short passage leads you to the old city area, which is where things become *really* beautiful. Nearly every moment walking through Bratislava's old city is a postcard moment. Nothing here is too grandiose, and still, prettiness is all around. Many pictures were taken, and very few of them will be filtered out.

You could understand, then, why Bratislava's old city area is the focal point of tourism in this city. Restaurants, cafes... you name it, it's there; and for westerners, this place offers great deal for the money: things here cost more than they would in the non-touristic parts of the city, but still low when compared to touristic areas in western Europe.

Walking down the path, arrived at the old city's Hlavné Námestie, which means "main square". Eventually, most tourists end up finding themselves hanging around this square, taking photographs of themselves ruining otherwise postcard-perfect buildings.

A short walk to the south, there's the Danube again. Seems like everywhere I go in this tour, the Danube is lurking somewhere.

Very clearly visible from both banks of the Danube is the pylon of the *Most Slovenského národného povstania* (meaning: "Bridge of the Slovak National Uprising"), simply referred to as *Nový most* (meaning: "New Bridge").

The bridge is known for the UFO-shaped structure positioned upon the bridge's pylon (there's a restaurant inside). The bridge was built between 1967 and 1972; most of Bratislava's Jewish quarter, as well as some of the old city's historical walls, "had to be" demolished in order to create the road leading to that bridge from the old city.

A short walk along the Danube…

… And back to the old city. A bazaar took place there, drawing tourists of all types, shapes and forms.

Perfect afternoon, walking around a beautiful city. Sipped some coffee in a local coffee shop, then headed back to the hotel (see the saffron-coloured building in the following picture).

The concert venue was located about 2km away from the hotel, which called for careful planning of when to leave the hotel, where and when to have dinner (it was a Sunday, which made things a bit more problematic in that regards)… the usual concert attendance planning routine which became second nature here (one of the things I learned the hard way is to never go to a concert when I'm hungry, or in the likelihood of becoming hungry during the concert. I can't enjoy anything on an empty stomach).

Somehow Jeroen dug up a place called Cafe Estremo, on the way to the venue.

Just like in Budapest's case, I was getting ready to mock the Dutchman for his pick as this cafe is located in a rather uninviting location. Still, this place currently ranks #9 in Bratislava by *TripAdvisor* so there must be something to it… and there is. It's an Italian restaurant offering absolutely fantastic food. Gnocchi in a sauce made of cream, walnuts and pears. Sounds screwed up, right? I know it does, which is precisely why I ordered it. It was all devoured before I knew it. Brilliant.

No time for desserts; off to the venue, located about 10–15 minutes walk up the road.

The NTC Arena (also called "Aegon Arena") is actually a tennis arena (NTC stands for National Tennis Center), also hosting concerts. It's a small venue, can seat very few thousands.

A good concert, fortunately featuring *Kingdom of Gold* which keeps getting better and better with (almost) each time it is being played.

Out of the venue and a long walk back to the hotel.

Was a very good day, actually. Short travel from Budapest, plenty of time to see a beautiful city, and a good concert to finish. Felt almost like a day off.

Monday: a new week. Early wakeup and breakfast at the hotel. The evening prior, we booked a taxi for the next morning, to take us to the central railway station: €5, saving us a kilometer worth of walk… no brainer. Sold.

Train was scheduled to leave 9:42am. Taxi was booked for 9:15am, the ride to the train station is about 10 minutes. When it was 9:20am and the taxi didn't show up, I started getting nervous and, once again, found myself questioning my belief in all living things. I have an extremely low level of tolerance towards people who aren't too good with keeping time, especially when I depend on such people, for example, to catch trains.

It did arrive, eventually. After taking all sorts of weird turns into side streets and whatnot—at times, I was sure that this driver didn't quite know where he's heading—the central railway station was at plain sight.

Relief.

The itinerary from Bratislava to Salzburg is tricky. From Bratislava, it's a regional train to Vienna's central railway station (*Wien Hauptbahnhof*). From there, one needs to take two underground lines in order to get to Vienna's western railway station (*Wien Westbahnhof*), in order to catch the train from Vienna to Salzburg. As Vienna's central railway station is still under construction (supposed to end in a couple of years), you need to walk about 10 minutes between the train's platform to the underground… outside. And it was raining.

Raining? yes, raining. After about a week of a horrendous heat wave in Europe, temperatures fell dramatically overnight. It felt weird to wear my red rain jacket again after spending about a week with the burning desire to peel my own skin off.

Hopped on the underground, quick ride to the city center, then change to another line… and there's *Wien Westbahnhof* again. Looks exactly the way it did a few days earlier. Nothing's changed.

As we arrived earlier than planned, we decided to ask whether we could take an earlier train to Salzburg than the one originally planned. Asked someone who initially appeared to be knowing anything, we got a strict "no".

Well, alright then. An hour to kill in this train station. Had lunch (to get it over with), and looked for a coffee place. Found a place called "Don's Espresso Bar", located inside the train station. From outside its glass door, it looked fabulous: everything that an espresso bar is supposed to have. Great decor, soothing dark colours… the works.

Opened the door and almost choked to death. The entire place stunk up from cigarettes' smoke. So, apparently, this place caters exclusively to those who are happy to smoke either actively or passively. Interesting concept.

Fun in the train station didn't end there. Found another coffee place, put the bags down and headed to the cashier. Asked what I want, I replied. Great. How much does it cost, I asked. Cashier points at a random direction and mumbles something in German.

Whatever; I'll sort it out with you later. Sat down waiting for the coffee to be ready. As it was ready, I went ahead to grab it, grabbed it, put it on the table and tried to pay again.

"How can I pay?", I asked a seemingly simple question, now for the second time.

Again, fingers pointed at a random direction. Now, that got me a bit peeved. Look, dear: I really, *really* want to pay you. There's money in my pocket that I worked *really hard* to save—penny to penny—just so I can gather it all up and pay you for the (hopefully) delicious cappuccino that you had just prepared for me and I'm *dying* to drink already.

I WANT TO PAY YOU, TAKE MY MONEY.

Again, a finger pointed at a certain direction. Then I noticed that she's pointing at some guy who appeared to be picking things up from tables and taking orders. Well, fantastic: this is a sit-down cafe, then? thanks for allowing me to place my own order at the cashier, then. How could I miss that?

Of course, took a while to grab this dude's attention—not surprising, as he was serving 900 tables at once. It was of the few times that I was actually happy to pay just so I could leave.

Up to the platform and to ÖBB's Lounge, fortunately accessible to us as first class passengers. Standing in line there, to be validated (you need to prove that you're allowed access). The bloke currently getting service appears to fill the receptionist in with his entire life story. Clock is ticking, damn it, I just want to sit down and chill out from this noisy train station. Five… long… minutes, approved, yes, you may sit down, thanks. Bottle of water and it was already time to leave.

Boarded the train and was happy to get that stress over with.

(If you feel stressed after reading the last few paragraphs, then I'm happy. Means that I properly delivered an emotion. Hell, I got upset just re-reading it.)

I've never been to Salzburg before. I also didn't know much about it until I got there. What I did know, however, is that many consider it to be a very pretty city. Because of that, the original plan was to stay in Salzburg during the day off after the concert, taking a night train to Paris—so I have enough time to explore this city.

These plans were later scrapped as I decided that I'm over and done with sleeper trains for the remainder of my life.

Arrived to Salzburg Monday afternoon, close to 4:00pm, due to some train delays (of course). Concert was scheduled to begin at 7:30pm, which meant almost no time at all to do anything in the city. That's fine, though: plans were to leave Salzburg the next day (Tuesday; a day off) late, allowing for a few hours to explore the city the day after the concert.

Camped at the hotel—the Ramada Salzburg City Center—attached to the railway station. I was dead tired: power-napped for an hour, woke up at 5:30pm and we headed out, hoping to get some good dinner before the show.

Unfortunately, the restaurant we had in mind turned out closed. Even worse: that was the only proper restaurant on the path leading from the hotel to the venue, some 2km later. What do you do? of course, you backtrack and look for the first viable option.

That was not a good thing to do. The first place turned up was a restaurant that belonged to a shady hotel. Serving Austrian, Italian and Indian food at once. Think about it for a second and tell me whether you think that such a restaurant can *ever* produce food that makes any sense. If you think it can, then I am smarter than you. It can't, and it didn't. Horrible expensive food. Ordered a "Parisian" schnitzel, which was allegedly based on turkey meat; got a sponge-like substance that only remotely reminded me of turkey. And I'm pretty sure it wasn't a happy turkey either.

Disgusting.

Off to the venue...

It was raining—not an ideal situation to take photographs—but still, even by merely walking (fast) towards the venue, I could easily tell that Salzburg is an immensely pretty city. Was looking forward to the next day, to get some time to explore it.

The venue, Salzburgarena, is a sporting arena also used for concerts, seating around 6,700. Pretty from the outside... nothing very special from the inside.

My friend Philipp from Switzerland made his way to this concert. Philipp is an amateur pilot, so he was planning on flying to Salzburg; however, due to the weather conditions, he had to change his plans so he drove instead. Six hours. Way to go for the tenacity and not giving up. Was good to see Philipp, as it always is.

The concert was slated to begin 7:30pm, and it was the first time so far in this tour (that I can remember) that the concert *really started right on time*.

Another good concert—*Kingdom of Gold* played again, that's two nights in a row—and, for the first time this tour, the set consisted of less than 16 songs. A 15 songs set (dropping *Haul Away*), slightly under two hours. Encore played in front of a crowded standing audience in front of the stage. Good times.

Concert ended; raining outside. Quick walk to Philipp's hotel to pick up a battery charger he was so kind to lend to me for the next couple of weeks, then back to the Ramada for a bit of writing, work, catching up with things.

Unfortunately, the Ramada's internet connection was a total failure, which is why this post is so late.

Signing off this post from my hotel room in Stuttgart, Germany. Brilliant day off today—details (and amazing photos) will be published in the next post. Tomorrow morning: heading to Paris.

Isaac

Wednesday, June 26, 2013

Salzburg, Austria to Stuttgart, Germany (June 25, 2013)

Tuesday, June 25, was a day off. The original plan was to check out of the hotel in the morning, hold the luggage there, spend the entire day in Salzburg and take the night train to Paris, arriving Paris Wednesday morning. However, after that terrible night sleep in Copenhagen and my decision to avoid night trains altogether, plans were changed. Instead of taking the night train, it was decided to take the 3:51pm train to Stuttgart, spend the night there and proceed to Paris the next morning.

The good news is that, in retrospect, that was a wise decision.

Woke up easily Tuesday morning, looked through the window and noticed that it was raining. It's likely that it never really stopped raining since the night before. Didn't rain hard, though; something between a drizzle and a light rain. Not something that will make you lock yourself up in a hotel.

Other than offering Wi-Fi service that hardly worked, that Ramada hotel showed interesting ambition asking €19 per person for breakfast. Yeah, right. I'm definitely going to buy a few slices of cheese, bread and yogurt for the price of one month rent in Bulgaria. Shove it, folks. Checked out, kept luggage there, put on rain jackets and went out to explore the city.

Salzburg is the fourth largest city in Austria. It is located on the banks of the Salzach River, at the northern boundary of the Alps. Wolfgang Amadeus Mozart was born and raised here before moving to Vienna when he was 25 years old. Salzburg's Old Town area is listed as a UNESCO World Heritage Site for its baroque architecture. For tourists, Salzburg is a preferred destination for its scenery... as shall be demonstrated soon.

From the hotel, headed towards the old city, with the intention of grabbing some good breakfast along the way. Just before the bridge, there was a Cafe Sacher—the same cafe that sells the famous Sachertarte.

There are three Cafe Sacher shops in all of Austria: one in Vienna, one in Salzburg and one in Innsbruck. Funny that within a few days I came across two of them already. We were standing in the rain speculating whether we want to have breakfast there, when I noticed another cafe located right next to it—Cafe Bazar. Jeroen then remembered that he read about Cafe Bazar online and it's supposed to be good. Not surprisingly, then, we went in.

Right upon entering this establishment, you know that you're in for a treat. It is surprisingly spacious: I am not a big fan of crowdedness, let alone before breakfast, so this place bode very well with me right from the get go.

The menu offered a few breakfast combinations as well as a few "a la carte" options. Took a while to ponder upon it all.

Waiter came by, asks what we'd like to drink. Cappuccino for me, thank you very much—so far I'm a big fan of what Austria has to offer when it comes to coffee.

Jeroen: "I'll have a tea."

Waiter: "English breakfast?"

Jeroen: "No, just the tea, I want to pick individual items for breakfast."

Now, you might think that Jeroen was sarcastic. He wasn't. He was completely serious, which explains why he initially failed to understand why both the waiter and myself were looking at him as if we were witnessing the discovery of a new planet populated exclusively by idiots.

Me: "I think he meant to the type of tea you'd like to have."

It was evident that the waiter was quite amused by it all. I know I was.

Beautiful breakfast. Never thought that even scrambled eggs on toast can be so delicious. Exceptionally creamy yogurt with fruit—savoured to the last bit. Brilliant cappuccino to finish it all up and I was a tremendously happy camper.

Go there. Don't miss it. It's a bit pricy but definitely worth it.

Breakfast was done and over with, the rain wasn't. We were considering just going back to the hotel, grabbing our luggage and take an earlier train to Stuttgart, until sense finally won. Heck, I'm in Salzburg already. I'm here. Rain isn't going to stop me from at least seeing a city that some people claim is the most beautiful one in Austria.

From the cafe, headed to the water and turned towards the bridge.

Crossing the bridge, you can already see that this city has at least some beauty to it. It's gorgeous even when the weather is lousy—I can only speculate what it looks like when it's sunny. Actually, no need to speculate: a decision has already been registered with me to visit this place again as part of a proper (non-tour) vacation.

Once the bridge is crossed, the old city is right in front of you. Tourists flock this area like termites. Mozart's portrait is all over the place, in every way shape or form that is sellable to passer byers who are looking to spend their money on souvenirs.

See that fortress up above? that's the Hohensalzburg Castle, one of the largest medieval castles in Europe. Decided to just go ahead and climb there. There's a funicular that takes you all the way up to the mountain, but we decided to walk instead.

How was that walk? one of the most beautiful walks I ever took in my entire life—despite the rain. The path leading to the top is steep (though well paved) and shorter than it looks like. If you're there and are capable of walking instead of taking the funicular—WALK. It'll take more time but you'll be greatly rewarded.

It's really amazing to find out that people actually *live* here, high up on the mountain, overlooking the city. The residential (fully detached, of course) houses here aren't extravagant by any means—for the most part, they appear simple and moderate in size. I can only speculate, though, regarding the land's worth in this place. Such a gorgeous environment.

I'll let the pictures do the rest of the talking.

The path leads to a few viewpoints, as well as a cafe. Didn't go all the way up due to lack of time (as we decided to take the 3:31pm train after all), but the first viewpoint was fantastic nonetheless.

I would have stayed up there for hours if I could. I liked being up there so much that I no longer minded the rain anymore. To get back down to the old city area, a few different routes are available, which means more scenery going down…

… before touching ground level again.

Having a couple of hours before the train's departure, we knew we need to grab some lunch before taking the 4 hours ride. So, that Cafe Sacher from earlier?… well, yes. That would be it. Decided to have a light meal, and have the day's primary meal later on in Stuttgart. The reason for this decision was driven mostly by the knowledge that Cafe Sacher specializes in desserts of all sorts, and partly by realizing that Salzburg's Cafe Sacher ranks #6 in all of Salzburg according to *TripAdvisor*, with raving reviews.

Indeed, it was brilliant. Soup to start, followed by a superb slice of cake and (of course) another cappuccino. The place's atmosphere is just so warm, cozy and inviting that, once in, you really don't want to leave. Same recommendation here: go there, it's pricy but completely worth it.

A quick walk back to the hotel…

… grabbed the luggage, and off to the train station.

Spent some time in the ÖBB Lounge. Train arrived a few minutes past schedule. Goodbye Salzburg—it's been fun and I will certainly visit again.

Off to Stuttgart on board the EuroCity train—this one's 1st class cabin having seats that can roll out into beds. Didn't use this feature, but it's nice to know that it exists.

Spend the time on the train revising the hotel plans for the night. Found a better hotel than the one originally booked—more expensive, but closer to the railway station and including Wi-Fi.

I have been to Stuttgart once before in my life, during the 2010 Get Lucky tour. I remember it being a pretty, cool city. Later on in the tour, I'll be spending two nights here which should be enough to cover some of what it has to offer—which is good, because weather sort of sucked as we arrived at Stuttgart's central railway station shortly after 6:00pm.

Stuttgart's central railway station—which is currently under construction for expansion—is located right at the city's center. From there, it's about five minutes walk to our hotel for the night—Hotel Pflieger, a small yet functional and proper hotel. Checked in and off to see some of the city center, with the intention to eat.

Just before leaving the premises, I decided it might be a good idea to ask the receptionist what would constitute a "local dish" in Stuttgart, and where would be a proper location to acquire such dish. The receptionist's eyes appeared to be lit with the bright light of a thousand suns as she uttered a word in German that I couldn't make any sense of and later figured it was Maultasche. Another dish mentioned was Zwiebelrostbraten (good luck pronouncing either of these), as well as a very solid recommendation about where to get access to such alleged delicacies.

Two kilometers walk (in the rain) later, we arrived at the location: Weinstube Zur Kiste. According to the hotel's receptionist, the cooks who were cooking the food in this place have been there for the last 43 years, and all food was fresh, home made... well, you get my point. That's the sort of place you'd like to go to.

Opened the door. So, this place was as "pure" German dining experience as it could possibly get. Essentially, this is a residential house that, at some point, was converted to be a combination of a restaurant and a bar. Very crowded: unless you reserve in advance, you are very likely to share a table with complete strangers. But you know what? for whatever reason—perhaps I was in a good mood after the fantastic Salzburg experience—I didn't care at all. I *wanted* that German dining experience.

For once, I was willing to let go of my deep desire to personal space. If this place offers proper, true German dining experience, then bring it on—I'll give it my best shot. Waited about 10 minutes or so for two spots to be vacated, and sat down next to complete strangers, in the upper floor right next to the kitchen. The room we were all in was definitely a bedroom in the house's previous life: it was small and and could contain up to about 14–15 people sitting one next to each other. Very friendly atmosphere, not at all intimidating despite the crowdedness.

One Maultasche and one Zwiebelrostbraten ordered, with the intention to share those. And, for the first time in *a while*, I asked for beer. A small, 0.3L glass. Praise the Lord, for the stuck-up snob decided to join the common people.

Big plates, delicious food. Couldn't ask for more. What's puzzling is, that if it wasn't for the receptionist at the hotel, I'd probably never find out about this place. Note to self: ask the locals.

Arrived back to the hotel at around 9:00pm. Early, but really, with this rain, there isn't much to do. Better end this day on a high note, I thought. Shoes off, laptop plugged in and stayed awake very late to catch up with things, chat for a bit and write this pathetic blog entry —not necessarily in that order.

Signing off this post from my hotel room in Paris. Arrived here at around 1:30pm. Will upload this and immediately head out—weather is perfect for a stroll outside this beautiful, fantastic city.

Isaac

Thursday, June 27, 2013

Stuttgart, Germany to Paris, France (June 26, 2013)

Wednesday, June 26, was a day I was really looking forward to: this tour around, that would be the first concert in France. Five concerts in a row in various places across this beautiful country, before heading back to Germany for a week (and returning to France for a few more dates, some time in July).

Not sure how many of you, who are reading this, had the chance to read my 2010 Get Lucky tour blog. If you did, then you should already know my feelings towards France: I love it.

My first time *ever* in France was during that tour in 2010, and I approached it with care, as I was told more than a few things about the French people: that they're arrogant; that they're snobbish; that they won't help tourists if they need help.

This is all complete rubbish.

Arrogant and snobbish? give me a break. The fact that they're not as polite as people in many other countries (notably Canada and the United States, where politeness is, more often than not, artificial), doesn't make them rude. They're direct, they're passionate about what they say and do—which is precisely why I think I can connect with the French mentality more than I can connect with many others. I myself am direct, upfront and passionate about what I say and do—a trait that I preserved rather well through ten years living in Canada, even though it closed a few doors for me (but opened a few others, probably better ones).

Combine this with the fact that the French cuisine is of the best that this planet has to offer, and you should understand why I was looking forward to visit France again; and what would be the best place to start, if it's not for the country's capital city?

From Stuttgart, there are a few high speed trains (TGV) headed to Paris every day. The ride takes about 3.5 hours, during which the train reaches speeds in excess of 300km/h. TGV rides that span multiple countries are usually *very* expensive: even EURail and Interrail pass holders are required to pay a hefty supplement fee to ride these trains. This particular train, for example, resulted in a supplement of €30. Without a rail pass, the price would be much more.

Having said that, the TGV's 1st class cabins are more comfortable to ride than the 1st class cabins of, say, the ICE trains. Seats are wider and more comfortable, and they also recline (slightly) better.

For international travellers—those who pay that extra fee—a light meal is also served on board. I can't remember whether I took an international TGV train during the 2010 Get Lucky tour; anyway, neither of us knew of the coming meal which is why we bothered consuming breakfast at the hotel as well as buy sandwiches from Le Crobag. Most of that meal, then, was left untouched.

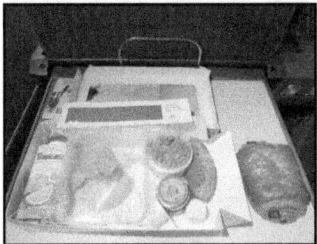

It was an uneventful ride to Paris, as I spent the time partly for attempting to doze off and partly for writing the previous post. These posts are surprisingly difficult to complete without proper internet connection—best I can do is to bring them into "almost finished" state, and finish them off once I have access to a hotspot. TGV, unfortunately, doesn't offer on-board Wi-Fi (other railway carriers, such as *Thalys*, do).

Train arrived to Paris-Est ("Paris East") railway station on time. Leaving the train, I took note of the weather: not too cold, not too warm, a bit cloudy but not too much—in other words, this should be a good day to spend outside.

The hotel for the night, Corail Hotel, was chosen for its location: a short walking distance from the concert's venue, as well as from Gare de Lyon—a major railway station in Paris. It takes two metro rides to get to Gare de Lyon from Paris-Est, which took a bit of time to figure out as I don't have much experience (read: hardly have any experience) riding Paris' metro system. It was around 2:00pm, and the metro was flooded with people. Much like a sardine, I got cramped up in a cabin on the M7 line, then changed in Châtelet to the M14. One more station… done. Off the train, up to the platform and exited Gare de Lyon onto the street.

Welcome to Paris.

From the station, it's a five minutes walk to the hotel. Checked in, and instead of heading straight out, I decided to sit down and complete the previous post. Believe you me, that was a tough decision to make. Weather outside was fantastic for a walk in the city, and the hotel's central location made it seem all to easy to just forget about writing any blog and head outside, being sucked into the rush that is Paris.

I hate deadlines (although I do insist to meet them, especially in my profession), and when I'm writing, I hate to be reminded that my time is up. Therefore, uncertain as to how long it would take, I informed the Dutchman that he should not wait for me. He didn't. Took me about 15 minutes to finish that post. Took a quick shower and headed to the streets.

A short walk north, there's the Place de la Bastille:

When the 2011 joint Knopfler-Dylan tour arrived at Lille, I remember going to an amazing desserts shop there called Meert. Those sweet memories (pun intended) prompted me to search whether there's a Meert store in Paris: Google Maps found two. Went to the closest one of them, but it turned out to be a very small store, offering mostly candy. Still, I earned about 10–15 minutes of walking around, taking photographs of this beautiful city.

Coffee time. A quick search in *TripAdvisor* brought up La Cafeotheque as a potential provider of coffee. It's currently ranked #563 in Paris… out of 9,774. Approximately 94% of all dining places in Paris are worse than this place, and in a city like Paris, that means a lot. Headed there…

Not a regular coffee shop. This place is divided into several "parts", a couple of which have dining tables and chairs, while one particular room—pictured below—was organized differently. A few random seats, plus one long cushion along the inner wall, and a few small tables (more like stands. They were very small) scattered around. Gives you the feeling that people here come to sit back and sip some coffee over a good book or something. I appreciated it.

The atmosphere there was so nice and charming that I didn't even pay attention that I spent about a full hour (!) there, sipping coffee and enjoying a delicious cheese cake while… well… hard to admit here, but yes: playing online chess. I lost more than I won.

Back on the streets, I just wandered around aimlessly. Crossed Pont Louis Philippe (*Pont* = Bridge), taking a few photographs of the Seine.

I couldn't possibly take good enough photographs to capture just how breathtaking this city is. You could easily spend a couple of weeks here and still have a few things left to see and do. Merely walking in these streets—even without any predetermined destination—is itself an enjoyable experience.

South on Rue Jean du Bellay, crossed Pont Saint-Louis, leading to Île de la Cité—one of the two remaining natural islands on the Seine within the city of Paris.

Accidentally, I entered a street that was flooded with tourists. Headed there. To the side, a beautiful square—Square Jean-XXIII, named after Pope John XXIII.

Right behind it, even more tourists were rambling around like maniacs. Turned out that, incidentally, the world famous Notre Dame de Paris is right there.

I could have kept on wandering around for hours; however, it was time to head back to the hotel and figure out technical issues such as... well... you know... dinner.

The Dutchman was already at the hotel when I arrived. He had his fair share of nice walks around the city as well. Of course, he took a few interesting photographs. I chose these two to include here: pictures from Pont de l'Archevêché—also called the "Padlock Bridge" because... well...

An attempt to look for a place online didn't go well. Well, that's the thing about using something like *TripAdvisor* or *Yelp* in a city with about 10,000 restaurants (that is, about 10,000 restaurants known to those search engines. Who knows how many more are there): the variety is so huge that you really don't know what to pick anymore. It's much easier to use such engines in smaller places, showing you 10–15 top places to pick from: in a city like Paris—especially in a central location such as the one where the hotel was located—you could easily sift through hundreds of restaurants, completely losing track over things.

One of my all-time favourite books was written specifically about this subject: The Paradox of Choice by Barry Schwartz. This book is a must read for anyone with the slightest interest in what motivates people to behave the way they do. Truly an eye-opening book. Read it.

Completely unwilling to spend too much time looking for a place, we decided on a place called Cafe Aux Cadrans located very close to the hotel and the railway station. Grilled salmon with pesto and wild rice, drinks and I was good to go.

The venue, Palais Omnisport de Paris-Bercy (often referred to as simply "Bercy"; "Bercy" is the name of a neighbourhood in Paris), is an indoor arena and concert hall in Paris. I am no stranger here, as I was here twice before: once during the 2010 Get Lucky tour and once during the 2011 joint Knopfler-Dylan tour. The Bercy is located a short walk from Gare de Lyon, even though there's a metro station (perhaps not coincidentally named "Bercy") steps away from it. The venue is surrounded by a myriad of dining places—cafes, pubs, bars, restaurants… really, endless. I'm pretty sure that this venue doesn't make a lot of money selling food: you need to be particularly negligent to arrive hungry to a Bercy concert (unless you were rushing or something).

Tickets pick-up took place in the regular place, through one of the side gates. As usual in the Bercy, an exceptionally long line-up for ticket collection (note: this is ticket *collection*, not ticket *purchase*. When you're in that line-up, you already have a ticket purchased: all you need to do is display some ID and get your tickets. Not rocket science). My friend Laurent joined a few minutes later and informed me that this is French efficiency at its best. I couldn't believe it when I was told that there were actually *three* people working inside, handing tickets to people. It really took forever. That's about 45 minutes of my life that I'll never get back.

Tickets collected, a group of friends decided to head to a nearby bar for a drink. As I had my annual third litre of beer just the preceding night, I opted out of alcohol. Everyone was ordering beers and other alcoholic beverages, and this stuck-up snob asked for a cappuccino. Laurent, communicating with the bartender, informed me that I can't get my cappuccino. Why? because the bartender doesn't have time to make it, he's too busy.

I still don't know whether Laurent was joking or not.

A minute later, I spotted a couple of familiar faces outside. My friends Jordan and Steve, from California, flew in for a few shows in France. Mike joined a couple of minutes later. Was good to see these good folks three years after we had a lot of fun getting together before, during and after concerts in North America and the UK.

Time ran out: headed to the venue. Entering through the gate, you are being checked by three different people. One checks that you're at the right gate, another checks your belongings (if any), and another scans your ticket. Again, French efficiency at its best.

The Bercy, while not too sophisticated a venue, is still impressive to look at.

Ruth Moody and her band are back to the opening act spot for Knopfler in France. Was good to see these folks again. As the Bercy was sold out for this concert, I'm gathering that close to 12,000 people watched Ruth perform—which is, if I recall right, the largest audience she performed in front of during this tour. Must have been quite an experience for her, but she and her band did very well.

Half an hour break after Ruth's opening act, and the lights went out again. Immensely loud cheers all over as the band was introduced: Mark's music is, and has always been, very popular in France, and the typical French audience isn't particularly known for it being of the laid back, quiet ones.

Of course, the audience and the band work in some sort of a feedback loop. Stronger audience reaction triggers better performances, and vice versa. This concert would definitely be considered of the top ones so far this tour, and Ruth joining for *I Dug Up a Diamond* and *Seattle* was a major push forward.

The audience… well, the audience went nuts. That, again, wasn't unexpected. That's one of the reasons why I like attending concerts in France: just being a part of the audience is already exciting. There's a lot of passion flying everywhere.

The *Running of the Bulls* commenced very early, as someone from the back decided to head to the stage way, *way*, before the encore. That triggered a major rush. I tried to avoid it, walking slowly towards the stage, when I was pushed by someone. I instinctively pushed back as my sore right wrist was hit, only to find out that it was my friend Vincent standing there. Apparently he was pushed by someone else right onto me. Sorry again Vincent… that was instinctive. Perhaps, with my wrist's condition, I shouldn't even have got up from my seat.

Beautiful encore played in front of a standing audience. As *Piper to the End* started playing, I was sure I heard some sobbing behind me. Turned around and noticed a guy who was obviously extremely excited and obviously emotional by whatever was going on (I wouldn't be surprised if this had something to do with the actual song, rather than the event itself: *Piper to the End* is a very touching farewell song, written by Mark about his uncle—a piper in the Scottish infantry, who carried his pipes into the battlefield, where he eventually died). I realized that his view of the stage was rather blocked, so I offered my spot to him—an offer that he appeared to be very happy to take. Glad to have been of help.

After the concert, a group of friends decided to head to that same pub for drinks. Sure, why not. Vincent was there as well with a few friends for a while—thanks for the drink, pal, and sorry again for that push!—and it was already after midnight when Nelly and I bid everyone else goodbye and headed back to Gare de Lyon, where our hotels were located.

Great, fantastic day in the gorgeous city of Paris. Hell, it's about time I head there for a proper vacation. A day is *far* from being anywhere close to enough.

Signing off this post from my hotel room in Caen. Will head for dinner now, and then to tonight's concert.

Isaac

Friday, June 28, 2013

Paris to Caen, France (June 27, 2013)

After a wonderful evening in Paris, woke up feeling not much more than half rested. The hotel's air conditioner didn't seem to work during the night—only circulating air around, not cooling it. I have low tolerance to heat when I'm asleep, which is why I woke up a couple of times during the night.

Of course, the air conditioner started working wonderfully, cooling the room to the temperature of 17°C, as soon as I woke up.

The hotel, Corail Hotel, was centrally located and reasonably priced. Of course, you can't have it all in this world, so the great ratio between price and location came on account of the room's size. Two single beds, short gap between them, almost no room to walk around.

Jeroen's headphones' battery ran out, and he was sure he had some extra batteries lying around in his pack. The reason I'm telling you this has nothing to do with my level of interest in Jeroen's portable energy reserves (which amounts to no interest at all), but has to do with the fact that there wasn't enough room around to open the pack comfortably and mess around with it. That's how small the room was.

Left the room feeling a tad claustrophobic, back to the railway station's area for a glorious (and expensive) breakfast, watching Paris go by. Back to the hotel, grabbed the luggage and off to the metro station. A few stops to Paris Saint-Lazare, arriving way, *way* too early.

The schedule: easy. From Paris, it is about two hours direct train ride west to Caen. It wasn't the TGV, but still a fast train boasting an excellent 1st class experience. Split the ride between trying to catch up with sleep and writing: writing didn't go well because I kept losing 3G signal along the way, and sleeping didn't go to well because I can't fall asleep for more than a minute in a rattling cabin.

Arrived at Caen right of schedule.

"Caen? hold on a second. Isn't it where they have that famous film festival?"

—That's what I thought to myself when I first read the Privateering tour's schedule. Yes! The French Riviera. I only wish it would be for more than one day.

So, no.

Even Wikipedia, under the Caen entry, states—in the very first line:

> *Not to be confused with Cannes.*

Caen is a small town located in France's north west, a few kilometers south of the English Channel. The city is located in the region of Normandy: shortly after the Invasion of Normandy during World War II, much of this city was destroyed before being liberated by British and Canadian troops.

Its population count is around 120,000 and whoever I asked about this town said that there's nothing really interesting to see or do there.

I still had quite a bit of writing to do, so I passed on the opportunity to explore the area and spent a couple of hours in the hotel room, writing and writing even more, as the Dutchman set off to see what this small town has to offer:

Isaac's "Privateering" Tour Blog

Finished writing in just about the time the Dutchman arrived back to the hotel. Post uploaded—it always feels good; some feeling of accomplishment—and stormed out looking for a pre-concert meal.

During the 2010 Get Lucky tour, I often encountered serious trouble feeding myself in France and Spain. This is because restaurants there tend to follow certain opening hours throughout the day, and this problem is magnified the smaller the city you're in. If you are to dine out, you better adjust your dining time to certain timeframes—which is not necessarily bad overall, but extremely problematic when you crisscross the country by train. Why? simple: often, train rides take place during the time when restaurants are open, and once you arrive at your destination, it's too late for lunch and too early for dinner.

What do you do in that case? well, you have the obvious option to starve to death; but, assuming you are not a masochist, you simply have to find a place offering lighter fare—usually sandwiches, desserts and such. At times, you may come across proper restaurants offering food outside the normal dining hours: you are likely to run into those in the more tourist-centric areas, and food there tends to be way overpriced considering its quality.

That's exactly what happened in Caen. Looking for proper food had us walk through the (small) city center a few times to compare between the available options. There was no place that could offer what we were looking for, so ended up getting a small wrap in Big Apple Coffee, then heading to a nearby Paul shop where I was refused a cappuccino (again—second time in two days!) but allowed a proper sandwich, and then head back to Big Apple Coffee for… well… coffee.

That's quite the effort to exert when you're hungry.

A lesson was learned: in France, Italy and Spain, research will be done ahead of time to decide where to eat upon arrival.

Nevertheless, Caen's town center area isn't too cruel on the eyes. It is small, and maybe there's not too much to see and do, but I wouldn't call it a total failure. Took some photos myself.

Came across a restaurant that offered tartars made of lawyers:

I don't have much against lawyers, but I still wouldn't want to eat them.

Back to the hotel to grab a rain jacket—as weather forecast called for some drizzle later on—and out again, heading to the concert.

The venue, Zénith de Caen, is located about 2km away from the city center. It is a part of the Zénith "chain" of indoor arenas. It can seat about 7,000, and it did—as this show, like most other shows in France, was sold out.

First thing was first: collecting the tickets, quite expectedly going through French efficiency at its best. Long line to a small booth. Two people working inside, and still the line takes forever. The two seemed to not really understand what they were doing there in the first place. Are the tickets in this pile? no… let me look… maybe in this one? yes. Ah, no. Asking her colleague now. Meanwhile, it gets crowded inside, as the booth's entrance also serves as an exit (otherwise people's lives might be comfortable).

Fifteen minutes in line to collect the tickets, then trying to enter the venue through the wrong gate. Forget the fact that entrances' lines were pretty much vacant: still, no, you have to enter through *that* gate. Yes, Sir: please, control me. Correct me. Lead me. I will learn an awful lot about life if I am redirected from one empty queue to another.

Entered the venue and headed to the hall itself. Approaching the hall, I noticed yet another long, *long* line-up of people standing on some reddish carpet. OK, that's a first: I can't recall seeing a line-up in such a strange location and in such a strange context—not even in Canada, the mother land of all queues, where people fight for their right to queue anywhere, anytime, for any reason.

What is that queue for? I didn't know. Now, the entrance to the hall was very wide, and the queue was very narrow, so we just entered the hall. An usher came over and mumbled something in French. At that point I already lost patience towards any sort of bureaucracy or protocol: really, screw this. Just headed to my seat completely ignoring my surroundings.

I can't speak French to save my life, but the Dutchman can (to some extent). Turns out that we were asked whether we were "already seated". According to this venue's protocol, you need to be seated by staff upon your first entry to the venue.

Excuse moi? no, I wasn't "already seated". Here's my seat, right in front of me. It's two meters away. Are you really expecting me to wait in line just so your colleague can peek at my ticket and prove to me that they know how this venue is organized—let alone that the line is huge and the concert starts in just about three minutes?

Don't think so, but really, thanks anyway.

Apparently, though, I was a minority in my line of thinking. That queue just kept growing.

Ruth Moody and her band, the opening act for Mark et al in France, showed up on the stage performing their usual set. Apparently, her parents were in the audience. That didn't do much to affect the performance, which was, as usual, lovely.

Of course, ten minutes into Ruth's performance, people were still being "seated" by the courteous staff. Now, what happens once an usher seats a person? they have to go back to the line-up, to collect the next victim. How do they go about doing so? AH. Good question. They do so by running through the aisles. Imagine that, staff running through the venue through the first 10–15 minutes of the show.

Ruth's act concluded: about 20–25 minutes break and Paul Crockford arrived at the stage, asking the audience to welcome Mark back to Caen, setting of a stellar concert, not at all less impressive than the one performed just 24 hours prior in Paris. I was expecting a shorter set (as the band had to fly back to Paris), but no: a good 17 songs set, including the "Golden Moody Trio"—*I Dug Up a Diamond*, *Seattle* and —performed with Ruth for the first time since the Amsterdam show—the mighty *Kingdom of Gold*.

During *Marbletown*, certain people decided it'd be a great idea to applaud during the performance's more subtle part, prompting someone from the audience to emit a rather strong shushing sound, stopping the applause but starting a wave of laughter instead.

For the first time in quite a while, *Speedway at Nazareth* was skipped, triggering a rush of enthusiastic bulls towards the stage. Learning my lesson from the night before, I walked forward very carefully. No injury this time. Let a short nice girl in front of me (she seemed to be way overly ecstatic of whatever was happening on the stage); joy, happiness and peace for all.

Looking at the stage, I noticed a large piece of paper, on which there was written—

I was at the Royal Albert Hall. Please play Sultans tonight!

—which made me wonder perhaps I should bring my own piece of paper to the stage, with something like the following written on it:

I have been to all concerts so far in this tour, please skip Sultans tonight as well. Thank you.

(Unfortunately, I don't have a photograph of that paper to share here, but I will in a few days.)

After the concert, a light drizzle through the 20 minutes walk back to the hotel. I was planning on doing some writing but was so tired I decided to skip.

Signing off this post from my hotel room in Rennes. Will try to take a nap before heading to the venue. Need to catch up with some sleep.
Isaac

Tuesday, July 2, 2013

Caen to Rennes to Clermont-Ferrand to Dijon, France (June 28-30, 2013)

The last few days in France were characterized by moderate to severe tiredness, difficult travel, difficulties eating… too many difficulties that made it rather unfeasible to sit down and write anything.

In fact, I hardly even used my laptop at all since I left Caen on Friday morning.

From Caen, the shortest train ride to Rennes requires you to change in Le Mans. Early 9:02am train to Le Mans, about an hour and a half spent trying to catch up with some sleep and failing. About half an hour stop there, then a TGV train to Rennes arriving 12:30pm.

My experience shows that, when planning to follow a tour, relying solely on public transport, your best bet is to always book your accommodations as close as possible to the port of travel from which you're heading out the next day (a central railway station, an airport etc.), and worry about getting to and from the concert venue later. So, the good thing about the Rennes experience was that all key locations —the central railway station, the hotel for the night and the concert venue—were all located within a few minutes walk from one another.

Having learned the lesson from the miserable experience in Caen revolving around looking for food, the intention in Rennes was to go out for lunch as soon as possible. Arriving at the hotel, Hotel le Sevigne, the room wasn't ready yet so luggage was stored there and the search for food began. It didn't take long. Less than one minute walk from the hotel, there's a French restaurant that received excellent reviews online: Le Galopin. It was my first French dining experience in France, and it was nothing short of amazing. Three course lunch menu for under €20.

> One thing I like about French restaurants—and I am referring not necessarily to restaurants serving French cuisine, but restaurants that are "behaviourally" French—is the dining experience. It's not only about the delicious food that often makes you wonder "how on earth did they come up with *that*?"; it's about the experience involved in actually spending time in that restaurant. From the moment you're led to your table until the moment you leave, you get the sense that you're not only there to eat, but also to enjoy yourself.

Happy that I got dining and nutrition sorted out for the day, I headed back to the hotel and worked on finishing the previous post. That took a while. Then, instead of heading out to the beautiful day and explore the city, my brain signalled that it needs a rest; my body complied by crawling under the blanket and falling asleep within approximately 4 seconds.

> It is indeed disappointing that, often, I need to give up some time in the sun exploring new places. However, that's a risk I was already aware of when I decided to write this blog. It does take an awful lot of time—time which could otherwise be spent sleeping (at night) or exploring (at day). But if it wasn't for the writing, I wouldn't have followed this tour to begin with.
>
> So please, if we happen to run into each other, please don't bring this point of "but you don't get to see anything" up. I am well aware of it.

Woke up at around 6:00pm feeling fresh. My friend Laurent and his wife Carole were in town for the concert: the concert in Rennes being a general admission one, Laurent has decided to arrive at the venue early in order to catch a good spot. Carole decided to pass, so we opted at taking a walk around the city center and grab a bite together before the show.

The city of Rennes (pronounced "Renn") is located in France's northwest, and is the capital of the French region of Brittany. A little more than 200,000 people live here. Comparing to Caen, which I had visited just a day before, Rennes had much more to offer in terms of scenery.

Spent less than an hour in the old city area, which was enough for me to determine that this place deserves a spot in my list of places deserving another in-depth look in the future.

Jeroen, who went to see the city earlier by himself, took a few photographs as well:

Before heading back to the venue, it was time for a quick bite. Being asked what is it that I wanted to eat, I told Carole that I simply don't care, and that I grant her full authority (and responsibility) to decide where it is that we're going to eat, and what it is that I'm going to eat and drink. When in France, let a Frenchwoman decide such minutiae for you, that's what I say. Delicious crepe with salmon, spinach and other goodies, finishing with some apple cider. Apple cider? yes. I wouldn't have thought of that my self, but Carole said that it's either apple cider or I don't drink anything at all. You know what? fine. Hit me.

Was great. Big thanks to Carole for showing me around and telling me what to do.

Headed back to the venue, a short walk from the old city center, arriving about 5–10 minutes before the scheduled start time.

The venue, Le Liberté, is located near the city center. For this concert, there were seats only at the perimeter—about 10 rows of seats or so—while the entire area between the stage and the back seats was open. The entire venue was "general admission", including the seats: therefore, even if you opt at sitting at the back rather than standing, you need to show up early in order to grab a seat.

Arriving a few minutes before the concert's start time, the venue was absolutely jam-packed with people. I can't recall other general admission concerts that were as packed as this one. In his diary, Richard Bennett wrote that you couldn't possibly shoehorn another person into that venue: that's exactly what it felt like.

When entering the venue, I didn't stand much chance looking for Jeroen, who was already at the venue. We had agreed to meet in the venue earlier, an agreement that I violated by opting to spend more time in the old city center. Asking him through the mobile for his location, he responded with "right in front of FOH". Now, apparently I was expected to know that "FOH" means "Front of House", but for the life of me, I had no idea what "FOH" stood for and, even if I knew that it referred to "Front of House", I wouldn't even know what "Front of House" meant.

As I was struggling to figure out the meaning behind the secret acronym of "FOH", it turned out that Laurent and a few other friends were seated right above the entrance. Asking them for help locating the Dutchman, nobody really stood a chance doing so as there were too many heads around. As I was still pondering what to do, Laurent called my name again saying that a seat was vacated right in front of him, upstairs. A couple of minutes to show time, I decided to head upstairs and be seated.

As a consequence, I ended up watching the concert with no Dutchman around, for the first time since autumn 2011 (the joint Knopfler-Dylan tour).

At the back of the venue, sound is usually better than in the front section, so the loss of visuals is often compensated for by better audio. As usual for standing audiences this tour, *Cleaning My Gun* was played (*Haul Away* just doesn't fit such concerts), and it was surprising to find *Gator Blood* played at the encore. Loud concert, loud audience, good experience.

As Ruth Moody and her band are opening for Knopfler in France, and concerts in France typically kicking off at around 8:00pm, it's usually around 11:30pm when you leave the venue. All of the energy gathered during that afternoon's sleep seemed to have flown out the window. Had to pass on drinks with Laurent et al, bid everyone goodbye and headed directly to the hotel.

Tired, hungry… and tired again, which wasn't very pleasant knowing that it was going to be a very short night.

After Rennes came Clermont-Ferrand. Now, getting from Rennes to Clermont-Ferrand by public transit is far from being pleasant: leaving Rennes at 7:07am (!) to Lyon, arriving 11:30am; then a very short 10 minutes connection time, departing Lyon at 11:40am arriving Clermont-Ferrand at 2:05pm. That journey was one of the closest calls in the tour with respect to missed connections: any delay during the journey from Rennes to Lyon would result in a severe delay arriving to Clermont-Ferrand. Unfortunately, so far in the tour, train delays have been more common than I would have expected.

Woke up at around 5:30am after a short, insufficient night sleep. Got everything ready and went to the hotel's dining room for breakfast as soon as breakfast became available at 6:30am. Nothing beats eating breakfast in a rush, after a short night sleep: a day starting like that is bound to be far from perfect. Mediocre breakfast—which appears, by the way, to be the norm in French hotels—all consumed within 10 minutes and then a short walk to the central railway station to catch the TGV train, right on time.

The long train ride from Rennes to Lyon—more than four hours—was spent mostly trying to fall asleep. When the journey began, I pulled my laptop out and started writing this post. Two sentences later, I realized that my eyes can't quite focus on the screen anymore; shut the laptop down with a great deal of frustration and spent the entire ride trying to fall asleep. Didn't manage except for a few naps.

These are the moments—when your eyes are glazed; focusing on nothing; your brain feels like a mush; you're tired, but can't fall asleep; and all within a train riding at 320 km/h—these are the moments that make you wonder what it is that you're actually doing here. It's not a new feeling—I have experienced it many times during the 2010 Get Lucky tour, especially towards the end. Almost three months away from home, out of which two months spent in extreme travel, homesickness kicked in right above and below the belt.

Homesickness, towards either homes.

On one side, there's the city of Vancouver—whose standing as the best city on this planet to live in (*in my eyes*. Don't start getting sensitive and defensive on me here) has been strengthened even further during this intense travel in Europe. The more I travel in the old continent, the more I learn to appreciate how fortunate I am to be living in that beautiful city in Canada. I fully understand now why Vancouverites are perceived as snobs in the eyes of their fellow Canadians—it's just that the city of Vancouver is such a damn fine place to be in. I long to once again live in its beautiful city center, surrounded by beaches, parks and snow peaked mountains.

> Those who think that I am exaggerating in my appreciation of that city are well advised to attempt living there for a while. I have heard of many, *many* cases of people who came to visit and never went back to wherever they came from. Try and see for yourself.
>
> On the other side, there's the metro area of Tel Aviv, Israel. Israel… that exciting, troubled, constantly misrepresented and undervalued country to the eastern shore of the Mediterranean Sea, and where I happened to be born and raised. The country that is portrayed by worldwide media as the constant violator of human rights; as a war-mongering monster seeding worldwide political instability. The country that was condemned by the ridiculous United Nations more times than North Korea, Syria (I suppose the United Nations isn't intervening there because it's still busy counting the casualties), Iran, Iraq, Libya, and Saudi Arabia (where they still behead criminals. Well, at least they're considering stopping doing so, as they're running out of swordsmen. They're considering crucifixion and firing squads instead) combined. The country which is currently undergoing a profound, immense change led by the younger generation who is sick and tired of the conflict- and corruption-laden mentality of their predecessors. Scenery-wise, it can't compete with much else: it has no snow-peaked mountains; even fresh water is scarce. Life is *very* hard—virtually nothing can be taken for granted there nowadays—but this is where my entire family, as well as the vast majority of my circle of friends, live.
>
> Two homes I have, and I am spending three months crisscrossing the old continent which is right between them. Visions of Vancouver's Stanley Park mingle with recollections of Tel Aviv's beaches; visions of my beautiful apartment in the 27th floor of a a high rise located in the very center of Vancouver's downtown—with my five guitars all laid up next to my piano just begging to be played—are mingled with those of the poor, neglected neighbourhood in Tel Aviv's suburbs where I spent my first 25 years of living.

Eyes went shut…

… And then reopened. 11:30am, stormed out of the TGV train as if I was on fire. Ten minutes to catch the connecting train. Line-up to get out of the train: an annoying small kid refuses to leave the train, prompting his mother to attempt all sorts of methods to convince him to comply, and holding dozens of other innocent passengers hostage. "Pick the kid up and just leave the damn train", I said. To myself, of course.

YES! Mr. Prince Charming finally agreed to leave the train. On the platform, running towards the exit. A flight of stairs. And another one. Now where is the damn departures board? oh, there it is. Wait, which one is our train? YES—there it is. Hurry up! another flight of stairs. Carry luggage up—of course, with my left hand, as the right hand is still out of commission—

—Made it. Arrived at the platform about a minute before the connecting train arrived. *Phew*. Boarded the train, 1st class cabin… which left much to be desired.

Slow ride, again spent staring at nothing in particular with thoughts running in virtually all directions. Two hours and a half, and arrived at Clermont-Ferrand on time.

Clermont-Ferrand is yet another city in France of which existence I knew nothing of before looking at the tour's schedule. It is located almost at the very center of France—about 400km south of Paris—and is known for being surrounded by (dormant) volcanoes (the Chaîne des Puys). As implied by the city's name, what's known nowadays as Clermont-Ferrand used to be two separate towns—Clermont and Montferrand—joined together in the days of Louis XV.

From Clermont-Ferrand's central railway station, it was a long, hilly 2km walk from to the hotel for the night, Kyriad Hotel Clermont-Ferrand Center. As the hotel was located very close to the city center—two minutes walk, maybe—we decided to look for a place to eat before even checking in: we were *that* hungry. Quickly enough, we realized that carrying luggage around while looking for food wasn't going to work out: headed to the hotel, checked in and went back to the city center area.

In the meantime, my friend Ingrid was making her way from her home in The Netherlands to Clermont-Ferrand, to attend the concert (now, I should tell you that the distance involved is just about 850km). The three of us agreed to get together in our hotel, and catch a pre-concert dinner together; however, the Dutchman and myself were so hungry that we couldn't really wait anymore.

Looking for lunch in Clermont-Ferrand turned out, quite expectedly, to be a nightmare. Many tourist-centric cafes around the city's main square—places that you just know are bound to provide mediocre food for stupid prices. On the other hand, there's *TripAdvisor* recommending a French restaurant, Le Dome, located inside a big shopping center right by the city's main square. Problem: expensive. That resulted in us walking around the main square looking for other options, failing to find any. It's either that places are closed, or not offering any seating space, or are obvious tourist traps… one restaurant—an Italian one—was actually open, but once we sat down inside, we were informed that it's only open for drinks and snacks: no lunch. I suppose nobody there thought it might be a good idea to put up a huge sign in front of that place, saying "NO FOOD HERE, PLEASE GO AWAY".

Somehow, I get the impression that my most useful suggestions are often ignored.

Nightmare, I tell you. Being hungry in small cities in France, while outside normal dining hours, is a nerve-wrecking experience. I wouldn't recommend it to anyone.

What a mess.

Eventually, resorted to that expensive French restaurant located in the shopping center. At least they agreed to serve lunch. Good food (though not as good as that wonderful experience in Rennes), blood sugar level back to normal. Sanity restored, you can talk to me now.

Back at the hotel, and Ingrid showed up moments later. Whenever Ingrid is present, you get the sense that things are going to be OK from now on (that is, assuming that Ingrid is on your side. If Ingrid is not on your side… well… mercy on your soul). Asked Ingrid what it is that we should be doing next, as I was too tired and too apathetic to my surroundings to even care; but this is Ingrid, and you can trust Ingrid to come up with good, solid plans for pretty much anything.

Out of the hotel again to the city center for a few snacks and some coffee.

Now, I have to tell you this: as good as the French cuisine is, and as good as restaurants in France are, their coffee generally sucks. Well, "sucks" is not a strong enough word; I would use another word, but then I would violate my own rule of not using that word ever again (in writing) after receiving some constructive criticism from a reader (who just happens to be the mother of my ex. You see, I learn from everyone). At any rate, I keep giving it a chance and I keep getting disappointed.

As we were sitting in Clermont-Ferrand's main square, suddenly the drums started banging. What the heck? what's going on? well, it was some sort of a parade. If any of you knows what this parade is for, or what it represents, please add a comment to this post and explain. Thank you.

Update, July 5, 2013: According to a commenter by the name Benoit, this parade is a part of the Saint-Jean celebrations in France. Thank you Benoit for the info.

Back to the hotel as it was time to head to the venue. Luckily, we had Ingrid on our side as the venue was located far away from the city center so a car was needed to get there. As a matter of fact, it wasn't even located in Clermont-Ferrand.

The venue, Zénith d'Auvergne, is located in Cournon-d'Auvergne, about 10km away from Clermont-Ferrand's city center. It is yet another venue in the French Zénith series of venues: opened in 2003 and has the capacity of 8,500. Located right off the nearby freeway, the entire area seemed scarcely populated, and perhaps as a consequence, a *huge* parking lot was adjacent to the venue, free of charge.

My friend Nelly, who lives a couple of hours away from Clermont-Ferrand, was on site along with her parents. Many other familiar faces and figures made it to the concert. After the Rennes concert experience, it was good to be seated closer to the stage in a much less crowded venue.

Good gig, after which a group of us gathered together in front of the venue, chatting, passing the time until the parking lot clears up a bit (that's usually the problem with arriving to a concert venue with a car: it takes forever to leave the parking lot). Half an hour after the show, there was still a traffic jam leaving the venue. Ten minutes to ride approximately 50 meters. Finally hit the highway… minutes later, Ingrid dropped us off at the hotel and went on her way to spend the night in Saint-Etienne, about an hour and a half away.

> Altogether, Ingrid drove a little more than 1,000km in 18 hours. She attended the show and didn't seem tired *in the slightest*. I have not the tiniest clue how she did this. A normal human being should not be capable of driving so much and still maintain such level of energy. I call for a DNA check on Ingrid. Something must be wired a bit differently there.

At the hotel, I discovered I'm starving. Held to my guns and decided to go to sleep hungry. Time to lose a couple of pounds I gained over the last two months.

Sunday morning in Clermont-Ferrand was beautiful:

And, as it was beautiful, it was quiet. The usual morning routine and we were ready to go traveling again. Next destination: Dijon.

The original plan was to take the train from Clermont-Ferrand to Lyon; then change and proceed to Dijon. That, however, would have us arrive at Dijon outside normal dining hours… *on a Sunday*. The day before, I discovered how awful such an itinerary might be. As Ingrid was going to attend the Dijon concert as well, the revised itinerary was to get off the train in Lyon, wait for Ingrid there (as she would be making her way up north from Saint-Etienne), have lunch together in a proper restaurant in Lyon and then go by car to Dijon.

That idea (to which I take the credit for coming up with) seemed to work well for everybody. Everything worked as planned: Left Clermont-Ferrand at 8:57am, arrived to Lyon's Part-Dieu station at 11:20am. Ingrid was still about an hour away by car, so we went on to look for a nearby restaurant.

Nothing was available, which is not very surprising as we were looking at the wrong place. Lyon Part-Dieu, while being Lyon's prominent railway station, isn't exactly located in the most interesting area of the city.

> I have been to Lyon before, during the 2010 Get Lucky tour. Wish I had more time, this time around, to look around. Lyon is a gorgeous city.

Agreed to meet Ingrid at the railway station and explore from there. A quick look in Google Local hinted at a place called Brasserie Georges, receiving raving reviews left right and center. What can I say? another extraordinarily delicious meal in a French restaurant.

> I also got to try what turned out to be the spiciest Dijon mustard I ever had in my entire life. Put a respectable amount of that mustard on a piece of bread, ate it and felt as if my eyes were coming out of their sockets. Really, it felt as someone was setting my throat and nose on fire; and just as it was spicy, it was irresistible.

Spent about a couple of hours enjoying fantastic food in the restaurant's patio, enjoying the beautiful weather. Was hard to leave the seat… I'd camp there for a few days if I could. Alas, time was running out: need to get on our way.

From Lyon to Dijon, Ingrid drove about 200km. Now, rumours are that I was asleep during the entire ride—rumours that I passionately dismiss. I did take a nap, two or five hundred, but I wasn't asleep the *entire* ride.

Dijon is located in the Burgundy region of France. Around 150,000 live in this small city, which is famous for the International Gastronomic Fair it holds every year, but perhaps more famous for the Dijon mustard which was invented here—the same type of mustard that almost set me on fire two hours before I arrived here.

After arriving at the hotel, Hotel Montigny, took another nap for an hour and then the three of us headed outside for a pre-concert snack. Oh, how lucky we were for having a big meal in Lyon earlier: virtually *everything* was closed.

Found one place that was open. Sandwich, terrible coffee and headed back to the tram station to take the tram to the venue. The machine selling tickets for the tram appeared to be broken: whatever we tried, we just couldn't by tickets—the machine didn't let us. We decided, then, to board the tram and do some explaining if and when an inspector comes on board, which they didn't.

The venue, Zénith de Dijon—yes, another Zénith—seats 7,800. Again, many familiar faces made their way to this concert.

Unfortunately, due to other commitments, the Dijon concert was the last one for Ruth Moody and her band to perform as an opening act for. To me this is a shame: for twelve times this tour, Ruth and her band delivered excellent performances that left the audiences in the UK and France in awe. I cannot recall such a fantastic reception of a Knopfler opening act before: after each and every concert, dozens over dozens of people lined up to purchase Ruth's albums. During her band's performances, you could feel that the audience was very appreciative of whatever was going on on the stage.

Hats off to Ruth, Adrian, Sam and Adam for delivering fantastic performances. Good things are coming their way, no doubt about it.

If you don't have Ruth's albums (there are two of them: These Wilder Things and The Garden), then I strongly suggest that you buy them.

Half an hour after the opening act, the band of eight took the stage to deliver another good performance. Unfortunately for me, I couldn't quite stand the heat in the place (although it wasn't as hot as, say, the Frankfurt concert) so I watched a part of the concert from the back. It was funny to witness the *Running of the Bulls*—essentially, it looks as if a huge magnet sucks entire rows of people into the stage. I watched it all from the back, sipping cold water. Let the kids have fun, I say.

After the concert, a late night tram back to Dijon's city center and off to a good night sleep.

Special warm thanks to Ingrid van de Maat for being the golden hearted woman she is. It's always fun to be in the vicinity of such a lovely woman, and she *did* help a lot. Many hugs and kisses headed your way, darling!

Signing off this post from my hotel room in Köln, Germany. It was a much needed day off today... concert tomorrow, the first one of five in a row, all in Germany.

Isaac

Thursday, July 4, 2013

Heartbeat Check

Just a quick one for now.

It's been very busy few days since getting to Germany. As I have been rather tired recently, I didn't finish the Köln post until fifteen minutes ago, and now I can't upload it because the Holiday Inn Express' Wi-Fi connection is just too slow, making my blogging software time out whenever I try to upload it.

Stay tuned… It will come.
Isaac

Friday, July 5, 2013

Dijon, France to Köln, Germany (July 1-2, 2013)

Note: this post is being uploaded along with its successor. Had to accumulate a couple of posts due to Wi-Fi availability issues. Make sure you check out the next post: Köln to Halle (Westfalen), Germany (July 3, 2013).

Monday morning, July 1st: Woke up at around 8:00am in Dijon, with mixed feelings.

(No, it's not that I had mixed feelings about waking up: I love waking up. As far as I'm concerned, it's better to wake up eventually than… well… not waking up.)

On one hand, I didn't really want to leave France (even though I'll be back to France for a few days, as the tour arrives at Nîmes, St. Julien en Genevois and Carcassonne); on the other hand, the difficult travel and the difficulties in proper dining (due to the French's standard dining hours) made me feel good about heading back to Germany.

So far, Germany proved to be the most convenient country to follow a tour in, logistics-wise. An advanced, developed railway network; relatively organized mentality; and, of course, restaurants in Germany *ARE USUALLY OPEN*.

As Monday was a day off, it made sense to use it for the purpose of travel, in order to avoid travel as much as possible on a concert day. Packed whatever was unpacked and headed to Dijon's town center for a short pre-travel breakfast.

Now, you would think that, after travelling for so long, experiencing so many quirks and oddities in different countries, there would be less and less to learn as time goes by. Well, that's what I had thought and hoped for. Whatever doesn't kill me, makes me stronger; I have been bruised and battered by the oddities of so many places, nothing can surprise me now.

Headed to a random cafe in Dijon's town center. No menu on display, so we decided to ask what they offer. The owner, in return, asked us what we would like to have.

Alright, no problem. "Well, you know… sandwiches, tea, coffee…"

Sure, that's fine, folks. Sit down.

We did.

Beautiful morning. Sitting outside, observing the people of this small town going about their day. The owner (now functioning as a waiter) approaches, asking us what we would like to have.

– "Can we see the menu?"

– "We don't have a menu. Just tell me what you'd like to have."

Jeroen looked at me, I looked back at Jeroen, already knowing that nothing good was going to come out of this.

– "Two sandwiches, one tea and one cappuccino."

Now, a reasonable diner would expect the waiter to enlist what types of sandwiches are offered, and then ask what sandwich the customer would like. Maybe it's only me, but that was quite the automatic expectation. The word "sandwich" simply happens to cover too large of a spectrum of options.

– "OK, no problem."

So, one possible course of action would be for me to chase the waiter back to where he came from and require some explanation as to what it is that he had in mind when he said "OK, no problem" as a response to the (arguably) generic wish for a "sandwich".

Another possible course of action was to simply remain frozen and see how things unfold, which is exactly what we ended up doing.

Five minutes later, the waiter comes with a cappuccino, some tea, and two sandwiches, each of which consists of a dry baguette with a hefty portion of ham inside.

Terrible coffee, terrible breakfast I didn't even ask for. Should I jot this down as a note to myself that a "sandwich", unless begged for otherwise, means "a dry piece of dough filled with ham"? Is this normal in France? who knows. Moral of the story: "we don't have a menu, just tell me what you'd like to have" is not the beginning of a love story between a man and his sandwich.

OK, whatever. Consumed the sandwich with a negligible amount of passion, paid and backtracked to a small pastry shop we had noticed earlier. Delicious few pastries did much to mend the culinary damage inflicted by the unwelcome breakfast.

Time to leave. Headed to the station—some fifteen minutes walk away—and hopped on the train.

The schedule: Take the TGV from Dijon, France to Basel, Switzerland; about 45 minutes wait, then hop on an ICE train to Mannheim, Germany; about 15 minutes wait, then hop on another ICE train to Köln. Altogether just over 6 hours of travel, spanning three trains.

Easy.

TGV train from Dijon left on time and arrived at Basel SBB on time. Left the train and looked for a way to kill 45 minutes as functionally as possible, that is—seek a proper place for a quick lunch before travel continues. Instead of buying something to eat later, it was decided to sit down in a small cafe named "Hallo", located right inside the train station. Approximately 30 minutes left for the next train to depart, and the cafe was located right above the platform so we could even see the train arriving when the time comes.

No brainer, huh?

OK, so after decrypting the menu (which was written in Swiss German, which is effectively German, so Jeroen decrypted it for me), the request was simple: two sandwiches, plus water. Not hard.

How long could it take to prepare two sandwiches in a cafe that isn't even close to being full? two minutes?

Three minutes?

… Four?

Alright. So about ten minutes later, I noticed that our sandwiches were already prepared, placed on a shelf and waiting for pickup by the waitress, who, by then, both of us already concluded that was entirely, completely and utterly clueless. The sandwiches just stood there on the shelf, ready for pick up. For how long? One minute?

Two minutes?

Alright. So about five minutes later, it was time for action. Jeroen sprang on his feet and headed to grab the sandwiches from the lonely shelf himself. The clueless waitress gave him a look that clearly demanded some sort of an explanation, and such explanation was duly provided: *"WE ARE IN A HURRY"*.

Disgusting sandwiches, by the way.

About 12 minutes or so left to the train's departure. Looking down to the platform, I noticed our train coming.

> Trains arriving early simply wait at the station for longer than planned; they don't just go away. So we knew that the train wasn't going to leave before schedule. But still, there's something disconcerting in looking at your train standing on the tracks as if waiting for you.
>
> I don't want trains to wait for me, ever; I prefer waiting for them.

Time to pay.

> This is the part I dislike the most about dining out. Not because I don't want to pay, but because of the actual process: get the staff's attention; ask for the bill; wait for the staff to come back with the bill; provide means of payment; have the payment processed (which usually takes longer when you pay with a card). It simply takes time, for no useful reason at all.
>
> If you ever happen to be so misfortunate to be my waiter/waitress, how about you do the following: once food is provided to the table, ask me if there's any chance that I'm going to be ordering something later. If I say "no", just give me the bill. Wait a few seconds, I'll provide the payment and you can go about processing it while I chew on what I paid for. I'll be happy because my time was saved; you'll be happy because you (1) made me happy, and (2) managed to reduce further interaction with me, which is good for your mental well being.
>
> The best service I can ever be given is a service that saves me the one resource I can never have back in any way: my time.

The indented rant above doesn't appear here just out of the blue. I think we caught the attention of two different waitresses, about three or four times each. "We need the bill because our train is leaving". Now, you would assume that people, working in restaurants located inside a terribly busy railway station, would not be strangers to the idea of clients being in a hurry. After about six minutes with nobody even handing us the bill (all waitresses were under the impression that it's much more important to seat new clients, and take orders from said new clients, before releasing two prisoners who happen to follow a Knopfler tour), I simply got up, grabbed my bags and was ready to go to one of the cashiers there (the cafe had a "to go" section as well) and give her a piece of my mind. Miraculously, the clueless waitress from before finally realized that some hell was going to be raised; payment was done and we stormed out of that hell hole, down to the platform and into the train.

Arrived at Mannheim on time, and went straight to the departures board, only to see that the connecting train to Köln is being delayed by about 20 minutes. One of us decided that the best way to use this gap is by devouring a cheesecake in a bakery right there in the station; the other one was me.

Sat down watching a Dutchman arranging a meeting between a cheesecake and its maker, resisting the temptation to steal half of it. Then off to the platform, hopped on the train… and about an hour and a half later, finally arrived to Köln's central railway station.

Köln (in English: Cologne) is the fourth largest city in Germany. Its metro area is home for about ten million people, and it is situated on both banks of the Rhine.

The city has a rich history dating back to the 1st century, when it was founded by the Romans. During the Middle Ages, Köln was a major trade route connecting eastern and western Europe. During World War II, Köln was one of the most heavily bombed cities in Germany: 95% of its population abandoned it, and the city was almost completely destroyed. After the war, much effort and resources were put into trying to restore some of the city's many cultural and architectural landmarks.

I have been to Köln before, during the 2010 Get Lucky tour. Other than that, I have been to the city's central railway station a few times as it serves as a major railway hub in Germany's west. I never, though, had the opportunity to actually explore this city. In that regards, a day off in Köln was definitely called for.

Out of the station and into the hotel, Best Western Grand City Hotel Köln, conveniently located right across the street from the central railway station. Originally, the plan was to stay in a different hotel, but once Germany was hit with a ruthless heat wave, the reservation was changed to a hotel that provides air conditioning, of course for an added price.

(We will get to that air conditioning part later.)

Up to the room and I was extraordinarily happy: spacious, comfortable… excellent for two nights' stay. Nice view, too.

Turned on the air conditioning and sat down to finish the previous post. That took a while, during which I noticed that the room isn't really getting colder. Checked the air conditioner: fan is on, thermostat set correctly… nothing but plain unconditioned air comes out. Decided to open the window, which helped reducing the temperature but resulted in extreme noise coming in. As the room was facing the central railway station, I could clearly hear all train announcements (in both German and English); the despicable screeching sound of all trains, halting to a stop; and, of course, the loud noise emitted by drunken creatures who gathered in front of the station with alcohol supply equivalent in its volume to satisfy the needs of a small country.

Shoes on, and down to reception.

> I don't like arguing for the sake of argument. I'm OK with arguing in order to reach some sort of a common understanding, common grounds; to achieve something, most preferably something that is mutually beneficial.
>
> What I'm not OK with is arguing with stupidity.
>
> My problem of arguing with stupidity is that I have no common grounds with stupid people (or, as will be demonstrated below, nice people who are forced to argue in favour of stupid policies). My desire to reach common understandings and mutual gain is far superseded by my reluctance to bring my intelligence down to that of idiots.

Once reported the problem, a more senior staff came in. Nice lady, with nothing but goodness in her eyes. She said that cooling was turned off for the entire hotel because guests were complaining that it's "too cold".

That didn't sit well with the fact that the air conditioning system in the rooms had an on/off switch as well as a thermostat, both of which in perfect working order.

– "So you're telling me that the thermostat and the on/off switch really do nothing?", I inquired.

She nodded for "yes". She was either lying or just demonstrating complete ignorance.

– "So you're turning off the air conditioning for the entire hotel, because guests claimed that it's too cold?", I inquired, just to confirm.

– "Yes."

– "And I'm guessing that, if I told you that I was too warm, you wouldn't turn the air conditioning on. Right?", I said, trying to sound as sarcastic as I could.

– "No."

– "And that is because I'm just one person."

She looked at me and tilted her head to the side, as if she's trying to show compassion towards a miniature three legged dog with an apparent bowel movement problem.

– "Yes."

Well, at the least, I learned something new.

– "OK, so what are we going to do about that?"

– "We can try to move you to a different, quieter room tomorrow."

Sure, whatever.

> The fact that a hotel room has an on/off switch for its air conditioning system, as well as a thermostat, goes to imply that guests have independent control over their room's temperature. The only conclusion out of that argument was that the hotel was disabling the cooling system in an attempt to save energy (which means, save money. For them, that is. Guests still pay the same).

Back in the room, it was decided to give things a chance for the night and see how things go.

So, as I mentioned above, I never really got the chance to see this city, despite being here a couple of times before. Evening time, wonderful weather outside… off for a walk.

Perhaps the most famous attraction in Köln is the Köln Cathedral. A UNESCO World Heritage Site, this cathedral is Germany's most visited landmark, attracting about 20,000 people a day.

The building of this cathedral started in the 13th century. In the 15th century, it was abandoned and left unfinished. Work restarted in the 19th century, and was completed in 1880.

You can't stay apathetic to the sight of this astonishing building. It is about 155 meters tall (!), gorgeous and, well, massive.

The Köln Cathedral is right in your face as you exit the central railway station to the south. Once there, the old city (*Altstadt*) is all around you. Due to the fact that the city was almost completely destroyed during World War II, you would often encounter mixtures of old and new buildings as you walk along.

First—dinner. A place called Oma's Küche was suggested by *TripAdvisor* for good, traditional German food right in the heart of the old city.

Steps from it, a building carrying two symbols of Corporate America, Food Division:

Long walk south, then west towards River Rhine, and north along the river. The scenery—both involving the river and the nearby houses—is very pretty.

Some of these colourful houses now serve as hotels. Numerous traditional German-style pubs are scattered along the walkway, attracting tourists and locals alike.

Refreshing walk, and back to the hotel, where I did some more writing. Time flew by, and before I knew it, it was dark. The Köln Cathedral is lit brilliantly at night, which provided for a superb view from the hotel room's balcony.

After a relaxing day off, another beautiful morning. The hotel was asking an insane amount of €19 per person (!) for breakfast (if you're clueless about Germany, you're likely to fall into such traps. Dining out in Germany is not cheap, but not expensive either. €19 is a ridiculous amount of money to spend on a breakfast there), so we headed out.

On our way out, we decided to speak to the receptionist again about the air conditioning problem. Asking for explanation, we were told that "the hotel's director decided to turn off the air cooling system".

– "But why?", we inquired.

– (with utmost seriousness) "Because he doesn't think it's warm enough."

Well then. How could one possibly argue against such a profound, objective observation?

Before I was able to fully compile this last sentence in my head (admit it: you didn't see it coming), another receptionist came by and informed us that it was decided to enable air cooling for the entire hotel.

Wonderful.

Headed out to the city center, looking for something to eat. Located in a side street off the city center's main shopping walkway, there's Cafe Eigel, offering brilliant breakfasts for the staggering price of about €7. For my money, breakfast doesn't get much better than that.

Due to the fact that we had cancelled a couple of sleeper train reservations, it became unclear how we should be getting a refund for those. Decided to get it over with now, during the day off. So, breakfast done and over with, we went back to the central railway station to sort things out.

Pushed button; got a number. Waited. The guy just before us ended up going to booth number 5, where he was met by a staff member who looked like, and sounded like, someone who is in the habit of barking things at people. Something about the tone of his voice, combined with his body language, made me predict that discussing heavenly matters with this fellow is going to yield an interesting experience.

After a short argument, involving hearing the word "No!" (exclamation mark included) way too many times, the guy realized that perhaps the issue needs to be escalated. Some senior staff was called in and the matter got (for now, until further notice) resolved. A part of the resolution required the Dutchman to provide his email address, which he spelled out… until the "@gmail.com" part arrived.

– "What?", asked the representative.

– "@gmail.com", responded the Dutchman.

The representative looked a bit confused; took out a piece of paper and a pen, and ask Jeroen to spell it, which he did. Receiving the paper, the representative mentioned that he had never encountered this domain name before.

THERE'S SOMEONE ON THIS PLANET WHO KNOWS WHAT AN E-MAIL IS, BUT HAD NEVER ENCOUNTERED THE "gmail.com" DOMAIN BEFORE.

Excellent.

Spent the next few hours by myself—it's good to do so, every once in a while—walking around this beautiful city.

Late afternoon: time for a pre-concert dinner. A bit north of the hotel—away from the rush of the touristic city center, there's a place called Max Stark. Upon entering, a nice waiter welcomes us offering us a seat, and immediately asking if we would like a couple of pints of their "local beer".

– "No, thank you."

The waiter looked at us in amazement.

– "No?"

– "No, thank you."

– "Really?"

– "Yes", and I couldn't avoid smiling. The waiter obviously looked shocked.

– "No beer?"

– "No…"

– "You know where you are, right?"

The expression on the waiter's face once he realized that no beer is going to be ordered here was priceless. Food-wise, this is a great place to dine in. Good food, very reasonably priced. Check it out if and when you happen to be in the city.

Back to the touristic area of the city center for some (non-alcoholic) drink, an experience that provided yet another hilarious dialogue. The waiter, an Italian who speaks fluent German but very flakey English, didn't quite understand what I meant when I asked for an ice-based espresso drink. He just couldn't perceive how espresso, steamed milk and ice cubes could fit into a drinkable beverage. To his credit, he really *did* try to understand. While doing so, he apologized for his English and told me his life story in a nutshell—having worked in the USA before etc. etc., and that he would have liked to be in his home country but (quote) "Italy—kaput".

Nice to meet interesting people along the way.

Time was up—off to the train station to head to the venue. From the central railway station, there are trains headed to the venue every 2–3 minutes (!), and the venue is located about 2 minutes train ride away. In other words, there should be no worries getting to the venue on time, right?

Think again.

Turned out that the city's S-Bahn lines were suffering terrible delays due to shortage in personnel. Virtually all S-Bahn trains headed towards the venue were suffering delays of 10 minutes or more, which is terrible news to get 35 minutes before show time. It was one of the most stressful experiences in getting to a venue, which is ridiculous considering the fact that the venue is located right on the other side of River Rhine.

Eventually, though, found a regular (non S-Bahn) train heading that way. Arrived at the venue 20 minutes to show time, collected the tickets, had to circle around the venue to find the applicable entry…

Done. Made it on time.

As Jeroen was headed to the hall, I stayed behind to get us a couple of drinks. I didn't even look at the sign showing the prices of everything. I had a vague idea of what to expect.

– "Two waters, please."

– "OK."

Man pours water into two cups, about 250mL each.

– "Ten Euros and sixty cents."

I looked at him.

– "Excuse me?"

– "That would be ten Euros and sixty cents."

– "Ten sixty?!"

– "Yes."

– "For two cups of water?!"

– "Yes."

I looked at him, astonished. I know he wasn't to blame—he's a poor guy just working there.

– "Are you sure? Ten sixty for two cups of water?"

Another staff member showed up.

– "You get one Euro back if you return the cup after you finish using it."

I did some really, really quick math in my head.

– "So, nine Euros and sixty cents for two cups of water?"

– "Yes."

I looked at them.

– "No thanks, that's fine."

The two looked at me as if awestruck as I simply walked away.

In a totally unrelated subject, the water from the tap in the men's room were just fine.

Made it to the hall a few minutes before the concert. The concert went well, again with a very receptive audience. If you happen to have purchased the USB stick for this concert, pay attention to the Marbletown outro, as Mike & John took things to a completely different direction than usual—a minor-scale, touching melody that turned the song into a different, unique experience.

These guys just keep coming up with ideas… and still people often ask me "why would you see the same show so many times?".

On a side note, this was the first concert in which I bothered to look into something that looked a bit odd. *Gator Blood* is played on a white Fender Stratocaster, with a capo on the third fret, plus, of course, a guitar slide. For the guitar slide to work well on this song, a normal tuning simply wouldn't be the right approach. Plus, the finger work for the song's main rhythm theme didn't make sense.

Then it dawned on me: the guitar is tuned for "Open G".

Glad to have figured that one out.

After the concert, took the train back to the hotel. No train delays this time around.

These were good two days in this beautiful city. Looking forward to visiting again.

Signing off this post from my hotel room in Dresden. Took a while to complete this post, but the main problem was Wi-Fi availability as well as tiredness. The next post is already 95% done, and will be uploaded later tonight.

Isaac

Friday, July 5, 2013

Köln to Halle (Westfalen), Germany (July 3, 2013)

Note: this post is being uploaded along with its predecessor. Had to accumulate a couple of posts due to Wi-Fi availability issues. Make sure you check out the previous post: Dijon, France to Köln, Germany (July 1–2, 2013).

Slightly less than two days after arriving at the beautiful city of Köln, it was time once again to decamp. Woke up tired: all energy that was regained during the day off in Köln seemed to have evaporated. Opened up the window to find out that weather decided to play another trick: after two days of sunshine and fantastic weather, the buildings and sidewalks were all wet. People walking around with umbrellas. The rain was back.

The original plan was to leave Köln at 9:48am; however, as Köln proved to be such a fun place to be in, it was decided, the day prior, to push the schedule a little bit and depart at 11:48am instead—allowing time for breakfast in that wonderful restaurant discovered the day before.

Nobody, however, took into consideration that the weather might change.

Armed with rain jackets, two wanderers made their way through the rain and through the city center all the way to the promised land—Cafe Eigel, exactly where breakfast was consumed the morning before. Great breakfast, followed by a prolonged period of chilling out. There was no desire whatsoever to even leave the restaurant: what for, really? they have everything required for human survival. Great food (including mind-numbingly gorgeous desserts), lots of space, free air to breathe… and where the hell is that "Halle" place that I need to get to later today, anyway?

But, plans are there to be followed. Back at the hotel, grabbed everything, checked out and headed to catch the train. No incidents this time as the train left on time.

The original plan called for travel from Köln to Halle and spend the night there. It was tricky to book a hotel in Halle as there weren't many options to begin with—not even one twin room available anywhere, which is why two separate single rooms were booked.

Later on, a closer look at the travel schedule revealed an inefficiency. To get from Köln to Halle, one needs to take a train from Köln *east* to Bielefeld, and then *west* to Halle using a regional train; and in the next morning, to get from Halle to Dresden, a change of trains in Bielefeld is required once again. To avoid this redundancy, it was decided to spend the night in Bielefeld instead, as it would save some train rides. From Bielefeld, it's an easy 30 minutes train to Halle for the concert.

Intended to do some writing during the train ride to Bielefeld, but shut the laptop down after a few minutes as I realized that I can't really concentrate on anything due to tiredness. Less than two hours later, the train arrived to Bielefeld.

The hotel booked for Bielefeld was called B&B Hotel Bielefeld. Now, I may not have enough travel experience but, for me, a "B&B" and a "Hotel" are two different things. I would associate the term "B&B" with a nice quiet house, privately owned, in which rooms are offered to guests along with home made breakfast. Also, it was rather suspicious to find that the rate offered by this "B&B Hotel" didn't include the second "B" of the "B&B" package: breakfast has to be paid for separately. Silly. Call it "B(&B)" instead. Or "B&maybeB". Or "B&mayB".

That hotel, located right across the street from the central railway station inside a complex that includes a movie theater and a few restaurants, looked brand new.

Checking in. Two nice ladies in reception. I started suspecting that something might be wrong with the reservation as soon as one of them mentioned that we had reserved a "French bed". I don't know what a "French bed" is, and I can't recall ever encountering that term before. I wouldn't book a hotel room with a "French bed" unless I know exactly what it meant, and I trust Jeroen wouldn't do so either. For once, I am not entirely confident in the properness of assigning nationality to furniture; and for twice, the plural suffix "s" was missing.

Luckily, the mishap was corrected on the spot. Then, I was informed that there are available rooms in certain floors of the hotel—which one do I want?

I thought about the first, most important criteria.

– "Are the hotel rooms quiet?", I asked.

The receptionist looked at me as if she has just unravelled a brand new type of frog yet unknown to science.

– "Sorry?"

– "Are the hotel rooms quiet? is it quiet in the rooms?", I elaborated.

– "No."

(????!)

– "… No?"

– "No."

(Gulp.)

– "So I guess it doesn't really matter which room we get, then."

At that point, Jeroen, who speaks German, decided to intervene and translate my question to German. So, the hotel rooms *are* quiet after all. Good.

– "Would you like to have breakfast tomorrow?"

– "Can we decide tomorrow morning?"

– "Yes, but we would highly prefer that you decide today, so we can call the breakfast provider to let them know."

We decided to think about that one. Up to the room, did some writing and before I knew it, it was time to head out for dinner. That's one of the downsides of staying the night far away from the venue: you need to have your dinner early (unless you're planning on having dinner at the venue, which is a very risky thing to do. Don't do it unless you know exactly what the venue offers).

On the way out from the hotel, a different receptionist. As the hotel's reception is closed late at night, it was unclear how one would enter the premises afterhours—say, upon returning from a concert located 30 minutes train ride away. Also, the hotel doesn't provide keys, or cards, to enter the hotel or the room: instead, they give you a code which you're supposed to be punching on a keypad.

– "So, the reception is closed after 11:00pm, right?"

– "Yes."

– "So, can we enter the hotel if we return late?"

– "No."

(??????????!)

– "No?"

– "No. There's nobody in reception after 11:00pm."

– "We don't need to check in after 11:00pm. We're already guests here. But can we enter the building if we return late?"

– "Yes. Just enter your code on the keypad outside, by the front door."

Sigh.

TripAdvisor suggested a place called Westside Lounge, about ten minutes walk from the hotel: an Asian-Italian fusion restaurant. Sitting outside on the patio, beautiful weather: fantastic dinner for a very affordable price. Jeroen's starter arrived with a small bread that was baked on site, over coal: I can't remember when was the last time I had such a tasty bread—France included.

Terrific. Great food in affordable prices—I'm developing a whole new opinion about dining in Germany. It's convenient—restaurants are open most of the time; it's very affordable; service is usually very good and efficient. What's not to like? I'll need to dig up some of my old notes from previous tours to see why I wasn't a fan of dining in Germany to begin with. Something has changed… either Germany or myself.

Back to the hotel, to get prepared for the concert. Weather forecast suggested that it might be raining, and as we were going to take the train back to Bielefeld after the concert, it was necessary to prepare for the possibility of spending some time outside.

Back to the reception, as we decided to have breakfast at the hotel. Same guy as before.

– "Is it early enough to order breakfast for tomorrow?", asked the Dutchman. Now, a normal person would phrase the question in a more simplified manner, such as "*is it still possible to order breakfast for tomorrow?*", but we're talking about a Dutchman under stress.

– "No."

Applying some logic to the aforementioned question & answer, it's easy to conclude that it was too late for ordering breakfast.

– "What? So we can't order breakfast anymore?"

– "Oh, sure, you can."

Sigh.

Arrived at the station, regional train to Halle left on time. Two or three cabins, all 2nd class. The difference comparing to 1st class is evident: it's noisier here. More crowded. More children, which amounts to more noise. Half an hour train ride, passing through rural hilly areas…

certainly not the landscape in which one would expect to find a concert venue. One station past Halle's central railway station, arrived at the very small railway station servicing the venue; left the train and followed the crowd.

The venue, Gerry Weber Stadion (*Stadion* means *Stadium* in German), is an indoor arena located in Halle. There is another city named *Halle* in Germany—a larger one, by River Saale. To differentiate between the two, the larger city is referred to as *Halle (Saale)* and this one—the one where the concert took place—as *Halle (Westfalen)*, or *Halle (Westf.)* in a shorter form.

You might think that the Gerry Weber Stadium is named after an individual named Gerry Weber. Seems reasonable… but I couldn't find any reference to such a person. There is, however, a tennis tournament called *Gerry Weber Open*—a tournament that takes place at (drumroll, please) the Gerry Weber Stadium.

Walking from the stadium's railway station to the venue, I couldn't really believe that there's actually a venue there. The surroundings were such that a tennis stadium simply wouldn't fit in—almost farmland.

After picking up the tickets, I went ahead and walked for a bit around the venue, to take some pictures. Turns out that this is a residential area. There are houses located within less than 20 meters away from the venue's area.

It was nice to get a breath of fresh air in these quiet surroundings. Time was up—back to the venue.

The venue being a tennis stadium made the concert experience very different from the usual indoor experience. For once, the ceiling wasn't opaque, and didn't cover the venue's perimeter shut; as a result, there was pretty much free flow of light from outside. It gets dark late in Halle during the summer, so most of the concert was performed in daylight. Strange feeling… you're indoors, but still watching a concert in daylight.

The stadium can hold 12,300 spectators for tennis events, but the seating configuration for the concert allowed for up to 7,000. Still, the venue felt surprisingly small. The feeling of a small venue, together with the daylight, cast a special atmosphere of casualness and intimacy.

The band started with the usual set, featuring Nigel Hitchcock who is going to be joining the band for all shows in Germany this week. After *Song for Sonny Liston*, I was going to take a quick toilet break when I noticed that Glen Saggers was holding a Gibson guitar, to be played by Mark in the next song. This is very strange, considering the fact that Mark was already holding a Gibson guitar in his hands. That meant that the guitar switch was needed either for a different Gibson sound, or a different tuning.

Richard grabbed the Telecaster, which prompted me to think that maybe it's *Back to Tupelo* again. To confirm, I looked at John: John plays a ~~mandolin-like instrument (can someone comment and shed some light about the exact name of this instrument?)~~ cittern (*thanks, Benoit, for the information. I was under the impression that citterns are bigger, but apparently they come in different sizes*) during *Back to Tupelo*, but instead was holding a flute.

– "Look, they have Nigel", the Dutchman mentioned. I looked, and there was Nigel there, but he wasn't holding a saxophone. What is this? a clarinet?

Can someone please explain what's going on?

Eyes back at Mark, and I noticed the capo on the third fret. Third fret? what could these guys possibly play in *Cm* (or *Gm* or E♭ or B♭)? My brain started emitting smoke for all the computing it was required to perform along this time span of about six seconds, when Guy played the initial *Cm*.

And so, yes: in the small venue in Halle, a small town in the middle of seemingly nowhere, a new song was introduced to the set… and what a song it was. *Dream of the Drowned Submariner*—as far as I'm concerned, the most moving piece of music in Knopfler's latest double album. I have listened to this song so many times before and, admittedly, already lost any hope of listening to it performed live.

An unexpected arrangement, too. In the studio version, Mark plays both an acoustic guitar and an electric one: in one particular section, both guitars sound at once (I'm guessing that both guitars were recorded in separate tracks, then mixed together). All the while, an electric rhythm guitar is played in the background. The studio arrangement can't, therefore, be played live; instead, the acoustic guitar went away; John and Mike played flutes, Nigel on clarinet, Richard on the telecaster for the rhythm part and Mark with the Gibson.

It was evident, though, that Mark was quite undecided as to which direction he wants to take the outro solo to. Much like *Kingdom of Gold*, the outro of *Dream of the Drowned Submariner* can wear millions of shapes and forms. I can only hope for this song to be played again during this tour (preferably, 21 more times) and see where it gets.

The tiredness I was feeling all day to that point, simply vanished.

The rest of the concert went well, followed by a rush to the stage which I preferred to avoid altogether. A much awaited quick toilet break, and back to the hall to watch the encore from the side, near the entrance.

Once the concert ended, it was time to head back to Bielefeld. The next train to Bielefeld (which also happened to be the last train heading that direction for the day) was scheduled to arrive to Halle in more than an hour. Initially, when planning to stay in Bielefeld instead of Halle, the one hour wait seemed reasonable; however, when it was time to face the music, it was decided to just forego a few dozens of Euros and hail a taxi instead. €35 and 25 minutes later, we were back at the entertainment complex adjacent to the hotel.

I've been trying to reduce my food intake recently, with some success. Still, as dinner in Bielefeld took place very early (around 5:00pm), by the time the concert was over I already developed some sort of hunger. There were a few restaurants in the entertainment complex. Walking through them and inspecting the menus, came across an Italian one.

Needed to check whether the kitchen was open at all. Jeroen headed inside.

– "Is the kitchen still open?"

– "Yes."

– "Good. So, can we eat here?"

– "No. The kitchen is closed."

Sigh. I'm wondering if there's something in Bielefeld's air, or water, that makes people's listening comprehension go a bit off.

Found a nearby Asian restaurant. One roll of sushi was ordered, two were provided. Yum. Back to the hotel and off to bed.

Signing off this post from my hotel room in Dresden.

Isaac

Sunday, July 7, 2013

The 197th and 198th: Halle (Westfalen) to Dresden to Bad Mergentheim, Germany (July 4-5, 2013)

Thursday, July 4th. Woke up in Bielefeld, organized everything and went downstairs to the hotel's breakfast room. Piled a few edible substances and sat down to eat, reading the news. Only the day before, there was a coup in Egypt: the military took power after putting the (democratically elected) president under house arrest. I'm not an expert in Egyptian politics (although, due to my background, I'm inclined to say that I know more about it than most) but my entire family happens to live in a country that borders it. Any sort of instability in that part of the world can easily cascade to neighbouring countries.

"Why can't we all just get along", I kept asking myself as I was chewing on something—can't even recall what it was. Done eating and went back to the breakfast stand, to check out the drinks.

In front of me, there stood my arch-enemy: An automated, all-in-one, "push a button and I'll prepare your coffee" kind of coffee machine.

I hate "push a button and I'll prepare your coffee" machines. When checking out coffee places, the very sight of such automatic machine is sufficient to make me draw a virtual huge red X on the establishment and move on. Espresso drinks should be prepared manually, or not prepared at all.

I looked at the machine, it looked at me.

None of us moved away.

Knowing that pressing the "Cappuccino" button will result in a disgraceful beverage, I opted at the button labeled "Latte Macchiato". Hard to screw that one: 99% warm milk, with a shot of espresso. Even if your espresso is garbage, the milk should be able to at least save the day.

Altogether a gloomy morning—one of those that you'd like to get over with already. One of those mornings when you wake up in a town in the middle of nowhere, and your plan involves six hours of travel to a city in east Germany—almost on the border with Poland; I was worried that Poland has some sort of an "halo of awfulness" around it.

The plan: depart Bielefeld at 9:37am, arrive Hannover 10:28am; depart Hannover 11:36am, arrive Dresden 3:29pm. No ICE trains—InterCity only: that did much to ruin whatever expectations I had left from that day. Six hours of travel, all the way east…

Arrived at Hannover's central railway station. I have been to Hannover before, during the 2010 Get Lucky tour. I remember it being a beautiful city. What I also remembered is that convenient cafe located right in the central railway station, called World Coffee. They make proper coffee there, have lots of seating space—but the highlight is that they have a large patio right in Ernst August Platz, a small nice square located right outside the station. When the weather is good (as it was), it's a perfect spot to enjoy a good beverage.

They also provide exceptionally long spoons along with your coffee.

I asked the barista whether they have a bigger spoon than that. Failing to sense my sarcasm (many people do), she replied with an apologetic "no".

Wish I could stay longer in Hannover; however, the one hour connection time seemed to have flown by. Back to the platform, and on to another train, heading to Dresden. Four long hours, during which I was haunted by Jeroen's earlier statement about East German cities being grey and boring.

I didn't know much about Dresden before arriving there. The only thing I *thought* I knew about Dresden was that the first bomb that the allies dropped on Germany in World War II killed a single elephant in Dresden's zoo: turned out I was wrong—the incident indeed took place, but it was in Berlin. Realizing that I was wrong, the number of things I knew about Dresden decreased by one, yielding zero.

Not only I was wrong about that bombing, but I couldn't be further from the truth. Dresden was indeed bombed by the allies; however, it was towards the *end* of the war, and while there is no record as to how many elephants were killed in that bombing (if at all), the bombing *did* kill between 22,000 and 25,000 people.

Apparently, it was a massive bombing. 3,900 tons of high-explosive bombs were dropped on the city over three days, causing a series of firestorms that demolished much of the city. So serious was that beating, that it triggered worldwide debate—even within the allies—as to whether that bombing was really necessary.

Arrived at Dresden's central railway station, which was under construction (are all central railway stations in Germany under construction nowadays?). From there, it was about a kilometer walk to the hotel. During that walk, it occurred to me that if Poland indeed has a "halo of awfulness", it certainly doesn't hover over Dresden.

From the station, heading north, there's a pedestrian walkway called *Prager Straße* (that is, *Prager Street*), which looked as if only recently built. Many people in the streets, lots of shops… wait, am I really in east Germany? am I missing anything?

Checked into the hotel, Holiday Inn Express Dresden City Center. I was in such a mood that I was numb to whatever was happening around me, even while checking in. Totally distracted, totally not caring about whatever was going on around me. Later, I was told that the receptionist was shaking her head at me while I was filling out the check in form, as if to gesture "this guy is a moron". I was so apathetic, that I didn't even care *after* I was informed of that head shaking.

Internet connectivity in that hotel costs money: €5 per device. The reason I booked this hotel was, that even factoring the Wi-Fi costs in, it would still be cheaper than most other hotels around. Jeroen bought one, I decided not to, in order to see how it works first.

Up to the room. Jeroen headed out almost instantly, I stayed in the room to complete the previous post and the one before. That took a while, and then, happy that I was done, I started uploading it.

It failed.

Tried again… failed. Timed out.

Tried again. And again. And it just didn't work. Possibly the worst Wi-Fi setup so far this tour.

Headed downstairs to the lobby, hoping that maybe better reception will speed things up a bit.

Tried once, twice, thrice… Nada. Timed out.

Furious, I went back upstairs, dropped the laptop on the desk and notified Jeroen that I'm on my way to the old city, where he was having an early dinner by himself.

Very shortly after leaving the hotel and heading north, I realized how wrong I was to assume anything about Dresden. The city's "old city" area is nothing short of stunning, featuring baroque-style buildings—some of which have been restored after being severely damaged during World War II.

The first thing you see heading north from the hotel is this:

This is the Dresden Frauenkirche, a Lutheran church. I can't describe the awe I felt when I first saw this building: it is *gigantic*. Its dome is one of the largest domes in Europe. The church was destroyed during World War II, and was restored after Germany's reunification.

Walked over to wherever the Dutchman was having his dinner—somewhere around this spot:

The Dutchman then decided that he's interested in getting to the venue relatively early. I'm usually against that—I have nothing to look for in a concert venue more than twenty or thirty minutes before the concert starts—but as the Dutchman owned the tickets for this show, I had to abide by the Dutch rules.

Fled back to the city center, looking for something to eat. Hey, what's that? an Asian restaurant? good. Upon entering, I realized that it's one of those places when you pick certain items from display, and they box it all up for you. But I don't want a box: I want my food on a plate, please. I'm not going to walk around the city with your food in a box. But no, they don't do it. Box only. And this entire exchange lasted about 5 minutes, because none of the people working there could speak more than one word in English.

Eventually, resorted to a sandwich, a few buns and was given a cake for free, all for the staggering price of €2.63. Things tend to cost less in the eastern part of Germany, so I learned later.

Rush… rush… and more rush… only because some Dutchman decided to be in a concert venue one full hour before the concert starts.

Back to the hotel, changed my shirt, and headed north again towards the venue.

The venue… well, I'm not even sure it has a name. The Elbe runs through the city of Dresden, and on its north bank, there's a film festival called "Filmnachte am Elbufer" (English: *Film Night on the Elb's Bank*). The area is called "Freilichtgelände Koenigsufer" (*Freilichtgelände* in German means "Open air", and *Koenigsufer* is… well… a name. OK, this is being too confusing already).

I never thought I'll have to put so much effort into explaining what a venue's name means.

One of the bridges that connect Dresden's old city area with the north bank of the Elba is called *Augustusbrücke* (in English: *Augustus Bridge*). That was the bridge you'd need to cross in order to enter the venue (as the venue could only be entered from its west side). Crossing that bridge provided excellent views of Dresden's old city.

The next panoramic photo was an attempt to capture the old city's view from the north bank of the Elbe, but the picture turned out… well… curved. Sorry. That's all I have for you at the moment.

As Jeroen had already entered the venue, I collected my ticket from the box office and went inside. It was already very busy everywhere.

In general admission shows when the venue is more than just a pile of asphalt (such as a field, or a castle for example), I tend to prefer watching the concert from afar. As I have been watching many, *many* shows, I find it refreshing, once in a while, to forget about having a visual on the band and just walk around interesting venues (I remember the concert in Würzburg, of the 2010 Get Lucky tour, being a very interesting experience in that regards).

Therefore, I spent the concert wandering from one place to another, getting a "feel" of the venue from multiple locations. I hardly even *seen* the band at all.

During *Cleaning My Gun*, I was to the side of the stage, and the angle between myself and the stage was such that I didn't see the band at all. Still, I realized that something went awfully wrong for Richard right at the beginning of the song: a string seemed to have gone out of tune. Strange noise. Richard then stopped playing for about 10–15 seconds, and then continued. Later, I was informed that Richard was playing the remainder of the song with a red Stratocaster. The sound where I was standing was so bad that I couldn't even tell the difference.

Wandering around the venue, I took a few more photos. I should really work on my panoramic shooting skills.

As it grew darker, the scenery became better:

Was good to listen to *Dream of the Drowned Submariner* again. For this song, I climbed up to the very top of the venue, and went for the middle, to get some good sound quality. The performance of this song was slightly better than in the previous show in Halle, as Mark's work on the guitar was a little more involved. As I mentioned in the last post, I wouldn't be surprised if it's going to take a few more runs for this song's performance to become incredibly pleasant.

After the concert, exited the venue very quickly (I prepared myself by watching the encore in the vicinity of the exit) as I figured it might take hours to leave the venue once the masses start marching towards it. A few more shots of the city at night time, and off to the hotel.

Back at the hotel, I tried uploading that blog post again, and failed. Went downstairs to speak to reception.

– "Are you aware of the fact that you have terrible problems with your internet connection?"

– "Yes, we do."

Nice. At least he was honest.

– "Are you going to do anything about it?"

– "Well, we tried telling management, the director, the owners of the hotel… but nothing is done."

I love honest people.

– "Interesting. So, do you think it's fair to continue selling Wi-Fi for €5 per day when you know that it's not working?"

– "Well, I'm sorry… this is not my decision…"

– "I know, I know. I'm not blaming you. I'm just asking you if *you* think it's fair."

– "Oh. Did you pay for the internet access here?"

– "I didn't. My friend did, and I'm using the voucher he bought."

And then, something wonderful happened. He went to the cash register, pulled out a €5 bill and handed it to me. I was less impressed with the actual money than with the gesture itself.

Back upstairs for some sleep; the next day was going to be a long travel day.

Friday, July 5th. Woke up... yawn. Fired up my mobile device, took a look at the schedule: Leave Dresden 7:53am, arrive Fulda 11:42am; short connection—leave Fulda 11:55am, arrive Würzburg 12:28pm; leave Würzburg 1:10pm, arrive Bad Mergentheim 2:13pm. More than six hours of travel, starting so early in the morning.

> To better explain how that day went for me, I should take you a couple of weeks back, to the Regensburg experience. While in Regensburg, I decided to see a doctor about a pain I had in my right wrist for the preceding two weeks, after I had a nasty fall in Delft, after the UK shows. X-rays were taken, the doctor saw nothing, and advised that I should simply let my hand rest, which I did. I was also advised to have a follow up visit if the pain doesn't go away within two weeks.
>
> So, those two weeks were just about to end. The situation improved, but still, I have pain when bending the palm of my right hand upwards. Unbearable pain, actually.
>
> I heard a joke a few days ago, saying that "men are never sick. They're either healthy, or dying"—obviously referring to the fact (yes, it was actually proven) that men have a lower tolerance to pain than women. Whenever I'm ill, or in pain, I'm a complete mess; not only that, but in such times, I tend to move between complete apathy to anything around me, and extreme agitation.
>
> In other words, I'm not your ideal companion in such times. Ask all of my ex girlfriends, they'll reaffirm.
>
> So, this time, as the pain didn't subside within the prescribed time (two weeks), I became *really* worried. Two million different scenarios of "what if" kept popping in my head. Therefore, keep in mind that, for the entire day, I was completely apathetic to *everything* around me. I'm pretty sure I didn't even speak to the Dutchman at all for the entire train ride to Bad Mergentheim. Felt completely disconnected.
>
> All I wanted was for that day to be over, so I can catch the earliest train the next day to Stuttgart and get the follow up check done. I desired to hear good news—that this pain is going to go away at *some* point—and became completely oblivious of *anything* else that was happening.

Moderately acceptable breakfast courtesy of the Holiday Inn Express, and off to the central railway station.

Spent the entire first leg of travel—almost four hours—dozing. I think I actually got a lot of sleep done, somehow. I didn't even *try* to write: not only I was not in the mood for anything, but the frustration over the inability to upload the last two posts was really distracting me from writing anything that would please any sense.

Approaching the end of the first leg of travel, an announcement was made that the train will be late at its destination, now scheduled to arrive 11:54am. This was horrible news, considering the fact that the connecting train was scheduled to depart on 11:55am. That's one minute to change platforms—and the platform you arrive to, and the platform you're connecting from, may as well be in two different ends of the station.

Brilliant.

So, I spent the next little while figuring things out. Turns out that the train I'm on was supposed to arrive at platform 3, and the connecting train was supposed to depart from platform 4. There was a good reason to believe that platforms 3 and 4 were adjacent to each other, which means that all you have to do is simply depart your train and jump to the other side of the platform, a few meters away. But, then I remembered that I had seen stations before where this arrangement was inapplicable.

How to do figure things out, then? of course: by downloading the train station's platform plan from the internet. Neat. Unfortunately, I lost data connectivity too many times so I couldn't download the damn thing.

Fortunately, as the train approached Fulda, another announcement was made, saying that the connecting train is indeed at the other side of the platform, and the departing train was instructed to wait for connecting passengers.

Phew. Good. Thanks.

Everything worked like a charm. Arrived Würzburg on time; spent the break consuming a sandwich, then hopped on the last train for the day, heading to Bad Mergentheim. That was a "regional train"—of the simpler trains that Deutsche Bahn operates, used mainly for travel in rural locations.

And, indeed, the train did go through rural locations. Beautiful scenery of green hills and postcard-like views of beautiful, simple, old houses along.

Finally, arrived at Bad Mergentheim.

Bad Mergentheim. Ha. Interesting. I remember when the tour's schedule was first published, I was looking at the name "Bad Mergentheim" and instinctively started wondering whether there's a "Good Mergentheim" somewhere which might be more worthy of a visit.

It goes without saying, that I had never heard of Bad Mergentheim before. "Another place in the middle of nowhere", I thought to myself. Indeed: it *is* in the middle of nowhere.

Turns out that the word "Bad" in German means "Bath", or "Spring". There are many small towns in Germany having the word "Bad" in their names, and they all essentially refer to spa towns, or resorts of some sort. Those "Bad" places is where Germans go on holidays to.

The hotel for the night, Kurhotel Alexa, was located a few minutes walk from the (small) central railway station—to the north, while the town's "old city" area is in the south. Heading away from the busy area, the scenery became fantastic (see photos below).

Booking accommodations in Bad Mergentheim was a problem, because we couldn't find affordable rooms offering twin beds. Therefore, we ended up picking a hotel that offered single rooms, and got two single rooms. For the first time in over three months, *I had my own room.* Oh, how I missed being *completely by myself.*

Extremely friendly staff on site. Up to the room and the first thing I did was upload those two posts I didn't manage uploading in Dresden. As soon as they both uploaded successfully, I felt as if some weight was lifted off my soul. It was good being back in business again.

My friend Ingrid made her way from The Netherlands to the concert, picking up Maarten somewhere along the way. The two stayed in a hotel nearby, and plans were made to get together at around 4:00pm.

The concert in Bad Mergentheim was a general admission concert, scheduled to begin at 8:00pm. Ticket collection was scheduled to start at 4:30pm, with *markknopfler.com* ticket purchasers being allowed early entry to the venue at around 5:00pm, before the doors open to the general public. That's paradise for people who insist on being in the front in a general admission concert—but it comes with the price of having to wait quite a long time inside the venue, before the concert even starts.

Everyone has their own preferences. My preference is to avoid the wait, and use that time to wander around.

The other three decided to enter the venue early, which is the reason for that early meeting.

The venue, *Schlosshof* (German for "Courtyard"), was located right in the old city area: approaching the old city area, you'd take a turn to the left and you're already inside the venue. So, as soon as I got my own ticket from the Dutchman, I bid the trio goodbye and went on my way. I had more than three hours to see this beautiful place.

TripAdvisor pointed me at a restaurant called Zunftstube Poseidon, offering a Greek menu. Food hit the spot really, really well: delicious dish made up of rice, lamb, vegetables… excellent.

Kept wandering around the picturesque old city area…

… And after some good coffee in a cafe nearby the venue, I decided to go north of the old city, towards the hotel and the peaceful scenery around.

A really nice river by the name of Tauber flows through the city, right behind the hotel. That provides for excellent greenery and an extremely nice walk, which I, of course, took.

The walk along the green was a truly refreshing experience. I spent eight years of my life being based in southwestern Ontario, where the scenery isn't much different: overall, I didn't like it that much but what I *did* like was the easy access to such peaceful environments (of course, British Columbia offers that as well). While living in Ontario, I spent quite a few days taking day trips to places with similar scenery, often accompanied by a guitar.

I really miss playing my guitars.

Time was nearly up, so I headed back to the old city area.

A quick walk, and then entered the venue.

markknopfler.com ticket purchasers also had access to an area called "Front of the Stage", which is the immediate area to… well… the front of the stage. Such ticketholders were given a red wristband, which allowed them access into that area. I headed there, but upon arrival, realized that the place was already jam packed. Again, I decided to listen to the concert simply sitting on the grass, often walking around to see the venue.

I was then identified by someone who happens to be reading this drivel that I write here. A guy named Dirk, who was accompanied by his girlfriend Sabine. The two are from Stuttgart. We started chatting, until I remembered what I was going to do in Stuttgart the next day: hospital visit.

To my extreme fortune, the two took the time to explain to me exactly where I should be going to seek medical care. Not only that, but Dirk went ahead and made phone calls to a couple of hospitals in Stuttgart, and later came back telling me exactly where I should be going —a clinic specializing in wrist injuries and the like.

Wonderful people. Thank you very much Dirk and Sabine for your kind help!

Concert started…

And was, well… very good. Very receptive audience, except in the back and in the sides where people seemed to be much more concerned about consuming insane amounts of beer and chatting with each other. I will never understand why people would pay so much money to go to a concert and then spend the time there drinking beer (which would cost much less in a proper pub) and chatting with others.

But still, what can you do.

I believe it was before *I Used to Could* when Jim Cox decided to show off a nice piano riff, prompting Mark to ask him to "do it again", which he did. Sounded lovely. Mark then looked at Jim, looked at his guitar, looked back at Jim and said "I can't play", triggering laughter at the audience.

Similar set to the day before, and the concert ended after just about two hours.

After the concert, I took another short walk through the old city, taking blurry photographs. I shall carry my regular camera from now on; the phone's camera doesn't do a good job when in darker environments.

Right after, late night snacks at the restaurant that operates at the hotel where Ingrid was staying. An hour or so spent over drinks, desserts and good chat, and then back to the hotel to catch some sleep before catching an early train to Stuttgart the next day.

Signing off this post from my hotel room in Stuttgart. Been a very eventful day today. 3:19am... better catch some sleep.
Isaac

Monday, July 8, 2013

The 199th: Bad Mergentheim to Stuttgart, Germany (July 6, 2013)

It's July 6th already. Hell, time flies.

The hotel I stayed in in Bad Mergentheim, Kurhotel Alexa, was located by the river in the quieter area of town, amidst a bunch of green. As a result, not even a peep could be heard while in the room. Also, the room featured curtains that could be turned completely opaque, which meant no light could enter the room in the morning. The result: very good night sleep.

The original schedule for the day called for departing Bad Mergentheim close to 12:00pm, arriving Stuttgart about two hours later. Very easy schedule, which would have been perfect had I not been terribly worried about my wrist. The day before, while my brain was working overtime worrying about my wrist's fate, I decided to change the schedule and arrive to Stuttgart much earlier (hospital visits usually take hours, and I didn't want to risk missing the concert). The Dutchman decided to tag along instead of spending a few more hours in this beautiful relaxing environment of this spa town, so by 8:30am we were already on the platform.

I'll miss this place.

Short ride north east to Lauda (about 10 minutes), in a 2nd class cabin full of suitcases and—even worse—people. Those rural trains... I dislike them. Started hypothesizing about what would happen if the longer ride—from Lauda to Stuttgart—was to take place in a similar train: nightmare. Luckily, after about half an hour break in Lauda, a more proper train arrived carrying good 1st class cabins.

> I cannot possibly stress this enough: if you are planning on a long trip to Europe, relying on trains, upgrading to 1st class passes is one of the best investments you could make.

The train ride from Lauda to Stuttgart passes through typical German country scenery. Germany is beautiful. Those of you who live in North America might not think of Germany as a travel destination, and I understand why: it's not really promoted as such by travel agencies or airlines. In North America, destinations such as Paris, Amsterdam and London are most of what you would hear about with respect to European destinations. I have never seen any advertisement *anywhere* promoting *any* German destination.

Shame, really: it's a beautiful country. I find it dumbfounding that people will buy into trips to Amsterdam and would consider it not exciting to visit, say, Köln; the latter is a more exciting destination than the former in almost every parameter.

(At least, that's my opinion.)

It was once again a train ride of silence. I was almost as apathetic as I was the day before. I wanted to get to Stuttgart already, just so I can go to the hospital there and get a better idea of what the hell was going on.

About half an hour before arriving to Stuttgart, the Dutchman bothered to look at the reservation for the hotel we were booked for: Hotel Unger, right at the city center. The price was €230 for 2 nights, and the reservation said that "some of the rooms are air conditioned". Internet connectivity? Wired only, for €5.50 per hour. Who booked it? myself. Why? I have *absolutely* no clue. I'm pretty sure that, when booking it, I had a good reason to; still, it's not a reason to not at least try to change things around.

Two travel ninjas then fired up their mobile phones. Five minutes later, the reservation for the "possibly air conditioned" hotel was cancelled, and a reservation to a much better hotel (judging by the description) was made, for €62 less—for a 4 star hotel nearby the station.

Arrived at the hotel—ARCOTEL Camino—and immediately recognized that I'm lucky to be staying here. Beautiful. Room wasn't ready yet, so I quickly changed to a slightly lighter attire (it was getting really warm outside), left the luggage with the hotel and rushed to the hospital.

The evening before, in Bad Mergentheim, I met a reader of this blog, by the name of Dirk. He happens to be living in Stuttgart, and gave me excellent advice which hospital to go to: Karl-Olga Krankenhaus, about 6 minutes ride by underground from the central railway station. A small mix-up in realizing which entrance I should be using—well, I don't understand German at all—but eventually, found myself at the emergency department.

By myself.

I mean, I was the only patient there. The entire emergency department worked for me.

After a quick diagnosis, the doctor said that he'd like to see the X-rays I took two weeks prior, in Regensburg. Loading those on his computer, he noticed a faint line that, in his opinion, was a fracture. It was very faint; still, I am not a doctor so I don't know what doctors are trained to look at when inspecting X-rays.

A new set of X-rays was then needed. Done on the spot. The new X-rays showed that the fracture (assuming that it was indeed a fracture; the doctor said he's pretty sure about it) has almost disappeared. Instructions: continue wearing that wrist brace for a couple more weeks, and see how things unfold. These things are known to take a long time to heal.

If you are a doctor, or happen to know one, here's the two applicable X-rays: The one done in Regensburg two weeks ago is on the left.

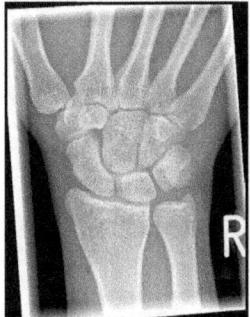 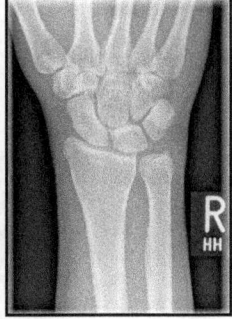

Overall, I was there for just about two hours. Great service, and I'm indebted to Dirk and his girlfriend Sabine for helping me out with this. Hats off to them.

Back to the central railway station and went to the hotel. The room was located on the very first floor, and once the door opened, I was shocked: the room was almost as big as my apartment in Vancouver. **HUGE**. I don't think I ever stayed in a hotel room that big.

> Once I took a look at the bathroom, I figured it out: it was a room for the disabled. That explained the fact that the room was located on the first floor, and had ample space for disabled people to move around in.

Quick setup, sat down to do some writing, and before I knew it, it was time to leave again. Last time in Stuttgart—about two weeks ago—we got a lead to a place offering excellent local food. As Ingrid and Maarten were in town this time around, it was decided to have an early group dinner. Delicious food again, good conversation, good times. A couple of hours flew by as nothing.

Took some pictures on my way to the restaurant and back. Stuttgart is certainly a beautiful city.

Back to the hotel, but not for long. As Ingrid's hotel was located right next to the venue, it was decided to meet there and head to the concert together. Knowing that I'll probably opt to stay near the venue for (non-alcoholic) drinks afterwards, I took my laptop with me so I can do some writing while the others enjoy themselves. The idea of writing my blog in Saturday night in a bar, surrounded by dozens of people who treat Saturday night as a "night out", did nothing to deter me.

Dropped the laptop in Ingrid's hotel, and off to the venue, a few steps away.

The venue, the Hanns Martin Schleyer Halle, is located in Stuttgart and named to commemorate Hanns Martin Schleyer, a former Nazi SS officer. Sounds a bit odd? I know it does. Sounds odd to me too, and I wrote about it last time I was here. I never quite understood what prompted the City of Stuttgart to commemorate a Nazi SS officer by naming one of its biggest arenas after him. Nobody bothered to explain it to me, either.

Arrived at the venue about 10 minutes before the concert started. Tickets picked up, and I went to buy some water for the group as everyone else headed to their seats. As I got to my seat, it wasn't long before *Feelin' Good* was played and the concert started.

And it was certainly not boring.

Before playing *I Used to Could*, Mark demonstrated the opening sequence as he tends to do recently. As he was done, he asked Richard whether this is "too fast for him", to which Richard responded with "everything's too fast for me" (which is, of course, false. I suggest you get a hold of Richard's albums—all four of them—nothing is "too fast" for this guy)—prompting Mark to report to the audience that "everything [indeed] is too fast for Richard".

As the band lined up to play *Dream of the Drowned Submariner*, Ian Thomas started performing the opening percussion sequence of *Postcards for Paraguay* instead (the percussion sequence during which Ian is normally being introduced. We'll get to that below, read on). That was odd. I looked at Ian; the entire band looked at Ian; and the entire audience looked at the band looking at Ian. He then understood that something is amiss, stopped and said something along the lines of "oh, I thought we're doing the [*something I couldn't decipher*]".

That triggered quite a bit of laughter from everyone present in the arena; all in good spirit, of course. Once the laughter was over, the band proceeded to play *Dream of the Drowned Submariner* the way I was waiting for it to be played. So, as I expected (and wrote about), this song indeed needed a few runs to catch substance; and in this particular song, most of the substance (again, that's my personal opinion) is in the outro solo, which is Mark's territory. Up until now, it seemed like Mark was experimenting, trying to figure out where to take things to—and in Stuttgart, for the first time, it simply sounded "complete". Stunning performance of this song.

Get the USB stick for this one. Not only the performance of *Dream of the Drowned Submariner* was absolutely stunning: in my opinion, the Stuttgart concert was one of the top gigs in the tour. That shouldn't be taken lightly, considering the fact that it was the fifth concert in a series of back-to-back concerts in Germany. Takes a lot of energy to perform this way after four concert days in a row.

Postcards from Paraguay is when Mark introduces the band. Ian Thomas is introduced first. This time, Mark mentioned Ian's name and added that he was "dying to be introduced"—referring to Ian's error from before, as he was performing the percussion sequence of the band's introduction.

Quite an eventful concert, but by far, the oddest event took place at the very end. At the very end of the last song (*Going Home*), Ian struck the drums as he usually does, then got up, threw the drumsticks away and just left the stage. By "threw", I mean simply throwing them high up in the air without aiming anywhere in particular. One stick flew to the back, and one stick flew forward, almost hitting Glenn's upright bass once gravity kicked in to bring the flying stick back to the ground. The entire band, minus Ian, stayed on the stage to bid the audience farewell.

I have absolutely no idea what prompted the throwing of the sticks and the early departure from the stage. I have never witnessed such an occurrence before, and as this post's title suggests, the Stuttgart concert was the 199th time I watched this band perform. I can only hope that everything's OK back there.

> Oh, yes. 199. I was going over my records a few months ago, and unless I'm missing something, the Stuttgart concert was the 199th time I watched this band perform—the first time being July 5, 2005 in Toronto.
>
> 199 concerts in 8 years, out of which 193 since June 2008.
>
> I am privileged to be able to do this.

As the band left, something appeared to be going on at the left hand side of the stage. Someone seemed to have been trying to steal something from the stage. A figure (a crew member?) ran from the back of the stage to its front, and there certainly was some contact going on. Seconds later, I saw security pushing away a young idiot wearing a white T-shirt.

Earlier today, I was informed that the idiot actually went on the stage, in an attempt to grab the drum stick that Ian had thrown away before. The person who informed me of this stood closer to where the action took place, so perhaps they are more accurate in their description of what really happened there.

One thing is for sure: it involved a selfish idiot.

After the show, went to a pub/restaurant nearby and spent a couple of hours chatting with friends. Did almost no writing at all, despite my plan to do so. Good times, made me almost completely forget that wrist thing. There aren't many chances to socialize when following such a busy tour, but still, I'm happy to have had the chance to do so.

Signing off this post from my hotel room in Stuttgart, after a great day off here. Tomorrow: train ride to Nîmes, France—for another day off. Next concert—the 200th—on Tuesday, in one of the most stunning venues I have ever seen.

Isaac

Thursday, July 11, 2013

The 200th: Stuttgart, Germany to Nîmes, France (July 7-9, 2013)

After a tough travel week in Germany—it was the time for a well-deserved break: not one, but two days off. As travel from Stuttgart to Nîmes takes about seven hours, it was decided, when planning this trip, to spend one day off in Stuttgart, and use the second day off to travel to Nîmes. Such arrangement made most sense, balancing between time spent unwinding and time spent travelling, all the while reducing the risk of missing the show in Nîmes due to… well, who knows. This is France, and every day without a railway strike is a day to savour.

Sunday, July 7th, was used to take things slow in Stuttgart. What a beautiful city, I tell you. Together with Köln, these two cities make for a great case to travel to Germany. The more time I spend in Germany, the more I grow to like it.

> Germany has not always been a preferred destination for travellers born and raised in Israel. World War II, which ended less than seventy years ago, saw six million Jewish people losing their lives to the atrocities of the Nazis. The Holocaust, being one of the most studied subjects in the world, is a subject that Israelis become well aware of since early days in primary school. I am not sure how the Israeli education system works now, seventeen years after left it; but in my time, the tight association between the country named "Germany" and the atrocities of the Nazis was instilled in people's minds as early as they could possibly understand, if only at the outset, what The Holocaust meant.
>
> As years went by since World War II, however, Germany turned to be one of Israel's closest allies in Europe. At least at the government level, German governments over the years showed a great deal of support in Israel in international forums. Trade and tourism ties strengthened significantly. Still, of course, nobody forgets World War II. Contradiction? in a sense, it is. But it is that contradiction that serves as a platform for the unique relationship between the two countries.

The day started with a late breakfast at the city center. Same group of people that met just the night before after the concert for drinks, minus one, were once away having a good time over breakfast out in some cafe's patio. Weather? perfect. Clear skies, around 22°C. Good healthy breakfast for a very reasonable price, even though the place could hardly be more tourist-oriented, being located at the very beginning of Königstraße, facing the central railway station. Time flew by, until we all bid each other goodbye. One left back to France, one to Belgium, one to The Netherlands… United Nations, really.

The day off was also used to do the laundry. There's a Laundromat right at the city center. Luck had it and some inconsiderate bloke was doing the laundry of his entire family and closest circle of friends, occupying multiple machines at once. Other machines were idle, but with clothes in them—belonging to people who weren't considerate enough to stay on the premises and unload their machines on time.

> Of course, that was enough to make me lose yet a bit more faith in humanity; mind you, faith is really running out here. The more people I find myself in the presence of, the more I long to be in the presence of less people. When I find myself dependent on other people's courtesy (not kindness; not looking for favours. Just plain, simple, basic courtesy), more often than not I end up getting disappointed.
>
> The world is probably full of nice people; where the hell are they?
>
> On the other hand, perhaps a cheap Laundromat off the most touristic area of Stuttgart is not the best place in the world to start looking.

My friend Dirk, who saved the previous day by recommending a good hospital for me to visit to look after my wrist problem, also recommended a good spot to see Stuttgart from above. Stuttgart's city center is located in some sort of a valley, as it is surrounded by mountains. Of course, the mountains' sides are dotted with beautiful red roofs, reminding me of the sights of West Vancouver when viewed from English Bay or Stanley Park. A short ride via U-Bahn line 15 to Bubenbad station, then a short walk along Richard-Wagner-Straße and you can't miss that viewpoint:

Along with the Dutchman, decided to walk a part of the way down instead of taking the U-Bahn. It's a moderate decline, making for an easy quiet walk through what seemed to be one of Stuttgart's more affluent areas.

Just as if the day couldn't be more relaxing, I noticed a nice cafe on the way down. Short sandwich and beautiful coffee, but my mind was set elsewhere. The place featured a beautiful black grand piano right in the middle of the cafe's interior; everyone was seated at the patio, so at first I considered trying it out, eventually decided that I'm way too shy to have a go at it.

Tram back to the city center…

… and we split up as the Dutchman went away for dinner and I headed back to the hotel to do some writing and upload the previous post.

Later on, met with a friend who just happened to be in Stuttgart for the concert. A nice walk from the Schlossplatz where there was an open air Jazz festival going on, to a cafe nearby and back.

It was Sunday night. Hundreds of people were sitting on the grass in the huge Schlossplatz, biding their time with friends, listening to the live music playing in the background. As busy as this city is, there was a sense of calmness in the air: piles of people just enjoying a breathe of fresh air as the sun sets. I could have stayed there for hours.

As the night was falling, I realized that the next day was going to involve quite a bit of travel starting earlier than 7:00am. Still had most of my clothes to fold and repack. Bid my friend farewell and headed back to the hotel.

One of the most interesting books I have read is James Surowiecki's "The Wisdom of Crowds". The book discusses the concept of crowd wisdom: when you present a challenge (such as a question) to a large enough group of people, aggregate all answers and analyze them, you often come up with the conclusion that, on average, the crowd is very smart—even though the variance in answers may be great. The book discusses the theory behind crowd wisdom, famous cases in which it was put in use and other interesting related topics; it is also usually high in the reading list of social sciences students.

I decided to do a little experiment. On my Facebook page, I posted the X-rays I took in Regensburg about three weeks ago, as well as the X-rays taken in Stuttgart just the day before, and asked people what they thought. Some of my friends are doctors, and some of them chose to respond privately. Some of my friends know other people who are doctors, and they also responded. I wasn't particularly seeking medical advice; I just wanted to know two things:

1. What a group of people, dealing with medicine, may come up with; and
2. Whether the group, as a whole, thinks that I should be stopping following the tour and return to Canada immediately in order to not worsen things.

I know nothing about medicine. All I know about the status of my wrist is what I actually feel. I was surprised to find, however, that opinions vary. Some claimed that the X-rays were just fine; some raised suspicions over a faint hairline in one of the bones, implying a fracture; and one suggested that I indeed had a minor fracture, but it is healing very well. I combined all opinions with the assessment given by the doctor at the Stuttgart hospital, and derived the most restrictive and conservative conclusion: returning to Canada now will not speed up recovery; and I should be wearing that compression brace for a few more weeks to let things heal properly.

Tour goes on. For now.

The next morning started early. Woke up shortly before 6:00am, got ready quickly and was already at the station before 6:40am. The itinerary: leave Stuttgart 6:54am, arrive Strasbourg 8:10am; then leave Strasbourg 9:16am, arrive Nîmes 2:30pm. Both rides are with the TGV, 1st class.

1st class international travellers on the TGV are served a complementary meal on board. With that in mind, it was decided to buy one sandwich each from Le Crobag, for lunch (Le Crobag has officially been nominated the trusted provider of sandwiches for the tour's leg in Germany).

Shortly after boarding the train, I felt that I'm starving. Turned out that the on-board meal on the TGV is served after the last stop in Germany, which is in Karlsruhe, 35 minutes into the ride. As the train left Karlsruhe, it took fifteen more minutes until TGV staff handed in those small boxes with "breakfast", hereby placed within quotes in order to not offend real breakfasts. Garbage. Really, garbage. Worse than most airlines' food.

That had to do, though.

Arrived at Strasbourg for a full hour wait. I have never been to Strasbourg before, and for some reason, I was under the impression that I was going to visit a beautiful city located on the mountains (where the hell do I get these ideas, I really don't know). Approaching

Strasbourg, I realized that there's no scenery here whatsoever. Didn't even leave the station; instead, bought a couple of croissants from a bakery on site and devoured it along with some cappuccino which was surprisingly adequate.

Nowadays in France, there seems to be a trend of placing pianos in public places so you can simply sit at one, and play. I seem to recall a commenter on this blog informing me about this. Anyway, there was one in Strasbourg's central railway station. Once again I had doubts, but then decided that, what the hell, I'm unlikely to see any of these people around anymore in my entire lifetime.

So, this particular piano had a very soft sound, as if its una corda pedal was permanently set. Wouldn't be surprised to find out that this was true for all of the pianos scattered around France. It was good to touch a keyboard again, for the first time after more than three months, although I had to stop after a few minutes as my wrist was hurting.

Back to the platform, and boarded the next TGV train. Five long hours ride to Nîmes, as the train rides through a couple of places visited before in this tour—Dijon and Lyon. During the ride, I experienced a little of this, from the passenger seated right in front of me (needless to say, he opted doing so while his seat was fully reclined).

The direction was, in general, south; and the more you head south, the more sparsely populated the area appears to be. So sparsely populated, that a couple of minutes before arriving to Nîmes, it seemed as if the train was still riding through France's rural areas. The city of Nîmes appeared as if suddenly, out of the blue.

Left the air-conditioned train right into the platform, feeling the most unwelcome jab of hot air right in my face.

Welcome to Nîmes, and welcome to (possibly) the warmest part of the tour.

The city of Nîmes is located in the south of France. 140,000 people live here. Its history dates back to the Roman Empire, and the city still has some of the best-preserved Roman structures in France. The city's name is pronounced as "*Neem*", with a dominant "*ee*" sound.

> I was always wondering what that strange letter î (that little "hat" on top of it is called "circumflex") was all about and how it should be pronounced. A Facebook post I made ended up getting really useful information about the subject.

I have been to Nîmes before, during the 2010 Get Lucky tour. Back then, I was only there for a day, which I remember was a very hard day due to the immense heat and the inability to feed myself due to the French's somewhat strict hours of restaurant dining. I was ready, then, to make amends: was going to spend two nights in this city and try to make sense out of it.

The hotel, Ibis Styles Nîmes Gare Centre, is located right behind Nîmes' central railway station. From there, it's about 800 meters walk to the city center: the closer you are to the city center, the pricier hotels become. For the purpose of following the tour, though, the location was perfect: a stone throw away from the central railway station (good for the next train heading towards Locarno, leaving very early in the morning), and about 10 minutes easy walk to the city center which, coincidentally, is also where the concert venue is.

Checked into the hotel and started the air conditioner even before *considering* putting my luggage down. The temperature outside was around 31°C, which is a temperature that I simply can't agree to and think it should be outlawed.

A short while later, went outside to explore the city. Chose to take the stairs as the elevator was occupied by a clueless couple who didn't quite understand the concept of inserting your key card in order to activate the elevator. Now, you might think that once you reach floor "1" and proceed downstairs, the next one will be "0". Well…

From the hotel, it's about 10 minutes walk north west, on a nice walkway featuring an artificial waterway. Due to the immense heat, people were sitting by this waterway with their feet inside it, to cool off. Children were bathing in it, too.

The walkway ends in a garden, bounded by two major boulevards—Boulevard de Prague to the east, and Boulevard Victor Hugo to the west. The old city center is located between the garden to the south; these two boulevards to the east and west; and Boulevard Gambetta to the north. Tourists in Nîmes are likely to be spending most of their time within those boundaries, and you can certainly see the entire old city center in one day.

Once you reach the garden at the end of the walkway…

… and look left, you see one of Nîmes' most precious prides, which also, coincidentally, was to serve as a venue for the next day's concert: the wonderful, splendid arena. We will get to that arena later on in this post, but for now…

(In the picture above, the arena is to the left.)

Walking west on Boulevard Victor Hugo is a good way to start exploring the old city center. From that boulevard, all you need to do is just pick on a random side street heading east and you're already in the old city center's core. Like most other old city centers I had seen so far in France, this one, too, isn't too bad on the eyes.

The people in Nîmes appear to exhibit slightly different lifestyle than in other places I have been to in France. Casualness seems to be prevalent: people seem to be more vocal, less formal. This may have something to do with the fact that Nîmes is located in southern France, and Italy and Spain are very close. I wouldn't be surprised to find that this proximity to Italy (to the east) and Spain (to the south west) has a lot to do with the impression you get out of people here.

It was hot. *Very* hot. How hot? I'm pretty sure I witnessed a cigarette setting a smoker on fire. So hot I wanted to peel my own skin off. There should be a bylaw in Nîmes allowing people to walk around naked. So hot that I was breathing fire. So hot that you couldn't possibly throw ice cubes at people—they'd melt before hitting their target.

How on earth could I survive 24 summers in Israel—which is hotter than Nîmes in the summer—is beyond me.

At some point, it was time to eat something. Horrific memories of my last time in Nîmes, looking for food, crept into my consciousness. Wandering around the city center following recommendations by *TripAdvisor* for about an hour, all attempts ended in restaurants that were either closed altogether or open for drinks only.

By complete chance, I noticed a place that was open, selling baked goods, yogurts and fresh fruit. Well, at least I *thought* it was yogurt; it was, in fact, *fromage blanc* (French for "white cheese"). Absolutely delicious: together with a cup of fresh fruit, that small snack was enough to keep me going until dinner.

Back to the hotel as it made no sense at all to be outside for long in those temperatures. First thing I did was to ask my French friends & followers, on Facebook, what was that *fromage blanc* thing and how is it different from a yogurt. Many useful responses came through. Unfortunately, it's not something I would prepare on my own. Hopefully they sell this stuff in Vancouver. It's addictive.

A couple of hours spent in the hotel to escape the heat, then back again to the city center for dinner. Cafe Leffe on Boulevard Victor Hugo offers an interesting menu, and even though it is located in an area that attracts many tourists, prices are reasonable. Delicious beef portions simmered in a broth that was based on… beer. Quick dessert, and back to the hotel again.

Second day off—check. Off for a good night sleep.

Waking up in Nîmes took a long while. Until the end of the tour, there aren't going to be too many mornings not involving an alarm clock, so such mornings are very well used to get out of bed as late as possible. Breakfast, included in the hotel, turned out to be mediocre

—not unlike the breakfast experience in many other French hotels. Seems like, in France, you simply can't expect your hotel's breakfast to be very good.

The plan was to take a walk from the city center to a large stain of green on the map—a place called *Bois des Espeisses*, some 4km away. Quite early in the journey, I already knew that I wasn't going to make it all the way there: the weather was just unforgivingly hot, and as the concert for the night was scheduled to start 8:30pm and include an opening act, I wasn't quite in the mood to aggregate much tiredness anyway.

Crossed the city center and then headed west towards another, smaller green stain on the map: a park called *Jardins de la Fontaine*. I knew nothing about this place before setting foot there: all I knew was that, on the map, it was represented by a green stain with some smaller stains painted blue, implying water.

Heading west from the north end of the city center, you walk by a nice canal that leads to a fountain:

The fountain marks the south entrance to the gardens. I couldn't be happier about deciding to visit these gardens—the scenery is absolutely stunning. I could hardly find any location in these gardens not worthy of a photograph.

These gardens were built in the 18th century, surrounding a then-recently discovered ancient Roman thermae.

Walking north inside the park, the path inclines...

... until you reach the top, where another famous Roman site is located: the *Tour Magne* ("Great Tower"), a ruined Roman tower.

Once arrived to the north end of the gardens, Jeroen decided to proceed to *Bois des Espeisses* and I decided not to. That's it for me: can't take this heat anymore, I ran out of water, please leave me alone, thanks. The Dutchman kept going towards the forest, I headed back.

Back in *Jardins de la Fontaine*, I took a different route to the city center, going through a different part of the gardens. I was happy I did: came across a few small tiny caves, where you can sit and watch water drop into small little ponds in front of you.

All that was missing in this picture was my beloved Taylor acoustic guitar; that guitar in my hands, it'd take a bulldozer to force me out of that spot.

On my way back to the hotel, I came across a cafe in the city center featuring the word "*Saladerie*" in its name. Salad? sure, why not. Might be a good healthy lunch. Lots of greens, walnuts and slices of duck breast. The French... what can I say, they know their food.

Back to the hotel and I decided to forgo of any other activity, and get a good nap instead. The heat outside wore me out, and with a long evening ahead, I figured I should probably get some sleep now when time is on my side.

Quarter by 6:00pm… concert time approaching. The plan: grab dinner before heading to the venue, as the concert was scheduled to end close to midnight, and with an early train ride the next morning, going for a post-concert snack was out of the question. Went to Cafe Leffe again, good hamburger. Ate too much. The search for a pre-concert coffee yielded no coffee bars—couldn't afford the time for coffee in a full sit-down restaurant. No worries: coffee in France sucks anyway. Headed to the arena, got impressed once more with how fantastic it looks from the outside, and went inside.

> Last time I was here, I was involved in a miserable incident: just before heading to the concert, I went to buy a deodorant in a drugstore. Entering the venue, some thug working for security grabbed my newly-purchased deodorant, assumed that it was a spray-on and simply tossed it into the garbage without even trying to explain what he was doing. I recall being livid afterwards, as I searched for an on-site staff member who understands more than a word in English. That deodorant was then saved when the stupid thug had to immerse himself in a bin of dump to restore my precious purchase.
>
> That thug's face remained engraved in my memory; I was *that* upset. So, when approaching the venue this time, I was wondering whether I'm going to come across that lowlife scum dressed as a human once again. Lo and behold—he was right there. Didn't even bother changing his appalling haircut.

I was looking forward to visit the Arena of Nîmes again, as my recollection has it as being once of the most beautiful venues I had ever been to. The arena was built by the Romans during the 1st century, and was changed in 1863 to function as a bullring.

Nowadays, the arena is used for all sorts of public events. In the realm of concerts, Knopfler's own Dire Straits' *On the Night* DVD features much of a concert performed right here in May 1992. On another end of the musical spectrum, *Metallica* recorded their 2009 DVD *Français pour Une Nuit* in this arena as well.

Stepping inside, you feel like you're going back in time. Imagine: watching a concert in a place that was built nearly 2,000 years ago.

I was seated at the second row facing the stage, but was actually more than willing to give up my seat for a seat somewhere in the back. I'm convinced that, in such a venue, watching the concert from the higher terraces would be a memorable experience. However, all seats in the venue were numbered and I was in no position to start asking staff for something as involved as this.

At around 8:30pm, Paul Crockford took the stage and introduced a very special opening act for the night: Bap Kennedy, an Irish songwriter that recorded his last album, *The Sailor's Revenge*, in Knopfler's *British Grove* studios in London. Knopfler himself plays on it. *The Sailor's Revenge* is a great album: I listened to it for the first time last October, as the Dutchman and I were scorching the USA's west coast following a few Knopfler-Dylan performances, and I still listen to it once in a while. Bap's voice is soothing, accurate, and beautiful, and I was wondering what he would sound like performing live.

Bap took the stage along with another guitar player, Gordon McAllister. Bap himself played rhythm on a brown acoustic guitar, while McAllister played the more involved parts. Listening closely to the tone of McAllister's guitar, I knew it sounded familiar. Looking at the guitar's headstock, I confirmed my hypothesis: you just can't go wrong with the Taylor sound. McAllister, if I'm not mistaken, was playing an *x*14CE. As much as I know Taylor Guitars' naming scheme, the "14" stands for their Grand Auditorium series; the "C" refers to their "cutaway" variant; and the "E" refers to the guitar's ability to be connected directly to an amplifier (an "acoustic-electric" guitar). I just wasn't sure about which series that guitar belongs to (that's the "x" part): I wouldn't be surprised if it was of the 800 series, or even the ridiculously expensive (and *such as good*) 900 series.

> Back when I was shopping around for an acoustic guitar, I tried quite a few. Each and every *HD Martin* I tried turned out to be a failure: I just couldn't play them (although I did hear that the Knopfler signature *HD Martin* guitar is different in that regards and has excellent playability; never tried it myself). Tried many other brands and models. At the end, there was no competition: Taylor Guitars, period. Bought the 314CE, and two days later exchanged it for the 414CE which I enjoy to this day. The better sounding models, unfortunately, were unaffordable for me back then. I may reconsider this.

It was the first time for me to listen to Bap Kennedy perform live. I enjoyed the performance—essentially, "thinned down" arrangements of a few of his songs—but something was missing. It was hard, at first, to understand what it was that was missing, until it hit me: the audience. The audience just didn't seem to "be there". I don't think it was any of Bap's fault—his performance was very good—instead, I just think that the audience wasn't the perfect match for this kind of a thinned-down, "down to earth" performance. Another indication that it wasn't Bap's fault at all was that the audience "wasn't there" right from the beginning. Shame, really: they missed on a great performance by very gifted performers.

Thirty minutes after Kennedy and McAllister left the stage, the lights went off and the band kicked off its 53rd concert for this tour, and their 200th concert with me in the audience.

Two hundred.

So what did we have there? Nigel Hitchcock is no longer performing with the band, so we're back to the original, Nigel-less set. *Dream of the Drowned Submariner*, as expected, wasn't played (as you'd need Nigel for the clarinet part; although, to my knowledge, Mike plays the clarinet as well); *Gator Blood* was played instead, like in the pre-Nigel days.

A short audio mishap took place at the beginning, about a minute into *What It Is*; most of the speakers simply stopped working at once, so unless you were in the front, you probably couldn't hear much of the concert for about 10–15 seconds. Not sure what went off there, but it was all over and done with quickly.

The band itself seemed fresh and rested, the audience—well, it's France, so it doesn't get much better than that, except for the endless chatter. Behind me, a group of 3–4 humans just kept talking and talking for about half an hour, until a guy sitting two seats to my left turned to them and yelled something at them in fluent French. I don't know exactly what he said but an argument quickly ensued and just as quickly ended. They stopped talking from there on. Chatter was evident elsewhere as well. I'm not entirely sure why people bother going to a concert if they're going to be sitting through it chatting their guts out. Then again, any attempt to understand stupidity is bound to make you feel stupid yourself.

Last time in Nîmes, I recall a rather violent *Running of the Bulls* taking place, followed by repeated calls by the back rows to sit down. Neither happened this time: there was hardly any running, and I couldn't see much violence. Heck, people ran wilder in England. No calls to sit down, either: good encore played in front of a standing audience, on the floor as well as on the terraces in the perimeter.

Beautiful.

Concert ended. Headed back to the hotel for a good night sleep, expecting a long, *long* travel day to follow.

As I am writing these lines on my way out of France and into Switzerland, I think it would be a good time for a confession.

Over the last few years, these modest travel blogs of mine have been receiving a great deal of attention. "No man is an island" (although I'd consider myself being as close to an island as a person could possibly be); naturally, over the years travelling following this wonderful band, I have met so many people—some of which I get to see more frequently than others.

There aren't many opportunities to socialize when following a tour—at least not when the subject is Mark Knopfler, who doesn't shy away from scheduling concerts back-to-back in cities that span vast distances between each other; and at times when socializing is actually possible, I often prefer to pass on the opportunity because I'm either tired or have to conserve energy before a long travel day.

Having said that (and here comes the tough part), when I socialize with people, I prefer to talk about… well, many things: life; the lives of the people I meet; my life; common interests. On the other hand, I dislike overly excessive discussions about topics that, for some reason, people assume that I'd be happy to discuss. Examples are aplenty:

- Any particular band member, their history and/or their personal lives.
- Past concerts, especially comparisons between them (which show was better than others. As if I can remember, really).
- What motivates Mark to do one thing or not the other; play one song and not another; wear one shirt but not another (as this is none of my business).
- Bootlegs, recordings, collectibles, signatures (not my thing at all).
- Set lists.

Why? Well, that's a topic I wanted to write about ever since the first tour I followed, back in 2008. Perhaps I will, some day—when I find the right words. For now, I hope you will not find the preceding text offensive or condescending, because it certainly isn't meant to be so.

Signing off this post from the patio of my hotel in Cardada, 1,340m above Locarno, Switzerland. Yesterday was a very challenging day, full of strange occurrences. Heck, it was so challenging and tiring that I went to bed at 10:00pm.

You'll definitely want to read the next post.

Isaac

Friday, July 12, 2013

Nîmes, France to Locarno, Switzerland (July 10-11, 2013)

After great two days in Nîmes—following great two days in Stuttgart—it was time to decamp and travel north east, for another expected great two days in Locarno. When following such a tour, you learn to appreciate and embrace time periods that involve no travel: travelling by train is more tiring than not travelling at all, even when you travel in 1st class cabins all the time. Being able to wake up whenever you want without subjecting yourself to the whims of alarm clocks… savour these mornings.

The punishment: wake up early enough to grab breakfast at the hotel and make it to Nîmes' central railway station to catch the 7:29am train heading to Lyon; about an hour connection time, then catch the 10:04am train heading to Mulhouse Ville; ten minutes connection time, then catch the 1:07pm train to Basel; and lastly, about 40 minutes connection time, then catch the 2:04pm train to Locarno.

I'll save you the math: it's just under 11 hours of travel, over four different trains. Three of the trains were TGV, so I knew that travel wouldn't be *that* hard anyway: TGV's 1st class cabins are excellent—spacious and comfortable. It's the last leg—the four hours ride from Basel to Locarno—that I wasn't sure about: the train's code began with "IR", and while I might have ridden one during the last tour, I couldn't remember anything about it.

Long, long travel day, one of the longest ones in the tour.

The first layover in Lyon was used to look for, and buy, packed lunch of some sort. The next opportunity to do so would be in Basel, which would be too late as I'd starve to death by then. Exiting the station, it was decided to go for a safe bet: the good old American mega food corporation of *Subway* has a shop conveniently located right outside *Lyon Part Dieu*.

After much debate, it was decided to buy two types of sandwiches—two "foot long" ones—and share them. As the sandwich connoisseur was completing working his magic on the second sandwich, and we were debating between ourselves how on earth we were going to divide the two sandwiches so we can share them (if you have ever been to *Subway* before, and know how they pack sandwiches to go, then you should be familiar with the challenge we were facing), the Dutchman decided to start the day with a giant leap over language barriers.

– "I am going to ask him to cut each sandwich in half, separate the halves, mix them and pack them."

"Yeah, right", I thought to myself.

– "Yeah, right", I then said out loud.

– "What?"

– "Do you speak French?", I asked a rhetorical question.

– "No, but we'll see how it goes."

I was curious to see how this would work out, considering the language barrier and the fact that the Dutchman was going to assign an unusual task to an individual who lives in a country where bar owners often refuse to serve you cappuccino because "it takes too long to prepare".

The Dutchman then proceeded to explain his wish to the sandwich God in plain English. The sandwich God responded with one of the most vile, dumbfounded look I ever witnessed on the face of a Frenchman—but then, surprisingly, did exactly what he was asked to, no questions asked.

> Some of you may wonder why I was so surprised to see that this minutiae worked out just fine. Well, some background information is needed: I live in North America. While exceptions exist (of course), people in North America whose jobs involve a great deal of routine work tend to perform their duties "by the book": any request for a slight deviation from what they have been trained to think of as "standard" is perceived with a great deal of suspicion and helplessness. There are strong reasons for such mentality, concerned with strong obedience to authority; I have done a lot of reading on the subject and I'd recommend that you do, too. Fascinating subject.

Sandwiches grabbed, and backtracked a few steps to a nearby cafe, to kill some half an hour left to departure. Lovely lady barista eagerly tried to convince me to add some sugar to my specialty cold cappuccino—smiling all throughout—that I was starting to think she might be flirting. Then again, I have no idea how flirting works and I couldn't tell when a lady flirts with me even if she smacked my face with her bra. At any rate, I was never persuaded so strongly to add sugar to my drink.

Back to the platform, off to the next train… arrived at Mulhouse, off the train, back to another platform, hopped on another train… then arrived at Basel SBB for a much awaited forty minutes break.

The black wrist brace I had bought in Vienna started wearing out, as the Velcro there wouldn't attach well anymore. That, combined with my decision to be more conservative about how I treat this wrist of mine, prompted me to try something else—a firmer brace, one of those featuring a metal bracket that prevents you from bending your wrist altogether. Luckily, this is Switzerland, and in Switzerland there appears to be a pharmacy in every block; expectedly, there was one in the train station itself. Quite a few Euros later and I was the proud owner of a beige wrist trap.

Back to the platform for the last train for the day. Those "IR" trains… who knows what they are made of? would there be 1st class cabins at all? are they crowded? air conditioned? how would the next four hours look like?…

… Senseless fears. That train ride turned out to be the best train ride in the tour so far. Modern, spotless 1st class cabin with panoramic windows—almost floor to ceiling—and for a good reason: the ride from Basel to Locarno is really, really, *really* scenic, once you leave the big city and head south east.

How scenic? well, I was very busy writing the previous post, and still, at times, I just couldn't let go of my camera. Memories of British Columbia kept creeping in—mountains, valleys, snowy peaks, gorgeous lakes. The same British Columbia that is my home, and that I chose to leave for 3+ months to wander around European destinations of all sorts. The more natural scenery my eyes transmitted to my brain, the happier I was that the tour is coming to an end, and in three weeks time, I'll be home again.

Time for some pictures.

With scenery like that, and the 1st class cabin being almost completely devoid of other people, it's no wonder that the four hours train ride passed quickly. At 6:13pm, finally arrived at Locarno's central railway station.

Locarno is located at the foot of the Swiss Alps. About 15,000 people live in this tiny town, and some might say that these are 15,000 exceptionally lucky people: it only happens that Locarno is a very popular tourist destination, as people from Switzerland, Germany and Italy flood its streets year round. Why? well, it is, as written before, located at the foot of the Swiss Alps; plus, we are talking about an immensely picturesque place.

Amazing natural scenery aside, the city *itself* is beautiful, featuring beautiful, colourful houses, narrow streets and a great deal of history. Now, that scenery that we had put aside before… add it back into the picture, and you get a total eye-candy of a place.

Much of the Locarno's beauty has to do with the fact that the town lies on the shore of Lake Maggiore. This huge lake, shared between Switzerland and Italy, boasts clear water that blend perfectly with the beautiful mountains all around. You need to see it to understand just how majestic that entire natural ordeal is.

And, of course, seeing it from an altitude of 1,340m may just be the best way to go about doing so.

I have been to Locarno before, during the 2010 Get Lucky tour. During that tour, I was in the bad habit of planning my itinerary while on the go, resulting in a financial catastrophe in Locarno: ended up booking an outrageously expensive room in a mediocre hotel with no air conditioning at all, right by Lake Maggiore: that's what happens when you book accommodations in short notice for staying in a Swiss resort town during one of the busiest periods in the year—the famous Moon and Stars Festival, taking place annually in mid-July and attracting big names in the music industry.

For this tour, however, planning was done well in advance. The problem, though, was that it was next to impossible to find rooms with two separate beds in them. Very few options came up, and after factoring in others' reviews of these hotels, three options came up: one in a town neighbouring to Locarno (still, very close: about 3km away); one in Orselina, which is about 300 meters above Locarno, accessible by walk, car or a funicular; and one in Cardada, located even further up the mountain (1,340m above Locarno).

The latter hotel, Albergo Cardada, was shown to offer magnificent views over Locarno, Lake Maggiore and the surrounding mountains. There was one caveat, though: it is only accessible by a cable car, or walk. You can't drive a car there.

Considering the options, and figuring that it would be nice to spend a couple of days in a hotel offering such peaceful, magnificent views, it was decided to book Albergo Cardada: reasonably priced, and the views are fantastic. The hotel also received very good reviews, so why not?

A few weeks ago, I received an email from the hotel asking whether I'm going to be attending the Moon and Stars Festival. Odd question. I asked why, to which they replied that they were going to book a "special cable car" late at night for those who want to attend the festival and go back to the hotel afterwards.

I shrugged. Well, sure, OK, put me down for this. In hindsight, though, the amount of details I neglected to look into turned out to be scary to the extent of ridiculousness. The fact that everything worked out at the end is a matter of mere luck.

So, here's how it goes: to get to the hotel from Locarno's center, you need to take *two* methods of transit: first, you take a funicular to Orselina, and from there, you take a cable car to Cardada.

The funicular from Locarno to Orselina operates daily between 7:00am to midnight, every 15 minutes (starting 8:00pm, every 30 minutes). Sounds reasonable, but things start getting scary when you consider the schedule of the cable car that takes you further up to Cardada: operating daily, from 8:00am to 8:15pm (!). If you miss that cable car, you have no way of arriving to the hotel except for walking, and we're not talking about an easy walk in the park: the difference in altitude is about a kilometer. It is said to take about 3–4 hours to walk your way to the hotel.

We didn't know all of this.

Instead, as soon as arrived to Locarno's central railway station, we started looking for a place to eat. Locarno, being a resort town, is obnoxiously filled with dining options, most of which cater to tourists. Prices are stupidly high. Looking online, we found a vegetarian Indian restaurant by the name of Govinda. Prices were so expensive that we ended up taking a one person's meal and splitting it half way.

Then, went back to the funicular station, paid and went up to Orselina. It's a short 5 minutes ride up, then a short few meters walk to catch the cable car station to get you up to Cardada.

By complete and utter luck, we were in time to catch the *very last cable car available for the day*; and we didn't even know it.

Arriving at the cable car station, there was nobody there. Knocked on the ticket office's windows… no response. Knocked on the only door I could find there… no response. Ten minutes before the scheduled departure, someone finally made it to the receiving end of the counter. Good. Tickets purchased, and we waited by the entrance for the time to come.

At 8:07pm, eight minutes before schedule, the cable car's doors closed and it started making its way up.

We were not in it.

I approached the control window, where the dude controlling things was sitting and appeared to be pushing buttons. He noticed me and immediately had the look of "oh, crap" on his face. He looked up, pushed a few other buttons, and the cable car came back.

Gee.

Heading up to Cardada was… well… a lot of fun. I captured it all on video, and I might publish it on my Facebook page soon. It's a very fast ride—the cable car reaches maximum speed of 10m/s, climbing to an altitude of 1,340m above Locarno in about 5 minutes. Not for the faint of heart, I tell you. With every second of the cable car climbing up, I got a better sense of what it would be like to be up there, watching the view.

Cable car reached its destination. Doors opened, and the hotel was right there. Looked to my left, and saw the magic of mother nature right there—but it was cloudy so I didn't bother taking pictures. Weather seemed to be worsening every minute, so the first order of business was to check in first, and see what was going on around later.

Stepped into the hotel, which looked more like a gigantic two- or three-level house. Checking in, I already got the idea of how things were going to look like interacting with these people: almost no ability to communicate in English whatsoever. Locarno's official language is Italian (as it is located in the "Italian part" of Switzerland), and, despite what you might think, knowledge of the English language isn't considered to be a "must have" here, even if you're in the tourism business.

Up to the room, which had three single beds and a playpen. Why a playpen? because I asked for one. No, just kidding: I didn't ask for one. But a playpen was there. Also, all three or four rooms on that floor had access to one shared huge patio, offering excellent views of Lake Maggiore and the town of Locarno, far below.

But first, before enjoying the Alpine air, some room setup is needed. Very awkwardly organized room, and what do you look for first when you're setting yourself up in the room? That's right: electricity sockets.

Now, I wonder how many of you have ever encountered this:

There were three of these in the room: one (pictured above) inconveniently located at the room's entrance by the door; and one on each side of the two single beds that were attached together. The ones by the sides of the bed were behind the beds' frames, and a round hole was sawn in the beds' frames to allow access to them.

It took us about 30 minutes to figure out how to optimally use those. These outlets look like they cater to all sorts of plug types, but they don't. The holes are either too thin, or too close to each other, or too far apart. A "normal" European plug, consisting of two prongs, will *not* fit in all pairs: there's a slight width difference between the various pairs, and it takes some trial an error to figure things out.

Now, when one travels, one usually carries some sort of a socket adapter. My adapter was just too big to fit through the bed frame's hole. That took five minutes to fight with until I gave up.

The good thing about these sockets (and I can't believe that I'm writing that there's a *good thing* about these sockets. Probably the *only* good thing) is that you could fit three normal European 2-prong plugs in one socket.

Wi-Fi connection took forever to work, as my devices kept stuck on the adapter's "obtaining IP address" phase, which, in geek speak, means that the device is waiting for the router's DHCP server to assign it with a unique NAT address; and in laymen terms, it means that the device is waiting for the Wi-Fi router to "accept it". That's not uncommon in Wi-Fi infrastructure setups that use cheap equipment that is geared towards home use.

All the while, thunders were sounding around. Rain. Minutes later, a lightning. Electricity went down, and then back up again after a second. All electrics immediately plugged out from those fancy sockets—last thing I need was a lightning to burn my laptop and my phone.

What a rush.

Wi-Fi down. That's another common thing with low-end routers: a sudden fluctuation in electricity may cause them to lose all touch with the world. Agreed with the Dutchman (actually, didn't "agree"; I simply refused to go downstairs to speak to these people—all I wanted was to take a shower and go to bed) that he steps downstairs to report the Wi-Fi problem while I take a long shower to wash this long day off.

Out of the shower, and I thought I'll chat with my family for a bit. Still no Wi-Fi. The Dutchman reported that he went downstairs to speak to the staff, but couldn't quite explain to them what the problem is, as he couldn't speak Italian.

Whatever. What time is it? 10:00pm? good. I'm going to bed, good night.

(Luckily, 3G connectivity was available.)

The next morning started much, *much* better. Beautiful weather. Quick wakeup procedure and downstairs for breakfast, not before taking a quick panoramic shot of the view from the room's patio:

The hotel offers a huge patio for breakfast, and in a sunny morning, that's where most people I know would have liked to have their breakfast, and here is why.

That was a sign that this was going to be a good day. Took my time with breakfast—I had nowhere to hurry to. Once done, went upstairs to bring my laptop so I could finish my previous post and upload it. Post finished, started uploading…

And continued uploading…

(All the while, I was wandering aimlessly around the patio just breathing pristine air.)

And continued uploading…

And then Wi-Fi signal was lost.

AAAAAAAAAaaaaaaaaaaaarrrrrrrrrrrrgggggggggggggghhhhhhhhhhhhhh

Went back to the room and found out that there was no electricity at all. A quick calculation of cause and effect in my head led to the conclusion that Wi-Fi was down simply because there was no electricity in the entire hotel.

You know what? alright. Might be nice to disconnect from the grid. Packed a few bottles of water and an apple, and together with the Dutchman headed off to a nearby chairlift station: the plan was to take the chairlift to Cimetta—even higher than where we already where—and hike down.

Approaching the chairlift station, we noticed a bunch of people sitting on the stairs leading to the station, as well as on benches around. Hmmm, interesting.

– "Can we buy tickets?"

And the man on attendance there informed us that the chairlift doesn't work at the moment due to a power outage. Apparently, one of the cables connecting Cardada with the main electricity grid went kaput.

That's not the kind of news you'd be happy to hear when you're high up on a mountain with no way of getting down. I mean, I wouldn't *that* mind it if there wasn't a concert to attend, some nine hours later.

After waiting about 20–30 minutes on site, electricity was still not restored. While it was possible to walk up the mountain, it was decided to return to the hotel and try again later.

The hotel offers a few plastic beach-like benches so you can sit (or lie down) and watch the view, basking in the sun. I was therefore forced to spend the next couple of hours like this:

I didn't quite know whether I'm supposed to enjoy the total and complete serenity around, or get worried about the fact that electricity is out on that mountain and there's no way down at all. I ended up striking a balance between the two. A quick discussion with the chairlift's operator revealed that the cable car, connecting Cardada with Orselina below, gets its power supply from Orselina, so the power outage wouldn't keep people stranded in the mountain. That being heard, I was able to enjoy the surroundings.

Possibly the most relaxing couple of hours in the tour so far. It's futile to attempt to describe, in words, the feeling you get when you're sitting like this watching Mother Nature at its best, in perfect weather, breathing pristine air into your lungs; it's either futile to try, or my English vocabulary isn't rich enough.

Either way, if you can, then I strongly suggest you try it at least once.

Once I had enough of the sun, went back to the room and got a good nap. A long day was ahead, and I wasn't going to spend it being tired: tried to gain as much energy as I could.

Woke up… hey! what's that? electricity is back! YES! Published that previous post and fled the scene to the chairlift.

From the moment I sat on that chairlift, until I was back at the hotel an hour and a half later, I found it very difficult to let go of my camera. The views were insanely difficult to ignore. Everywhere you look, there's a postcard opportunity. I took so many pictures, and writing this post now, I find it hard to filter them: almost all of them turned out really, *really* well. Here are some.

And of course, some of these had to be taken, otherwise my sister would kill me:

Brilliant! Twenty minutes there flew by, then it was time to hike back down. About forty minutes give or take, with picturesque views every step of the way.

On August 2nd, I'll be back in British Columbia. I'm going to crisscross it until my car dies. I really miss it.

Definitely, the best day of the tour so far.

Back to the hotel and prepared to take the cable car down. Weather forecast (at least on my mobile app) called for a slight chance of rain. Also, once it turned out that it would be impossible for us to take the cable car up to the hotel right after the concert—we'd have to wait until 12:45am!—it was decided to grab rain jackets just in case.

Down with the cable car… then the funicular… and back into the tourist-laden town center. Grabbed the tickets for the concert, and then met my friend Philipp and his friend Thomas. Philipp flew in to Locarno for the concert, and by "flew in" I mean "flew *himself* (and his friend) in", as Philipp happens to be a pilot, was good to see him again.

markknopfler.com ticket purchasers were allowed early entry to the venue, an option that I was very much happy to forfeit. I have been to the front row in this venue three years ago (in what turned out to be one of the best concerts in the entire Get Lucky tour), and I was more curious to find what the concert experience would be like from the back, given that the venue, *Piazza Grande*, is tantalizingly beautiful. The group therefore opted at a nearby Italian restaurant for some pre-concert pizza.

Philipp and Thomas went to the Piazza…

… and the two remaining ones decided to take a look at Lake Maggiore.

Time was up—back to the Piazza.

The venue, Piazza Grande ("Large Square"), is located in Locarno's city center. It is, really, a square: what makes it so beautiful is the fact that it is surrounded by beautifully coloured houses.

At the sides of the Piazza, there are about five thousand restaurants and ice cream stands. The day before, walking through the Piazza on the way to dinner, I noticed fences around the perimeter, effectively separating between the restaurants' area and the venue. These fences weren't there now: you could really easily just sit in a restaurant, have dinner and watch the show over a glass of wine. Perfect. Too bad I didn't know about it; many others, though, did.

The concert started a few minutes past schedule. A shorter set (15 songs), and it was quite an experience to watch it from the far back. It felt, really, like a festival. The concert was also broadcasted on two big screens positioned at both sides of the stage.

So, I liked the concert, liked the venue, liked the setting… but of course, something negative must (almost) always pop up. As this was a general admission show, I was once again witnessing all the typical annoyances of general admission concerts: at least at the back, people kept on talking loudly—even on their phones; drinking alcohol all the time, getting hammered to the sound of music; beer done? why throw it in the garbage, if I can just squeeze it with my foot and wait for some other sucker to pick it up later? in summary, a huge bunch of losers who clearly weren't there for the music. It was, after all, a festival: people are there *just for the sake of being there*. I wouldn't be surprised to find out that many people in the audience yesterday weren't really appreciative of Mark's music—that is, assuming they even knew who Mark was.

Why do people behave this way? why would a group of people buy concert tickets, just so they can enter the venue, get hammered with alcohol (isn't alcohol more expensive in concert venues, anyway?), chat loudly with their co-losers and interfere with others' enjoyment of the concert?

It is what it is, though. What can I do? nothing much, except for complaining digitally.

Still, it was a nice experience to be a part of. Good music, and the Piazza prettier as the sun sets.

Concert ended in just under two hours. There was still an hour or so left until the hotel's special cable car service. Time spent with Philipp, Thomas, their friend Barbara and two other strangers. Bid everyone goodbye and headed to the funicular en route to Orselina.

Once in Orselina, it was still 40 minutes or so before the cable car was scheduled to arrive. I was a bit worried that the "special service" might end up being forgotten altogether, which would really, *really* ruin the night.

Near the cable car station, there's a viewpoint over the lake and the mountains. Spent some time there taking photographs with long exposure:

A nice couple from Switzerland, also staying at that hotel, joined shortly after. Was good to speak with locals. Time passed quickly, and fortunately, the special cable car service showed up on time.

Was good to be up there again. Packed everything that needed packing, and off for a good night sleep.

Brilliant and adventurous couple of days in the beautiful city of Locarno. Lucky to be doing this.

Signing off this post from the hotel room in Padova, Italy. Will go hunt for food now, and then to the concert—some 20km away.

Isaac

Monday, July 15, 2013

A Sign of Life from Italy

The last few days were just too insane. The tour's current leg in Italy involves a lot of insane travel, late shows, complete insanity when it comes to getting to and from venues… almost no time to write at all.

2:00am now, after the concert in Napoli. Day off tomorrow, I'll try to catch up then.

Night.

Isaac

Tuesday, July 16, 2013

Locarno, Switzerland to Padova and Rome, Italy (July 12-13, 2013)

The first cable car from Cardada down to Orselina departs 8:15am. As I wasn't quite aware of the cable car's schedule until I actually arrived in Locarno, I felt lucky as 8:15am departure fitted well with the rest of the schedule for the day: depart Locarno's central station at 9:03am, arrive Bellinzona 9:26am; depart Bellinzona 10:05am, arrive Milano 11:50am; depart Milano 12:05pm, arrive Padova 2:12pm. Five hours over three trains.

The Albergo Cardada hotel, situated in Cardada, some 1,340m above Locarno, offers breakfast starting 8:00am, so things had to be done quickly. By 7:55am, two hungry travellers were already checked out, luggage set aside and started piling food on plates. Less than

15 minutes later, breakfast was over and done with and the journey to the cable car station—a staggering 10 meters walk from the hotel's entrance—began.

One last look at the mountains and Lake Maggiore. It was grey and foggy, but you could still see some majesty.

I will miss this, but it's time to move on.

8:15am sharp, the cable car went on its way down. Each second passed made me realize how lucky I was that everything worked perfect in Locarno, schedule-wise, with all the funiculars and cable cars along. Last sanity check: do I have everything with me? let's see. Train pass... here. Passport... here. Laptop... well, my laptop is so heavy that it's impossible to not notice. Yes, everything's here: nothing's left on that mountain.

Arrived at Orselina. A few minutes wait for the funicular down to Locarno... boarded... check. Felt good to be back on the ground again. Not because I preferred Locarno's city center over the mountains, but because now, on the ground, with 30 minutes or so left to the train's departure, I knew that I no longer depend on cable cars.

Philipp, Thomas and Barbara were in the station as well, en route to Locarno's airport, where Philipp had his airplane parked. Imagine how nice it must be: you fly your own airplane, land in an airport, and park it there. You wanna go home? no problem: train to the airport, start your airplane and fly out.

> That also allows for an exceptionally good pick up line. "Hey, how about I'll pick you up at 6 o'clock, we'll fly somewhere nice."

Hopped on the S-20 S-Bahn en route to Bellinzona. As Philipp is such a nice person, I agreed to lower my standards temporarily, join the "common people" and board the 2nd class cabin for the first few stations. Not that bad. Trains in Switzerland seem to provide very high standard of travel even in 2nd class, and even for S-Bahn trains, which are usually short-haul ones.

Arrived in Bellinzona and had some time to kill. I thought I had never been here before, but once I exited the station and crossed the street to a nearby pharmacy, I looked around and the place looked awfully familiar. Yes, I have been here before: here's the cafe I sat in, exactly three years ago, waiting for my train...

The reason for visiting a pharmacy was to attempt to buy an adhesive tape, so I can attach a few gauze pads together when wrapping those around my wrist under the wrist brace (won't bore you with the details about why). Of course, not even one living soul in the pharmacy was able to communicate in English, leaving me with the only option of looking around the pharmacy myself, which I did and found nothing.

Hopped on the train, quick two hours ride to Milano Centrale. A short delay, but we still made it to the connecting train which was conveniently located on the other side of the platform.

Looking at the seat reservation for the train from Milano to Padova, we noticed that the seat was a 2nd class seat. That was odd: we wouldn't book a 2nd class seat for a train ride unless the ride was very short and the price difference was substantial. As EURail and Interrail train passes cover 1st class fares in Italy (but not seat reservations: seat reservations, if required, still have to be paid out of pocket), we assumed that we could just board a 1st class cabin, find two vacant seats and enjoy the ride.

That was a mistake that resulted in one of the most chaotic train rides in the entire tour.

First, it turns out that train rides from Milano to Padova during this seasons were extremely busy. In hindsight, that's not surprising considering the fact that these trains' final destination is Venice, which only happens to be one of the most popular tourism destinations in the world. Boarding the 1st class cabin, I thought I was entering hell: I don't think I have ever seen so many suitcases inside a train before. *Loads and loads* of tourists—single travellers, couples and families—were all over the cabin, with their suitcases located pretty much everywhere: overhead, between the seats, on the aisle, between the train's cabins... bloody everywhere. The cabin had air conditioning going on, but apparently not strong enough to battle the heat generated by the bodies of so many tourists scrambling around the cabins to either find a vacant seat, or to find their own seats.

Luckily (or so I thought), two vacant seats, opposing each other, were found; however, the LCD panel above them showed that they were reserved between Milano and Venice. That meant that either the people who reserved these seats are not on this train, or that they *are* on the train and currently battling to find their way to their seats. We stood by the seats—the train ride had already started, mind you; and it's a fast train, reaching speed in excess of 200km/h—waiting to see whether the seats' rightful owners were going to show up or not.

Eventually, they did. Fortunately, they were sympathetic of the situation and weren't mad or anything. Frustrated, we decided to head back to the 2nd class cabin—a walk of about 3–4 coaches in a moving train. On the way there, I found one vacant seat in 1st class and parked myself there. A minute later, Jeroen appeared and reported that these trains require seat reservations, and if you own a 2nd class seat reservation, then you must be seated there even if you own a train pass (this information was provided by the train's staff).

Defeated, we marched back to our rightful seats. Total time spent walking back and forth in a moving train: about half an hour, out of a 2 hours train ride.

Chaos didn't skip the 2nd class cabin, either. *So... many... tourists. So... many... families... with... noisy... kids*. Where the hell am I? am I on a train or in a damn kindergarten? *WILL SOMEONE TURN ON THE AIR CONDITIONING?*

All I wanted was for this train ride to pass. Eventually, it did. Was happy to leave the train. Exited Padova's central railway station and headed to the hotel—Hotel Grand'Italia (no typo; they put the apostrophe in the hotel's name)—located right across the street from the station.

Even though the tour's schedule mentions Padova as the city/town where the concert was to take place, this information is incorrect: the "real" location would be Piazzola sul Brenta, and Padova just happens to be the closest sizable city. I knew this, because during the 2010 Get Lucky tour, a concert took place in exactly the same venue.

Still, I have never been to Padova before. In 2010, I was subject to the mercy of two wonderful Italian sisters who live in northern Italy and were going to the concert anyway (by car), so I tagged along with them.

The feeling I got as soon as I exited Padova's central railway station—even before arriving at the hotel, which was a mere 40 meters away or so—was not good in the slightest. The area looked, felt and smelled like a slum. Typical central railway station scenery in Europe: those who weren't as fortunate as I am to live capable life—along with those who were probably given a chance or two and blew it—call the area home. Dirt, filth, everywhere. Everything looks dusty, neglected. Questionable individuals leaning against the buildings, some drinking alcohol in broad daylight (you could get arrested for doing so pretty much anywhere in North America).

Shady, dodgy place; the hotel, however, was very pleasant. Checked in, chilled out for a bit and then went out to look for some food.

Before heading out, we asked the receptionist about how we were to go about getting to Piazzola sul Brenta, which is located about 20km away from Padova's city center. We knew that there was a bus going there, but the problem was about getting back; we presumed that, if no other options exist, we'd simply take a taxi.

So, here's a tip: while in Italy, you must *never* presume anything. The receptionist informed us that a taxi back from Piazzola sul Brenta to Padova's city center is likely to cost about (sit *very* tight) €140. Mind you, that's for a 20km ride (I found out the reason later; read on). The Dutchman then said that he does recall reading about taxi cab riding in Italy being a stupidly expensive thing to do.

It's funny, though, how things end up working out at the end. The hotel's receptionist mentioned that they have a "private car" service, and that two other guests in the hotel booked it in order to get to the very same concert. She phoned them, and the good news were that they were willing to share the expenses. A "private car" service means that a driver picks you up from the hotel, takes you wherever you want for a duration of a few hours and then gets you back to the hotel—all for a price of about €130. Split four ways, you can't say it's a bad deal.

Nothing suitable was found to eat in the immediate vicinity of the central railway station. There was a McDonald's there, and if you took some time to observe the people who hung around in the area, you'd know why. Searches in *TripAdvisor* showed nothing useful, so we decided to just walk towards the city center—about one kilometer south. Once you cross the San Gregorio river, the scenery begins to look more like what you'd expect from Italy, and less like what you'd expect from hell.

Of course, this is Italy: a restaurant is to be considered closed unless proven otherwise. *Google Local*, the online tool I'm using for looking for places to eat whenever *TripAdvisor* fails, suggested a restaurant by the name of Brek. Arriving there, it turned out that it was going to open 20 minutes or so down the road, so the time was used to wander around the city center and taking pictures. Meanwhile, looked for some other dining alternatives, which turned out to be overpriced tourist traps.

This part of the city is indeed nicer. I would have, perhaps, continued to traverse the old city's narrow, picturesque streets but time was pressing. 6:30pm and we stormed into that restaurant found earlier. The way it works there is that you're supposed to walk through multiple "booths" and ask for the items you want, then pay at the end. Problem: it's all in Italian, but fortunately, there was an exceptionally nice lady working there who explained each and every item in the menu.

Simple, excellent filling dinner for two for about €26. Can't go wrong. Go there if you're in town.

Back to the hotel, chilled out for a bit and went downstairs shortly before 8:00pm, as we were supposed to meet the other passengers there. Minutes later, a big (big? huge!) guy with the haircut and the attire of a heavy metal fan stepped out of the elevator escorted by an older woman. Their accent meant either English or Australian; turned out to be Australian, a mother and her son. The son, in his early 30's, recently quit his job in Australia and decided to spend a few months in Europe following all sorts of music festivals. I asked him whether he's aware of the fact that Mark Knopfler isn't quite considered the purveyor of heavy metal music—you know, just to help him set his expectations right; he replied that he knew that, and it's all good.

Hopped on the private taxi. 25 minutes and an interesting conversation later, the driver dropped us off right at the entrance to the venue, and promised to be there when the concert ends, to pick us all up.

The venue, *Anfiteatro Camerini*, is located in the area of a huge Italian villa called Villa Contarini. The villa is named after the House of Contarini—a rich and respected Venetian dynasty. The venue hosts a live music festival every year.

A few bars and restaurants are available outside the venue, along the nearby streets and near the adjacent park. I remember, last time I was here in 2010, I went along with the Italian sisters and their family to a nearby cafe—a couple of blocks away from the venue and away from the typical festival noise. Somehow, I managed to find that cafe (actually, "somehow" doesn't fit well; memory is associative. Being placed in the same venue, three years later, helped resurface hidden memories from the back of my mind).

Interesting concept: you can't just go inside, say what you want, get it, pay and get out. No, that would be too simple. Instead, you are more than welcome to browse what they have—but then, you have to go outside, where a cashier can be found. You tell the cashier what you want, she types it all in, gives you a receipt and sends you back in to grab your goods.

Inefficient (which, in Italy, means "business as usual"); but what I was really wondering is whether any of you could guess, by this receipt, what it was that we ordered.

For those of you who weren't able to guess it, we ordered one cappuccino and one small 2-scoops ice cream. Shame on you, really, for not being able to tell. Now, mind you, this didn't confuse only you: it also confused the poor lady who had to prepare the order. Eventually, it turns out that what we *said* we would like to have isn't exactly what the cashier *thought* we should be getting. There was a very loose connection between what we asked for and what we ended up paying for. At the end, those missing €0.40 were gladly paid. Perfect cappuccino, thank you very much.

Back at the venue.

Villa Contarini provides for an excellent outdoors concert venue. The beautiful villa located to the right; green all around; lots of space; and the weather was excellent—what else could you ask for? not much. It was a great concert experience with a lot of energy. Well, this is, again, Italy: the audience in Italy is an integral part of the concert. Cheers and applauses are usually *very* loud, and when you factor in the amount of passion built into the Italian language itself, you should get the idea why attending concerts in Italy is a pleasure.

Ian—perhaps for the first time in this tour—chose to stand up for the opening sequence of *Hill Farmer's Blues*. I'm guessing it's easier hitting all those cymbals that way.

After *Speedway to Nazareth*, I was expecting the usual *Running of the Bulls* which, in Italy, might get rather nasty. What happened in reality, though, was far from anything I could have imagined. A group of people from the front couple of rows indeed walked (didn't run, though. Walk. Puzzling) towards the stage with the intention of staying there until the end of the concert. That, naturally, obstructed the view of people sitting behind. People then started yelling at the bulls—I don't exactly know what, but it sounded like "*sedotti*" (maybe an Italian-speaking reader could comment and explain?). At any rate, I believe what they meant to yell was "sit the !#@# down". The calls grew louder and louder until the group of people, standing in the front, simply took off and went back to their seats.

Update, July 19, 2013: the correct word is "seduti". Thanks, Valeria.

After *Telegraph Road*, however, nobody could stop them. Good encore, show ended and we exited the venue through the main exit.

With every step towards the agreed-upon meeting place, I was praying that things will turn out well. It was comforting to know, though, that there's a business association between the private driver and the hotel, and if something goes wrong, I would be raising hell the next morning. To my complete surprise, though, the driver was already at the meeting point, waiting for us outside the car. Now that's what I call service.

Quite expectedly, the Australian and his mother weren't there yet. Long minutes passed before they showed up, during which the driver explained, in a nutshell, how taxis work in Italy.

If I understood things correctly, there are two types of taxi cabs in Italy: white ones and yellow ones. The white ones can't be hailed spontaneously: you must call their respective company in order to get them to your location. Once you call the taxi company, a taxi is dispatched your way *and the meter starts running as soon as the driver is dispatched*. That is, if the driver happens to be located half an hour away from you, and they are dispatched at your direction, you have to pay for that half an hour.

I don't think I ever encountered such a standard before. It raises interesting questions. For example, what happens if you call a taxi company, and they have two taxis that can serve you: one is two minutes away from you, and one is half an hour away. Which one will they send over? the one closer to you? not necessarily. While it would cost *you* less, remember that it's in the best interest of the taxi company (and the driver) to get as much money out of you as possible.

Yellow cabs, on the other hand, work differently. You may hail them at will but there's no telling how much you're going to be charged. According to our driver, the taxi world in Italy is a mess—everybody's ripping everybody else off.

The Australian family finally showed up, with Alex (the son) holding a cup of beer. Before entering the cab, he remembered that he needed to urinate and voiced his frustration over the inability to simply take his manhood out of his trousers and urinate on a nearby tree. He then had to go back inside the venue, empty his bladder and get back. That's another 10 minutes.

I didn't care, though. All I knew was that I'm going to be glued to this driver and I'm going to go anywhere he goes; at the end, I'll likely end up in my hotel.

Fortunately, that's how things turned out. Paid the driver, left the car, bid the Australians goodbye and off to bed.

Funny how these things work out.

The next morning started easy. Being in a hotel so close to the central railway station carries the advantage of being able to sleep in, have breakfast at ease and still be certain that you're OK, travel-wise.

The plan: leave Padova 9:53am, arrive Rome 1:10pm. One train, around three hours. You're kidding, right? come on. That's easy. One train? that's it?

Yes.

I was excited to get to Rome. I have been there once before in my life, during the 2010 Get Lucky tour—for one night only, a time period barely enough to do anything in this great city. Also, the early arrival time made it possible to do some sightseeing.

The three hours train ride was divided into two: *hell* and *paradise*. *Hell* took place between Padova and Florence, and was characterized by millions of tourists riding that poor train. Again, so many suitcases…

> I moved to Canada a little more than ten years ago. I had to take my entire life with me, for an indefinite length of time, to a country located about 10,000km from where I was born and raised. Everything fit well into two suitcases.
>
> Why people take so much luggage with them when they go on vacation is beyond me. Women tend to pack more than men (see this) for incredibly stupid reasons; but that aside, the way I see it is that the more you pack, the less "true" vacation you're going to have.

Paradise took place once all said tourists left the train in Florence.

Arrived in Roma Termini on time. The hotel, Hotel Mozart, was located about three metro stops away, near the Piazza di Spagna (the "Spanish Steps"). Metro… now how do you go about doing that? oh, here's a machine. Good. In Italy, I prefer using such machines over talking to people, if only for the fact that these machines can communicate in English, which too many Italians can't. In Rome, you can get a day pass for €6, covering the two metro lines and all buses until midnight; a bargain.

There are two metro lines in Rome: Line A and Line B. Line B actually came first: it's old (dating back to 1955), and the trains running that line are old as well. Line A is more modern and is even air conditioned: not only the trains are air-conditioned, but also the entire waiting area.

We needed Line A. Good. Mind you, you don't see many clouds in Rome nowadays as the temperature was approaching 6,000°C.

Three stations to Spagna, and from there it's a short walk through a sea of people to the hotel, located in a narrow side street. Very good hotel right at the city center—although it does get noisy at times, because… well, because it's right at the city center.

Checked in and decided to go do some sightseeing. Being in Rome and not going to witness at least some of what this city has to offer in terms of history is insane, and what's more insane is doing it *twice*. The itinerary: first, go to see what's that Vatican thing is all about, then head to the Colosseum. The reason was that the venue—located outside the city center—was closer to the Colosseum than to the Vatican, and we were prepared for the possibility of running out of time and having to head to the venue directly.

Off to the metro, and the Vatican City is a few stops away. Exited the station and started following the crowds.

Five minutes later, and the Vatican City was right there. It looks like a mass of architectural beauty amidst a mass of… well… "regular" old buildings. Entering from the east, the first thing you see is Saint Peter's Square, a huge square located in front of one of the most famous sites in the Vatican City (and, considering the number of Christians in the world, I'm betting this is one of the most famous buildings in the world)—the Saint Peter's Basilica.

While the place is indeed beautiful and very impressive, for some reason, I started feeling anxious.

> I'm not saying that religion is a bad idea. I'm not saying it's a good idea, either. "Live and let live" is my motto: as long as you let me live by my own values, and as long as your lifestyle doesn't violate my rights, I really don't care how you believe the world was created, or who (or what) God is. Whatever floats your boat, really.
>
> My problem is with religious "authorities". It appears as if religion is such complex an idea, that people often seek some sort of an "authority" to tell them exactly what they should be thinking or doing. This, however, is a slippery slope: people who take religious authorities too seriously can quickly become controlled by said authorities. If you are used to some authority always preaching to

you and telling you what you should and should not do, you are likely to, eventually, lose the ability to question such authority. You then blindly follow whatever someone else says.

And *that* is where things go awry. Too many crimes against humanity were committed in the name of religion. Religion, by being preached to billions of people, became a tool to differentiate between people rather than uniting them. Competition between different religions (and different groups of people having different interpretation to the same religion!) led to terrible wars and millions over millions dead.

Why? because "some authority" decided that religion is an idea worth killing for.

What I say is simple: the moment you (either directly, or indirectly through some sort of a preacher) decide that someone else's life is less precious than your own because of religion-related factors, you don't belong in my society anymore. For all I care, life is more important than any sort of deity, be it called God, Jehovah, Allah, Buddha or $E=mc^2$.

The moment some else's life becomes less worthy in your eyes because of your spiritual belief, your spiritual belief is immediately rendered as complete and total garbage: please commit yourself to an asylum and relieve us from your presence, thank you.

That explains, in a nutshell, why I become slightly anxious when I get to think about religious authorities of any sort.

And I won't even get started with the Catholic Church's issues with child molestation, their divisive and hate-mongering approach towards homosexuality, female rights and so forth. There comes a person, delegitimizes people based on his interpretation of the "holy books", and in the same sentence calls for peace and unity. The only people stupider than such abusive "authority" is those who blindly subject themselves to it.

In the Vatican City, there usually is a long line for visiting Saint Peter's Basilica. Standing in line for hours is not something I'm capable of doing without losing my mind, let alone on concert day; therefore, after about 10 minutes wandering around Saint Peter's square, we left the scene and headed back to the metro.

Like many other touristic locations in Europe, many streets in Rome are laden with individuals who sell possibly-stolen, possibly-fake, definitely-illegal fashion goods on the sidewalks. Goods are being placed on some sort of a blanket; upon noticing a police officer, all goods are wrapped into one big bag in a matter of a couple of seconds, and all you get to see are innocent-looking people walking around with strange big bags hanging off their shoulders. The first time I saw it was in Barcelona in 2010, a few days after the end of the 2010 Get Lucky tour as I stayed an extra few days in Barcelona to unwind.

From the metro, it's a long ride (including a metro line change) to get to the Colosseum. Now *there's* history for you. What a magnificent sight. Seeing it in pictures and in movies really doesn't do the trick: you need to be there to fully grasp the magnitude of this thing. I took so many photographs trying to capture how amazing this thing is in real life… almost consistently failing.

The place was, of course, filled with tourists. The Colosseum, mind you, is not the only piece of history in the area: Rome's history dates back about 2,500 years, and, to this day, contains numerous important historical sites. I love places that are rich with history, which is why I often visit the city of Jerusalem whenever I'm home for a visit. I'm not even going to try to cover a fraction of Rome's history in this blog

—there's simply too much to say. But one thing is for sure: you need to be there to believe it. No still photograph and no video can ever do justice to the immense ancient beauty that Rome has to offer.

(I took the last panoramic one just for that kissing couple.)

Rome, therefore, has been added to my list of places to revisit in the future—not an easy list to get into, as I have been to so many places already and I have to be very picky.

The weather was too hot to bear so decided to go back to the hotel and chill out. I knew it was going to be a long day still: the concert was scheduled to start at 9:00pm, and getting back from the venue to the city center was still a big question mark (we'll get to that later).

The hotel offers a nice terrace on top, offering fantastic panoramic views.

Back to the room, to get some rest, and then off to the venue.

The venue, Ippodromo Capannelle, is—listen to this—a *horse racecourse*. There's a first time for everything, I guess: more than two hundred times watching this band perform, and I never thought I'll watch a concert in a horse racecourse. I didn't know it was a racecourse before arriving, though; all I knew was the venue's name and that *Bruce Springsteen* performed there a few days earlier.

The problem with the venue, though, was its location: the venue is located about 20km away from Rome's city center. To get there, you need to take the metro almost all the way east, and then take a bus. An annoyance, but not a huge problem: the problem is getting back to the city center. While the metro in Rome is active until very late at night, buses become less and less frequent. Due to the huge distance involved, walking back to the hotel is not an option: missing the metro and/or the bus would mean having to hail a taxi, which is very hard to do on the spot due to how taxis work in Italy (you have to call them first).

Arrived at the venue, and the first thing done was to ensure we know where the departing bus leaves from. That's much easier done in daylight than otherwise. Once done, headed to the venue, collected tickets and entered.

Italians love their scooters…

Once inside, before arriving to where the concert was actually going to take place, there were many food and drink stands, plus a few "rooms" dedicated to particular products for the sake of promotion (*Samsung*, for example, had a "room" there to promote their *S4* device). Some band played "music" to the "pleasure" of passer byers. Torture. A couple of minutes walk through this nonsense and arrived at this.

It was then when I realized that the venue is a horse racecourse.

markknopfler.com ticket purchasers were allowed early entry to the venue, a privilege I was very happy to forfeit. I opted, instead, at watching and listening to the concert from the very back, as the Dutchman held a convenient spot closer to the stage, leaning against one of the drink stands.

How far back did I go? as far as I could possibly go. At the far back, there were a few benches. Laid down on one and listened to a part of the concert looking at the sky. What a relaxing, great experience! sound was not bad at all, too—even fifty meters away or more from the stage.

The concert ended at around 11:30pm and we were the first ones to leave the venue. We were in a hurry to the bus station—in such a hurry, actually, that we left the venue's area seconds after the band did. The bus was supposed to arrive at around 11:40pm, and nobody wanted to take chances.

Of course, the bus didn't show up around 11:40pm. As time went by, more and more people arrived at the station, each one wondering where the hell the bus was. A different bus, also headed to the city center, drove by the station without stopping.

The last thing you want happening after a concert is to be stranded 20km away from your hotel. It was slightly comforting, though, to realize that many other people were waiting for the very same bus: it meant that there was a good reason to believe that the bus will arrive *eventually*, which it did—about half an hour late.

Stormed into the bus as if I was getting out of jail. Fifteen minutes later, we arrived at a metro station, just in time to catch the train back to the city center.

It was late—around 1:00am—when we arrived back at the city center. The next day's travel schedule was going to be easy, so it was decided to see some of Rome at night. The city's streets were far from being devoid of humans: it was Saturday night, and Italians don't seem to believe in sleeping at nights to begin with. Many bars, pubs, clubs were open, and people—old as young—seemed to be having fun.

Not far from the hotel, there's the Trevi Fountain. What a magnificent sight at night. Being one of the more famous touristic attraction in Rome, there were many tourists and local nearby the fountain, having a good time at the immediate vicinity of this masterpiece.

Tired… headed back to the hotel and crashed into bed.

Signing off this post from Napoli's airport, waiting to board a flight to Catania.
Isaac

Tuesday, July 16, 2013

Rome to Napoli, Italy (July 14, 2013)

After a very busy day in Rome—including noisy train rides, some sightseeing, and immense mental battle to keep my sanity in check while waiting for the bus heading to Rome's city center after the concert—the compensation came in the form of a very easy travel day: depart Rome 10:40am, arrive Napoli 11:50am. One hour, one train. Brilliant.

Mark, here's a small request for your next tour: more easy travel days such as this one. Thank you.

Woke up late, easy breakfast at the hotel and headed to the nearest metro station. Sunday morning, and the streets of Rome's city center were as empty as they can possibly get: still moderately full with people. Weather was warm, but still too early to be a scorcher.

Feeling upbeat for the upcoming easy travel day, entered the *Spagna* metro station and headed to the ticketing machine (the day pass purchased a day before was only good till midnight).

Two single tickets... €3.00... no problem. The entire transaction was done in under 25 seconds.

That is, the entire transactions except for the part where tickets are actually printed. Checked once, twice, thrice... nothing. What do you do in such a case? of course: you turn to on-site staff for assistance. Piece of cake.

Approached the staffed ticketing office. Jeroen did the talking, explaining to the attendant what had happened.

She didn't immediately respond. Instead, she took out a piece of paper, wrote a number on it, handed it to the puzzled Dutchman and instructed him to call that number to complain.

At that moment, I already realized what was going to happen. I already knew that there was no chance in hell we will ever get those three Euros back. Turned to the Dutchman, and told him that there really is no hope—lets try another method, maybe a different machine.

> I grew up in Israel, and Israelis are very similar to Italians in many behavioural aspects. I know what it is like facing authorities in a highly bureaucratic environment; I know how to detect when nobody is going to help me with anything. While not being the primary reason, the Israeli mentality of being harsh to each other was one of the reasons I left Israel for Canada to begin with: I was tired of a society where people care less and less about others as time goes by.
>
> The Dutchman, however, grew up in The Netherlands. Much like in Canada, in The Netherlands, people in general want to be helpful. Chances are higher for a service provider to walk an extra mile for you in The Netherlands or in Canada, than, say, in Italy.
>
> As such, the Dutchman *really believed* that he could somehow demonstrate to that rude lady that he was right and she was wrong.
>
> I therefore opted at standing aside and watching the dialogue evolve.

Two more minutes of an increasingly heating dialogue didn't help at all. The Dutchman kept being more and more amazed at the immense rudeness and unwillingness to help exhibited by the tantalizingly stupid attendant, and the latter kept demanding that worrying about issues like this is not her job, and "call this number". Eventually, she simply said "I am not helping you" and gestured with her hand that we should step aside.

None of the aforementioned was surprising to me; yet, it was fun watching the Dutchman reveal the multiple layers of stupidity, ignorance and rudeness from the attendant. At the end, he muttered an expression involving the F-word and walked away.

Time was pressing, so I decided to head back to the ticketing machines and try another one. Tried to issue one ticket first (so if the machine is broken, we waste less money)—done. Second ticket printed too. Good.

Heading to the platform, we came across another attendant. Jeroen told him that, at the least, they should be putting an "out of order" sign on that machine so people won't continue wasting money on it; alas, the attendant wasn't much inclined to help either. In the meantime, more and more people were using the broken machine, losing money to Rome's metro station.

Three stops, and back in Rome's central station, *Roma Termini*. Easy train ride to Napoli, except for a mature man sitting behind me and constantly talking on the phone, with a very heavy Italian voice. Every sentence he said sounded as if it was taken out of *The Godfather*. I spent a few minutes listening to his voice and imagining Don Corleone speaking. It was very amusing, and once it was done being amusing, it started becoming annoying.

Fortunately, it was a short ride until the train arrived in Napoli's central railway station, Napoli Centrale.

I knew very little of Napoli (in English: *Naples*. Why? beats me) before coming here. I knew that Diego Maradona played for Napoli's soccer team back in the times when he wasn't doing drugs (at least not publicly) and I actually cared for soccer at all; I was also informed that food in Napoli is very good. All and all, I didn't quite know what to expect.

What I encountered was a very different experience than what I had experienced in the northern parts of Italy.

It started at the central railway station. There, you could already feel that Napoli lives somewhere in the distant past. You could see it on people's faces, too: to me, people seemed tired and unmotivated. Old infrastructure—older than what you'd expect in the third largest municipality in Italy (after Rome and Milano).

Figured out that we need to take the metro. Down to the platform, expecting to find ticket selling machines there. None. Instead, we found small machines into which you should be inserting some ticket for it to be stamped. OK, that means that you need to buy the ticket *somewhere*. But where?

Backtracked to the main level, and started looking for information. A lady working on site asked what it was that we were looking for. "Metro tickets", we said. "Tabacchi, Tabacchi", she replied.

I already knew what it meant.

> OK, so here's a very useful tip for tourists in Italy. "Tabacchi" means "tobacco shop". In tobacco shops, you buy cigarettes so you can smoke and kill yourself faster (except for Ingrid. I don't think there's a cigarette on this planet strong enough to harm this superwoman); BUT—you also buy other useful things there. One of these things is metro tickets and bus tickets.
>
> Public transport ticketing works differently in different municipalities in Italy. Sometimes, you can buy public transport tickets at the station itself from machines or manned booths; and sometimes you buy those tickets from external vendors. Where public transport tickets are sold by external vendors,

usually tobacco shops are your best bet to get those. Sometimes, you can buy such tickets from other vendors—even in your hotel.

Better do your research before leaving home.

We already had too much research to do, so some things were left out to figure out "on the spot".

Finding our way in Napoli's metro system was one of them.

Bought those damned tickets and back to the platform. Oh, the humanity: what an old, out-dated metro system. Prehistoric trains, prehistoric tunnels… prehistoric everything. Boarded the train, and the short ride to *Cavour* seemed to take forever. These aren't the advanced, modern metro trains you'd see elsewhere in Europe.

Exited the metro station and started walking towards the hotel. The path reminded me more of the older parts of Tel Aviv or Jaffa than of Italy: very old buildings—I'm surprised some of them are still standing—and man, oh man, how crowded they are. Living here means no personal space for you, ever.

It was Sunday afternoon. Not many living souls outside, most shops were closed. The mostly empty streets reveal sights of neglect and slight decay. Weather was hot, and I was counting down the meters left to get to the hotel; was happy to finally make it: Hotel Piazza Bellini, located by Piazza Bellini, turned out to be an island of beauty and relaxation in that area.

Already late afternoon, we decided to go out for a bite. Before heading out, we asked at the reception what would be the best way to get to and from the concert venue. The concert venue was located about 8km west of the hotel, easily accessible by metro, which makes it great for getting there, but useless for coming back as the metro's last train on Sundays run before the concert's anticipated end time. The hotel's receptionist suggested that we don't rely on buses because Napoli's public bus system sucks in royal levels, and instead gave us the number of a local taxi company to call.

Great. Was really looking forward for another hectic night, figuring out ways to get back to my hotel. At least, we had a feasible "last resort": walking. It's not fun walking 8km at night, but still doable in just under 2 hours.

The hotel's receptionist gave us a general direction for lunch—just go towards Piazza Bellini and there should be "a few open places". Those "few open places" turned out to only serve drinks and snacks. Incidentally, I turned my head at some point and noticed people dining in some patio. That looked promising: Antica Pizzeria Port'Alba.

I was told before, by my friend Daria, that pizza lovers, while in Napoli, must try a simple Pizza Margherita as it is a "Napoli thing". Who am I to argue? the pizza, along with some spaghetti and a side order of vegetables, were all consumed with pleasure. The pizza was fantastic.

> As I am sitting down writing this blog post, I used Google to find a link to the *TripAdvisor* entry for this pizzeria. I was surprised to also find a Wikipedia entry. Well, what do you know: this restaurant is believed to be *the world's first pizzeria*.

Too much food was ordered and eaten. That, together with the fact that the preceding few days were hectic, prompted me to decide to go back to the hotel, do some writing and never leave the room until the time comes to head to the venue. I followed my decision through, and added a good, healthy nap to the mix.

Time's up—let's go. Left the hotel…

... and entered the metro station again. Couldn't find any ticket selling booth. Where do you go to to buy metro tickets in Napoli? right: the good old Tabacchi. There was one a few meters away from the station.

Again, those ugly, noisy trains. Long, noisy ride. Left at the closest metro station to the venue and started walking towards the venue, guided by an online map. It was a long walk through a major, busy avenue.

We were a little unsure where the venue really was: in the online map, the arena seemed to be a part of a huge complex, so it wasn't clear where we should be turning off from the main avenue. Shortly after, I found an indication where to go: the fake concert T-shirt stands. You can always count on those to show up nearby a Knopfler concert venue. Turning right from the main avenue, I was in the middle of a huge complex, still not having a clear direction where to go so. Others seemed to know where they were going, so following them seemed like a great idea.

It worked: *Arena Flegrea* was right there.

Collected the tickets, and then decided to see whether the people working in the ticket booth know anything about how to get back from the venue to the city center. Again, Italian service at its best: there were two women working in that booth—one handing tickets to people and the other, facing another window, typing on her phone, looking completely apathetic to whatever was going on around. Asking her, she gestured as if to say she has no idea, and turned to her co-worker who then said "don't know", followed by a shriek.

The ticketing booth now had two panicked women in it. Ticket collection stopped. The entire world stopped for a few seconds. The reason? one of them discovered a huge bug underneath some paper.

Up the stairs and entered the venue. It was a little weird: the area where the concert was to take place was outdoors, but to get there, you had to go through some sort of a building. That building looked relatively well kept, and I'm guessing that it was new (I can't find much information about this venue online).

Looked like a small venue with one strange feature: between the front row to the stage, the distance was about 10 meters. A fence separated between the front row and that 10 meters gap, and the gap's height was about 2–3 meters: clearly no *Running of the Bulls* tonight, as that would involve jumping over a fence, breaking a few limbs while doing so, and then being completely unable to watch the concert as the stage was a few meters high above the gap area.

Another feature of this venue was the two concrete walls to the side. I immediately realized that acoustics were going to be a problem. For added scenery, the venue backed into tall green trees, giving you the feeling that you're watching a concert inside a forest (if you were to ignore those huge concrete walls).

Seats?

A few readers of this blog came to say hello: one from North Carolina, one from Manchester and one from Switzerland. Another United Nations sort of thing. The common to all: nobody knew exactly how to get back from the venue to their hotels, and everybody who tried to get any sort of information about the subject ended up encountering a huge wall of complete ignorance.

It was decided, then, to get together in an agreed-upon spot (conveniently located right in front of my seat) after the concert, so we could figure things out as a group.

The concert started pretty much on time, and right at the beginning I realized that I won't be able to watch the concert fully from where I was seated. I was seated to the left, and the high volume was going to kill my sensitive left ear. A few songs into the show, I decided that I'm not risking going deaf so I watched most of the concert from the very back rows, high up the stairs.

Was a good concert overall, with *Brothers in Arms* being played for the first time in a while. I watched the last few songs from my seat: people kept sneaking to the front for the purpose of taking pictures, then hurrying back to their seats. The guy sitting to my immediate left videotaped the entire concert.

During Telegraph Road, someone decided that he was going to Skype the entire song to his friend, using his tablet. He arrived, armed with a tablet and his girlfriend, fired his tablet, Skype-called his friend and held the tablet so his friend could see and listen to what was going on. During the quiet part of Telegraph Road, the recipient of the Skype call decided that it'd be a good time to start talking.

So many idiots live on this planet that I start feeling lonely.

Concert ended, and five tourists gathered together trying to figure out how to get back to the city center. We decided to head back to the main avenue and try hailing a taxi. One taxi signalled that he was turning around to pick us up, which he did—but while doing so, he was hailed by someone else and let them in. Great service.

Went to a nearby bar. Amann, a nice fellow from Switzerland who was in our group, happened to be speaking Italian so he grabbed the phone number of a taxi company from the bar's owner and called for a taxi. A minute later, a taxi showed up, but it wasn't the taxi that we called for; plus, it could only hold three passengers.

We had no choice, then, but to break up: Jeroen, Amann and myself went into the taxi, and the others remained behind waiting for the taxi that Amann called for minutes earlier.

The ride to the hotel was one of the scariest taxi rides I took in my entire life. I would *never* drive in Napoli. People here drive like complete and utter idiots. Sort of like Istanbul: you can never anticipate who's going to do what. You can't take anything for granted. Numerous scooters ridden by people who were under the impression that they owned the road.

One of the scariest moments took place as we drove through a tunnel. In front of us, three scooters—two people on each. At the left shoulder of the tunnel, a girl was walking by. The people on the scooter right in front of us decided that this would be a perfect time to stop the scooter to chat the girl up. May I remind you, again, that we were *in a tunnel*. How our taxi driver got out of that one—I don't know. We nearly hit them.

The drive took about 10 minutes but it felt like forever. I was sure we're going to end up in a hospital somewhere: *insane* drivers. Luckily, got back to the hotel safely. Took a few minutes to see what was going on in Piazza Bellini, right in front of the hotel: seems like a popular destination for youngsters in the evening, a few cafes full of people, and others enjoying their time by the fountain. Some police was present on site, to maintain order.

Back to the hotel and off for a good night sleep, knowing that the next day was going to be hell.

Signing off this post from the hotel room in Taormina. So much happened over the last couple of days... what a rush. Off to the concert now. Will try to complete the next blog post during the ferry ride to Malta tomorrow.

Isaac

Thursday, July 18, 2013

Napoli to Taormina, Italy (July 15-16, 2013)

Almost three months into the tour, July 15 signified the beginning of the Sicily-Malta mayhem.

Why mayhem? The short period of the tour, from Sicily to Malta and then back to northern Italy, was the hardest period to plan for in the entire tour. Most other destinations were planned out down to the smallest travel detail; a few destinations were planned out, and then altered along the way; but only one period of the tour kept being altered throughout the tour—and it was this period, from Sicily to Malta.

There were simply too many "moving parts" to consider, and too few options for travel—some of which remained unknown until just a few days ago.

Many readers, who were courteous enough to introduce themselves to me during the tour, were interested to know what it was like planning this enormous journey.

Well, here's a taste. Buckle up: it's going to be long.

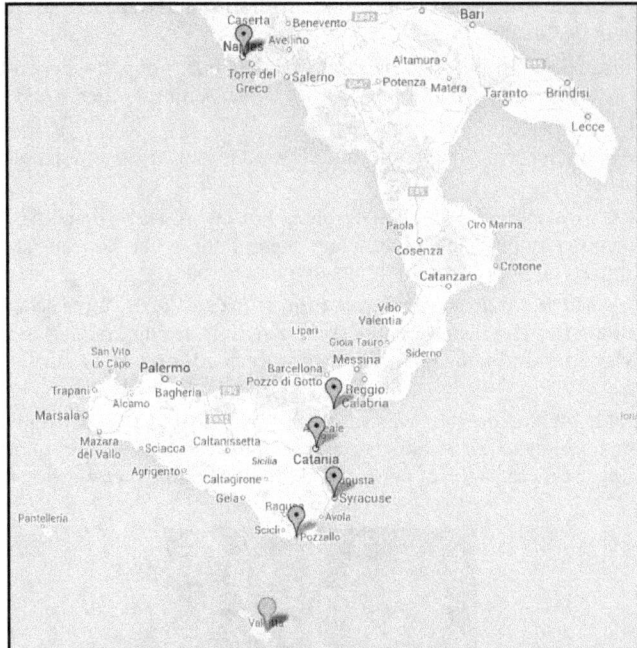

(Image captured from *Google Maps*. The marked locations, from top to bottom: Napoli; Taormina; Catania; Siracusa; Pozzallo; Malta).

To get to Malta, you can either swim, fly, or take the ferry (if your name is Jesus, you might be able to walk it). Swimming was out of the question as Jeroen isn't in good physical shape, so we had to resort to either flying or taking the ferry.

Flying would mean selling a few internal organs on the black market, which left the ferry as the only viable option.

The ferry to Malta departs from Pozzallo. There are two ways to take that ferry:

1. Board a bus in Catania (not far from Taormina), which takes you straight to the ferry terminal in Pozzallo.

2. Get to the ferry terminal yourself.

Of course, option (1) would make most sense, as Catania is easily accessible by train from Napoli *and* is very close to Taormina.

This ideal option is available every day of the week except for Wednesdays. Commensurable to my luck in life, July 17 happened to be a Wednesday.

The meaning: after attending the concert in Taormina, we needed to somehow get to Pozzallo—at the very southern tip of Sicily—for the next morning (there are two ferry departures every day. To catch the concert, the 9:15am ferry is the only viable option). No public transport exists in Sicily to take you to Pozzallo from Taormina so early in the morning (just under two hours drive).

So... a car rental was required. One-way car rentals are almost always a problem: they're either too expensive or altogether impossible to do (from the point of view of a car rental agency, one-way car rentals present logistical challenges).

The plan we originally came up with, then, was to head as south as possible in Sicily during the day off—ideally spending the night in Pozzallo. A hotel room was booked in Pozzallo, as well as a car (pick up and drop-off both in Pozzallo).

The question now became how to get to Pozzallo. It is possible to do this by train in one day from Napoli, but we're talking about a *very long* ride with tight connections. Therefore, we decided to do the following: use the day off to fly from Napoli to Catania; take the train to Siracusa; spend the night in Siracusa; take the train early morning to Pozzallo.

Then, another problem surfaced. There was only one car rental agency in Pozzallo: *Hertz*. Now, Hertz in Pozzallo are open only during certain hours in the day: in the morning until 10:00am, and then from 5:00pm to 7:00pm. The first train from Siracusa to Pozzallo leaves 10:00am, which meant that, once in Pozzallo, we couldn't pick up the car before 5:00pm. We assumed it would be OK because the drive from Pozzallo to Taormina takes about 2 hours, and the concert was scheduled to start at 9:30—tight, but possible.

To summarize, the original plan was as follows:

July 15:

- Fly from Napoli to Catania.
- Train from Catania to Siracusa.
- Spend the night in Siracusa.

July 16:

- Take first train to Pozzallo.
- Check in to the hotel in Pozzallo.
- On 5:00pm, rent the car and head directly to Taormina for the concert.

- After the concert (approximately 11:30pm), drive back to Pozzallo.
- Spend the night in Pozzallo.

July 17:

- Return the rental car.
- Board the ferry.

Hectic, but it is what it is: we couldn't see any better option.

Until Nîmes.

Arriving at Nîmes, we realized that energy levels are going down. The extensive travel over the past few months started taking its toll, so we sat down together to review the rest of the itinerary and see whether we can improve things a little.

Surprisingly, I was able to find a one-way car rental from Siracusa (where we already had a hotel booked) to Pozzallo. The only problem was, that the rental had to be confirmed first with the local Hertz dealer in Siracusa and the confirmation was said to take a few days. We still held on to the previous plan, but now, an alternate "path" was made possible (pending the rental car's confirmation):

July 16:

- Pick up the car in Siracusa (after having spent the night there) in the morning.
- Drive to Pozzallo, check into the hotel there and put the luggage in the room (for safety).
- Drive back to Taormina.
- After the concert, drive back to Pozzallo.

The advantage of this alternate path was that we wouldn't have to wait until 5:00pm to leave Pozzallo, thus reducing the risk of missing the concert *and* reducing the amount of time had to be spent in Pozzallo, which seemed to be a dodgy town with absolutely nothing to do in it.

A few days after requesting the one-way car rental, it was approved.

Still, as you shall see shortly, the plan changed even further later on.

Woke up in Napoli and headed to breakfast. It was a slow wake-up as the flight to Catania was scheduled to depart at 4:40pm. The hotel, Hotel Piazza Bellini, boasts a really nice patio so I my plan for the day is do nothing except sitting there.

I would, of course, not mind going to see some of Napoli's attractions—I had heard that their harbour area is very nice—but, knowing how hectic the upcoming couple of days were going to be, I decided to conserve my energy and do as little as possible until all difficult travel is done with. The Dutchman had different thoughts, which prompted him to flee the scene shortly after breakfast as I stayed behind.

Started writing but couldn't quite concentrate. Remembering that there's a nice looking cafe right around the corner, in Piazza Bellini itself, I decided to take my backpack, sit there and do some writing while sipping cold coffee.

As I was walking the short (even less than 50 meters) distance to that cafe, something prompted me to just keep on walking. Piazza Bellini is located in one of Napoli's older, much less touristic areas, so I decided to take a short walk around to see what Napoli would look like without annoying tourists and their even more annoying noisy children.

It was, for some reason, more exciting than I initially expected.

The feeling walking through these narrow, old, crowded, dusty streets wasn't entirely pleasant: it was a somewhat "rough" feeling. Here is life in Napoli, unabridged. Real, unpolished. No significant attempts to please tourists' eyes.

In fact, as I was walking down this street—a mere 100m walk; I already said that I wasn't in the position to take long, excruciating walks—wearing my backpack and holding my camera, I received quite a few suspicious looks from locals. People there were probably asking themselves what the hell would a tourist look for in this place to begin with.

Narrow alleys, showing just how crowded life can get here. A woman hanging clothes to dry on her balcony; the balcony—actually the entire building—is so old that I was wondering what's keeping it upright. So crowded, you could spit into your neighbour's balcony.

Small, authentic stores selling fruit and vegetables for ridiculously low prices. All sorts of locally-made pasta's are wrapped in small bags and offered for sale, again for ridiculously low prices.

With each and every step, I just *felt* how old that street was. People here are clearly not in a rush anywhere. Back in Vancouver, when my FiOS-based Internet connection doesn't work as fast as I'm used for it to work, I get anxious; here, they probably don't care at all what FiOS Internet connection means. And, somehow, they live on.

Fascinating.

Back to the cafe in Piazza Bellini; ordered cold espresso with milk, got something different than what I was asking for, and sat down to do some writing.

An hour or so later, the Dutchman decided to return from his excursion discovering Napoli's tourist areas and joined me in the cafe. A small fruit salad for lunch, and headed back to the hotel, where our luggage was stored.

Sitting down at the hotel's patio, just waiting for the time to pass by, it was evident that nobody was really looking forward for this day to unfold. The preceding few days were very hectic, especially with respect to getting back to our hotels every night after the show. Energy levels were very low.

Alas, a plan is a plan. Got up, grabbed luggage, dialled for a taxi and fifteen minutes later we were in Napoli's airport.

Through the course of my "normal" life (that is: my life when I'm not following Knopfler's tours), I fly a lot, both domestically and internationally. During 2012–2013 alone, I visited Israel five times; inside Canada, I fly a few times a year for business. I am no stranger to airports, which is why I have a rule: I always show up at the airport about an hour and a half before departure. That's because I'm used to Air Canada's efficiency and the entire airport experience in Vancouver's, Toronto's and Tel Aviv's airports.

In Europe, though, I become a little stressed. I already noticed that public transport companies in Europe tend to be less efficient than their North American counterparts, and in Italy, merely mentioning the word "efficiency" will prompt people to point their finger at you and laugh. That's why I wasn't very disappointed to find out, upon arriving to Napoli's airport, that Meridiana's check-in counter wasn't even open yet.

> Oh, talking about efficiency: Meridiana does offer online check-in, but still requires you to print the following documents and bring them with you to the airport:

- Your boarding pass.
- Your seat assignment (if you chose your seat online).
- Your baggage receipt (proving that you paid for your baggage).

Between Jeroen and myself, we ended up with eight printed pages. Well, maybe I'm crazy, but I thought that the deal about "online check-in" was to reduce paperwork and streamline processes.

When I fly with Air Canada, all I need to show at the airport is my smartphone, showing a barcode that I received in an email.

Spent about 30 minutes or so standing up doing nothing while waiting for the check-in counters to open. They were scheduled to open two hours before departure; in practice, it took an extra 15–20 minutes for the staff there to stop chatting between themselves and finally allow people to check in.

Got all airport bureaucracy done, and headed to the gate. Grabbed a short snack from a bakery on the way there—a cannoli filled with cream, a Sicilian "thing"—meh. Not something I'd kill for. Down to the gate, where nothing interesting seemed to be happening with the exception of two particularly noisy kids that were yelling (not crying; just yelling) all the time with their parents (or guardians, I don't know and I don't care) not even trying to attend to them.

Time passed slowly, but the flight departed on time. Of course, one of those kids kept on yelling during the entire flight, making a 55 minutes flight feel like 55 hours. Was happy to finally leave the aircraft.

Baggage claim: that's the best place to realize that, at least in Catania (although this is true to Italy in general), the concept of "personal space" doesn't exist. You stand by the conveyor belt waiting for your luggage so you can grab it and get the hell out of there, but that doesn't stop someone else to stand right next to you, hardly leaving you any space to breathe. For them, it seems normal; where I live (sorry, folks: as time goes by, I miss Vancouver more and more so I can't possibly avoid doing comparisons), such behaviour would be considered extremely rude and intrusive.

Have I lost the ability to adjust to new places, new habits, new values? obviously, one of the purposes in doing such a trip is to experience new things, but how willing am I to actually allow such experiences to sink in?

The answer seems to head in one direction: not willing in the slightest.

Baggage collected. Outside the terminal, a taxi driver wanted too much money to take us to Catania's central railway station, so we decided to go on a bus instead. €1.00 buys you a one-way fare from the airport to the central railway station. Took 25 minutes or so for the bus to arrive. Boarded it, and one station later, a group of 5 females—three adults and two kids—boarded as well. The amount of noise this group generated during their 15 minutes presence on the bus was UNBELIEVABLE.

"People demand freedom of speech as a compensation for the freedom of thought which they seldom use." — Søren Kierkegaard

The train from Catania's central railway station to Siracusa was scheduled to depart on 7:08pm, with the next train one hour later. During the bus ride, there were times we thought we were going to miss that train—a rather depressing thought, because all we really wanted was just to get this travel day over and done with. Fortunately, the bus made it to the central railway station on time. Stormed to the platform and found the train, which was just a tad behind the high-speed trains I got used to, technology-wise.

Two coaches.

One of them had a 1st class section!

There was no difference at all between the 1st class seats and the 2nd class ones.

"Great, that's what I needed", I thought to myself. "To end this long travel day with a train ride in a train that predates most dinosaurs". Indeed, the ride was slow and *very* noisy, but on the other hand, it was scenic. The railway tracks from Catania to Siracusa mostly go along the eastern shoreline of Sicily, so the wonderful Mediterranean Sea was visible for a long part of the ride.

At some point, the sun started to set.

When the train finally arrived in Siracusa, it was already getting dark.

I have never heard of Siracusa before planning the itinerary for following the tour. All I cared for, regarding Siracusa, was its location on the map and how well connected it is to the railway network in Sicily. Thus, once I exited the station, I didn't even bother looking around me. Jeroen already had the map to the hotel showing up on his iFail, so I followed his steps blindly, not caring at all to whatever was around me. It was a long, 15 minutes walk to the hotel; even though it was getting dark, the temperatures were still high and so was the humidity. I was sweating all over and all I wanted was a good shower.

Was happy to finally arrive at the hotel, Grande Albergo Alfeo. With the old, dusty setting surrounding it, it was actually a pretty nice looking one. Checked in, rushed to the room and set the air conditioner to the lowest temperature it could possibly yield.

It didn't. The room featured very high ceilings, and the air conditioner wasn't strong enough to cool the room.

"The water taste very bad", said the Dutchman.

Nightmare.

Hungry. What's to eat?

Where the hell am I? what the *hell* am I doing in Siracusa?

Down to reception, and the receptionist explained that Siracusa's tap water isn't very suitable for drinking. The city does employ machines to clean water before it gets to the tap, but the water in Siracusa are so terrible that even those machines can't do a good-enough job cleaning them. Advice: don't drink tap water there.

None of us had any motivation to look for a place to eat, so we asked the receptionist, who recommended a place called Osteria AmUnì, a few blocks away from the hotel. Started walking there. It was already dark. Dust, grayness everywhere. Passing by a couple of alleys, a despicable scent of sewer filled my nostrils.

Then, I saw the restaurant. Nice setting. A few tables inside, a nice patio outside. Went inside, greeted by staff that could barely speak a word in English. After repeatedly asking to see the menu and not receiving any, we were referred to one of the walls, that had the menu written on it. Of course, the menu was in Italian so it was of no help.

The owner of the restaurant, a cool chap by the name Pio, came by. He could barely say a word in English but really tried his best helping us out. Trying to make things simple, he asked just one question: "what type of an appetizer do you want? meat or fish?".

We went for meat.

He then proceeded to determine the main courses mostly by himself: all we needed to choose was whether we'd like to have beef, fish or chicken—and Pio took it upon himself to complete the rest of the details.

And it was, hands down, *the best meal we have had in the entire tour*. A large plate containing 12 different appetizers, each one tastes better than the other. I had a couple of small steaks with truffle sauce, the Dutchman had some chicken bits covered with olive oil, spices and some other vegetables—absolute, complete, utter delight. Service was excellent, the food was simple and perfect. The very *thought* about that meal makes me hungry.

That's why I love Italian food so much. It's not sophisticated: on the contrary—it is *very* simple. All you need is just pick the best ingredients, make clever use of oil and a few key spices and you got yourself some delightful food.

Pio was very excited to hear that this was the best meal we have had in our entire three months trip (and counting). He was so excited that he rushed into the kitchen and called his cook to come over and hear it directly from us. You should have seen the happiness in these guys' eyes. So happy they were, that we were treated for another side dish (which was magnificent, but was mostly left untouched. There's a limit to how much I can eat), as well as a shot of some alcoholic beverage at the end.

What a fantastic dining experience. If you ever happen to pass by Siracusa, don't dare skipping this place.

As we were consuming ridiculously great food in that restaurant, we started talking about the next day and how horrific it was going to be. Then, as motivation was close to hit rock bottom, an interesting idea came up: how about we forfeit the hotel reservation in Pozzallo (too late to cancel it), and just stay in Taormina instead?

It took a couple of minutes to discuss, and eventually, we decided to make our lives much easier. Upon returning to the hotel, the plan was changed *once again*:

July 16:

- Pick up car in Siracusa.
- Drive to Taormina.
- Check into hotel in Taormina.
- Next morning, around 5:00am, drive south to Pozzallo to catch the ferry.

Could hardly get any easier than that. Hotel booked and motivation kicked in. The next day, then, was going to be a great day.

Off to bed, and I realized I can't sleep in such a hot room. The air conditioner was as useful as an ashtray is on a motorcycle. Took a towel, soaked it in cold water and used it as a blanket. Slept like a baby.

July 16, Tuesday. Got up, quick breakfast at the hotel including some sour milk. Terrible breakfast selection, much unlike what I got used to in Italy already. Got the luggage, checked out and headed to Siracusa's harbour, where Hertz's agency is located.

Signed up for a car: a small red Fiat 500L (you don't see many Fiat's in North America; mostly in Europe), manual shift. I can drive manual shift, but really dislike it.

I know that some people prefer manual shift because it helps you "feel the ride"; I don't subscribe to that. For me, a car is a helper object to help me get from point A to point B safely, quickly and with the least amount of effort involved. Beyond that, a car is just a pile of metal cleverly put together.

Of course, the car was parked less than one meter away from the water: an accidental drive forward would mean driving right into the sea. A few attempts to put the car into reverse resulted in the gear shifting to 6th instead, until the Dutchman realized that there's a hinge you need to pull with your finger in order to allow the gear stick to switch to reverse. Good to know, and I'm happy I didn't drive the car into the sea.

Google Maps' Navigator at hand, and within 10 minutes we were outside of Siracusa, heading towards Taormina: three months into the tour, and yet another transportation method was added to the list of methods used for the tour: a rental car.

Now, for some reason, I was expecting Sicily's roads to be old, narrow and rough to ride. I was shocked to find exactly the opposite: pristine roads in perfect condition. The ride, other than being much easier than expected, was also scenic: many hills along the Mediterranean's coast, spotted with red roofs and small buildings. Almost no high rises at all.

Less than an hour later, took the exit from the highway, paid the toll and entered Taormina's city limits. I was looking forward to that, not only because I longed for the safety of a roof over my head, but also because I had heard that Taormina is beautiful.

Taormina is not a big city. It's actually not even a city: it's a small town. Still, it has been a major tourist destination, and being there, you'd understand why. The town is built upon hills, rolling down into the Ionian Sea. Most tourists spend their time in Taormina's "Village", which is located on a cliff overlooking the Ionian Sea (we'll get to that later); in lower altitudes, life seems to be simpler and much more "authentic": beautiful houses, some of which are really old; streets are narrow and almost completely devoid of sidewalks. The Ionian Sea is visible from pretty much everywhere. It is *very* pretty.

Arrived at the hotel, Hotel Villa Sirina, and was glad to park the car. Got out and took a deep breath of warm Mediterranean air. That's exactly the same "air" as you get when you take a deep breath along Tel Aviv's less polluted beaches: in a sense, I missed it. Luggage unloaded and entered the hotel.

Checked into the room to find out that the air conditioner wasn't really working: fan only, no cooling. Tried to do some writing but couldn't—the heat was terrible. My "towel trick"—wetting a towel with cold water and covering myself with it—didn't work at all. Down to reception, where I was informed that the cooling is usually off while housemaids are cleaning the rooms (*very* strange), and that it should be back within an hour.

And it was. And Isaac was happy.

Hungry, and less stressed over things because *I made it to Taormina*, it was decided to go grab a bite. Got some instructions from the receptionist and headed outside.

A couple of pictures of the hotel…

As we decided to walk and not use the car unless absolutely having to, we were guided to a restaurant down by the sea.

The walk down was moderately steep, and almost completely devoid of sidewalks. Here, you're expected to walk on the side of the road, I guess.

Reached down and there was the Ionian Sea in all of its glory.

The restaurant we were guided to was closed, so we settled for sitting in a patio, owned by a different restaurant, by the sea.

Good home-made Sicilian food, followed by another short walk along the coast, an ice cream from a nearby gelateria and many, many pictures.

Isaac's "Privateering" Tour Blog

Back to the hotel, now in an incline, beneath a scorching sun.

Remember what I wrote earlier about "no sidewalks"?

Arrived to the hotel, sweaty as nobody should be allowed to be. Heat makes you tired, so I decided to go for a nap.

The concert was supposed to start at 9:30pm. The venue, however, was some 2.5km away from the hotel, including a significant elevation gain. We didn't want to take the car because we didn't want to mess around with parking at the area (none of us has been here before, and we didn't want to take any risks), so the only other viable option was to walk up. Knowing it might take a while, and wanting to leave some time to take some pictures of the venue (which, I was told, was magnificent), we left the hotel quite early—not before taking a few shots from the room's balcony.

When searching for walking directions in *Google Maps* (at least on Android phones), you also get a graph showing your elevation as you go. A quick peak revealed that the walk is going to be *very* steep. We really didn't know what to expect: we were expecting to walk 2.5km, and then arrive at some venue.

We were wrong.

The walk indeed started very steep, providing excellent views over the Ionian Sea:

A short while afterwards, a very narrow walkway forked off the road. Only scooters and pedestrians could use that walkway. Suddenly, we arrived at at intersection that appeared busy.

Nearby, a police officer was directing traffic. Behind him, there was a huge building serving as a parking garage, about 7–8 stories high.

(The last picture in the group above comes to show what the walk was like: essentially, walking on a road, with no sidewalks. Was interesting to see that they still bother painting crosswalks there.)

Despite *Google Maps'* instructions, I decided to ask the police officer whether there's a shortcut to get ourselves up the cliff as it was obvious that that's where we should be going. Fortunately, there *was* a shortcut: simply enter the parking garage, look for the lift and get to the 7th floor. Saved quite a bit of time, sweat and blood.

Leaving the elevator and stepping out…

… it felt like a completely different world. As I was expecting to be walking along a deserted walkway and eventually arrive at a venue, I found myself right at the beginning of Taormina's Village: full of tourists and, just as it was full of tourists, it was absolutely, unequivocally, ridiculously pretty. Being there, walking the narrow streets, you could see why Taormina attracts so many tourists: this is tourists' paradise. Of course, it looked a little overdone, but you could still sense history. Beautiful, romantic place.

Taormina's Village is located high up on a cliff overlooking the Ionian Sea. Many opportunities for landscape pictures.

Decided to head to the ticket booth to grab the tickets. Italian efficiency at its best: three people working in the counter. On the left, two women doing nothing. On the right, one man on the phone serving about 4 people at once. Approached the women and informed them that we're collecting *markknopfler.com* tickets. They had no idea what we were talking about and referred us to the man standing nearby, still on the phone. Waited there for five minutes until he finished talking and taking care of people in front of us in line. Finally, my turn. I showed my ID, looked for an envelope—couldn't find it. Asked how we got the tickets, I answered that these are fan club tickets.

"Oh, fan club!", he called, *referring us back to the two idle women*, telling them "pre-sale, pre-sale". "Oh, pre-sale", they called back. *Now* they were actually willing to do something.

Got the tickets and headed to the venue, some 200m away along a narrow walkway full of tourists and lined up with many gelaterias and other booths. Arrived at the venue, entered and knew right there and then: this is the most beautiful outdoors venue I have yet to set foot in, in Europe.

The venue, Teatrico Antico di Taormina ("Ancient Theatre of Taormina"), is an ancient Greek theatre, dating back to the 7th century BC. Not only it is well-preserved, to the point that you feel history being injected directly into your brain, it is also situated in such a location that, when sitting in the arena, you see the Ionian Sea and the rolling hills of Taormina right behind the ruins.

Our seats were in the second row, but looking at the venue, it was decided to forfeit these seats and look for alternative seats higher up. Watching a concert in this venue from the front rows is, in my opinion, a completely wasted opportunity. Quickly found my way up, where I discovered a series of unoccupied seats, almost at the center.

What a stunning setting.

The venue felt very intimate. The stage was low, virtually no gap between the front rows and the stage. The stage had to be adjusted to the venue's peculiar format: no overhead lights, very "thinned-down" arrangement. That, together with the breathtaking scenery just behind the ruins, were enough to determine: this was going to be the best concert experience in the tour, regardless of the actual performance. I just can't imagine a more profound, exciting concert experience: perfect temperature, cool breeze, astonishing scenery and a very special arrangement of the stage.

The concert itself was very good, and featured a surprisingly long set, comparing to the last few concerts.

Sultans of Swing made a comeback to the set, sending the audience to the sky, and prompting one of the police officers on site to film the performance.

Good concert, well-received by the audience.

As the concert ended, it took forever to leave the venue due to the narrow exits. Before heading to the hotel, stopped by a local booth and got a few snacks: the next day was going to be very busy, and it wasn't clear when we were going to have breakfast, if at all.

One last photograph before leaving the wonderful Taormina Village…

… and a quick walk back to the hotel. The walk wasn't quick because we were rushing anywhere; rather, it was quick because it *had* to be quick. The path was downhill, and so steep that it was very hard to maintain slow pace. It was also very dark at times, which is when the Dutchman's iFail proved useful (using the camera's flash as a flashlight).

Twenty minutes later we arrived at the hotel, set the alarm clocks for 4:30am and off for a good (but short) night sleep.

Signing off this post from a cafe in Malta. In a couple of hours, will head to the airport to catch a flight to Pisa, then Lucca tomorrow.

Isaac

Friday, July 19, 2013

Taormina, Italy to Valletta, Malta (July 17, 2013)

Woke up in Taormina at 4:30am, ready to go. It was a good decision to take an afternoon nap the day before: I felt fresh and ready for the 2 hours drive south. Packed everything that needed packing, and shortly after 5:00am I was already in the driver's seat, trying to navigate the car, in reverse, out of its parking spot. Small car, but still, it takes time to get used to the size of a car you had hardly driven before. A few attempts and I was out.

The drive to Pozzallo, in the southern tip of Sicily, takes about two hours. The ferry company demands that you're on site to check in one hour before departure, scheduled for 9:15am. Theoretically, we could have left later but it was decided to err on the side of caution: a traffic jam anywhere along the way could result in the ferry leaving without me, and we all know that world order wouldn't allow for that.

Taormina's roads were nearly devoid of cars as we left. Long two hours ride with no incidents at all. Beautiful scenery: looking to the left, I could see the sun rising above the Mediterranean Sea. Sicily is beautiful and I will definitely visit again.

Arrived to Pozzallo at around 7:30am. First thing's first: figure out where to drop the car off and where to line up for the ferry, *before* heading to breakfast: it's better to do these investigations when time is still on your side. Once things were figured out, we found a nearby gas station, filled up the tank and headed to Pozzallo's town center looking for a place to have breakfast.

Blimey, what a dead town. Nothing there. The very thought that I could have ended up spending almost an entire day here (had plans were not changed in the last minute) gave me the chills. Such a boring place. Almost nothing was open in the morning: incidentally, came across a cafe that was open and sold baked goods. The owner didn't speak a word in English; a portrait of Castro was hung proudly on the wall, cleverly positioned so you couldn't avoid looking at it even if you tried.

Nutella croissant that tasted like crap and a cappuccino that tasted almost entirely unlike any cappuccino in the world should be allowed to taste. Alas, nobody had the will and patience to look for an alternative place to dine in in this God forsaken town, so I had to pay my dues and eat the garbage being served.

That done, drove back to the Hertz booth to return the car. Again, Italian efficiency at its finest. When entering the section of the harbour where Hertz is located, you need to pass through a security guard. The security guard was sure that the car was intended to be loaded on the ferry, and him not being able to comprehend a single word in English, it was tricky conveying the message that no, this isn't the case. The guard then went to call his friend, who happened to be speaking English, only to inform me of what I had already known: yes, I can drop my car off at Hertz; and yes, once it's done, I need to check in to the ferry.

That exchange took 5 minutes of my life, that I will never get back.

Thought it ended here? wrong. Drove to the Hertz location, only to find out that the entrance to their parking lot is blocked with a long metal chain (the Hertz booth itself was closed, but they do have an afterhours key drop box). Backtracked, trying to find a way out of that mess. Two guys on site approached, asked what it was that I was doing. I told them that I'm trying to get to Hertz's parking lot, so they sent me back to where I just came from. Drove back there, and the chain was still there. Not a complete surprise, if I might add. The two guys then looked at me, as if they were surprised to find me there; then, finally, they held the chain up high so I could enter the parking lot.

As this is Italy and I wouldn't trust Italian vendors to tell me that the sky is blue in a warm July day, it was decided to take pictures of the fact that the car was indeed returned and the keys were placed in the key drop box.

Phew. OK, what's next? headed to the only place that made sense: a particular spot where a guy was standing checking people's passports, then letting them go on through a maze of fences to some sort of a waiting area. Passport—checked. "Boarding pass please", he asked. What boarding pass? here's all the printed documents I have. Choose one. "No, you have to go *there* to check in". Great, thanks. Off to the booth: two windows, only one attendant. Checked in and received a boarding pass along with a voucher for a €10 credit if I play in Malta's casino.

Back to the boarding line. Boarded, then was let into a "security check" area, where no security check was done at all. Once in the screened area, you can't go back. Time: about 8:05am, more than an hour to departure.

No seats. Wanna sit down? there's plenty of asphalt and gravel for you to sit on. More and more tourists came coming in. Families with noisy children. The clock ticked and I practiced numbing my senses as to minimize any connection with the outside world. Luckily, my chess partner was online so I spent most of the time playing eleven (yes, eleven) chess games with him, simultaneously.

FINALLY, the ferry arrived. Now, how long does it take to unload a ferry? 5 minutes? 10 minutes? more than 20 minutes passed until all passengers and vehicles were unloaded. Boarding commenced, prompting everyone to remove any trace of personal space of one another. Checked my luggage and went on board.

No assigned seats: sit wherever you'd like, just don't dare cross that elastic band that blocks access to the stairway going up, as the top floor is for VIPs. Did what I always do first when I'm on a ferry: looked for the door leading to the deck. Sat on the deck, overlooking the beautiful Mediterranean Sea, and decided to do some writing under the sun. It went well for a couple of minutes, until it turned out that my laptop's screen was too dusty and dirty, resulting in sunlight reflecting back to me, resulting in me not being able to see anything.

A sudden drop in energy level prompted me to head back inside, find a seat and try to pass out, which I think I did but no evidence to that exists as the Dutchman himself was already seated, mouth wide open sleeping his guts out (he didn't take my advice to get an afternoon nap the day before).

Somehow, the ferry ride which should have taken less than two hours ended up taking two and a half hours, and feeling like nine hundred hours. Have I mentioned Italian efficiency already in this post? have I? good. Once the ferry docked, it took about fifteen minutes until passengers were allowed to leave. Why? first, of course, you need to wait for the honourable VIPs to depart: "Everybody please stand in a circle and watch the VIPs as they gracefully go down the stairs and leave the ferry before you". As the ferry was carrying independent travellers (such as the Dutchman and I) as well as organized tours, some guidance had to be given as to which tourist group needs to go to which ferry deck, so they're collected by the applicable buses. These announcements had to be done in multiple languages—Italian, English and *I'm guessing* Maltese. They even went more fine-grained there: "buses number 3 and 4 will have the tour instructor speaking Russian and English; buses number 5 and 6 will have…".

To add salt to injury, not all passengers necessarily listened to the instructions given to them over the speakers, so they came by and asked the staff personally.

If the above description is causing your brain to sweat, then I'm doing an excellent job conveying to you what I was feeling.

What a mess.

Was happy to leave that damned ferry. Went down the stairs and all I saw was beige.

And more beige.

Everywhere I looked, I saw beige.

I knew nothing about Malta before coming here. Sorry, erase that: I knew a few things. I knew that it's an island and that it's a part of the European Union. I knew that there's a language out there called *Maltese*, and I was inclined to believe that it was Malta's formal language. I also knew that it is a popular tourist destination for Israelis.

Plus, of course, I knew everything that there was to know about how to get from Sicily to Malta (see the previous post).

Temperature kissed the 9,000°C mark, and as Malta is an island in which you're never too far from the see, humidity levels were just above 815,000%. Hot. Too hot. Collected my luggage and headed to the nearby building which is supposed to be an "arrivals hall" but seemed to be functioning solely as a passage to the outside world.

A glance in *Google Maps* revealed that the hotel for the night, Luciano Valletta Boutique Hotel, was located more than 2km away with a positive elevation gain. Take a taxi? sure, why not. Followed the sign saying "Taxis" and we found ourselves outside the station, a few taxis lined up and shady people approaching us asking "taxi? taxi?".

If there's something I learned throughout my adult life, it is this: when a stranger approaches you on the street, they want your money. If a stranger approaches you on the street suggesting things to you, then "no" is *always* the right answer. Read any European travel guide and it will tell you that people approaching you and asking you if you'd like a taxi, in close to 100% of the cases, are complete crooks.

The Dutchman, however, decided to be smart.

– "How much is it?", he asked.

– "€15", the driver said, *without even asking where it is that we wanted to get to*.

Finally, a taxi driver with a sixth sense.

The Dutchman, apparently, missed on that crucial detail.

– "To the city center?", he asked.

– "Yes."

– "We need to get to a hotel called 'Valletta Boutique'."

The taxi driver squinted.

– "I can take you very close to the hotel for €15. For €20, I'll take you all the way to the door."

That was when I already lost my patience and just muttered towards the Dutchman "come on, let's go" and started walking towards the hotel. The Dutchman was still processing the new data in his mind as the taxi driver started persuading him to hire his services. "But you're going the wrong way!", the driver said in a last attempt to extort cash out of innocent tourists.

The march towards the hotel was excruciating. I felt as if I was in the middle of a boxing ring, surrounded by professional boxers, each one landing their own blows onto my face in sequence. The weather on one side; hunger on another side; thirst on another; tiredness on yet another. How I survived that walk without passing out is beyond me.

AND WHY IS EVERYTHING HERE COLOURED BEIGE???

And it wasn't just beige: it was light beige. And you know what happens when the sun shines upon light beige, right? right. The light reflects back to you. So now, not only I was tired, hungry, thirsty and sweating like a sprinkler, I sometimes couldn't even see clearly where I was going.

At some point, I did notice some green.

About half an hour walk in hell, and I stood where *Google Maps* claimed that the hotel should be.

I didn't see any hotel. I saw many restaurants, but not a hotel.

Took a few minutes to figure it out: the hotel was actually located above a restaurant by the same name. It was crowded inside, but at least the air conditioner was on. One of the waitresses checked us in, asked us to leave our luggage behind and come back a couple of hours later as check-in time was 2:00pm.

Fine.

Grabbed my backpack (as I thought I may use the time to do some writing) and we went to resolve a burning issue: hunger. A couple of recommendations in *TripAdvisor* turned out to be closed, so the final honour of having me over for lunch befell on a place called La Mere Restaurant, located right at the main street in Valletta's city center. The restaurant serves Maltese and Indian food, as well as fusion of both. Delicious.

From there, to Cafe Caravaggio, simply because they had a nice patio. Food prices seem to be relatively low in Malta, comparing to other European destinations.

Malta's economy is small and very fragile. It produces about one fifth of the food needed to feed its inhabitants, and has no domestic energy sources: all energy in Malta is produced from oil (even though it could mitigate energy prices by using solar power), and all oil is imported as, again, Malta has no domestic energy sources.

What do people here live from, then? manufacturing and tourism. Tourism generates 35% of the GDP in Malta, and this is supported by the capital city, Valletta, looking like one huge tourist trap. Without tourism, Malta would be in trouble.

2:00pm sharp—back to the hotel/restaurant, where one of the waitresses showed us the room. Really funky place, doesn't look like a hotel at all. Taking the elevator the second floor, you leave the elevator straight into what looks like a maintenance room of a restaurant. Three doors there—one to each room. Definitely not your usual hotel corridor. The room itself, however, was great and very comfortable.

What wasn't comfortable was being neighbours to a stupid family that kept talking loudly outside their room.

About a week prior, we noticed that the hotel reservation for Malta specifies that air conditioning is provided for an "extra charge". Puzzled, I sent them an email and got the following reply:

Dear Mr. Isaac,

We thank you for your reservation at our Boutique Accommodation. Kindly note that air- conditioning is according to consumption. We will give you a 5 euro card upon check in which will give your around 6 hrs of air conditioning free of charged. If you would like more hours you can top your card by another 5 euro to have another 6 hours.

(All typos in source.)

I was therefore very intrigued to see how that would work. I inquired about this, and to my puzzlement, the waitress/hostess told me that there's no reason to worry about it, we'll have air conditioning running for the entire time for no extra charge.

Thumbs up.

Did some writing as the air conditioner cooled the room off until it felt like an Igloo. Eyes started to shut down, so I went to bed and took a royal, fantastic nap.

markknopfler.com, this tour around, has reported wrong concert times for a few concerts already. Not sure why exactly, but in general, I believe that there simply are way too many intermediary parties between the person determining the start time and the person who ends up sending emails to ticket purchasers informing them about the start time. Like most inconsistencies in life, this one can also be attributed to human error.

Decided not to trust the reported start times anymore. As the venue was located close to the hotel, and the tickets for the concert were under the Dutchman's name, he volunteered to simply go there when the box office opens, collect the tickets and then proceed to see the city (if there is enough time); I stayed at the hotel, writing some more after waking up.

Lo and behold: the concert tickets reported a start time 30 minutes earlier than the one reported by *markknopfler.com*. OK. Time to wrap things up and get ready to go to the concert. Left the hotel late, and decided to grab a bite before heading to the concert. On the way to the venue, nothing special really popped up so we decided to share a *Subway* sandwich. That did the trick: last meal for the day.

The concert venue in Malta is called *Il-Fosos*, which means "Pits" in Maltese (and Spanish). The place is also called "The Granaries" in English. Nowadays, this place is a public square; but what's more interesting is what this place was used for up until not too long ago.

The place is called "The Granaries" in English for a reason: the square itself is built upon multiple pits where wheat and grain used to be stored to feed the population of Malta. The pits were constructed in the 17th century, and they were constructed underground in order to protect that food during times of war. These granaries were used to store grain up until 1962, when a new above-ground silo was constructed.

This square is located in front of St. Publius Church.

The venue configuration allowed for seating in the front, and standing in the back. A fence separated between the two sections.

One thing that was of particular interest was this:

The stage was high. Between the stage and the front rows, was a thick wooden surface, supported by metal pegs.

The square itself seemed to be on a slope. I concluded that because the distance between the wooden surface and the floor remained more or less constant from left to right, but the height of the stage (relatively to the wooden surface) decreased as you headed towards the right hand side of the stage (the stage itself, obviously, must not be on a slope).

The venue quickly filled in, however the concert didn't start before 8:30pm—half an hour past the time written on the ticket. You see, now I am confused. I have absolutely no idea why it is so difficult to coordinate these things—it's frustrating and, more than being frustrating, it's outright ridiculous.

A few songs into the concert, Mark noticed that there were people watching the concert from the roof of one of the buildings surrounding the square. Seemed like a government building of some sort, which led Mark to ask whether it's the "Prime Minister or something" watching the concert from there.

Also about half way through the concert, a helicopter was flying around the square's perimeter, then vanished. Mark again asked who could it be in that chopper, to which one audience member shouted "The President".

Good concert, with a good receptive audience, except for a group of idiots sitting right behind me who chose to talk nonstop during the entire concert. I don't even think they were listening to the music. That, puzzlingly, didn't stop them from cheering *between* songs. Well, as I said many times before, the world is full of idiots; and the problem with alcohol is, that in most cases, when consumed without moderation, it intensifies one's idiocy and turns it from being the problem of one person (the idiot) to a problem of many (all people surrounding said idiot in a concert).

Towards the encore, people started leaving their seats and approaching the stage. *So Far Away* was played while people were dancing (harmlessly) in front of the band. *Piper to the End* and the show was over.

Back to the hotel, made a small detour to see what the colour beige looks like in the dark, when lit with yellow light.

Back to the hotel and I was happy to see bed again. Looked forward to the next day: a day off, used to take the *very last flight* for the tour departing in the evening, leaving enough time to see more beige.

Signing off this post from my hotel room in Lucca, Italy.

Isaac

Friday, July 19, 2013

Valletta, Malta to Pisa and Lucca, Italy (July 18-19, 2013)

Thursday, July 18: woke up late. Very late. The day's itinerary was simple: at around 2:20pm, take a bus to Malta's airport; an hour and a half flight to Pisa, departing shortly after 5:00pm; get an airport pick-up by the hotel's shuttle. It's a day off, and the next day's concert was to take place in Lucca, which is half an hour train ride from Pisa. I've never been to Pisa before, so spending the night in Pisa before heading to Lucca seemed to be a good idea.

Woke up fresh. The room's air conditioner did a great job cooling the room throughout the night, providing for an excellent night sleep. I was ready for the day, eager to spend my last few hours in Malta doing exactly what I like most: be stationary most of the time and write.

> I felt no passion whatsoever to see what Malta has to offer. I already got the idea: beige buildings, more beige buildings and, to top it all, even more beige buildings. Call me when the start growing some trees here: I want out and I'm unlikely to ever come back. This place must be nature freaks' hell.

The hotel I stayed in offered breakfast—a small selection of items from the restaurant on top of which the hotel rooms were. Very restrictive menu. Opted for an omelette inside something called "Maltese bread". I didn't know what "Maltese bread"—I assumed they were talking about a bread coloured beige, as everything in this island seems to be in beige—but I was willing to give it a shot. Delicious. Apparently there's a Wikipedia entry for it, too.

Back to the room to do some writing until 11:00am; time to check out. Left the luggage at the hotel—they ran out of space in the luggage room (which also functions as a general storage room for the restaurant. Repulsive) so luggage had to be stored outside that room, by the wall in the restaurant itself. Now how about that for feeling confident that you'll meet your luggage three hours later?

Took my small backpack containing my ridiculously heavy laptop (I should have bought an ultra-book before doing this tour, it'd save a lot of headache and a lot of sweat). Jeroen decided to go explore the city, I decided to do some maintenance.

First task: find a pharmacy. I ran out of gauze pads, and decided that I'd be better off with a gauze roll instead. Makes much more sense for my situation. There are many pharmacies in Valletta's city center. The first one I picked didn't have what I was looking for, the second one did. Good. Now, I asked them whether they have a sink or something so I can wash my hand, apply some gel and wrap my wrist with one of the newly purchased pad. The attendant there didn't know what I meant, so I had to rephrase. The mistake I did was mention the word "toilet": as soon as that word was heard, the attendant went into complete defensive mode and nodded for a strong "no". I guess that this place is so touristic that even pharmacies tend to get their toilets abused by careless travellers.

Whatever. I was planning on going to a cafe to do some writing anyway. Found a cafe nearby the hotel, and asked to go wash my hands before I sit down. Sure, go ahead. Now, that cafe had its toilets located in the basement. To get there, one needs to go down a very narrow spiral staircase, ducking the entire time. Every extra step you take down, temperature raises by 500°C, and humidity gets much, much worse. By the time I arrived to the basement level, I was already sweating like an exceptionally out-of-shape pig. Entered those toilets, total area of about one square meter. Got whatever I needed out of my backpack, applied the gel, then the gauze roll... now how do you cut it?

Now, you see, I'm not experienced in this kind of things. I suppose I should have known that gauze pads are designed to withstand exceptional pressure. Whatever I did, I just couldn't cut the damned thing. Meanwhile, the energy I exerted caused me to sweat even worse.

BLOODY HELL. Held the remainder of the roll in my hand and sprang out of that toilet to breathe some fresh air outside. Before sitting down for coffee, I asked for a knife.

The waiter looked at me in a look that is specifically reserved to waiters that just encountered a diner asking for a sharp knife before even ordering anything. That was when I realized I should demonstrate *why* I need a knife. All sorted out then.

Sat down for some iced coffee (took me a full minute to explain what I wanted. These guys only know how to make iced coffee with ice cream and whipped cream on it. For some reason he couldn't fathom a simple request to leave the last two out) and started to do some writing, all the while trying to reduce my core temperature.

At around 1:30pm, I decided to stop writing and go for a quick walk around: if I'm going to see so much beige, why should I be the only one to suffer?

Approaching the north end of Valletta, the Mediterranean Sea is right there, serving as a perfect blue background for… that's right. More beige.

Isaac's "Privateering" Tour Blog

Finally, some green…

… and back to beige.

Dripping sweat, I made it back to the hotel at 2:00pm, to meet the Dutchman, grab the luggage and head to the bus station, to get to the airport. I was tired and frustrated from the heat, to the point that I started losing focus. Grabbed a sandwich from the hotel's restaurant—which, of course, had to be cooked as it was only half-cooked; great, that's what I need: *more heat*—and headed to the bus station.

Boarded the bus and started consuming the sandwich. As soon as I was done, the bus started to move. At least in that part of Malta, roads aren't in very good shape, and traffic is busy, resulting in the bus driver having to brake a lot. Now, you know the feeling you get when you ride a bus right after eating, and the ride is spotty? nausea. And the heat… blimey, the heat.

Finally, arrived to Malta's international airport. Left the bus and entered the air-conditioned space.

Step 1—reaching the airport—done.

Now came step 2, which I wasn't very much looking forward to: dealing with an airline that is considered by many to be the worst in Europe.

Ryanair is a low-cost airline based in Ireland. The airline is named after one of its founders, an Irish businessman named Tony Ryan. It's been in business since 1985, experienced rapid growth, went public in 1997 and used the money raised (by taking the company public) to expand its services across Europe.

The company was designed to be a low-cost, no-frills airline. As such, over the years, it has gained a rather questionable reputation among customers. The lengths that Ryanair go to in order to squeeze extra money from travellers are truly astonishing.

> Examples are aplenty: you must show up in the airport with your boarding pass (by checking in online), otherwise you pay a fee—if I recall right, it's about €70. No free baggage: must pay for each piece, online of course (otherwise you pay extra fee, about €100). The very act of checking in online costs money (about €6 per passenger). Basically, there is no way to check-in without paying *some* fee.
>
> Even water on board costs money.
>
> This airline is the closest an airline can get to a "flying bus". Their aircrafts' seats don't recline, and don't have those pockets behind them—all to cut costs. What else do they do to cut costs? at some point, the company proposed removing two toilets in each aircraft in order to add more seats; asked for permission to redesign its aircrafts so passengers can fly while standing up; suggested charging money to use the toilets while on board; suggested charging extra fees from obese people; and even suggested that passengers should carry their own checked-in luggage onto the airplane.

Customer service-wise, this airline is known to be as terrible as an airline cat get.

> How terrible?
>
> in 2002, they refused to provide wheelchairs to disabled passengers. Once that got to the courts, the courts decided that the responsibility for wheelchairs should be joint between the airlines and the airports. The result? all fares went up by €0.50.
>
> In 2012, they disallowed a 69 years old lady, suffering from colostomy, to bring her medical kit on board, even though she was carrying a document from her doctor explaining her condition. The airline's staff forced the lady to lift her shirt up, in front of all other passengers, to prove that she had a colostomy bag.

What else? false or misleading advertising; allegations for carrying less than the minimum amount of fuel on the aircraft in order to cut costs; and the list goes on and on.

I was therefore partly curious and partly horrified. As this tour is nearing its end, my energy level is low and I have less patience towards idiots than I have ever had before. I dislike rude people with passion, and I started envisioning how this airline's employees are going to make me finally lose my mind.

Fortunately, we were prepared. All documents printed beforehand, leaving nothing to chance. Checked in, then off to the security gates. Malta's airport is small, and security clearance there can get very hectic: it was very crowded, but things went quick. Security cleared; no gate assignment yet, so it was time to sit down and unwind in a cafe somewhere.

It was comforting to realize that a large part of the band's crew was also taking this flight. I could recognize most faces, and surprisingly, my face was recognized as well. It was comforting because of two reasons: for once, it always feels better to be in the vicinity of people who are familiar to you, even if you never actually talked to them; and for twice, well, without this crew, there *is* no concert: if the flight is cancelled or diverted or whatever, my best bet would be to simply head where these guys are going as they know best how to get to the next concert—they *must* be there.

Sat down in the cafe, gazing at nothing. Took my noise cancelling headphones out, put them on and activated them. I felt increasingly numb towards anything and anyone around me: my eyes were unfocused. Thought about everything and nothing at once. My brain was a mush. I'm pretty sure that, at some point, I was on the verge of collapsing: I didn't eat well, I wasn't rested, and the heat experienced earlier left me very frustrated.

It *must* have been the heat. I really, *really* can't function well in insanely hot places.

Finally, gates for the flight were announced: "gate 8–10". Sorry, what's that? which gate? 8? 9? 10? all of the above?

Walked towards gates 8, 9 & 10. Only gate 8 was open, and there was already a line-up to enter the gate's area. Why line-up? because your boarding pass needs to be checked *before* you enter the gate area, and passengers with carry-on luggage must prove that their carry-on luggage fits into a fixture made of metal poles, denoting the maximum size for a carry-on luggage.

That took forever. Finally at the gate, now waiting for the bus. One bus arrived, all passengers started walking towards gate 8's exit. The bus left, people continued to stand. And stand. And stand. 20 minutes, standing like idiots. Finally, another bus came, but stopped next to gate 10's exit. Announcement over the speakers: the bus will now collect everyone from gate 10, not 8. That caused an uproar: unless you pay for priority boarding, there are no assigned seats. People who want to ensure being seated together must board the aircraft quickly in order to ensure getting two (or more) adjacent seats. I didn't care at all about all of this, but others did.

Loaded onto a bus… here's the airplane. Got an aisle seat, so did the Dutchman. People kept boarding the aircraft, getting very frustrated because they couldn't sit next to whoever they wanted to sit.

> I really don't understand the big deal about it. For heaven's sake, it's a short flight—a little more than an hour; is it really *that* important to you to sit next to someone you know, that you will start asking people to move to other seats to accommodate your wish?
>
> My hypothesis is that there is a strong correlation between one's eagerness to sit next to someone they know, and their inability to keep their mouth shut for periods that span more than a few minutes.
>
> (The issue is not about why people *prefer* to sit next to someone they know; that is obvious. The issue is about being so enthusiastic about it, and being so frustrated when they can't get what they want.)

On-board baggage mayhem, too. Suitcases were flying in the air, being shoved into, and pulled out of, overhead bins. I practiced being numb, and I think I made good progress.

Flight took off a bit late, but arrived on time. Nightmare is over; welcome to Pisa.

I have never been to Pisa before in my life. Also, other than the fact that this city features a leaning tower, prompting hundreds of thousands of people every year to pose to the camera as if they're pushing or supporting the tower.

> It was funny when it was done once, a long time ago, by someone who was obviously much more original than you are. Let's move on, shall we.

Baggage collected, and headed to the arrivals hall. Arrangements were made with the B&B that was booked for the night, for an airport pick-up. Exited through the arrivals hall's door and looked for someone holding a sign with my name.

Found him: a simple looking guy, wearing shorts and a T-shirt, as well as a partly shy, partly suspicious expression. Now out to the car. Walking through the parking lot, I was expecting to find some sort of a shuttle or a minivan, branded with the B&B's name; instead, I was surprised when the driver stopped by a small black jeep.

…

OK, interesting. We started driving towards Pisa's city center, chatting with the driver who was showing a great deal of interest in his passengers. Before I knew it, though, the ride was over: Pisa's airport is unique for being extremely close to the city center.

It didn't look like a street that I'd want to spend too many nights in: more like a rough area of town. Oh well, I wasn't intending to do much in here anyway. Luggage collected from the car and the driver started walking towards a nearby building. At the building's entrance, there stood a guy repeatedly pushing an intercom button.

The driver approached.

– "Can I help you?"

The guy turned to the driver and a dialogue started. It was a confused dialog, during which each side was trying to figure out what the other side wants—partly in English, and partly in Italian.

Then, all became clear. The driver wasn't just a driver: it was the owner of the B&B. The intercom button that the other guy was pushing was the button to ring the B&B's owner's office. The B&B owner asked the new client to wait until he finishes checking us in.

Now: I wrote before, on a few occasions, about how I keep getting surprised with new things almost on a daily basis, even though I've been travelling a lot recently. How long, would you say, a check-in process (to a hotel or a B&B) takes, assuming that the individual checking you in has 100% of their attention dedicated to you?

1 minute? 2 minutes?

Well, some sophisticated and luxurious 5 stars hotels may take 4–5 minutes: they have to pretend to be working hard for you, to justify their ridiculous nightly rates.

So this one took 45 minutes, and to your immense surprise, you won't hear me complaining about it much because it was a very interesting experience. The B&B owner, Michele, is really just a simple nice guy, very talkative but very knowledgeable about many things. His passion is photography—those 45 minutes included a demonstration of some of his work—and, by the way he talked about Italy in general and Pisa in particular, you could easily tell that he loves his country.

Asked for a restaurant recommendation, and a reservation was made in a Tuscan restaurant in the city center. With that, came a recommendation for gelateria which is considered (according to the B&B owner) to be one of the top 5 gelaterias in Italy.

Occupancy wasn't full, so we were upgraded to a mini-suite with two bedrooms. Quickly arranged everything and headed out for dinner.

Pisa's central railway station, conveniently located by the B&B, also marks the south end of Pisa's city center. From there, it's a short walk north to River Arno that flows through the city, offering excellent city scenery.

The restaurant, Antica Trattoria il Campano—a name by which name the B&B's owner would be willing to swear—provided good food indeed but nothing out of the ordinary except for a brilliant home-made pasta. Let's face it: after that glorious dinner in Sicily just a few days ago, I can't really see how that Sicilian restaurant's record can be met, let alone broken, by the time the tour ends. Still, a good place. Go there, just don't order the lamb chops: hardly any meat in them.

Backtracked a little bit to get my hands on some gelato from Gelateria De' Coltelli. Here, the B&B's owner was right on the spot: the place claims to use only natural, organic materials. Faced with a variety of closed cans with only labels (in Italian) on them, it was very hard to pick so I just picked two in random. Great. That's a place to savour memories of.

Of course, no (first time) visit in Pisa would be complete without seeing a leaning tower of some sort. The countless pictures I had the chance to see of that tower somehow gave me the impression that we're talking about a very tall one; looking around me from the city center, I could see no tower at all. Fired up *Google Maps*, only to find out that it's merely five minutes walk away.

OK… started walking through dark narrow streets, turned here, turned there… looking above me… no tower. Then, finally, it appeared as if out of nowhere.

Appears much smaller in reality than what I had imagined. It is indeed beautiful, and brilliantly lit at night time.

One of the things that annoys me the most in wide lens cameras is the phenomenon of lens distortion. Finally, I found a good use for this annoyance: taking one photograph showing as if the tower leans much more than it really does…

… and one showing as if it hardly leans at all.

Here's one taken without any lens distortion, taken from the side to which the tower leans—giving the impression that the tower doesn't lean at all:

A corresponding Facebook post evolved into a few failed guesses, plus me being scalded for not appreciating the tower for its touristic value.

Even at night time, the place was full of tourists. The usual tourist-oriented kitsch—all sorts of shady merchants selling the usual souvenirs, trick spiders and other toys. Headed back to the hotel, and discovered a good opportunity for a long exposure shot.

The next day was scheduled to involve an extremely easy ride: 27 minutes train ride to Lucca. Good night sleep, no alarm clock set.

July 19: somehow, woke up early but fresh. The B&B's breakfast ends at 9:30am. That being consumed, it was decided to bid Pisa adieu and head to Lucca. Frankly, except for that tower and its beautiful surrounding buildings, I wasn't planning on seeing much in Pisa anyway: Lucca seemed much more interesting.

The train ride from Pisa to Lucca takes 27 minutes, offering very good scenery. Tuscany is gorgeous, as I can vividly remember from the last time I was here, 3 years ago. Green mountains, lakes, the works.

After an excruciating 27 minutes ride, arrived to Lucca's central railway station.

I have been to Lucca before, during the 2010 Get Lucky tour. Back then, I was driven around Italy by the two wonderful Italian sisters, Daria and Valeria, who helped making that Italian leg of the tour so memorable. Still, in 2010, we only visited Lucca for the concert (arrived by car) and left right after, so I didn't get much time to look around. This time around, though, a hotel was booked in Lucca's city center, providing plenty of time for sightseeing.

A few minutes walk from Lucca's central railway station, there's one of the main entrances to Lucca's old city area. Lucca's old city area is surrounded by its famous walls, left intact since the Renaissance era: once you pass through a nice little garden informing you that the Lucca Summer Festival is taking place…

… you enter through the ancient wall into the old city, and immediately feel history all around you. This place is very beautiful, and despite the numerous tourists around, I wouldn't say that it looks or feels like a complete tourist trap: Lucca's old city area definitely has character.

It was still early in the morning (around 11:00am), but surprisingly, the hotel room in Hotel La Luna, located right in the old city's center, was ready. Went to the room, quick set up and, for a few hours, did almost nothing but writing.

Once I was done uploading the previous post, I decided to go outside for a walk. Lucca's old city center is very small, and you can cover it all within a day; I decided to head north, climb on the ancient wall and just walk on it.

Walked through the city center…

… until I arrived at the wall, about five minutes later. You can climb up the thick, few meters wide wall in many locations around the perimeter, and the walk along the wall is a rewarding one: you get to see Lucca's old city center, as well as other neighbourhoods, along with some mountains in the back and lots, *lots* of green.

For the first time in quite a while, I decided to do that walk while listening to music. Nothing Knopfler, of course: I get 2 hours of Knopfler's music on an almost nightly basis. Bob Dylan's *Tempest* did the trick very well. Beautiful album.

Reached the southern tip of the old city center, climbed down and walked back to the hotel.

Having learned the lesson from the previous few concerts, when the announced start time didn't correspond much with reality, I decided to go pick up the tickets as soon as the box office opens. The venue, *Piazza Napoleone*, is a square in the heart of Lucca's old city center, and is where concerts are performed during the Lucca Summer Festival. I arrived to the Piazza just a few moments before they closed the entire area: I have no idea why they were doing this, but apparently, the entire Piazza Napoleone area is being evicted of people about 3 hours before concerts start, and you can only enter the area once again once the event's "door opening time" arrives. Then, once you enter the Piazza, *you can't leave and come back anymore.*

That's very odd, for a venue that is actually a square and is located in the very heart of the city. The question then became how the hell was I supposed to go back to my hotel once I pick up my tickets? the answer: extra ten minutes walk around the entire Piazza area.

I am willing to bet that there is no Italian translation to the word "efficiency". No reason to have one: they never employ it anyway.

Tickets collected, back to the hotel to rest. About an hour before the concert, left once again for a pre-concert snack. A tasty fruit crepe hit the spot well, then off to the Piazza, waiting in line to get in.

I remember that, last time I was here in 2010, entering the venue was a huge mess: it was then when I realized how inefficiently things work in this country and how Italians simply can't let go of this inefficiency (they apparently need it in order to survive). This time, it was less of a mess because we entered the venue about 20 minutes before the concert's start time. As the concert time approached, though, a significant number of people were crowded against the entrance. Of course, not all people made it into the seated area by the time the concert started, resulting in people crossing the venue almost half way into the concert!

Some bizarre, nasty incident took place at the beginning. Like in every concert, a few professional photographers (employed by the press, or the promoter, or whatever) were allowed access to the narrow gap between the stage and the fence separating the audience from the stage, to take photographs. As usual, Peter Mackay was in charge of guiding the photographers through and instructing them where exactly they should be standing (or, more precisely, where exactly they should *not* be standing. Such restrictions, I believe, are imposed by Mark and the band, and are not to the venue's discretion).

One particular photographer, though, didn't quite subscribe to the idea of following these rules. While all other photographers obliged and seemed to be content with these restrictions, this particular low-life scum decided that it wasn't enough for him: he wanted more. He started getting into an argument with Peter, who tried to explain to the photographer that he (Peter) was simply doing his job. That explanation didn't bode well with the rogue camera man, who proceeded to shout, yell, curse and throw the middle finger repeatedly at Peter.

How Peter was able to maintain his cool through all of that is beyond me, but he did. Peter is there in each and every concert, and I get to see him more often than not, dealing with all sorts of annoyances—primarily demanding that people respect the band's photographing and video-shooting policies. No matter where you are, there's always that punk who just *needs* to use the flash while taking a picture; and there's always that guy who just *has* to raise his tablet up and record the show, obstructing others' view. To me and you, these are annoyances; but it's Peter's job to actually deal with it. Not sure how long I could have kept my cool being in Peter's shoes: he must have a much higher tolerance to idiots than I do.

The concert itself was very good, featuring a shorter set. That seems to align with the last tour, as the set became shorter as the tour was nearing its end. Strong cheers from the audience who appeared to have appreciated the show. A *Running of the Bulls* session triggered before *Telegraph Road* ended up with people being sent back to their seats, only to perform a more vicious run later. The guy seated next to me simply sprang on his feet and ran amok towards the stage. I waited until the mess was all over before getting up and marching forward.

Good encore, during which I was able to capture a photograph of a moron recording the encore using his tablet.

Hey, moron, if you're reading this—please don't procreate. We're backed up with idiots already.

Concert was over—took a long while before the lights turned on once the band left—and the march back towards the hotel began. A five minutes walk turned into a 15–20 minutes walk due to the fact that the Piazza is located right at the city center and everybody was leaving the venue at once, often choosing to stand and chat with their friends along the way, creating traffic jams.

Back to the hotel for a short night sleep, facing a long travel day the next morning. Wake up time: 5:30am.

Signing off this post from my hotel room in Zürich. Will head out for dinner and then to the show: should be a beautiful venue tonight.
Isaac

Wednesday, July 24, 2013

Lucca, Italy to Zürich, Switzerland to Lörrach, Germany to Saint-Julien-en-Genevois, France (July 20-22, 2013)

After spending a relaxing yet interesting day in Lucca, the God of Travel decided to offset joy with yet another long travel day: leave Lucca 6:48am, arrive Firenze (English: "Florence") 8:06am; leave Firenze 9:00am, arrive Milano 10:40am; leave Milano 11:10am, arrive Zürich 2:51pm. Eight hours of travel in total, following an alarm clock assisted wakeup at 5:30am.

Woke up half asleep, which is all that was really needed: more than three months of travelling, I'm going through my morning routine like a robot. Not much brainpower needed to kick-start the day.

It was too early for breakfast in the hotel, and Lucca's central railway station doesn't offer much in terms of dining, at least not that early on Saturdays. Hungry, arrived to the railway station about 15 minutes before the train's departure, after walking through Lucca's (mostly) empty old city center. The *Piazza Napoleone*, the venue for last night's concert, was as empty as a post-concert Piazza can be: completely devoid of people, except for a few city workers cleaning up the mess. So many plastic bottles and other sorts of litter, left behind by people who are, themselves, litter.

The two clocks I passed by in Lucca's central railway station were both wrong: one was a few minutes ahead, one was about 10 minutes behind. It's a sad world when you can't even trust clocks in train stations: my mobile phone is my guide here, thank you very much. Short delay, train came by... short one hour ride to Firenze.

Firenze. Heard so much about this city. Had slightly less than hour layover there so exploring the city was out of the question, although I would have liked to do that at some point. Instead, ten minutes were spent looking for a proper place for a breakfast snack, and the search ended where it began—a nice cafe right inside the station.

Next train to Milano's central railway station, Milano Centrale. It's the fourth time this tour that I'm stopping in Milano Centrale, so it's a familiar one. Saw a sign leading to a coffee bar at the upper level; never been there before so thought I should try it. Three elevators there, two were not working—of course, remind me again which country I'm in?—and the third one got me up for another sandwich bar offering mediocre sandwiches and terrible service.

> I love Italy: it's a beautiful country, people are generally warm-hearted and nice... but having said that, for me, Italy is a great destination for a different kind of trip—certainly not for a trip involving being dependent on so many service providers and when time works against you. Service providers here seem to be cutting too many corners rendering things to go unpredictable at times—and predictability is key when you're following such a busy travel schedule.
>
> I wrote, in one of my earlier posts, that virtually my entire life consists of looking for inefficiencies, getting bothered by them and—to the extent possible—help fix them. Hell, that's exactly what I do for living, and I've been in the same line of work (although in many different roles) for 18 years now. Now, if you are like me—getting irritated by inefficiencies—then Italy would be a very interesting experience for you: disorganization and inefficiencies are almost everywhere.
>
> You may argue that "efficiency" is a subjective term, and what constitutes "efficient" for Italians may be considered "inefficient" in mine; but you'd be wrong. "Efficiency" means "doing more with less", and that's *not* subjective. For instance, having four people working in a ticket booth, when three of them are busy handling one client *together* at a time and a fourth one doing nothing—that's inefficient, no matter where you're from. Still, they do it. Why? because efficiency here is simply not appreciated. They don't care about it at all, and for those of us who cherish efficiency—well, tough luck: we're visitors here. Accept the Italian way of life, or suffer the consequences. Adjust your trip's style to correspond with how things are done here.

Departed Milano on time and bid Italy goodbye: with all the challenges involved in following this concert tour in Italy, still, I'll miss it. It's a great country to be in and I'll certainly be back.

The train ride from Milano to Zürich takes about four hours. As you approach Switzerland, the scenery becomes increasingly scenic, and once you're in Switzerland, you just want to get off the train and walk. It's such a beautiful country, and for me, it's as close as Europe gets to British Columbia: a rare combination of stunning natural scenery, and polite, courteous people. I would consider the Swiss to be very lucky: of course, this consideration is purely subjective, but as it is me who is writing these lines, I am in the liberty to say that, if I were to rank European countries based on parameters that I consider "important", Switzerland would rank first.

Arrived in Zürich and immediately went to the hotel, Hotel City Zürich, thinking I'll get some rest after this long travel day. As soon as I exited the city's central railway station and started walking towards the hotel, I already knew that I was going to love this city: in many ways, it reminded me a lot of Vancouver. It is far from being crowded (at least comparing to other major European cities); roads and sidewalks are relatively spacious; natural scenery is visible from virtually everywhere; and, contrary to Vancouver, it was evident that this city has very efficient public transport infrastructure: tram stations everywhere, with dedicated lanes and digital signage.

Switzerland is an expensive country to travel in, and Zürich, relative to other Swiss cities, is itself expensive. The hotel for the night was thus expensive as well, but it delivered: great spacious room, fantastic condition.

A few friends, including Philipp (who is local to Zürich) and Ingrid (who is not local to Zürich, but somehow makes herself local everywhere she's at), had plans for a get-together in a restaurant nearby, offering a great patio with excellent view of the water (we'll get to the scenery soon, hold on). I had to do some writing and could definitely use some alone time after the last few stressful days so I decided to stay at the hotel for a while, catch up with things and get social a bit later.

After uploading the previous post, I headed out towards the meeting point, while checking out that restaurant's offering via my mobile. Turned out to be German food, but I had the craving for something else. A bit more research and I decided to visit some Thai restaurant, located at the east bank of the river.

On my way there, I started realizing just how beautiful this city is.

Once crossing the bridge to the east bank, the terrain is no longer flat: various stairways provide opportunities to explore the city in different altitudes. Beautiful streets boasting clean, coloured buildings; strong attention is given here to clean looks—clean, but not boring: you won't find cheap dirty metal sign here, even for a simple tobacco store. If you own a shop in Zürich, its exterior should better be clean and appealing, otherwise you won't "belong".

The Thai restaurant I had set my eyes on turned out to be closed, so I ended up in another spot—a Lebanese restaurant called Noon. Everything in this city is expensive, and this restaurant was no exception. Good food though, going for price that's almost double what I'd pay for a similar meal in Canada.

> I am not from Lebanon, but as Israeli cuisine is a fusion of many other cuisines (mainly Middle Eastern), Lebanese "elements" made it to the Israeli culinary world. In Lebanese restaurants, I can easily feel at home. That's why, when I was given a home-made lemonade, I could detect that they've put something else in there. Turned out to be rose water—used, in the Middle East, as a common addition to lemonade. The fact that I was able to recognize it prompted the restaurant's owner to inquire about my origin, to which I answered fully and truthfully, which, to my knowledge, is something that many people with Israeli background refrain from doing in encounters such as this one due to… you know. "The situation".

Excellent meal over, and I decided to pop for a visit in that restaurant where Philipp, Ingrid et al were sitting in. That provided for another pleasant walk in Zürich's city center.

The last picture shows some sort of a bathing house (look closely, behind the boats on the right). I didn't notice it when taking the picture. Turns out that this is a *Frauenbad*—an area designated for women *only* to bath and bask in the sun in. Although perfectly visible from outside (it was reported that the men's room in a nearby restaurant has windows offering direct view of this particular *Frauenbad*), women here feel free to take their tops off.

Which is, of course, fine. But what I don't understand is why *Frauenbad*'s exist to begin with. Unless the Swiss society is a chauvinistic one (and I don't know enough about the Swiss to make a judgement on that), I don't see the point in such women-only establishments, just as I don't see the point in men-only establishments. You can't strive for feminism on one hand, and segregate your gender on another. In a way, you're shooting yourself in the foot.

After touching base with folks at that restaurant overlooking the river and nearby lake, it was time to plan for transportation to the venue. Folks at the restaurant made arrangements to make their way to the venue by cars, but I decided to head to the hotel first and take public transport. On one hand, that was a bit of a careless step on my behalf as I knew that the venue is located somewhere on a nearby mountain; on the other hand, for some reason, I had complete trust in Switzerland's public transport system, and took *Google Maps*' public transport-based route suggestion for granted. According to *Google Maps*, it should take about 25 minutes to get to the venue from the city center, involving a tram and a funicular.

Everything worked like clockwork, including tram #3 that departed about 20 seconds before I arrived at the station. No worries, though: public transport here is very efficient even in weekends. Seven minutes later—again, *exactly* at the prescribed time—another tram came by. A few stations, took off and followed the herd to the funicular station located right across the street.

This funicular system, taking you up to the mountain where the concert venue was, is called Dolderbahn. It's based in the city center and travels up the mountain, with two or three stops along the way. During the *Live at Sunset* festival, of which Knopfler's concert was a part, the funicular operates non-stop until past midnight, departing every 10 minutes. That was nice to know, especially after the last experience with depending on cable cars to get to and from a venue, in Locarno.

The funicular on its way up was full of people cramped together like sardines. The ride up took about 5 minutes, at the end of which everyone left at once and started going to a direction well pointed to by this:

It's a short 200–300 meters pleasant walk among pleasant greens, until you see a large white fence to your left, separating you from the venue which is located, actually, below you.

markknopfler.com ticket distribution for this concert worked differently from any other concert: while for all other concerts tickets had to be collected on site, the tickets for this particular concert were sent to the purchaser's mailing address. That presented a problem, as the tickets were going to be mailed after the Dutchman and I were already on the road. Fortunately, *markknopfler.com*'s ticketing office was sympathetic to the unique situation and agreed to arrange for our tickets to be picked up at the venue. These tickets were under the Dutchman's name, which is why I found him in the ticketing office figuring things out with the attendant. Tickets weren't there, and we were asked to inquire at the "info booth", located a few meters away.

At the "info booth", the Dutchman barely finished explaining the background to the two attendants there when one of them simply called out loud "Oh! You're Gerrits!". It was good to have had this settled well.

Why "good"? should it not be taken for granted?

ABSOLUTELY NOT.

It sounds simple: the ticket distribution agency from which you bought the tickets "made arrangements" for your tickets to be picked up at the venue. In many countries where organization and order are appreciated, you could safely assume that there's a strong chance that everything indeed went according to plan, but that's not the case for other countries following different social norms.

Between the ticket distribution agency to the actual people *on site* at the venue, from whom you get your tickets, there exists a line-up of middlemen which is longer than you might think. I can think of the following entities and won't be surprised if there are more along the way:

- *markknopfler.com* service representative.
- *markknopfler.com* ticket distribution service.
- The actual ticket repository held by the main distributor of tickets (such as *Ticketmaster* or *Eventim* or *Live Nation*).
- The concert's promoter.
- The venue's ticketing office (as tickets to events can also be purchased on site).

All you need is one screw-up along the chain and you can bid your tickets adieu.

I have been to concerts in other countries where ticket collection itself—with no special arrangements needed to take place—was hell: papers over papers containing lists of all sorts; envelopes everywhere, some of them open, some sealed; people looking frantically in multiple piles containing envelopes, unsorted. Italy and Spain "star" at the list of disorganization in that regards (although, believe it or not, things were also quite hectic at England's Royal Albert Hall). I don't even want to think what would happen if such an arrangement had to be made for a concert in Italy or Spain; might as well not even bother getting to the venue.

Once I got my ticket, I was considered taking a walk at the green nearby the venue, but then realized that much of that green was actually a golf course, and the other green looked as if it's encompassing a hiking trail. Would love to, but not now. Headed to the venue instead.

This festival is called "Live in Sunset", and I'm guessing this has something to do with being able to get a good sunset view during the concert.

The way the venue was organized, though, you could only see such sunset while being seated at the very back, or at the upper levels. Still, the scenery wasn't quite bad.

Inside the venue, there were many dining options—much unlike most other venues in this tour, leaning towards serving garbage—including actual restaurants. You could, for instance, sit at a restaurant up above and consume a good meal while watching the concert. Good atmosphere: long gone is the mess and noise of Italy, for good or bad.

Concert started on time, usual set followed by a few bulls running towards the stage before the encore while I was trying to make the opposite way—away from the stage and up to the upper levels, to see what this concert looked like from above: better, I should say. A celebration of lights, sound and very appreciative audience. I took a few photographs but they all turned out to be terrible. Sorry.

Concert was over and it was time to figure out how to get back to the city center. I knew that the funicular presents one option, but there were also buses waiting around, each marked as "Live at Sunset Shuttle". Good thing I inquired: those weren't heading to the city center. Headed to the funicular, then, only to be met by a group of about 100–150 people already waiting there. We started debating whether we should simply walk down—it's about 4km in a decline towards the city center, about an hour walk—but then decided to remain on site and let Swiss efficiency do its magic, which it did. Twenty minutes later, we were on the funicular heading down. Once touched the ground, tram #3 made its way through the station about one minute later; ten minutes after that, I was already at the hotel.

That's how public transport should work!

Was a good day in Zürich. Headed to bed for a good night sleep—expecting very easy travel the next day.

July 21, woke up at around 9:30am, heading to breakfast at 10:00am. Good breakfast at the hotel—not extravagant as in, say, Italy, but still good—a nice opening for a relaxed day.

The original schedule was to take a train to Basel, and then a train to Lörrach (Germany)—about 20 minutes away—and spend the night in Lörrach after the concert; however, later it turned out that the hotel in Lörrach doesn't offer air conditioning. That, plus the fact that Ingrid and Philipp were going to stay in Basel after the Lörrach concert (the cities are *very* close to each other), prompted us to change plans, spending the night in Basel instead.

What remained was a very simple schedule: depart Zürich whenever you want, as there are many trains going to Basel; then take the express bus to the airport, where our hotel was located (that airport hotel simplified things with regards to logistics)—about 10 minutes away.

Checked out, left luggage with the hotel staff and headed to see some more of this beautiful city. Sunday morning, very few living souls outside—perfect for a walk. Once you cross the river to the east bank and head south, almost every moment is worthy of a picture.

Noticed this cafe, and memorized it as a place to have coffee in later.

Kept walking almost completely randomly:

Eventually, found myself overlooking the river again, as well as the city's beautiful churches, with the Fraumünster trapping your eyes with its beauty; you can't look away.

More views of the water… can't have enough of those:

Looking over the water, it was time to do some calculations about train times, bus times and other logistics: turned out that it'd be best to leave before 2:00pm. Went back to the hotel, grabbed the luggage, then off to the central railway station located minutes away. This city is so convenient getting around in, it's amazing. Arrived at the station about 25 minutes before our train's scheduled departure time, only to find that there's an earlier train departing in just about 3 minutes. Good. Boarded into a 1st class cabin that was almost entirely empty, and it was a good, beautiful ride to Basel.

Arrived Basel's central railway station ("Basel SBB"); a quick look at the clock (well, not really a clock. Smartphone's clock. Not sure if that qualifies as "looking at the clock" anymore) showed that the bus, heading towards the airport, is leaving in about 8 minutes. Time to hurry.

More often than not, trains' 1st class cabins are located at the train's tail; thus, you earn a convenient ride but are punished by having to walk quite the distance on the platform, to exit the station.

OK, here's the bus… now, how do you buy tickets for this thing? oh, here's a machine; found one.

– "No, this machine says 'SBB' on it; it's probably only selling tickets to regular trains", said someone who claims to be understanding German and happens to be following this tour as well.

Instead of listening to my own intuition, I decided to defer to the German-speaking "authority". The end result? bus went away 5 seconds before tickets were purchased… right: in that same machine. Those automated ticketing machines, apparently, can sell you many types of transport tickets.

Another bus showed up 10 minutes later, and was quickly loaded to capacity. The ten minutes bus ride felt much longer—the bus' air conditioner couldn't keep up with the body heat generated by so many people—and at its end, the hotel for the night, Airport Hotel Basel, was right in front.

Ingrid was there at the entrance, having a smoke. Always good to see this lovely woman. When Ingrid is around, you know that things simply can't go wrong: reality seems to bend itself backward to align with Ingrid's expectations, rather than the other way around.

Went inside to check in, and noticed this:

Naturally, I was instinctively looking for the Hebrew writing which turned out to be nonsense. "ברהך הבא" means nothing. The correct writing is "ברוך הבא", and I can see why they got it wrong. Of course I notified them; turns out that each and every Israeli stepping into this hotel for the last five years have been telling them exactly the same thing, but management doesn't seem to care much about it.

Upon checking in, it turned out that when you reserve a room in this hotel, you get public transport in all of Basel for free. How could we know about it? it's written right there in the booking confirmation email. Oh well, this tour involves reservations for almost 60 different hotels, can't expect to thoroughly read each and every one of them.

Got set up in this beautiful room, and did some last-minute adjustments to the hotel reservation in Madrid. I tell you, folks—no matter how much time and efforts you put upfront planning such a tour, you'd always have to revisit things as you go along. When the Madrid hotel was booked about five or six months ago, it was perfectly valid to and sensible to book a hotel located about a kilometer from the station to save a few bucks; but once you're past 90% of the tour, spending some of it in scorching weather, you start seeing things in a different light.

Left the hotel late afternoon, for a short drive to Lörrach.

I have never heard of Lörrach before. It's a small city—about 50,000 people live there—located very close to the Swiss-French-German border. Philipp, who was born and raised in Basel, says that many Swiss people used to (and probably still) visit Lörrach for the sole purpose of doing shopping, as price differences are significant enough to justify this.

Lörrach is a short 20 minutes car ride from Basel, but still, once you cross to the German side, you somehow feel that you're not in Switzerland anymore. The cityscape becomes more and more "typical German". It's interesting to witness this, given the fact that there is no real border between the two countries (as both countries are signed on the Schengen Agreement).

Arrived at Lörrach, getting the feel that this is a city where nothing particularly interesting is going on, except for the *Stimmen Festival* that takes place here annually. There isn't much to see or do here; either that, or I have been looking in the wrong places (which is quite possible, as I wasn't really spending much time looking around).

A few minutes walk from the parking lot and we arrived at where the festival was taking place: a square right in the heart of the city center.

Same concept as in Lucca: the area surrounding the square is being evicted a few hours before the concert's kick-off, so only people with tickets can be present at the area once the concert starts. What was weird about this square was its size and its shape: the area in the square, from which you could actually see much of the stage, was very small. Technically, the square consisted of a few areas that didn't even offer direct line view of the stage; and even factoring those areas in, the total size of the venue was relatively small.

Sat down in a restaurant at the square for some dinner before the show. Typical simple German pub menu, with Flammkuchen being the only reasonable option. That consumed, we went outside to collect the tickets and see how to go about actually entering the venue: these procedures are usually different when the concert takes place in a city square, and better figure things out earlier than later.

Turned out to be a wise decision.

The ticket collection office, located about 50m away from one of the entrances, was virtually empty when we got there. The Dutchman, seeing that the entrance queues were pretty vacant, decided to go there and catch a spot while I was picking up the tickets. I usually pass on the opportunity to queue anywhere, including concerts, but decided to make an exception this time as I wasn't expecting to find any other, more useful ways, to spend my time in this seemingly boring city.

Gates were opened about 10 minutes ahead of schedule and bulls started running amok towards the stage from the three entrances. As I wasn't going to risk breaking another wrist, I decided to avoid running; fortunately, the two Dutch people I was with agreed to save a little space for me at the front.

Upon settling in, I ran a little survey and went ahead to buy some water for a few friends who were present. The weather was hot, humid... terrible. I made a grave mistake and brought myself only one cup of water—forcing me to spend almost the entire concert dreaming about the next time I'll ever get to feel the sensation of good drinking water on my tongue.

Short toilet break before the concert began—luckily, not much resistance at all in my voyage back to where I started, but I'd attribute it to the fact that I knew most of the people who were in the front: many good, familiar people made it from neighbouring countries for this concert, including Amann (who saved the day after the concert in Napoli), and Marco—a guy from Switzerland who I am sure is the most positive-thinking individual on the face of the earth: he could make people happy even if he was to live-broadcast an asteroid impact on earth.

Concert started and, for the first time in *quite a while*, I felt how it was to enjoy watching and listening to this band perform from the very front in a general admission venue: it is definitely a different experience altogether from a seated show. Even though you're standing for the entire duration of the concert, still you can lean against the fence, drastically reducing the pressure on your feet so it's actually manageable. The band-audience energy loop works differently in a standing show, and when you're right at the front, you fell it each and every second.

As the concert started before sunset, Ian and Guy made it to the stage wearing sunglasses. Temperatures were very high—I'm sure these folks would have loved the opportunity to go on stage wearing shorts (why don't they, really?). At some point, the floor-mounted fan aimed at Mark stopped working, prompting him to ask the crew to turn that thing on.

Sometimes, when in the front, you need to face a few challenges. In this concert, the challenge was the lighting. As it happened, the lights positioned at the back of the stage were aimed directly at the faces of those standing in the front: now, these are *strong* lights. There were times that I had to duck or look away; others, fortunate enough to carry their sunglasses, had to wear them and take them off repeatedly. Of course, this was more of a problem at the later parts of the concert, as the sun set.

Adjacent to the square are a couple of buildings—at least one of which was a hotel—which prompted guests (or residents) to watch the concert from their own balconies.

Took a while for the square to clear once the concert was over. Back to the car, short ride to the hotel and a few snacks at the hotel's lobby before heading to bed.

July 22 was originally carrying one of the most difficult itineraries in the tour: depart Lörrach (as the original plan was to stay in Lörrach) 7:31am, arrive Basel 7:50am; depart Basel 8:31am, arrive Bern 9:27am; depart Bern 9:34am, arrive Geneve 11:15am; depart Geneve 11:29am, arrive Bellegarde 11:57am; depart Bellegarde 12:09pm, arrive Saint-Julien-en-Genevois 12:29pm. That's a total of five hours ride over five (!) different trains. Why? well, what can you do. That's life.

A few weeks ago, Ingrid decided that she will be attending the concert in Saint-Julien-en-Genevois as well, and offered a ride. Needless to say, it didn't take long to ponder before responding with a resounding "yes, *please*". Once again, Ingrid saved the day; and instead of spending five hours in the morning hopping from one train to another, we had the luxury of being driven in the *Van-de-Maat-Mobile*—a convertible ride in perfect weather, allowing for a scenic detour off the main highway.

If you were to drive directly from Basel to Saint-Julien-en-Genevois, you'd be driving around 260km, which takes mere mortals about two hours and a half. The direct route heads south to Bern; however, following Philipp's advice, we set the city of Delémont as a via point, as that would allow for a more scenic route along Lake Neuchâtel and Lake Geneva. Good call: the ride was nothing short of breathtaking, featuring beautiful Swiss scenery of mountains, lakes, rivers, green… whatever it takes to make for a good, relaxing ride.

Needless to say, the roof was tucked away for the entire ride, much thanks to the weatherman's cooperation. Beautiful sunny day, would be a total waste to spend in trains.

It was decided to have lunch somewhere before crossing the border to France. Came across a place called Terrasse du Lac, located a few meters away from Lake Geneva.

We were all happy for finding this place: the view from the restaurant's terrace was second to none, offering direct view of the lake, which was there, a stone-throw away.

Grabbed an empty table, and realized that nobody's serving us. Headed to the counter, where we were told that the kitchen is closed, and they only serve drinks now.

This part of Switzerland is the "French" part: there's strong French influence in Switzerland's southwest, close to the French border, and apparently the French's typical dining hours' restrictions crept through the non-existent border into the paradise that is Switzerland. Attempts to find other places around, with an active kitchen, failed—even after visiting a tourist information center nearby. We therefore had no choice but to proceed. Fortunately, a few minutes down the road, we arrived at Nyon's touristic parts where a few restaurants were open. Good (and expensive!) food, followed by a magnificent ice cream, and we went on our way to the final destination: Saint-Julien-en-Genevois.

Saint-Julien-en-What?

—That was my initial reaction when I read the tour's itinerary. Never heard of this place before in my life, and I'm pretty sure that it was because there's nothing really going on in there.

Saint-Julien-en-Genevois is located in France, right on the Swiss border. I'm therefore led to believe that the tour made a stop here simply because it's so close to a big city—Geneva is about 10km away (although in Switzerland). You could therefore think of Saint-Julien-en-Genevois as a suburb of Geneva, but don't say it out loud as some French may take offense.

Weather was unbelievably hot. Ingrid decided to drop us off at the hotel and head directly to the venue, as this was a general admission concert. The city seeming to be completely devoid of any other action, we headed ourselves to the venue shortly after checking in at the hotel for the night—Hotel Savoie.

> Finding a hotel in Saint-Julien-en-Genevois was *very* difficult. There's only a handful of hotels in the area, most of them were booked months in advance, and the rest didn't even offer twin rooms.
> We found this one by complete luck.
> In hindsight, though, it might have been a better option to stay in Geneva instead.

The hotel—one of those family-run old houses turned into hotels—was far from providing a lovely experience. As this tour nears its end, I become less and less patient towards old, out-dated accommodations, and this one was just it. Huge step down comparing to the wonderful hotels in Switzerland enjoyed in the preceding two nights. That explained why I wasn't even hesitating whether to head to the venue more than two hours before the concert: not only Saint-Julien-en-Genevois seemed to offer nothing interesting, but the hotel room *itself* begged to be left alone.

From the hotel, it's about a kilometer walk to the venue; and after spending two days in Switzerland, enjoying the Swiss' perfect organization and tidiness in events management, it was time to experience the other end of the scale... and what a "treat" it was.

The instructions for this concert were simple: box office opens at 5:30pm; *markknopfler.com* ticket holders get an "early entry" privilege at 6:00pm; doors are open to the general public at 6:30pm; and the concert begins at 7:30pm. For the "early entry" privilege, there should have been a separate entrance located right by the venue's main entrance.

Nonsense.

Arrived to the venue at around 5:00pm, to find piles of people waiting by the main entrance. Now, by the instructions quoted above, a reasonable individual (I hope) would expect that the box office is located *outside* the venue, so you can collect your tickets *before* entering.

That, however, would be too efficient; and the French, much like Italians, consider "efficiency" to be a bad word. The box office for the venue was actually *inside*, behind the venue's locked doors.

5:30pm arrived and passed; no doors were open, no ticket collection, nothing. I believe it was around 6:00pm when the main venue's doors finally opened, and piles of people stepped on each other to get to the box office, located less than 10 steps away. There, again, the French sense of (dis)organization shone in its brightest lights: there were *five people* working at the box office; *four of them selling merchandise and only one handing out tickets*. Yes: one person had to give out tickets to dozens and dozens of people who were instructed to collect their tickets at the venue.

Line-up? HA. What line-up? people were climbing on each other begging the tickets' God for attention. Jungle's rule: the strongest you were, the earlier you got your ticket.

markknopfler.com ticket holders were given a shiny yellow wristband. Once past the venue's main entrance, wristband wearers were instructed to gather in a particular fenced location, where they'll be allowed early entry to the venue at 6:45pm.

Of course, 6:45pm came by and passed as if nothing. So did 6:46pm and 6:47pm. It was more or less 7:15pm when the fences were pulled away and dozens of shiny wristbands went running amok towards what looked like a huge tent. Again, I chose to walk instead, and was happy to find out that a spot was saved for me somewhere at the front.

Weather just became worse on everyone. As I arrived at the stage, I asked people if they wanted any water. The conclusion was to simply bring as much water as I possibly could. Sure, no problem: went outside that tent, exchanged some money for festival monetary equivalent notes, and use those notes to buy bottles of water. Surprisingly cheap—€1 each—but of course, they need to take the cap off.

Took eight bottles, placed them on a cardboard tray, and headed back to the tent. People set their eyes on the cold, cold water bottles as if we were cast away on a remote island with no running water anywhere. Some people thought that I was working for the venue, and asked me for a bottle—alas, these were all accounted for. Dropped those eight bottles and went back for another round.

This time, I decided to be enterprising: 10 bottles. Sure, why not, pile them up. Got those bottles, barely maintaining my balance (reminder: they took off the caps) and started marching back towards the stage.

Suddenly, I heard noise. You know those animated movies where they have scenes taking place in a jungle, and then, at some point, you see the entire jungle population running by insanely, as if there was a big forest fire behind them? you know that rumbling sound you hear in those scenes? you do? good, because that what it sounded like. As I approached the tent—less than 30 meters for me to go—the venue's gates opened to the general public and hundreds of people ran towards the stage; and there stands your truly, with an injured wrist, holding a cardboard tray carrying ten *open* bottles of water.

Trying to protect the transparent liquid gold I was carrying, I lost my balance and a couple of bottles dropped (still inside the cardboard container) and started to spill. Treaded carefully towards the front, asking people to move away so I can get to my destination. I was very proud to find out that I made it to the finish line with eight intact bottles, and only two bottles half full.

An ad-hoc repository of cold, chilled water was organized along the fence separating the audience from the stage. I drank two full bottles without even noticing, and was very happy about not being thirsty again…

… But I wasn't thinking of the consequences. Twenty minutes before the concert, I was dying for a toilet break. Around me there were approximately two million enthusiastic French people who, apparently, never before heard the term "personal space" (or heard about it and decided that it's not a useful concept to pay attention to). I had to choose between staying in my place and suffering through the entire concert, or go ahead and answer Mother Nature's call and risk not being able to get back to my spot.

My bladder won. Bid everyone goodbye in advance—as I knew that there wasn't much chance we'll be watching the concert together—and went to do what had to be done. Coming back, the pre-concert playlist was already played on the speakers; there was really no chance for me to get back to where I was, and I wasn't in the mood for starting to beg for people's acceptance of my situation. When the band took the stage, it was already too late.

Still, I got a nice experience out of it. I ended up watching the concert on one of the big screens located in the festival's area. Also, the venue offered many interesting dining options of which I was happy to take advantage.

People seemed to be as condensed as sardines inside that tent. There wasn't enough room for everyone; many were standing outside the tent, trying to catch a glimpse of the stage.

Isaac's "Privateering" Tour Blog

I was perfectly fine with enjoying the concert in a different way.

Walking to get some food, I ran into Bap Kennedy. Bap and another guitar player, Gordon McAllister, were the opening act for the concert in Nîmes, as well as for tonight's.

As you may remember from my post about the Nîmes concert, I was wondering, back then, what guitar Gordon McAllister was playing; I was sure it was a Taylor, but didn't know the exact model: must have been one of the high-end ones. So, after introducing myself to Bap—nice fellow—I asked him for Gordon's guitar's details. He said he didn't know, and suggested that I look for Gordon who was supposedly nearby, inside one of the small tents surrounding the venue.

Took a while to track him, but eventually I did. Turned out that I was right: the guitar indeed belonged to the x14CE series, and as I had imagined, it was the 914CE. This guitar is as high-end as Taylor's x14 series goes; you can't go wrong on that one. I considered buying one myself back in the days, but couldn't afford it so I settled for a lesser model instead (which, still, emits beautiful sound). Gordon and I ended up chatting for about 20 minutes or so, about all sorts of things. Very nice fellow; was happy to have run into him.

Went back to watch the concert, sitting on the lawn. I suppose this following picture would be best to describe the magical atmosphere outside that crowded tent:

Concert ended, bid everyone I knew goodbye and headed back to the hotel. After a couple of easy travel days, the next morning was going to be an early one.

Signing off this post from my hotel room in Carcassonne. Took a while to complete this post as I wasn't in the best of moods over the last few days. Let's all hope for better times. Will get some rest now and head for tonight's concert in Carcassonne's breathtaking medieval city.

Isaac

Friday, July 26, 2013

Better Late than Never: Facebook Comments Enabled

I should have attended to this earlier than 6 days to the end of the tour…

Better late than never, though. Starting now, you can comment on blog posts using your Facebook account. Right above the traditional comments' section, you should see the familiar Facebook commenting button.

Enjoy.

On to complete the ongoing post…

Isaac

Saturday, July 27, 2013

Saint-Julien-en-Genevois to Carcassonne, France to Barcelona, Spain (July 23-25, 2013)

July 23, morning. Woke up at the hotel's exceptionally uninviting room, tired. 5:30am. How long have I been asleep? about five hours. Clearly not enough. Fortunately, the hotel was located a few minutes walk from the city's central (and possibly only) railway station.

The itinerary: depart Saint-Julien-en-Genevois 6:30am, arrive Lyon (yes, Lyon again) 8:22am; depart Lyon 9:10am, arrive Carcassonne 12:26pm. Six hours of travel. Not that bad, but it's the short nights that are killers.

Saint-Julien-en-Genevois doesn't seem to offer much to do at all, let alone so early in the morning. Short snack at the railway station before departure? yeah, right. The station was closed: you could access the trains (of course) by following a sign leading you behind the station's building. Heck, this station is so small you are even allowed to cross the tracks to reach the other platform (as there's no underpass to get there).

Train arrived on time and I was happy to board it. 1st class cabin, and I was ready to embark on my usual attempts to fall asleep. Alas, two people seated a couple of rows ahead were in the middle of an important discussion; that is—important to them, and completely unimportant to me. They didn't stop talking for even one minute throughout the entire ride.

Arrived at *Lyon Part Dieu* on time. This train station serves as Lyon's main station and I think it was my third or fourth stop in this station so far this tour. Having skipped breakfast (as no breakfast was available anywhere in Saint-Julien-en-Genevois), food was top priority. Got a sandwich from a *Paul* shop located inside the station, demolished it within two minutes and headed to the same coffee place I had been two only two weeks earlier, en route to Locarno. Fruit salad, croissant and excellent cappuccino and breakfast was over and done with.

Back to the platform and took the connecting train, the TGV, en route to Carcassonne. No chatty people on board, but that's not to say that the cabin was quiet. Shortly into the ride, I was suddenly under the impression that the cabin was also moonlighting as a carpentry. Well, at least that was my initial impression; calculating the probability of the TGV carrying a carpentry on board, I arrived at pretty slim odds, which prompted me to resort to my second best guess: a snoring traveller.

So, yes. Two rows ahead of me, an exceptionally obese individual was squatting over one seat and a half—I pity the lady who was seated right next to him—snoring his lungs out.

Now, I'm not entirely sure what the etiquette is for such situations. Is it ethical to wake someone up because his snoring is a nuisance for more than two dozen other people? on one hand, you can look at it as if the person was talking loudly on the phone: in that case, it makes sense to ask him to keep things down ("makes sense" theoretically, but not practically. Who knows what kind of a maniac you'd be pissing off. You really can't trust anyone these days). But on the other hand, snoring is a symptom of a medical problem: would you get pissed at someone because their handicap impedes on your peace?

At any rate, nobody woke the dude up. My noise-cancelling headphones did much to eliminate the train's low frequency noise, but not much to battle the snorer. The only way out of this mess was to listen to music through those headphones—once music is played, you hear almost nothing of your surroundings; Bose did a great job—and so I spent the entire ride listening to music that I had long forgotten about.

Arrived to Carcassonne at around 12:30pm.

I have never heard of Carcassonne before in my life. Mentioning this fact to people throughout the tour often yielded a look on their faces, as if implying "this person must be ignorant". To an extent, they'd be right. Apparently, this city, located at the very south of France —close to the Spanish border—is quite famous.

When the name "Carcassonne" is mentioned in the context of tourism, a reference is usually made to Carcassonne's *medieval city* area. When planning for the tour, hotels in the medieval city area turned out to be vastly overpriced, so it was decided to settle for a hotel in Carcassonne's city center.

How bad could it really be, after all? here's a hotel, costs less than half of the common prices in the medieval city area, and it's located right at the city center, steps away from the railway station. Good reviews… can't be *that* bad, can it?

The answer didn't take long to become apparent. Walking from Carcassonne's central railway station towards the hotel, about ten minutes under the mean scorching sun, I didn't see anything that I could possibly relate to positively. Seemed like an old, dusty, grey, boring city center. "No wonder I had never heard of it before", I muttered to myself; and in my head, I already started counting down: as it was a day-off, I was going to spend two nights in this city. Two nights? here? why?

Arrived at the hotel, Hotel Central, located… well… centrally. Carcassonne's city center isn't that big, and the hotel is located on one of the main streets surrounding the city center. The minute I set foot in this place, I was already getting the idea that the stay here wasn't going to be pleasant: essentially a very old building converted to a hotel without really putting much effort into making it comfortable. Up a crooked flight of stairs, and you need to open two doors to get to the room.

What a lousy room. Uneven, carpeted floor—so uneven that you couldn't possibly open the bathroom's door all the way: it would simply get stuck at some point. Only two power sockets in the entire room, one of them located at the very corner of the room, almost hidden, behind the pillow of one of the two sad single beds. Beds? HA. You could feel each and every spring in the mattress separately.

Tiny desk with a crack along its width, making it uneven and thus unsuitable for placing a laptop on. Old metal "chairs" grossly painted purple. And the shower… don't get me started.

In short: it was one of those rooms that motivate you to stay outside the hotel for as long as you can. This room clearly didn't want me there. I grew to dislike that room within a couple of minutes… realizing that I'm going to be spending two nights there.

Two nights.

At least the air conditioning worked well.

As this is France, you really want to get through feeding yourself within the standard French dining hours, or you're in the risk of starving. As we arrived to the hotel just in time for lunch, it was decided to head directly to the city center: it's one thing to be in a miserable hotel room, and a totally other thing to be in a miserable hotel room when you're starving. *TripAdvisor* recommended a place called Le Saint Roch, located in that *La Fontaine de Neptune*—a large square in the heart of the city center, with lots of shops, restaurants and cafes around. Four minutes walk. Good—though not great—food, for affordable prices.

Weather… hot, humid, disastrous. Forecasts called for a storm later on, and you could feel it by the high level of humidity in the air. Walking through the boring streets of Carcassonne's city center felt almost like swimming. The combination of heat and humidity causes tiredness, which is why I headed straight back to the hotel afterwards for a good nap.

While I was twisting and turning in bed, I was sure I heard thunders. Was I dreaming? apparently I wasn't. Later on that afternoon, a thunderstorm hit the area and rain poured. I woke up after it was all over; still light outside, it was decided to go see what's this "Carcassonne medieval city" thing is all about.

It's a short five minutes walk south of the hotel until you get to a large square featuring a huge wheel—no, not a car wheel; an amusement park wheel—so huge that it really seems a bit out of place. Heading east, you come across a bridge.

It doesn't take more than a few meters walk on that bridge to see something magical in the horizon. It appears all of a sudden, and gives you the feeling that you are about to experience something very special. The medieval city is right there in your face, as well as a beautiful pedestrians bridge leading to it.

If you look closely at the river flowing by the city, you'll see that it has a light brown margin. This, actually, is *not* sand: what you see is the meeting of two different waterways—what appears to be sand is actually water (possibly brownish due to high sand content). This is a very peculiar phenomenon to witness.

The medieval city is located upon a hill. Once off the bridge, you enter the lower part of the old city—still not the medieval one.

It's another 10 minutes walk, mostly on an incline, as you get closer to the medieval city's walls.

Beautiful scenery. Shortly after, a flight of stairs leads you into the medieval city, where virtually each and every corner begs for a photograph to be taken.

Decided to have a small dinner at the cafe shown in the last picture: mediocre sandwich. Asked for a baguette with "steak", ended up receiving a dry baguette with two pieces of microwave-thawed hamburgers. Half eaten, half thrown away.

Continued to walk randomly. The medieval city is very small, and the best way to explore it is to simply walk aimlessly in it. As you walk towards the city's surrounding walls and then walk by them, you get fantastic views over the city of Carcassonne and beyond.

Isaac's "Privateering" Tour Blog

Many pictures were taken (as you can see), and quite frankly, it's very hard for me to decide which ones are worthy of posting so I'll just post most of them.

After almost a couple of hours walking in the beautiful medieval city, it was time to head back to the hotel. After thunderstorms, temperatures usually drop but even then, temperatures were too high and humidity was insane—and all energy I gathered during the afternoon nap was gone as if never existed.

One last photograph, walking down the hill away from the medieval city…

Isaac's "Privateering" Tour Blog

... and back to that miserable hotel room. Tried to do some writing but couldn't; the room was *that* depressing. Caught up with all other things happening in the world and then off to bed.

Terrible hotel room... but surprisingly, a good night sleep. Woke up fresh and hungry. The day prior, upon checking in, we were informed that we need to make up our minds about the following day's breakfast in advance, because breakfast is ordered from an external vendor; that's usually a sign that breakfast in the hotel is going to cost you way more than it should, and quality is going to be terrible. Hotel's breakfast was skipped, then, and off we went back to the city center, to that same square, looking for some breakfast.

Found a place offering sandwiches and coffee. Sat in the patio, enjoying the great weather (it was too early for the sun to start burning people around) and watching the people of Carcassonne go about their day. Sitting in that patio was so lovely, that I considered going back to the hotel to bring my laptop so I can do some writing—clearly, I wasn't going to do any writing in that sad hotel room I was staying in.

What else was there to do? no idea. Heading back to the medieval city didn't sound like a good plan: it's a long walk there, meaning that it'd be best to go there a couple of hours before the concert rather than now.

Back to the hotel and decided to just lie down doing nothing. My friend Nelly was already on her way to Carcassonne to attend the concert, and plans were to meet at around 1:00pm to have lunch together. Was good to see Nelly again. Lunch was consumed at the same place as yesterday... back to the hotel for a rest... woke up, checked on what's going on in the world and then got really upset with a particular news item involving Roger Waters and a floating balloon.

At around 5:30pm, Nelly showed up and the group headed together towards the medieval city.

The medieval city, as beautiful as it is, is also extremely touristic. Not only millions of tourists seem to be flocking the medieval city every second of the day, it is evident that some of the medieval city's "charm" was lost as, at times, it appears as if the God of Tourism threw up on the entire area. There are *way* too many shops here, to the point of ridiculous redundancy: you can't swing a cat without hitting two ice cream parlours, three creperies and one fashion store.

> The preceding paragraph should not be considered an encouragement for anyone to swing any cat, for any purpose, either within or outside Carcassonne's medieval city. It's just an expression.
>
> In a related subject, I like cats in much the same way I like most other types of pets, that is—none at all.

After scouring the medieval city for what seemed to be the third or fourth time overall, it was decided to sit down for a pre-concert dinner. In a small square, there were a few restaurants with patios, one of them boasting a sign claiming that their pizzas were ranked #4 in the entire world. Ranked by whom? who knows, who cares. Challenge accepted. Was indeed good, but I wouldn't rank it #4 in any world.

That restaurant also featured two youngsters, male and female, who were sitting side by side at the patio, singing together. The male held a guitar. They were not a good duo: guitar playing was tasteless and their duets just didn't work. At some point, after the performance of a particular song, one of the waitresses told them (in English) "hey, I'm the only one applauding to you". Ouch, but a well-deserved one. That didn't stop them from playing.

As *markknopfler.com* had a few flops this tour already regarding concert start times, it was decided to head to the venue's box office early, grab the tickets and verify the concert's start time.

The venue's setup allowed for reserved seating in the first five or six rows, and general admission seating (first comes first served) elsewhere. Those who bought general admission tickets were already queuing behind the venue's doors, under the brutal sun. The tickets we were going to collect were for the reserved seating section, so there wasn't even a hint of rush there.

As this is France, the box office opened about 20 minutes after its scheduled opening time. People were queued against the box office as well—these were people who were waiting to collect general admission tickets, and wanted to rush towards the entrance's queue as soon as tickets were picked up. What for, really? the entrance's queues were already ridiculously loaded (with people who had their tickets printed at home, or purchased ahead of time).

Tickets collected, show time verified... great. Two more hours to kill. What do you do in a small medieval city that you had already seen four times, and you have two hours to kill?

Of course: you have coffee. Nelly's desire for a sandwich led us all to a small cafe that seemed to have a proper espresso machine in there. Mentioned what I wanted, and went with Nelly to grab a table in the patio, as the Dutchman was put in charge of paying and bringing goods to the table.

Now, just like Italy... I love France, but there are some things that I just don't understand about how they go about doing things. In Paris, for example, I was refused a cappuccino because "it takes too long to make". And now, the Dutchman ended up joining the table holding a wonderful sandwich for Nelly and a paper cup for me.

No espresso-based drink is to be consumed from a paper cup.

I can't stress this enough.

The story? well, apparently they *had* mugs there but "they couldn't use them". Why? who knows. Also, the way that this place makes a cappuccino is add warm milk to "coffee", and add whipped cream on top. Without whipped cream, they call it "cafe au lait"—which means "coffee with milk" in French. Which is really what I got, except that I didn't ask for it (a cappuccino is made with steamed milk).

The end result was something that failed to please any sense. But what can you do, really? you're in the middle of one of the most touristic places in France; would you start explaining to idiots how to make a proper cup? no. You just bite the bullet and leave; which is what I did.

Another round in the medieval city and I already had it. Yes, it's nice and beautiful, but there's a limit to how many times I can walk through it. Headed to the venue, with plenty of time left for the concert to start.

The venue, Théâtre Jean Deschamps, is a theater located inside the medieval city. The theater wasn't there in medieval times: it was built in 1908, on the ruins of a monastery. The venue is used to host an annual summer festival.

As I was completely stunned with the Ancient Theater of Taormina—to the point that I nominated it as the best outdoors venue I had ever been to in Europe—some claimed that I should hold my horses and not rush to determining such things before seeing the Théâtre Jean Deschamps; therefore, I was rather curious to see what this place is all about. I found it hard to believe that anything could beat Taormina's ancient theater's stunning setting, but was willing to give it a chance.

No doubt, this is a tasty looking venue. The sight of the medieval walls around clearly gives you the feeling as if you were stepping back in time.

Impressive, yes, but… still. Taormina's ancient theatre is in a different league altogether.

Can't complain much, really. The Théâtre Jean Deschamps is of the most beautiful ones out there.

The French audience is known for its vicious *Running of the Bulls* sessions, but no bulls were to run anywhere this time. The distance between the front row and the stage was less than one meter: I could lean my feat against the stage and my knees would still be bent.

The stage was low as well, enabling excellent view of the performance.

The concert started on time, and the French audience didn't let anybody down—loud cheers, as usual here. Good concert, well-enjoyed.

Speedway at Nazareth was skipped this time. Nelly, seated somewhere at the sixth row, quickly made her way to the front and took advantage of the best seat in the house: my lap. Some things, I guess, I'm not trained to say "no" to. It was, after all, the last concert for Nelly to attend this tour around, so it was prudent to ensure that she ends her part of the tour on a high note… and watching the performance from the front row was an added bonus.

Concert ended and it took the audience forever to leave through the exits. Two other ladies from the USA joined us for a walk back to the city center, which took longer than anticipated as the medieval city looks beautiful at night.

Back to the city center…

… and once at the room, I decided to take a shower after this long, hot, humid day. Waited a few minutes in the shower for the water to warm up—nada. Cold water.

What a lousy hotel; easily nominated to be of the worst hotels for the tour so far.

Sleep.

July 25, woke up very early for the last early morning travel itinerary for the tour: depart Carcassonne 6:47am, arrive Narbonne 7:19am; depart Narbonne 8:23am, arrive Barcelona 11:48am. Five hours of travel over two trains. There were other routes available, but they all included a large number of connections; when planning for the tour, it was decided to keep things simple and just bite the early morning bullet.

Walked like a zombie towards Carcassonne's central railway station. Took a small detour to see if there's anything open in the city center to grab some breakfast from—nada. Headed to the station, waited patiently for the train, boarded… good.

Short ride, about half an hour, and arrived to Narbonne. Narbonne? yes, Narbonne. Have I ever heard about it before? no, I didn't. But there I was, 7:20am in a railway station in the middle of nowhere, seeking breakfast. Surprisingly, there was a restaurant inside the station offering all sorts of goods. Took a sandwich and was glad to receive a mug that seemed to contain a proper cappuccino... until I tasted it.

That was, I'm pretty sure, <u>one of the worst cup of coffee I have ever had</u>—not only in France, but anywhere. It was so terrible I wanted to spit it out and vomit at the same time. Whoever serves such coffee should be tried at The Hague for war crimes. Hey Frenchies, what the hell is your problem with coffee? how can you be so brilliant, coming up with all sorts of amazing foods, but you just keep screwing coffee up?

Of course, very little can be done to ruin a morning further once it was ruined by a disgusting beverage. Kept sitting in that restaurant, killing time. Finally, it was time to head to the platform to get the connecting train.

Cabin's door open, a mature couple boarded ahead of me. Now, they were trying to fit a large suitcase—one of a few that they were carrying—into the coach's luggage rack, without success. They kept trying, and as the luggage rack was located right at the entrance to the cabin, others couldn't board.

And they kept trying and retrying, for about a minute.

I was already inside the train, at the entrance (waiting for the couple to be done with their luggage limbo), and so was the Dutchman; others, however, were still on the platform. A staff worker called me and gestured that I should move forward; I pointed at the couple (who were still trying to shove that suitcase in), gesturing back that I am myself stuck and can't really do anything. I wasn't in the mood to start arguing with people—not even to ask these people to move away and let others board. The Dutchman, however, took a different approach and informed the selfish couple that there were people trying to board. Only then, the Royal Couple remembered that they're not the only passengers on that train, and cleared the way.

Train went on its way... and I realized that I won't be visiting France again this tour. Moreover, I realized that I'm entering Spain, and will remain there until the end of the tour.

Spain.

Distant, sour memories from the last tour crept in. I "vividly" recall the Spanish leg of the 2010 Get Lucky tour as being the hardest of them all: tough travel, insane heat, and inability to eat properly as the Spanish, like the French, have their own dining hours. I also remember being very close to a breakdown when <u>my luggage was lost en route to Santiago de Compostela</u>. And that <u>bus ride to Córdoba</u>...

I went through hell in Spain in the last tour, which explains why I started feeling anxious during the train ride to Barcelona. Yet, I had hope.

Please, Spain; I come in peace. I'm ready to make amends. Let's work on our relationship together.

Half an hour delay along the way, and finally made it to Barcelona's main railway station, <u>Barcelona Sants</u>.

Barcelona Sants is a big station, serving as a hub to many train services in Spain; and just as big and central this station is, it is also inefficient way beyond the point of ridicule.

Just to give you an example of how stupidly things are done here: for train reservations and ticketing, there are about 20 different counters. The counters are grouped as follows:

- First group of counters serves passengers who are interested to buy a ticket to a train leaving "soon". What is "soon"? well, I couldn't find an answer to this question by looking at any sign, either because this information wasn't available on any sign or because the information wasn't available in English.

- Second group of counters serves passengers who are interested in "advance purchase" *for long-distance trains only*; I suppose that "advance purchase" pertains to trains that are not leaving "soon" (see bullet above). Also, it raises the question: what constitutes "long-distance trains"? is this some sort of elementary knowledge that tourists are supposed to already know?

- Third group of counters serves passengers who are interested in buying tickets for *medium-distance trains only*.

Now: for the first and third groups of counters, you have to wait in line: that is, physically stand in a line-up—a separate line-up per group of counters. For the second group of counters, *you need to take a number*: standing doesn't really grant you any precedence.

In other words: if you're a tourist, new to Barcelona or to Spain in general, and you can't communicate in Spanish—good luck trying to figure things out. Such a scheme is so inefficient, that the very thought that there are people out there who deem this "acceptable" makes me not want to belong in this planet anymore.

> You don't need to be a genius in mathematics, or have any background in the mathematics branch of <u>queuing theory</u> (indeed, there is a branch in mathematics that deals specifically with queues, how they're formed and what's the best way to manage them) to realize that they way ticket reservations are executed in Barcelona Sants makes absolutely no sense at all. It's just ridiculously inefficient.
>
> Then again... just like in France... some cultures are perfectly fine with inefficiencies. "That's how it is, so shut the hell up". They prefer the familiar disorganization over any sort of change. Disorganization and inefficiencies don't bother them enough to trigger a drive for change for the better. How can that be? beats the hell out of me.
>
> Really, hats off to all those who are capable of subjecting themselves to such a lifestyle. Shows a lot of mental strength; I'd lose my sanity in such a place a million times over already.

Luckily, <u>I already suffered in this station before</u> so I had some background knowledge about how to find my way around. We had to do some travel arrangements:

- Reserve seats for travel from Madrid to Gijón, as these seats couldn't be purchased anywhere else, *including Renfe's website* (*Renfe* is the name of the Spanish railway company. Don't even get me started talking about their website: complete and total garbage); and
- Buy a train ticket for Ingrid, who decided, as a last minute thing, to catch the concerts in Madrid and Malaga.

Took a number... #444. Counters currently serving #340 or something. Great. 100 people in front of us. What do you do? you use the time efficiently, to simplify your life later:

- Find the metro route to the hotel.
- Find the actual entrance to the metro system.
- Calculate whether metro day passes should be purchased, rather than individual tickets.
- Figure out how to use the metro's ticketing machines.

> Oh, ticketing machines. Here's another example why Barcelona Sants is a stupid, obnoxious railway station: this station serves many types of regional trains, and each such regional train system carries its own ticket format. Now, in an efficient culture, you'd expect someone to come up with the bright idea of constructing a machine that will simply *ask you* what train you'd like to take, where from and where to—and will simply print a ticket for you. Simple, easy. Right?
>
> Right. I mean—right, unless you're in Spain. Over-complicating things is key. *Each train system has its own type of ticket and is served by its own type of machine.*
>
> And if you thought that wasn't enough... there's a particular regional train system called *Rodalies*, offering many stations labelled as *R1, R2, R3* and so forth. Now, as it turns out, there are *two types of ticketing machines* to purchase tickets for the *Rodalies* system: one type serves all "R" trains except for a few, and the other type of machine serves those few remaining "R" trains. Why? I don't know, just thinking about it makes me want to cry.
>
> Of course, there's a sign nearby telling you all of that, including how to distinguish between the two types of machines (which are very similar, externally)...
>
> ... and the sign is in Spanish only.

The time it took to do all of the above was enough to get us about 50–60 people closer to the start of the line. Another 20 minutes wait and finally, #444 came up on the screen and two travellers found themselves storming towards the counter.

Thought the mess was over? think again. Now came the language barrier between the traveller and the staff. Asking for 1st class seats for the train from Madrid to Gijón, we were told that the train we were asking for—pretty much the only train we could take in order to keep the schedule manageable—was full. It was rather unbelievable, and upon inquiring again, the guy simply turned his computer screen at us to demonstrate. It was in Spanish, but even I could notice that there are still seats available. Turned out that, somehow, he neglected to hear the expression "1st class"; 2nd class cabins were indeed full.

What a relief.

Ticket for Ingrid—done, and then decided to have lunch right in the station. A nice buffet-style restaurant provided acceptable food for acceptable prices. That done, went to the metro; a few stops to the *Catalunya* station, located in Barcelona's famous *La Rambla*, and then a few minutes walk to the hotel for the night, Hotel Turin.

I have been to Barcelona before, during the 2010 Get Lucky tour: not only was I in Barcelona for the concert back then, but I also chose to spend a few days in Barcelona *after* the tour to unwind. During those few post-tour days, I have seen much of Barcelona; thus, I really wasn't too enthusiastic about seeing it again. At a glance, it seemed as if nothing was different in *La Rambla*: still, piles over piles of tourists, street merchants selling nonsense... very crowded. As it was close to 3:00pm, weather was hitting hard, and Barcelona being located on the shore of the Mediterranean Sea, humidity kicked in pushing weather further up the ladder of intolerability. Altogether, that didn't provide for much motivation to see much of the city anyway.

Checked into the hotel—brilliant room, compensating for the ugly room I was forced to spend two nights in while in Carcassonne—and decided that the best place for me in Barcelona would be to stay in that room for as long as possible. This plan, of doing nothing, was carried out perfectly: didn't even bother to leave the hotel until it was time to get some pre-concert dinner.

The venue, Poble Espanyol, was located about half an hour by foot from the hotel... hand half an hour by public transit. Walking it is, then. Half an hour later, arrived at the venue, sweaty, sticky, thirsty... as sweaty, sticky and thirsty that half an hour walk through insane humidity could turn you.

The venue was already full when I got there, about 30 minutes before the concert's scheduled start time. It's a beautiful venue: "Poble Espanyol" means "Spanish Town", and the goal behind its design was to aggregate various Spanish architectural styles in one location. It was constructed in 1929 and was kept, ever since, as a museum.

The venue, shaped as a square, is surrounded by many shops, mostly restaurants and cafes, most of which were very active well into the concert. I spent my time watching the concert from the very back, often walking around the venue to get a sense of the atmosphere here—and didn't even begin to think about the mere possibility of even *trying* to find a way to the front: it was very crowded, and audiences in Spain are a tad crazier than their French and Italian counterparts: an "excuse me" isn't likely to grant you access anywhere.

Concert ended around midnight. Watched the encore while standing close to the exit, as I predicted that leaving the venue with the masses would be a terrible experience. Less than half an hour walk back to the hotel, and the streets of Barcelona appeared rather active: cafes and bars open all over the place. It's a city that seems to rarely be sleeping, much like Tel Aviv (although Tel Aviv, really, *never* sleeps).

I, on the contrary, prefer to be sleeping as much as possible nowadays. Up to the hotel and was very happy to call it a night.

Signing off this post while on board the train from Madrid to Malaga. I'm a little behind with posting, but tomorrow will be a great opportunity to catch up with everything: the longest train travel day in the tour, crossing Spain from south to north, about 11 hours of travel.

Isaac

Monday, July 29, 2013

Barcelona to Madrid to Málaga, Spain (July 26-27, 2013)

During the 2010 Get Lucky tour, the tough travel in Spain—then, also, the last leg of the tour—was a major contributor to my exhaustion and my inability to enjoy anything in this interesting, wild country. This tour, however, travel in Spain is (at least planned to be) relatively easy. The rest of Europe—the convenience of travel in Germany; the total and utter awesomeness of Switzerland; the drama of Italy; the passionate nonchalance of France—is behind me: time to face Spain again and try to make amends.

The first all-Spain travel was an easy one: depart Barcelona 11:00am, arrive Madrid 1:45pm. Less than two hours of train travel, one single train ride, although in 2nd class (for some reason, 1st class seats weren't available for reservation for this particular train).

Nothing to rush for whatsoever in the morning of July 26. Woke up late, headed for a good breakfast at the hotel—the standard for hotel-provided breakfasts in Spain is very good; almost as good as Italy's and far, far better than France's—and then off to the nearby metro. A few stations and there's Barcelona Sants again: all travel arrangements done already, it was good to know that I don't have to deal with inefficiencies here. Baggage up on the conveyor belt for security check and boarded the train.

> I am not sure whether this applies to high-speed trains or all trains in Spain, but at least for the high-speed ones, boarding these trains isn't as simple as it is in other countries. Just to enter the platforms' area, you need to have your ticket checked and scanned, and then put your luggage through an X-ray machine, much like in an airport. Once done, you enter the departures area; and before boarding the train, you have your ticket checked and scanned once again.
>
> Once on the train, though, there is no ticket inspections.

The train ride between Barcelona and Madrid is scenic, however not scenic in the "Switzerland way": you won't see great snow-covered mountains and turquoise lakes. Instead, you'll see endless ranges of hills with patches of green, occasionally dotted by very small communities.

Arrived in Madrid's Puerta de Atocha station on time. This train station is the largest one in Madrid—took 15 minutes walk just to get to the exit. Sorry, erase that: not "the" exit. "An" exit. Somehow found myself walking in the station's top floor, and from there, I discovered (by complete accident) a flight of stairs leading all the way down to the street level. That was fine: the hotel for the night, AC Hotel Atocha, was located two minutes walk from that side exit. The area itself didn't seem to be very exciting, featuring many old buildings and shops, but the hotel looked like some sort of a modern blob in that landscape.

So, this hotel is a part of the Marriott chain, and its ridiculously low price (comparing to other Marriott hotels and considering its quality) leads me to believe that something is not quite right in Spain's tourism industry. One of the best hotel rooms in the tour: modern design, spotless, has everything you need in it, all looking brand new.

The best thing about this room was, though, the shower: it was a "rain shower" installed directly on the ceiling and pouring massive amounts of water on whoever is the lucky individual standing beneath it.

The worst thing about this room was the shower's door, which was almost entirely transparent.

> I ran into more than a few oddities with hotel rooms during this tour, as well as past ones. You can easily tell a "designer hotel" when you step into one. Hotels compete with each other on many parameters, including rooms' design, which leads a few designers to take some interesting decisions.
>
> A transparent shower door may be a good fit for a couple, but makes things tricky when two unrelated individuals share a room.
>
> As odd as the transparent shower door was, nothing beats what we came up with while planning this tour. It was a *CitizenM* hotel but I can't remember in which city; it featured a shower located *right in the middle of the room*, of course with completely transparent doors. *CitizenM* dubs itself a "boutique hotel chain", but I'd say that a shower located right in the middle of the room is a bit too "boutique" for me.

Madrid is an interesting city. I was here before during the 2010 Get Lucky tour, and back then, didn't even have time to see much of what this city has to offer, but from what I *did* get to see, I got the impression that it was but the tip of the iceberg. A reader of this blog, a nice fellow by the name Alberto, was kind enough to suggest a guided trip through Madrid's best sights; unfortunately, I was way too tired and too irritable and decided it'd be best (mostly for others) if I just disconnect for a while and chill out in the hotel room for as long as humanly possible.

As this is Spain, and my memories of Spain consist mostly of being starving to death, lunch seemed like a great idea. A quick search in *TripAdvisor*, cross-referenced with a recommendation by the hotel's receptionist, led to a place called Bodegas Rosell, conveniently located right by the train station and less than one minute walk from the hotel. It is a family-run business that dates way back, and is frequented by locals and foreigners alike.

I am almost ashamed to admit that, until this visit to Madrid, I have never before had tapas in Spain—including the two weeks I spent in Spain during the 2010 Get Lucky tour. Sounds ridiculous, I know.

> Not a first for me. In 2003, I went for a short trip to Nova Scotia, exploring the stunning Cape Breton Island. I stopped by one of the restaurants there, best known for serving fantastic lobsters pulled out of the ocean right behind that restaurant. I still remember the waitress' stunned look when I asked for a chicken sandwich.

Well, as I said: this time, I'm making amends with Spain. Just opened the menu, and without much consideration, the Dutchman and I just started shooting names of tapas at the waiter. The end result: a wonderful tapas meal. I almost cried: *I'm in Spain and I'm eating properly.* I thought this moment will never come.

Great food consumed, and back to the hotel. This hotel happens to only offer free Wi-Fi in the lobby, and charge ridiculous amounts for in-room connectivity. Being the hotel's lobby such a peaceful, beautiful and comfortable place to sit in, I didn't mind taking the entire pile of electronics downstairs, park my rear end in one of the couches, write and catch up.

Hours went by; at around 8:30pm, dropped all electronics at the hotel room and the journey to the venue started. To get to the venue from the central railway station, two metro lines were needed—approximately 20 minutes of travel.

Needed to buy a couple of metro tickets. Once again, confusing user interface of these damn machines, but it was worth it just to see that "insert more need" label—showing just how seriously people here take translation to English in *the biggest railway station in Spain's capital city*.

I love these things… the laughter helped the metro ride pass quicker. About 20 minutes later, arrived at the *Ventas* station, named (I suppose) after one of the most beautiful buildings I had seen in Spain: the Plaza de Toros de Las Ventas—one of the most famous bullrings in Spain, which happened to be the concert's venue.

The exterior of this building, which dates back to 1929, is staggeringly beautiful. You can't possibly look at it and remain apathetic to its immense beauty.

As if out of nowhere, my dear friend Ingrid just showed up at the square just facing the bullring. Ingrid drove back home to The Netherlands the morning after the concert in Saint-Julien-en-Genevois—a distance of just under 900km, mind you—and flew to Madrid to catch a couple of concerts in Spain. Where she summons this energy from—I have no clue.

Hugs, kisses… and then Alberto (who had offered the guided tour in Madrid earlier) came by and introduced himself. Good to meet nice people along the way, always. Tickets collected and we all went inside.

The interior of this bullring is as tantalizingly beautiful as its exterior. As the evening falls, the strong lights positioned along the bullring's perimeter shine with the light of two million suns, and looking around, you feel that you're a part of something powerful.

Well, as "powerful" as bullfighting can be. Senseless "sport". I wish all other Spanish provinces follow Catalonia and ban this savage practice altogether.

I was seated at the floor, although I think I would have preferred watching the performance from somewhere high up on the terraces. However, as I arrived at the venue late, there was virtually no chance to catch a good spot on the terrace.

The concert started, as usual, accompanied by deafening cheers. This band is very popular in Spain, and Knopfler's Spanish audience has traditionally been exceptionally loud. People here were jumping in the air, screaming, dancing in their seats... an entire party. This is Spain, and that's how I remembered it from the last tour: things get very loud here, and when it happens in such a large, immense venue such as Las Ventas, you can't distance yourself from the excitement: you're a part of it, because it's all the way around you.

For *Gator Blood*, Mark uses a white Fender Stratocaster tuned for Open G. Incidentally, right before playing *Gator Blood*, the audience decided that it's time for the traditional "o-e-o-e-o-e-o-o" chant. Usually, Mark joins the chant by playing it on guitar; however, I'm led to believe that, this time in Madrid, was the first time he was "required" to do so using an Open G-tuned guitar. Not sure whether he expected it or not, but it did take a few moments until he figured out what's the best way to go about doing so. The slide used for *Gator Blood* was incorporated to the performance as well.

Half way into *Telegraph Road*, the *Running of the Bulls* commenced: people seated at the floor charged at the stage in full power. That run, practiced in most western European countries when Knopfler is in town, can get messy in France and Italy, but in Spain... it takes on a different level altogether. I waited until the entire run was over and only then dared getting up from my seat... only to find myself a few meters away from the stage. Things got really crowded around, and *Telegraph Road*'s outro solo didn't do much to calm things down. People were screaming, yelling and shouting recklessly—at each other, at the band, at the venue... at everything that can absorb noise. I think the audience in Madrid was of the louder so far this tour, if not the loudest.

Concert ended after a good encore, featuring two billion people raising cameras, phones and iPads up in the air recording the show and distracting everyone else's view. One particularly obnoxious individual recorded the entire performance of *So Far Away* with his phone, while obstructing others... and was cheeky enough to ask someone standing in front of him to lower his own camera. Brilliant.

Didn't take the venue much time to become devoid of people once the concert was over. Alberto was kind enough to give the three of us a ride back to our hotel, saving us an awful lot of time and effort. Thanks Alberto.

Up to the room and got a good night sleep.

July 27. Woke up in the morning, breakfast at the hotel and the three of us—Ingrid, the Dutchman and myself—went on our way. A short walk from the hotel to the central railway station. Itinerary: leave Madrid 9:35am, arrive Málaga 12:17pm. Piece of cake.

Arrived Málaga right on time, and for the first time this tour, didn't even have to leave the railway station to get to the hotel. The hotel for the night, Barcelo Málaga, is ranked by *TripAdvisor* as one of the best hotels in the city and is attached to the railway station: from the station, you enter the hotel through a couple of glass doors.

Long line-up to check in. Finally, my turn. I approached His Highness, Lord of the Keys, and handed my driver's license over.

Most hotels I have been to in Europe suffice with any government-issued ID for identification purposes, even when issued by foreign governments. Some hotels, however, require a passport if you're a foreigner.

The receptionist turned to me.

– "Thank you. Can I please see some ID, like a passport or any other document...?"

I looked at the counter. My driver's license was still there. I repeated the receptionist's question in my head, trying to see where it was exactly that we lost each other.

– "Here is my ID, right there", I said, pointing at my ID.

– "No... a driver's license is not good... no driver's license, no other card... only passport."

Inconsistencies bother me almost as much as inefficiencies do.

– "Oh, I understand. So you're saying that I can show some ID, like a passport or *any other document*, but not a driver's license, not anything else other than a passport", I blurted out in what was probably the most condescending tone I ever had the displeasure to emit out of my mouth.

He didn't seem to be too impressed with my tone. Admittedly, I agree with him: my tone was so condescending and sarcastic, that for a moment afterwards, I wanted to punch myself in the face.

While checking in, I noticed the following digital sign:

I think I mentioned before that, once a heat wave hit Europe about a month ago, we did some adjustments to our itinerary to ensure that all hotels we stay in provide air conditioning. So far this tour, I heard many strange excuses and restrictions regarding air conditioning: a hotel in Malta claimed that it charges €5 per six hours of air conditioning; some hotels indeed offered air conditioning — for certain periods in the year.

These, of course, aren't things that you can predict: when a hotel reservation mentions that air conditioning is provided in the room, you sort of take it for granted that you'll be able to... well... condition the room's air.

This hotel, though, came up with a scheme that I could have never predicted: air conditioning would work only at times when the outside temperature is over 26°C; heating (in the winter) would work only at times when the outside temperature is less than 21°C.

I find it disconcerting that even air conditioning in hotels is now subject to fine prints of all sorts.

I have never been to Málaga before, however I surely did hear about it: in Europe and beyond, Málaga is known for its beautiful beaches and "resort town" atmosphere. An ultra-popular sun destination, Málaga attracts visitors from all over — especially from western Europe — as its climate provides for a relatively warm winter (average daytime temperature between December and February is around 17–18°C). The sun shines here for around 300 days every year.

Stuff left at the room and the trio headed out for lunch. The central railway station in Málaga isn't quite located in the most interesting area of the city; with the aid of *TripAdvisor*, a place by the name Asador Iñaki came up, located a couple of minutes walk from the hotel.

Started walking, and the area didn't quite bode well with me. Upon arrival to the place, I took a look around and determined that, has it not been for *TripAdvisor*, I'd probably shy away from a place like this: it doesn't look too attractive or too inviting. Shady, dodgy surroundings tend to give me the creeps, and admittedly, living in British Columbia did turn me to be snobbier than I already was.

Gave this place a chance anyway, and it paid off. What a wonderful meal. This place is in the business of grilling: beef, chicken, pork, seafood, snails... you name it — it's there. They'll grill a shoe for you if you ask them nicely. Huge portions, delicious food, fantastic service. When we arrived, the place was empty; 20 minutes later, it was almost entirely full.

Back to the hotel and took a long, *long* nap. Nothing like 2–3 hours of a good afternoon sleep to recharge batteries. Up like a tiger, and decided to head where "normal" people head to while in this city, namely — the beach.

It's about 25 minutes walk from the hotel to the beach area. On your way to the beach (walking west to east), you walk by the harbour — also a popular area for drinks and snacks, especially for tourists or those who are tired of the beach scene located right behind the harbour.

About an hour killed just sitting down for a drink overlooking the harbour, and it was decided to head to the venue to grab the tickets and return to the beach later. The concert in Málaga was a general admission concert offering an early entry privilege for *markknopfler.com* ticket holders, but none of us was going to take advantage of it: the beach seemed like a more appropriate place to pass the time, than waiting hours inside a bullring for the concert to start. Still, we decided to get through with ticket pickup as soon as possible, to avoid stress later on.

The venue, Plaza de Toros de La Malagueta, is Málaga's bullring. It is located very close to the beach, a short distance from the city's main touristic areas.

Ticket collection took a while, about half an hour; that done, returned immediately to the beach, looking for a place to sit down, unwind, grab a pre-concert dinner, and then unwind again.

As it was evening—past 8:00pm already—the beach was almost entirely devoid of noisy tourists. Weather was perfect. Heck, everything was perfect. About two hours spent there in total and complete relaxation.

At around 10:00pm, another friend joined and we all headed back to the venue.

Upon arrival, it turned out that we had to split: two of us had to go to the floor, and the Dutchman and myself had to look for a place to sit somewhere on the terrace (unmarked seats; the entire venue was general admission). That was somewhat disappointing as we wanted to stay as a group; attempts to persuade the venue's staff to allow us to join our friends at the floor went unsuccessful, even though there was plenty of space at the left hand side of the stage.

Had no choice but to look for a place to sit. As it was close to show time already, all reasonable seating locations were already occupied. Standing was forbidden, so we were asked to walk all the way to the side, as that was the only place where seats were actually available. We were kicked out from one entrance to the next, until luck struck and we came across a couple of cool staff members who seemed to be OK with us just standing there. Not bad: high up in the bullring, a bit left of the center.

Concert started at 10:30pm, as scheduled: the latest start time for a concert in this tour. Again, exceptionally loud audience. The concert experience itself was great—seated high up (at some point, I just got tired of standing so I sat down on the floor), perfect weather, cool breeze. What else do you need, really?

Concert ended close to 12:30am and I thanked the universe for my decision to get an afternoon sleep. Out of the venue, and got a taxi back to the hotel.

As this was the last concert this tour for Ingrid to attend, drinks were in order. A good mojito from the hotel's bar, enjoyed at the patio —not before Ingrid decided to take advantage of the slide that the hotel so cleverly positioned between the first floor and the ground floor, heading directly to the bar.

Bidding Ingrid goodbye was a royal pain in the butt. Some of the best moments in this tour so far were spent with Ingrid nearby—you can't go wrong with this wonderful woman around. The more time spent in her vicinity, the more I learned to admire her—a remarkable persona with a charming personality and a golden heart. Hats off to Ingrid for wonderful times spent together, as well as for her much appreciated help along the way.

1:30am… time to bed. Last goodbye to Ingrid, elevator up, quick shower and off to bed after a fantastic day.

Signing off this post from my hotel room in Gijón. Wasn't the easiest day today: it was the last train day for the tour—12 hours over two trains from Spain's southern tip to its northern one. Truly knackered, folks. 2:30am now, time for bed.

Isaac

Wednesday, July 31, 2013

Málaga to Gijón to San Sebastián, Spain (July 28-30, 2013)

After a few days of easy travel in Spain (I never thought I'll be writing the words "easy" and "Spain" in the same sentence), there came the time for the grand finale: the longest train-travel day in the entire tour, which, coincidentally, was also the *last* train-travel day in the tour.

The (planned; we'll get to that soon) itinerary: depart Málaga 9:00am, arrive Madrid's Puerta de Atocha station 11:50am; take the Cercanías (commuter train) to Madrid's Chamartín station; depart Madrid Chamartín 2:40am, arrive Gijón 8:15pm.

That's ten hours and a quarter overall travel, over three trains. Long travel day, crossing Spain from its southern tip to its northern one. The two main train rides involved are high-speed trains, but the ride from Madrid to Gijón has very slow sections in it due to northern Spain's terrain.

> Feel like having another taste of how difficult it was, at times, to plan for following this tour? buckle your seatbelts.
>
> The very last train ride for the tour—from Madrid to Gijón—was also the hardest one to plan (the Málaga-Madrid leg was planned for and purchased in advance). When planning the tour's itinerary, Deutsche Bahn's website showed that a train indeed exists from Madrid Puerta de Atocha to Gijón, leaving 1:55pm. Hence, the schedule should have been very simple: no need to take the Cercanías from one station in Madrid to another.
>
> However, for whatever reason, that particular train ride couldn't be purchased through Germany's railway company (through Deutsche Bahn, you can book train tickets virtually anywhere in Europe). Also, it couldn't be booked through Renfe's website (*Renfe* is the umbrella company for Spain's railway carriers). The meaning was simple: you must be present on Spanish soil in order to purchase that train ticket.
>
> That particular train ride was a shining red light in the tour's plan. Maybe at some point I'll share with you a glimpse of the *Google Docs*-based itinerary we had prepared—I consider that spreadsheet a pure mastery; for now, let me just tell you that it was full of green-coloured cells implying "purchased & confirmed", but that one last ride was painted red, implying "to be done". Neither myself nor the Dutchman are fans of things that are "to be done": I am allergic to procrastination, and that one red-painted cell felt like a pain in the butt.
>
> That's why, as soon as we arrived at Barcelona, it was decided to get this thing over with (see the post telling the Barcelona story). Even *that* wasn't simple. As we asked for the reservation to be made, we were told that the train doesn't leave from Madrid's Puerta de Atocha station, but from Chamartín instead, at 2:40pm; we were instructed to take the commuter train between the two stations in Madrid. We tried explaining to the attendant that we had seen, online, that that it's possible to board this train in Puerta de Atocha; unfortunately, the language barrier was too high for him to even listen.

Back to July 28. Woke up at around 7:30am, packed and went downstairs for breakfast. The previous night was a late one, went to sleep close to 2:00am after having farewell drinks with dear Ingrid, so I didn't really wake up: I was half asleep when I approached the elevator. Door opened, we both went inside. By the elevator's door, there were two couples who were obviously very vocal and even more obviously drunk. At the last moment, they decided to take the same elevator down.

Few things beat spending some time in an elevator with two drunk, vocal couples at 8:00am, before you're even fully awake. Don't exactly know who stunk from alcohol more, I think it was the ladies—who were, by the way, not really dressed for breakfast: it seemed like they all just got back from some sort of a party.

Ate breakfast like some sort of a robot, often glancing at the drunk foursome who continued their vocal "conversation" in a table nearby. Breakfast done, up to the room, chilled out for a few more minutes and then embarked on the remarkably difficult journey to the train station, consisting of taking the elevator down and going through one set of doors.

> It was worth it to spend the night in a hotel located right at the railway station, even though it was very far from anything that's interesting in Málaga. Obviously, I'd prefer to stay closer to the beach, but when you're following a tour, other logistical factors take precedence: the distance from the beach to the railway station is more than 2km, and nobody had any intention walking such distance so early in the morning.

Arrived to Madrid's Puerta de Atocha, and decided to be enterprising: how about asking on-site staff whether it's possible to board the next train in this station, instead of taking the commuter train to the other one?

Approached the platform and asked the attendant, who then delegated to her colleague. Well, what do you know: yes, it *was* possible to board that train in this station.

Just think how ridiculous this is: Deutsche Bahn, which is the railway company of a different country altogether, is more knowledgeable in Spanish railway schedules *than an attendant working in Barcelona Sants, one of the largest, most prominent train stations in Spain.*

Why did the attendant in Barcelona not know about it? I have no clue. Anyway, these were good news: no need to take that intermediate train travel.

Knowing that the ride was going to be a long one, it was decided to head out of the station and look for lunch. Unfortunately, restaurants appeared to be closed: not surprising as it was a Sunday, around noon time. Went back to the station, found a restaurant. How good can a restaurant, located inside a train station, be? I don't have good history with such restaurants and the one in Madrid wasn't an exception. Cheap food that made no sense, but was enough to keep the body going. Killed some more time in the station, and then boarded the train —each of us boarding to a different coach (it was impossible to even explain to that Barcelona Sants attendant that we're looking for two adjacent seats).

Last train ride for the tour… what a strange feeling. I still remember having my EURail pass stamped in Milano Centrale, as soon as I arrived there from Milano's airport, arriving from Belgrade. When the *hell* was that? WOW. Almost three months ago. THREE MONTHS. Back then, the end of the tour seemed inconceivably distant: and now, there I am, boarding the last train for this tour.

All and all, using trains in Europe was more of a positive experience than a negative one. Not much seemed to have changed since I last used it extensively, back in the 2010 Get Lucky tour: same inefficiencies in the same countries, lack of integration… that's the empty half of the glass. The full half of the glass is that Europe actually *does* have a working, functioning railway system. It'll take ages before such a developed railway system will be implemented in North America. I suppose we, North Americans, are bound to continue using cars as the primary method of transportation for the next little while.

I had many plans for this long train ride, including doing some writing and slowly clear items off my post-tour to-do list. Unfortunately, this particular train didn't offer power sockets, and my dying laptop battery was enough for a little over two hours. Tried to pass the time playing online chess with a friend, but the ride went through so many tunnels and so many desolate places with no cellular reception, that I eventually got fed up with the intermittent connectivity and just sat in my chair doing nothing but thinking.

The ride itself was stunning. At first, it was just more of the same—lots of hills with plenty of trees and small villages; however, once you get north—at around León, the terrain changes dramatically, offering spectacular natural views rivalling those of, say, Switzerland— although the landscape itself is different. No snow-peaked mountains here (at least not in late July), and not too many lakes, but the rugged green ridges here are nothing short of awesome.

Northern Spain, in that regards, is drastically different than the south and the center. That wasn't all that new to me: I travelled to northern Spain before, during the 2010 Get Lucky tour, as that tour had a stop in Bilbao. I remember similar spectacular views when taking the train from Madrid to Bilbao back then, often not believing that I'm still in the same country.

Unfortunately, though, I was so busy thinking of all sorts of things; the type of thoughts that really don't motivate you to do anything, but to the contrary. Therefore, I didn't even take one single photograph in the entire ride. The Dutchman, however, did; but these turned out very bad due to reflection.

Looked at the time: it's close to 8:00pm already. Fired up *Google Maps* to see where the train is and how long it should take to get to the destination… not even close. It was close to 9:00pm—approximately 45 minutes behind schedule—when the train finally stopped in Gijón. Door opened. I looked around me. Took a last look at the train's cabin, realizing that I won't be riding any train anymore this tour. As always when I leave a train, I went through a list of important items in my head to ensure that I *know* that they're with me: laptop? here. Passport? here. Train pass? here, *and I won't be needing it anymore.*

Left the train, onto the platform and out of the station.

Like many other cities visited over the last few months, I have never heard of Gijón before. The city's name is pronounced *he-hon*, and it's located at Spain's very north.

The hotel for the next couple of nights, Silken Ciudad Gijón, is adjacent to the railway station, and both aren't quite located in the city center. It wasn't the original hotel pick: the reservation for the original hotel—don't remember its name—had to be cancelled once it turned out that it doesn't offer air conditioning.

Even though the entire day consisted of sitting inside a train, I was extremely tired upon arrival at the hotel. It was still light outside, but I decided that that's it for me for the day: going to get something to eat, then call it an early night. Not being quite in the mood to do research about restaurants, the hotel's restaurant had to do. Overpriced burger, some of which was rare (not the biggest fan of that), went upstairs, shower and bed.

The next morning I woke up with all intentions to have breakfast and go out to see the city. A few readers living in Spain mentioned that the city is pretty, as well as its beaches and its harbour. Somehow, though, I got carried away into doing other things. Kept looking at the clock, thinking what time I should be leaving in order to get some sightseeing time, and kept postponing it. I guess that, at some level, I wasn't too interested.

On my way to meet the Dutchman for lunch, about a kilometer away from the hotel, I took a few looks around and couldn't quite believe that I'm in Spain. Contrary to other places I had seen before in Spain, Gijón is spacious, clean and has a "laid back" feel to it. This city "feels" much more like a small Canadian town than a Spanish one, at least based on my own experience with Spain.

And the best thing? the weather. Oh, this northern weather. It's the end of July, and—lo and behold—you don't feel like peeling your own skin off when walking the streets here.

Met the Dutchman for lunch in a nearby restaurant (as he headed out earlier to explore the city). On my way there, and during the meal, I started feeling some pain in my right wrist, and the pain spread to my entire arm. I can't really describe just how frustrated I was with all of this: let's just say that, at that moment, I decided to simply return to the hotel right after lunch and just sleep, hoping that the frustration will go away throughout, and maybe the pain will subside. That completely pushed aside any plans for seeing anything of this city; I was *that* frustrated.

Went back to the hotel and slept for about 2–3 hours. Woke up, not much change in the pain, but at least I was extremely fresh. Some writing, some reading, and at around 9:00pm, took a taxi to the venue.

The venue, La Plaza de Universidad, wasn't very easy to locate online. We figured it might have something to do with a square inside a university: but which university? and where exactly, in the university, is that square located? I was later able to reach a high degree of certainty regarding the venue's whereabouts by using *Google Maps*' satellite imagery, showing a large square inside a university located about 7–8km south west of the central railway station. Later, this was confirmed by the hotel's staff, who already knew that Knopfler is performing in town, "in the university"—implying that, just maybe, there aren't many universities in town.

It is known that, in Spain, people's ability to communicate in English is very limited. Locals that I have been asking about this subject had one cause to point their finger at—the fact that TV programs and movies are dubbed in Spanish rather than being subtitled, so other than learning English in primary school, people don't really have much opportunity (or reason) to deal with English in their day-to-day lives. Still, in big cities such as Barcelona, you can somehow get by; in smaller, or less cosmopolitan cities, communication in English becomes much more problematic.

The nice taxi driver who was misfortunate enough to hail us to the venue tried very hard to start any sort of conversation, only to be stuck after one or two consonants. It was evident that he was somewhat embarrassed. Not sure why: clearly not his fault. He did know, however, exactly where the concert was taking place. Quick ten minutes ride and we arrived.

So: the university is called *Laboral*, and is located far from the city center, so neat hill views are available everywhere you look. To get into the "Plaza" part in "La Plaza de Universidad", you need to enter through the university's main gate. Before entering, took some photographs of the surroundings.

It was rather unclear where ticket pickup should take place. Asking around, it turned out that the venue's box office is inside a hall which I could best describe as a library.

From there, access to the square is very easy.

This was a general admission standing show, with an early entry privilege for *markknopfler.com* ticket purchasers—again, it was decided to not take advantage of it. It made more sense to enjoy this concert from the back. Weather was perfect—breezy, at the low twenties—providing for a great general admission concert experience: gone were the heat and the humidity of Barcelona.

Hunger, somehow, struck me shortly after the concert started. What do you do in such case? of course, you eat at the venue. Granted, I never expect much from food offered in concert venues. This particular venue sold food and drink out of a huge tent located right in the middle of the square, behind the sound technicians. Approached, and… get this: *they ran out of food*.

You see, there's always a first. I thought I had seen everything before; I never imagined that a venue, selling food, will completely run out of food (as garbage quality as that food may be), let alone 10 minutes into the concert.

(It goes without saying that they didn't run out of beer.)

The audience in Spain's north is different with respect to loudness. It is loud, but less (though not much) than in, say, Madrid or Barcelona. It was evident that the audience loved the show, but it was also just as evident that people here aren't in the habit of jumping out of their skins for cheering. People's temperament, overall, seems to be cooler here than elsewhere (I have been to) in Spain.

I wrote it before and I'll reiterate: this city and its people reminded me more of a Canadian town than a Spanish one.

During *Postcards from Paraguay*, a mishap took place when Ian finished the song one verse too early. For a couple of seconds, it looked as if the band was heading into complete mayhem—even Mark started singing the last verse—but within two seconds, somehow, they got out of it.

Similar events happened a couple of times during the 2010 Get Lucky tour, and really, I'm not sure I fully understand how they avoid complete disaster when such things happen. When you're used to play a particular song following a certain pattern almost on a daily basis, and suddenly something changes radically (and a premature ending of a song is, undoubtedly, a radical change), it is *extremely* difficult, for the inexperienced performer, to adjust. First, there's the element of complete surprise; second, there's the element of looking at what other band members are doing, to somehow try to end things gracefully and harmonically; and third, you actually have to carry out your unplanned sequence. All of the above has to happen within an exceptionally short duration, as these complications tend to grow exponentially the longer the performance goes without a unified "direction".

As I said before, I don't know of a band that performs as well as this one.

All other songs in the concert were played in full. Great experience.

Out of the venue and now it was time to figure out how to get back to the city center. Horrible memories of the Rome experience crept in. Fortunately, things were quite organized: a few buses were waiting nearby, each one heading to a different destination. None of the buses seemed to head to the railway station. An attendant—positioned right next to the buses (I love it how they're organized in here)—was very happy to help out despite the evident language barrier. Boarded one of the buses, waited until it was full… 15 minutes drive to the central bus station, and from there it's a 10 minutes walk to the hotel. Quick sandwich before heading to the room and off for a good night sleep, knowing that, the next day, I won't be riding any train and will be heading towards a city that many Spanish people consider to be one of the most beautiful cities in Spain.

July 30. Woke up and realized that this entire tour was going to be over within less than 48 hours. Quick breakfast at the hotel and it was decided to head out early: I wasn't going to see much of Gijón anyway and I was looking forward to spending as much time as possible in San Sebastián, based on the so many recommendations I have been hearing about it recently.

The quickest route between Gijón and San Sebastián takes about four hours, often right along the coast. For the life of me, my English vocabulary isn't rich enough to describe just how stunning the scenery was along the ride. Green-covered mountains as far as the eyes can see, and the clear, amazing blue waters of the Bay of Biscay are often in sight. These views were enough for me to determine that this part of Spain clearly deserves a more in-depth look in the future. I could easily spend weeks over weeks in this tantalizingly beautiful country.

The awesome scenery helped the long ride feel shorter. Somewhere along the way, it was decided to look for a place for lunch before the entire country of Spain closes all its restaurants. OK... but where? how do you look for a restaurant when you're in the middle of nowhere?

While driving through the highway, occasionally there were signs showing a symbol of a restaurant, implying that there's a restaurant nearby. Well, you can never tell by these: it might as well be just a small dirty restaurant inside a gas stop. Still, it was better than nothing. Eventually, I realized that these signs are really the only reasonable guide to get *anything* to eat around, so I took the exit right into a a town named *San Mamés de Meruelo*.

Needless to say, I had never heard of anything named *San Mamés de Meruelo* or even close to it. This town seemed to be as close to "in the middle of nowhere" as they can get. Fired up *TripAdvisor* and it turned out that there's a very good restaurant just up the road, which is ranked #1 in San Mamés De Meruelo. That is, ranked #1 out of the staggering total of 2.

OK... drove a few extra kilometers up the road, following the GPS' advice. "Arrived at your destination" but where's that restaurant? oh, there it is. Looked nice from the outside but was uncertain whether it's even open, so I waited in the car as the Dutchman went inside to inquire.

About five minutes later, he was back. Now, you'd wonder why it would take a person (even a Dutch one) five minutes to find out whether a restaurant is presently open or closed. Turns out that the restaurant, La Yaya, is of the more fancy ones, requires reservations and was going to open its door fifteen minutes later. The reason for the delay, then, was that the Dutchman actually had to go about making a reservation, as the restaurant is usually fully booked for lunch.

They also had daily menus: three course meal for €13.

Reservation was made, and we had a few minutes to kill before entering.

So far, the best meal in the entire tour was consumed in a restaurant in Siracusa, on the day-off before the Taormina concert. That one was as unexpected as they can get: stepping into that restaurant in Siracusa, would have never guessed that the experience would later unfold to be the best dining experience in a three months tour.

It happened again. I am proud to announce the second best meal of this tour so far: it took place right here in San Mamés de Meruelo. The food—just like in Siracusa—was simple, unpretentious; and just as it was simple, it was absolutely fantastic.

At some point, we were wondering whether the Dutchman was right about the price of the daily menu: it was possible that they meant to say "30" and said something that sounded like "13". Where on earth would you get such a great meal for €13? impossible.

But no, it wasn't a mistake. The bill arrived, clean €26. Even the (bottled) water was free.

If you're ever in San Mamés de Meruelo, go visit that restaurant. Once you're done eating, send me an email and let me know why you had to visit San Mamés de Meruelo in the first place.

About an hour and a half spent in that restaurant; time to go. Started the car and drove non-stop towards San Sebastián. The destination: Hotel K10 in Urnieta, about 10km south of San Sebastián. The reasons had to do with logistics:

- Hotels in San Sebastián turned out to be very expensive.
- The concert venue was far from San Sebastián's city center anyway.
- Being in the possession of a car, we were no longer bound to stay in city centers, or close to public transport hubs.

- The next morning, we'd have to drive south anyway. It made sense to stay somewhere along the highway south of San Sebastián, to save time battling with rush hour in the morning.

Arrived at the hotel, checked in, left luggage in the room and immediately fled the scene. Back to the car and headed north towards San Sebastián's city center, after getting some advice from the hotel's receptionist who seemed to be very enthusiastic to talk about San Sebastián, calling it a "very beautiful city". So far, everybody who's ever been there was claiming that San Sebastián is pretty; it goes without saying that I was really looking forward to see it.

From the hotel, it's about 20 minutes drive to San Sebastián's city center. Approaching the city center, a quick look around was enough to determine that this place is clearly a gem. Found a parking garage, which happened to be located right next to the beach; car parked, took the stairs up, and, two seconds later, realized that I'm in the most beautiful Spanish city I had seen so far, and one of the most beautiful places I have been to in Europe.

I have never heard of San Sebastián before reading the tour's itinerary (by the number of cities I had never heard of before, I'm starting to get the impression that maybe I should brush up on my knowledge of Europe at some point. I'm way more ignorant about it than I originally thought).

The two main beaches in the city face the *Bahia de La Concha*, with the gorgeous Santa Clara Island visible from everywhere.

Continued walking east towards the old city area. The old city area is very pretty and ridiculously touristic.

After crossing the old city, there was the water again—now looking to the other beach in San Sebastián, more frequented by surfers.

If only it was possible to look at all of this from above… oh, wait. It *is* possible. It was very warm, but nothing to deter me from walking up a steep incline. I will let the pictures do the rest of the talking.

And, of course, a panoramic one (not sure why the leftmost part appears as if skewed upwards… I tried taking that shot multiple times, and it always ended the same. Deal with it):

Found another path, kept walking up…

Indeed, this city *is* a gem: complete different from anything else I had seen in Spain so far in my life. No photograph could possibly do justice to the immense natural beauty of this place.

Walking down, hunger struck again. Everyone I was talking to about San Sebastián mentioned the term *Pintxos* as a must-eat thing there. A *Pintxo* (sometimes written *Pincho*) is northern Spain's version of the *tapa*. Typically, these consist of one or two miniature slices of bread, plus an arbitrary selection of ingredients, all held together with a toothpick or a skewer (the word *Pincho* in Spanish means "spike"). A *pintxo* may or may not contain bread: the term, essentially, is used to describe any sort of a very small dish. As long as there's a skewer holding things together there, it's a *pintxo*.

San Sebastián's old city area was full of bars offering those, which, naturally, raised the question how on earth was I going to go about picking the right one. *TripAdvisor* suggested a place called Bar Zeruko, which turned out to be closed for another 15–20 minutes once we got there. No problem. A quick walk around the city and a visit to the cash machine, then back, and the place was open.

It took the place about two minutes to be almost completely full of people. Only a few tables to dine on, and if you don't have a table —no worries, you are invited to just stand next to the bar and eat. The deal: you pick items (with your hands), put them on a plate, and then hand it to one of the people working there. They heat whatever needs heating, give you the rest, and bring the heated items to your table once they're done.

So much variety, but, what can I tell you... heavenly. Had I not had plans to attend some concert played by some band later on, I'd probably sit there for another hour or so. If you are ever in this part of the country, give those *pintxos* a shot. Once you do, I guarantee that you will no longer want to hear anything about traditional tapas again.

Back to the city center...

Tried for a low exposure shot...

A few last photographs (I promise)...

... and back to the parking lot, heading to the venue. Took a few minutes to the GPS to find itself, but still, it was a short ride to the venue. Upon noticing the venue on the right, it was decided to park the car nearby, rather than head to the venue's parking lot: this is based on past experience with getting out of venues' parking lots after a show. Found a parking spot nearby and walked for about 10 minutes to the venue.

The venue, Plaza de Toros de Illumbe, is a bullring with a retractable roof. Grabbed the tickets and went inside.

The concert was still 30–40 minutes ahead. Spent some time chatting with familiar people who made it to San Sebastián, as well as with a few readers of this blog who came by to introduce themselves.

Concert started a few minutes past schedule and was a very good one. During the concert, multiple references were made to the previous concert's incident of Ian prematurely ending *Postcards from Paraguay*: during the band's introduction, Mark introduced Ian and added "... who will be playing this song all the way through tonight", eliciting lots of laughter from whoever knew what he was talking about. When it was time for the song's last verse, Mark turned back, pointing a finger to the air (gesturing the number "1") and called towards Ian "one more". When it was time to conclude the song, Ian turned to Guy and asked him, jokingly, "… now?".

The song was performed, indeed, all the way through.

After the concert, ten minutes walk to the car, another 10 minutes ride to the hotel… a long, *long* shower and a good night sleep.

Signing off this post from my hotel's lobby in Llafranc, in Costa Brava. Will upload this and head out to catch tonight's concert, which will also be the last.

The last post of this blog will be posted later on tonight, or tomorrow morning at the latest.

Isaac

Thursday, August 1, 2013

The Last One & Conclusion: San Sebastián to Calella de Palafrugell, Spain (July 31, 2013)

No one should be allowed to leave San Sebastián after less than 24 hours; and no tour should be planned so people who follow it are required to stay in San Sebastián less than 24 hours.

Woke up at around 8:30am to the sound of the Dutchman's iPhone-based alarm clock, playing a song that must not be allowed as a wake-up alarm anywhere: not even in jail, not even in San Quentin. If there's one good thing about July 31 being the last day of the tour, is that I will never (hopefully) have to wake up to the sound of that iPhone alarm, ever again in my entire life.

(Well, except for Friday, as the Dutchman's flight home leaves early in the morning.)

Went down to the hotel's ground floor for breakfast, which cost about €11 and was worth incredibly less. Poor selection of… well… nothing interesting. Piled a few pseudo-edible substances onto a plate and sat down eating while reading the news on my phone. OK, let's see… the Israeli Parliament just passed a law to give elected governments more power and make it harder to topple them; hello, Mussolini, good to have you back. What else… yeah, another terrorist organization states that they want to kill me because my foreskin was removed when I was eight days old. Gee, thanks mates; wake me up when it's my turn.

Great bunch of news in the morning, isn't it. I should really stop doing that. I mean, stop reading the news altogether, not only in the mornings.

Finished breakfast in just about 15 minutes, up to the room, post-breakfast morning routine and by 9:20am I was already in the driver's seat.

The sun was shining, everything around was either green or of a colour that fits very well with green. 35 years I'm on this planet, and only now I'm learning about this part of Spain. Better late than never, and hear me when I say, you locals of northern Spain: I *will* be back.

Engine started, GPS started. Itinerary: 661km drive from Urnieta (a suburb of San Sebastián, where last night's hotel is located) to Llafranc, located in Costa Brava, not far from Calella de Palafrugell.

661km with a manual shift. I'm used to travel long distances—may I remind you of the 2008 Kill to Get Crimson tour and the 2010 Get Lucky tour? plus, hey, I live in Canada, and a few times before I drove 600km just for a restaurant—but not in a country where I don't speak the language, and not with a manual shift. I know how to drive those, but really, I find it too tiring.

The southbound ride from San Sebastián is scenic, sifting through green-covered mountains and valleys, although with much less natural bodies of water as you're getting further and further from the sea. The drive being scenic, plus the superbly comfortable weather, made that part of the drive a rather easy and enjoyable one. Once you hit Pamplona, though, the scenery changes dramatically—almost instantly—to a much less pleasant one.

> I often use the expression *Running of the Bulls* to describe fans' reckless run towards the stage before the encore. The *real* Running of the Bulls is a Pamplona tradition. The concept is simple: release six hot-tempered bulls to run through the streets, and have people run at the same direction that the bulls run—of course, said people would be running *in front of the herd*; otherwise it wouldn't be interesting—and see what happens. Injuries are very common (now that's a shocker), and sometimes (although much less frequently than I'd expect) there are deaths as well (fifteen people died in Pamplona bulls' runs since 1910).

The drive from Pamplona onwards, almost all the way to Costa Brava, was very difficult. Not only the scenery changed so it resembled more of a desert than anything else, but climate also changed to be rather vicious: intense dry heat, so intense that the car's air conditioner could no longer keep up. For a large part of the ride, it felt less warm to open the windows and turn off the air conditioning, than having the car sealed with the air conditioning turned on full power.

Other than stopping for gas once along the way, another 15 minutes break was taken for a quick sandwich in some service station along the way, located, more or less, right in the very center of the middle of absolutely nowhere.

Also, this ride was possibly the most expensive car ride I have ever taken in my entire life, toll-wise: overall, taking toll roads along the way saved about an hour of driving. The cost, altogether (there were five or six toll roads along the way) was—sit tight; that's going to hurt—more than €50 (that's about $68 CDN and $66 US). Absolute insanity: I have seen flights that cost less than that, covering greater distances.

Having said that, one good word must be said about the actual roads: all roads driven, both toll and toll-free (but mostly the toll ones), were in fantastic condition. Great infrastructure, good signing and numerous service centers along the way.

After many hours of driving, traffic started becoming a bit more crowded approaching Barcelona. Fortunately, there was no need to enter the city itself; instead, took a road north, heading towards Costa Brava. In mid-day during the working week, traffic there seems to be a breeze.

As you approach Costa Brava, the scenery becomes, once again, more and more interesting. The last half hour of driving was slower, and once sifting through the little towns along the coast, driving was even slower than that.

Finally, after a really long day of driving, arrived at the destination: Casamar Hotel in Llafranc.

Llafranc is a small town, one of three towns belonging to the municipality of Palafrugell (pronounced *pa-la-fru-hey*). One of the other two towns in this municipality is Calella de Palafrugell (*Calella* is pronounced *ka-le-ya*. Now try pronouncing the full name of *Calella de Palafrugell* correctly. Do it three times in a row. It's fun). The latter hosts the annual *Cap Roig Festival*, featuring Knopfler on its roster for this year.

I have never heard of Calella de Palafrugell before in my entire life. I did, however, hear a lot about Costa Brava. The latter is a world-class tourism destination, attracting herds over herds of tourists with its beautiful beaches and wild, rugged coastline (*Costa Brava* in Spanish means *Rough Coast*).

The first time I became aware of Calella de Palafrugell was when details about the show were made available. I woke up one morning, and as I usually do even before getting up, I reached to my phone and caught up with things. A message was waiting for me from the Dutchman, saying that a new show was added to the tour and tickets went for sale *immediately* upon announcement. Unfortunately, I was asleep at that time and the Dutchman was on a train; we therefore bought the tickets about one hour after the sale started.

Still, even though tickets were purchased late, we ended up getting the best seats that were available (third row, center. The first few rows, I suppose, were reserved for VIPs and the sorts). I wouldn't be surprised if that had something to do with the price: €180 *per ticket* (about $250 CDN), making this the most expensive concert ticket in the entire tour and one of the most expensive concert tickets I have ever purchased.

> To put this price in perspective: the 2010 Get Lucky tour made a stop in Monte-Carlo, Monaco. Two concerts, each going for the price of €140, and prices were inclusive of a full three course French dinner inside the venue.
>
> What's also interesting (at least for me) is that €140 in 2010 was worth almost exactly the same amount in Canadian dollars as €180 are worth nowadays.

Arrived at the hotel and found out that it's located right on the water. The hotel also features a one Michelin star restaurant and a patio, offering views such as the following one:

After checking in, it turned out to be too late for lunch in proper restaurants. A few restaurants were still open for business in the exceptionally touristic beach below…

… however, their kitchens were either closed or proposing non-interesting menus for annoyingly high prices. Fortunately, there was also a small bakery nearby selling sandwiches and other small snacks: a sandwich had to do.

Went back to the hotel and continued writing the previous post. That took a great while: about two or three hours spent pecking ruthlessly at the keyboard, while seated at the hotel's terrace overlooking the clear blue water and enjoying perfect weather. There are far worse surroundings for writing, believe you me.

> It is disturbingly funny to realize that, while the Spanish leg of the 2010 Get Lucky tour has been a nightmare, this time I'm having a ball here. I'm happy that I was given the chance to make peace with Spain after that horrendous experience three years ago. This last week in Spain has been great and I will certainly be back.

As the previous post was being uploaded over the hotel's slow internet connection, I took the time to get ready for the concert. Same routine that has been an integral part of my life for the last three months… and it felt very strange going through it for the last time in this tour. Felt very special, like some sort of a celebration. I even put on a new shirt: my favourite one.

The concert was scheduled to start at 10:00pm, and the main problem was that we just couldn't tell for sure where the venue was going to be. Calella de Palafrugell is a small town; but *where*, in that small town, was the festival taking place?

> I found this to be a common problem with concerts that are a part of a festival: when concert details are published, the (reasonable) expectation is that the target audience—the locals—are already somewhat aware of where the venue actually is. When the concert in Calella de Palafrugell was announced as being a part of the Cap Roig Festival, I'm led to believe that most people who were the target audience for this concert already knew what the Cap Roig Festival is all about and its whereabouts.

The hotel's receptionist handed out a map and pointed at a particular intersection. Turned out that the festival was taking place at the Cap Roig Botanical Gardens, located about 2km away from the hotel. While it was possible to drive, walking seemed to be a much better option: from the hotel to Calella de Palafrugell, there is a winding footpath going right along the coastline, offering stunning views of the surroundings.

With views like that, no wonder that a 25 minutes walk took longer to end. Once the path by the coastline ends and merges with the streets of Calella de Palafrugell, the terrain becomes steep. Guided by a paper map *and* the *Google Maps* app on my phone, we only became confident that we're in the right place once we arrived at the venue's parking lot.

That was when the sensation of "I made it" crept in for the first time.

Ticket collection didn't take place in the venue's box office; instead, it took place in a a small black tent right next to the venue's main entrance.

That was when the *second* sensation of "I made it" took place.

The third one took place once I actually entered the venue.

The venue was, as people were warning me beforehand, pretty; yet, I was so excited and dumbfounded by the fact that I actually made it here after three months of travel, that I didn't even bother taking pictures of this place before the concert started (you can find some online).

Upon entrance, I noticed piles of people were standing by small tables. The entrance leads you right into the venue's dining area, consisting of multiple tents located along the perimeter and a few high standing tables in the middle. Very crowded. Still, somehow, I heard the call "Isaac!". That was Mikel Camps, whom I already met a few times during this tour and who also helped a great deal in the last concert of the Get Lucky tour in Gredos. Always good to see this guy, who seems to be very familiar with the ins and outs of the Spanish entertainment industry.

Went to take a look at the seats…

… and stayed there for a few minutes, still trying to catch my breath after the climb up to the venue. Looking around, I noticed that this venue is quite small: I'm pretty sure this was the smallest venue for this tour.

Three quarters of an hour before the show, hunger struck; back to the dining area. As expected, prices there were quite steep. An assortment of tiny mini sandwiches went for €6 and had to do. It took less time to eat those six tiny sandwiches than it took to actually get them. That done with, went back to the seating area and waited for the concert to begin.

I looked at the stage, the stage looked at me. How familiar this stage is to me now, after seeing it approximately 220 times over the last eight years, about 180 of which during the last three years. I believe I know it by heart already. What a strange feeling it was, seeing this stage *for the last time*.

The seating area quickly filled with people. A couple of minutes past the scheduled start time, Junior Parker's *Feelin' Good* started playing; 10 seconds later, lights went out, Paul got the stage, introduced the band and the last concert of the Privateering tour went on its way.

The concert took on a great start, with the band appearing to be upbeat and fresh—possibly the result of an adrenaline rush due to this being the last concert for this tour and all.

Audience-wise… well, I don't know. Here's the deal: during the *markknopfler.com* presales, only rows 3 and up were offered for sale. At the venue, a new row was added in front of row 1 (let's call it "row 0"), making row 3 the fourth row overall. I am not entirely sure who or what entity sold tickets for the first three rows (0–2); at any rate, I have a feeling that those three rows were sold through some sort of VIP or private channels. The audience in the first three rows seemed less cheering and ecstatic than how you'd imagine them to be: most cheering appeared to have originated at the back and at the sides.

The cheering and immense support from the back and the sides, though, were of typical Spanish nature: very loud, very passionate. Richard Bennett, in one of his recent posts, wrote: "There is nothing like the Spanish audiences", and, now that the tour is coming to an end, I believe that I can concur. Yes, there are other loud audiences out there (France, Italy) but, overall, the Spanish seem to be consistently ecstatic (well, except for the north, when they're a little—though not much—quieter).

Just before *Song for Sonny Liston*, something went wrong. For the first time ever in my life, I heard Kerry's voice over the microphone, telling Glenn Worf to remove his in-ear monitor. Apparently, there was a buzz going on in the system, that made it to the speakers as well as to the band members' in-ear monitors. The buzzing prompted Mark and Kerry to exchange a few words in a technical language that I'm completely oblivious to.

At some point, the buzz was so loud that Mark cried "Ouch!" and removed the in-ear monitor from his ear. Kerry then sprang into action to locate the source of the noise, which turned out to be somewhere around Ian's drum kit. The chat with Kerry proceeded, with Mark saying that he was going to test something. Upon hearing the word "test", some smartass in the audience (naturally, from somewhere in the first three rows) called (loudly) "one… one" (as if testing a microphone). That seemed to annoy Mark, who turned towards the smartass and called *"Oh, shut up!"*, eliciting a wave of laughter from the audience.

The issue was sorted out a few seconds later. Mark, then, turned again towards the joker: "OK, you. What were you saying? what's your name?", to which the joker responded with a particular word that I'm not entirely sure of, followed by the expression "like anybody else". Not entirely sure what it was, but nobody laughed at this. Performance then went on as usual.

Once again during *Postcards from Paraguay*, the band urged Ian to continue drumming "one more verse" (in reference to his premature ending of the song during the concert in Gijón): I am happy to report that the song was, once again, played to completion.

Marbletown… Telegraph Road… a short break, *Our Shangri La, So Far Away* and it was all over. Band left the stage, lights kept shut for a few minutes, and once the lights went back on, it really sunk in.

It's over.

Bid Mikel Camps goodbye, took a few photographs of the venue at night…

… and proceeded with the 25 minutes walk towards the hotel.

Grabbed some ice cream along the way, which didn't help much to cope with the heat. It was incredibly hot and humid; I was sweating from body parts that I never knew I was in possession of. It was close to 1:00am when I finally arrived at the hotel; took a shower, verified with the Dutchman that it was indeed all over and went to bed.

Well, it's been quite a ride. More than three months on the road, with my world compressed into a travel bag (what a brilliant travel bag it is! thanks, Osprey), following what I still consider the best band around.

It was far from being easy. It was hard. *Very* hard. I recall the Dutchman saying something along the lines of "I knew it would be hard, I just didn't know how hard it could possibly be". Undoubtedly, this tour was much, *much* harder to follow than the 2010 Get Lucky tour —and that one, mind you, wasn't easy to follow in the slightest.

I could go on and on about the challenges that were encountered during the tour, and there were many. I will be the first to admit that I am more than a tad spoiled (later on in this post, you'll understand why): living in my own bubble in western Canada, I got so used to certain conveniences that I started taking them for granted. Thus, while I could write piles and piles of rants over why things don't quite "work" in many parts in Europe, this is all a matter of perspective: it's not that Europe "sucks"; it's just that my own bubble, headquartered very close to the Pacific Ocean in the stupidly awesome city of Vancouver, is… well… as good as it gets. FOR ME.

> One comment, written in French, accused me of being way too harsh and disrespectful towards certain Latin cultures (interestingly enough, it was the one and only negative comment I received, throughout the entire tour), and called upon me to "go home already"; I recall similar comments being made during the last tour. That comment failed to take into consideration one major factor: *everything* that has been written in this blog was written from the point of view of an individual who doesn't live here and has an exceptionally complex and convoluted schedule to follow. I never intended to perform full research of entire cultures and pass judgments on them; what I did was to just highlight certain aspects of these cultures that affect reckless travellers, such as myself. Chill out, then; your country

(or city, town, or whatever) doesn't suck. You're OK, too. Relax. Take a deep breath. No offence was intended.

It's been a tough ride and I must say that I feel privileged to have been given the opportunity to do what I had done.

Now, I suppose, would be a good time for thanks.

The first "thank you" goes to the one who deserves it the most: my travel partner, usually referred to as "The Dutchman" although some people prefer, for a reason I just can't comprehend, to call him "Jeroen Gerrits".

For months, we were planning the tour's itinerary together, and I can't even begin to tell you how difficult it was just to *plan* for this tour (let alone to actually follow it). The efforts put into planning paid off, though: together, we came up with a travel plan as meticulous and extensive as only two minds with strong scientific orientation could come up with.

We ended up spending the vast majority of the time during this tour together, and whoever knows me a little beyond this funny blog screen could easily tell you that my personality would render me a disastrous travel partner at times. I am forever indebted to Jeroen for his companionship and friendship along the way, as well as for helping me out by lifting my travel bag onto trains' overhead compartments ever since I fell down and broke my wrist in June. How he withstood those long nights when I was pecking at the keyboard writing this drivel while he was trying to fall asleep—is beyond me.

Special thanks also go to the almighty Ingrid—possibly the closest thing to "superwoman" that I had ever seen in my entire life. Many of this tour's best days were spent with Ingrid around, and I am indebted to her as well for her friendship, as well as for her help along the way.

Many thanks to all the readers of this blog, for your readership as well as for your comments. My goal in this blog was far from being about the actual concerts; instead, it was all about the travel experience. If I was able to convey at least some of the highs and lows of this tour to you, then I consider my job done.

Many thanks to all people I met during this tour, new and familiar faces alike: your support was, and still is, much appreciated.

And, of course, many thanks to (in clockwise order) Jim Cox, John McCusker, Glenn Worf, Ian Thomas, Mike McGoldrick, Richard Bennett, Guy Fletcher and Mark Knopfler, as well as the tour's management, for helping provide a perfect soundtrack for yet another amazing experience. No matter what happened during the days, watching this band perform on an almost nightly basis helped reverting things back to equilibrium.

There is no better band around. There can't be.

August 1, 2010. The Get Lucky tour had just ended, and I headed to Barcelona to spend a few days on the beach before heading home (back then, I used to live in Waterloo, Ontario). I knew I'd need a few days to unwind, so I had my flight home scheduled to depart a few days past the tour's conclusion.

I remember spending a few days on Barcelona's beautiful beaches. It was beautiful, peaceful, and beautiful again. I remember gazing at the beach and at the water, trying to comprehend the fact that the tour was over and what it meant; and more than anything else, I remember the feeling. It was a feeling of intense and profound emptiness: what used to be a daily routine—waking up, travelling, watching concerts, sleeping—had just ended: *what now?*

The few days spent in Barcelona after that tour were not enough to recover. In a sense, I don't think I ever recovered fully: I dislike clichés, but I'm willing to take a leap forward and admit that following the 2010 Get Lucky tour had an immense impact on my life, mostly positive but also negative.

I flew from Barcelona back to Toronto, took the one hour taxi ride to Waterloo, entered my house and…

Nothing.

It was that moment, that sensation of emotional vacuum that convinced me that my time had come: time to leave the boring, comfortable life in rural Ontario behind, sell my house, pack whatever still meant anything to me and move to where I had always wanted to: the wonderful city of Vancouver, located five hours flight west of Ontario, right on the coast of the Pacific Ocean.

I still had a few commitments to attend to. Those ended in December, and one month later I was already in Canada's west coast. I took with me five guitars, a piano, an espresso machine, an espresso beans grinder, a few clothes, and everything related to my computer; I gave away most of what was left.

Fast forward three years later. The move to Vancouver was one of the best decisions I have ever made. Life became exciting. From the deafening quietness and paralyzing boredom of rural Ontario, I moved to live in the very heart of a big city—a city which I still consider the best place (again, *FOR ME*) to live in on the face of this miserable blue planet.

After spending a year in a small apartment in an older building, I moved to a brand new apartment, in a brand new building, looking over the city from really high up.

And here's some very early morning view:

My passion to travel changed as well. Before, I was happy whenever I got the chance to travel far, very far—as far as an airplane could get me out out of southwestern Ontario; living in Vancouver, I still like to travel a lot—but I really don't need to put too much effort into it. Everything I'm looking for in a travel experience is located within a few hours drive from my apartment, and some of it can even be found in Vancouver's downtown area.

For example, it's less than an hour drive to the *Stawamus Chief*, for a lovely day hike that features, say, these:

Whytecliff Park is even closer:

Horseshoe Bay is just around the corner from there:

Or, say, this (I'm not even sure where I took it, I think somewhere around *Squamish*):

How about a hiking trail in, say, *Cypress Mountain*, conveniently located in West Vancouver, a bridge away from downtown (note: there are bears there, too)?

Highway 99 ("Sea to Sky Highway"), considered to be one of the most beautiful highways in the world, connects Vancouver with Whistler.

Isaac's "Privateering" Tour Blog

How about Whistler in the winter?

(Too bad I don't ski.)

Sitting here in *Porteau Cove* isn't half bad either, about 30 minutes drive away from home:

Feeling like going to the beach? why drive? *English Bay* is located at west side of the downtown peninsula:

Feeling like taking a day trip? here's the *Okanagan Valley* in the east, about four hours drive.

Further east, you get to the Canadian Rockies:

And the list goes on and on. The point of all of this was to illustrate that I no longer have to travel much in order to get up close and intimate with Mother Nature; it's all right here within reach.

That should explain why I was thinking really, *really* hard before finally deciding to follow this tour. I kept raising valid questions against doing it, and kept coming up with a "yes, but…". *Something* tipped the scale in favour of this tour, and given my immense love towards British Columbia (well, the Canadian Rockies are on the border between British Columbia and Alberta, and most famous sites are technically in Alberta's side; but work with me here), you could see why I had trouble rationalizing it. At the end, I gave up all rationalization and decided to just go with it.

When I say "at the end", I am referring, really, *to the end*. All tickets were purchased and virtually all travel was already arranged and paid for, *before* I took the final decision to attend the tour in its entirety. I can't recall exactly when it was that I took that final decision; I believe it was around March, about a month or so before the tour started.

And so, on April 8, I bid Vancouver goodbye, headed to the airport, and flew to Israel to visit my family and friends. Two weeks later, and two days earlier than planned due to aviation strikes in both my departure point (Israel) and destination (Germany), I arrived to Frankfurt to meet the Dutchman; a day later, flew to Bucharest and the rest is all (well, mostly) documented in this blog.

I am happy that I took myself through this immense challenge, and I feel a great sense of accomplishment for successfully going through it all.

Signing off this post from the terrace of the hotel in Llafranc. A good lunch was had earlier in the hotel's Michelin Star restaurant.

Will upload this post, take another walk around this beautiful place, and then head back to Barcelona, staying in a hotel by the airport.

Tomorrow morning, the Dutchman will take an early flight to Amsterdam. My flight to Toronto departs a few hours later, at around 12:00pm; a couple of hours break and then a connecting flight (in executive class; finally managed to upgrade) to Vancouver. Should arrive home at around 7:00pm local time, and head directly to the emergency room.

Wish me luck.

Until the next time,

Isaac